Literature and Culture Series

General Editor: Greg Dawes

Series Editor: Ana Peluffo

Other Books Published by Editorial *A Contracorriente*:

Marisol Montaño, Alejandro Solomianski y Sofia Wolhein (eds.), *Otras voces. Nuevas identidades en la frontera sur de California (Testimonios)*

Ana Peluffo (ed.), *Pensar el siglo XIX desde el siglo XXI. Nuevas miradas y lecturas*

Andrea Matallana, *El Tango entre dos Américas. La representación del tango en Estados Unidos, 1910-1939*

Carlos Aguirre (ed.), *Militantes, intelectuales y revolucionarios. Ensayos sobre marxismo e izquierda en América Latina*

The Generation of '72
Latin America's Forced Global Citizens

Edited by

BRANTLEY NICHOLSON
University of Richmond

SOPHIA A. MCCLENNEN
Pennsylvania State University

Raleigh, NC

©Brantley Nicholson, 2013
©Sophia A. McClennen, 2013

All rights reserved for this edition for:
©2013, Editorial *A Contracorriente*

ISBN: 978-0-9853715-4-8

No part of this book, including the cover, may be reproduced without expressed permission from the editor.

Library of Congress Control Number: 2013950780

Library of Congress Cataloging-in-Publication Data:

The Generation of '72 : latin america's forced global citizens / Brantley Nicholson, Sophia A. McClennen.

Raleigh, NC: Editorial A Contracorriente, 2013 / p. cm.

ISBN 10: 0-9853715-4-4
ISBN 13: 978-0-9853715-4-8

Interior design by Samuel F. Sotillo
Illustration on page 42 by Ivette Arends

This work is published under the auspices of the Department of Foreign Languages and Literatures at NORTH CAROLINA STATE UNIVERSITY.

Content

The Generation of '72: Latin America's Forced Global Citizens   11
Brantley Nicholson
Sophia A. McClennen

Literary Futures: Crime Fiction, Global Capitalism and the History
of the Present in Ricardo Piglia   29
Patrick Dove

Itinerant Citizens: Imagining Global Citizenship in the Works of
Osvaldo Soriano   49
Leila Lehnen

Connecting September 11's: Hemispheric Historical Ambiguity in
Ariel Dorfman's *Americanos: Los pasos de Murieta*   75
John Riofrio

The Psychosomatic Text: Re-reading Psychoanalysis and Semiotics
in *Como en la guerra*, or, The Sister(s) of Oedipus   97
Geoffrey Kantaris

El legado del exilio de Cristina Peri Rossi: un mapa para géneros e
identidades   119
María Rosa Olivera-Williams

Radiografía de un pueblo enfermo: la narrativa de Diamela Eltit   147
J. Agustín Pastén B.

Antonio Skármeta's Uniqueness   181
    Randolph D. Pope

Gazing Backwards in Fernando Vallejo   205
    Juanita Cristina Aristizábal

The King's Toilet: Cruising Literary History in Reinaldo Arenas'
Before Night Falls   229
    Lázaro Lima

Postdata

Apuntes sobre el espacio en las novelas de Diamela Eltit   259
    J. Agustín Pastén B.

Cristina Peri Rossi bajo la lente de la Generación del 72   273
    María Rosa Olivera-Williams

Contributors   285

The Generation of '72: Latin America's Forced Global Citizens

Brantley Nicholson
University of Richmond

Sophia A. McClennen
Pennsylvania State University

A very poignant moment stands out in Cristina Peri Rossi's "La influencia de Edgar A. Poe en la poesía de Raimundo Arenas." In a confrontation between the child narrator and her exiled father, the voice of the child-narrator breaks with the impersonal third person account and delivers an unexpectedly pithy knockout line: "Estoy segura de que lo que piensas acerca de nuestra generación es completamente falso" (52). The idea of generational rupture is certainly not a new feature of literary transformation, but there is something in the bold and decisive way that this line is delivered, something in the notion that the father cannot understand his child, that characterizes the break that takes place in the literary generation we refer to in this collection as the Generation of '72. In contrast to the generational testimonies and World Literary schematics that stand on either side of the Generation of '72, there have been no critical collections, definitive testimonies, or telltale autobiographies dedicated to the authors that fall between the *Boom* and the recently famed anti-*Boom*: Roberto Bolaño and the Generation X that is generally subsumed under the monikers *Crack* and *McOndo*. While this group has, at times, been studied as the post-boom or the writers of the postmodern turn, we think that there is value to be added to those approaches by framing this cohort of writers through particular attention to their historical context, one which, we argue, heralded a substantial shift in many of the intellectual practices and political realities that had previously influenced literary work.

The term "Generation of '72" is an extrapolation from the framework that Cedomil Goic created in his structuralist reading of the Latin American novel and sweeping analysis of the evolution of Hispanic letters, *Mitos degradados* (1992).[1] In his formal reading, Goic analyzes literary trends and peaks in Latin American narrative by dividing writers and intellectuals into groups based on the year in which they were born. A group, for Goic, spans fifteen years, and their name is based on the year twenty-three years after the youngest member of a generation was born, presumably around the time that the generation's writers would become intellectually and artistically conscious. Within the "Novela Contemporánea" of the twentieth century, for example, the "Generación de 1927" consists of writers born between 1890 and 1904, such as the *Boom predecessors* in which, "Eduardo Mallea, Miguel Angel Asturias, Leopoldo Marechal, Roberto Arlt, Borges, Augustín Yánez, Carpentier, Manuel Rojas, Enrique Amorín son los destacados representantes" (231). Following are the two generational tiers of the *Boom*, the first, the "Generación de 1942," born between 1905 and 1919 consisting of Cortázar, Onetti, Droguett, Bombal, Arguedas, Roa Bastos, and Rulfo, and the second, "Generación de 1957" whose members include, García Márquez, Donoso, Fuentes, and Julio Ramón Ribeyro." While unarguably rigid, Goic's framework is useful for exploring Latin American literary trends as collective responses to institutional and historical pressures that affect intellectuals as they mature. Goic, for example, separates Cortázar, Onetti, and Bombal from García Marquez and Fuentes, a rare critical division. He considers the urban narratives and "neorealista" tendencies that exhibit a "realismo tradicional" and a "polémico nacionalismo literario" of the former to contrast with the "irrealismo" of the latter that "se distingue por su renovada conciencia de la autonomía de la obra literaria y de la especificidad de la literatura", and whose "mundo destaca por la radicalización de esa autonomía por el distanciamiento que lo extraño, fantástico o grotesco, proporciona al mundo narrativo" (236).

---

1. While Goic originally lays out this framework in *Historia de la novela Hispanoamericana* (1972), he updates the categories for *Mitos degradados* (1992).

Goic's last generation is the "Generación de 1972," whose writers were born between 1935 and 1949. While he offers early candidates for his "Novissimi Narratores"—Vargas Llosa, Severo Sarduy, Reinaldo Arenas and Alfredo Bryce Echenique—judging by the one brief paragraph that he dedicates to this generation, it was too early to give the group a fleshed out reading or to successfully indicate which authors would leave their mark on the region or the world. And the formal characteristics that he uses to classify them are not as developed as they could be. Neither entirely off the mark, nor fully descriptive of the "Generación de 1972," he writes that their "disposición narrativa envuelve dos términos contrapuestos: uno de rígida y simétrica construcción, con otro de fluidez y movilidad en el montaje de tiempos y espacios diversos," and that they, "ilustran sectores sociales y humanos en su variedad y complejidad con ambiciosa contemplación de totalidad" (238).

Goic's preliminary understanding of post-*Boom* literature seems to affirm Donald Shaw's in depth theorization of a similar generation and their return to a realism that ponders sociopolitical totalities. For Shaw, whose post-*Boom* writers are typified by Antonio Skármeta, Rosario Ferré, and Gustavo Sainz, there is a formal breach between Goic's "irrealistas" and the "Generación de 1972" that has as much to do with the political reality of the time as any attempt to formally rebel against their predecessors. The "*Pinochetazo* in Chile," as he puts it, along with the *Guerra Sucia* around the River Plate, the insurrections in Central America, the massacre at Tlatelolco in 1968, and rising feminist discourses in Europe and the Americas, induce a break with both the glossy social distancing that had come to exemplify *Boom* literature and the stereotypical and voiceless female characters that had filled its pages.[2]

In theoretical and social terms, Idelber Avelar gets more specific about post-*Boom* writers, describing the group as intellectuals confronted with the doubly arduous task of finding a formal voice in an editorial economy steeped in the style of the *Boom* giants, on one front, and faced with the political realities of a wave of dictatorships and economic shock treatment amidst which they come of age, on the other. It is a generation that, for the first time in twentieth-century Latin America, experiences the roundly nega-

---

2. Two works serve for a thorough understanding of Donald Shaw's theorization of post-*Boom* literature: *The Post-Boom in Spanish American Fiction* (1998) and *Antonio Skármeta and the post-Boom* (1994).

tive aspects of globalization and whose writers make less voluntary trips to the cosmopolitan center than enter into acquiesced global citizenship through political exile. The battles of writers that for Avelar include Ricardo Piglia, Diamela Eltit, Silviano Santiago, and Tununa Mercado are both formal and political. They attempt to consolidate a voice that will capture the violence experienced in the seventies and eighties, while seeking out what Shoshana Felman and Dori Laub would refer to as an "authentic listener" through literature.

This collection aims to both affirm and move-beyond the primary readings presented by Goic, Shaw, and Avelar. It presents an attempt to update theoretical approaches to the Generation of '72 and to explore how its collective aesthetics holds up, as dictatorships give way to neoliberal democracies. The list of authors presented here is not meant to be a rigid schematic, but rather a jumping off point. Many authors have come and gone from this volume's short list. Our goal is not to define, canonize, and exclude but, along with the greatly talented scholars that have agreed to contribute to this collection, to add to the growing conversation on contemporary Latin American letters. With that in mind, the authors that comprise the Generation of '72 and receive criticism in this collection consist of Luisa Valenzuela (1938), Antonio Skármeta (1940), Ricardo Piglia (1941), Cristina Peri Rossi (1941), Ariel Dorfman (1942), Fernando Vallejo (1942), Osvaldo Soriano (1943), Reinaldo Arenas (1943), Diamela Eltit (1949), and César Aira (1949).

Between National and post-National Aesthetics

The Generation of '72 stands out from their predecessors and followers in many ways. They mark the first Latin American generation to experience a widespread post-war economic globalization that will lead to a darkening of the hemispheric cultural goodwill that the *Boom* enjoys. They are the first generation to *en masse* consider popular culture to be a viable aesthetic register that can be used for the sake of resistance as much as a tool of coloniality. More so than any other generation, they experience a rapid ideological ascension, following the Cuban Revolution in 1959 and the election of Salvador Allende in 1970, and collapse, following the coup in Chile in 1973 and the spread of dictatorships that will follow. They are presented with the task of mourning while questioning the very limits of a literature that undergoes a double affront through the strict control of symbolic systems by authoritarian regimes and the influx of new cultural referents that the abrupt liberalization of Latin American economies causes. They struggle to find and maintain a literary identity in the wake of publishing houses' expectation of them to reproduce *realismo mágico*, on one hand, and to maintain regional and national identities while in exile, or to perform the regional while increasingly becoming global citizens, on the other. And beyond the Latin American precedent, they are forced to express the exposure and fragility of a life in exile while their literary vocabulary experiences the turbulence of exile itself. In short, the Generation of '72 collectively negotiates tension between the regional and the global in a way that no other twentieth century cultural movement is forced to do so in Latin America.

While the Generation of '72 has been marked by ambiguity and few definitive accounts, José Donoso's *Historia personal del Boom* (1972) and Jorge Volpi's *El insomnio de Bolívar* (2010), representing generations that stand on either side of them, offer robust and celebratory renderings of their respective generations.[3] Not wholly literary, this owes a great deal to Latin America's position in the ebbs and flows of the geopolitics of the past sixty years. Donoso and Volpi's experience with the same political and cultural globalization that haunted the Generation of '72 has inarguably played to their favor more than it has hindered them.[4] The generations repre-

---

3. Volpi's *El insomnio de Bolívar* may be written in a tongue-in-cheek tone, but it is nonetheless celebratory and, generationally speaking, self-affirming. Additionally, we consider the employment of irony a part of the evolution of universal literary tone. What was the destabilization of the ego for the *Boom* is the prevalence of irony for the Generation X.

4. Two quotes point to the benefit of internationalism for the Boom and the Gen. X. The first being José Donoso's claim in *Historia personal del Boom* that "Al decir "internacionalización" no me refiero a la nueva avidez de las editoriales; ni a los diversos premios millonarios; ni a la cantidad de traducciones por casas importantes de París, Milán y Nueva York; ni al gusto por el potin literario que ahora interesa a un público de proporciones insospechadas hace una década; ni a las revistas y películas y agentes literarios de todas las capitales que no esconden su interés; ni a las innumerables tesis de doctorado en cientos de universidades yanquis de que están siendo objeto los narradores de Hispanoamérica, cuando antes era necesario ser por lo menos nombre de calle antes de que esto sucediera. Aunque nadie sabe qué vino primero, el huevo o la gallina, a mí me parece que todas estas cosas positivas y estimulantes en un sentido más bien superficial—siempre de dimensiones muchísimo menores a las creadas por la leyenda paranoica—, han sido consecuencia de, y no causa de, la internacionalización de la novela hispanoamericana" (17).

sented by Donoso (*Boom*) and Volpi (Gen.-X) are part and parcel of a literary cosmopolitanism and Latin American socioeconomic globalization that opened new avenues of literary exposure, fostered global intellectual exchange in a largely peaceful setting, and founded an unprecedented wealth of publishing forums. One might argue that the writers associated with the *Boom* inherit airs of the privileged intellectual abroad from their *modernista* predecessors, no matter how bohemian their aesthetics might have played out. And while the writers associated with the Gen.-X enjoy Latin American home cities that have become recently minted cosmopolitan spaces themselves, members of the Generation of '72 have been forced to travel to cosmopolitan centers in Europe and North American under duress rather than as part of an iconography of a national and post-national cultural world.

Politically speaking, the *Boom* carved out a niche during a three-fold cultural investment produced during the Cold War, whose incipient phases lent themselves more to literary expansion than repression: the soft-power inflected investments made by North American cultural institutions, similar tactics used by Cuba through the Casa de las Américas, and the bourgeoning interest in Latin American writers by Spanish publishing houses during the Franco Regime. As the *Boom* began its ascent, editors in Madrid and Barcelona dreamt up prizes that would help market a Latin American literature in order to fill a cultural void left in Spain under Franco and, in the midst of the Cold War, North American philanthropic institutions, namely the Rockefeller Federation, the Center for Inter-American Relations, and the American Association of University Presses, began a soft-power campaign in a battle for hearts and minds. This showing of "cultural good will", as Deborah Cohn puts it, facilitated the inter-American exchange of literary icons and the opening of new reader markets to Latin American authors, leaving an indelible mark on the international literary can-

---

The second is from Jorge Volpi's *El insomnio de Bolívar*, "Qué tienen en común, entonces? Quizás una relación con el Boom nada traumática, casi diríamos natural: todos admiran a García Márquez y a Cortázar y, en bandos antagónicos, a Vargas Llosa o a Fuentes, pero del mismo modo en que se rinden ante escritores de otras lenguas, Sebald o McEwan, Lobo Antunes o Tabucchi; ninguno siente la obligación de medirse con sus padres y abuelos latinoamericanos, o al menos no sólo con ellos; ninguno se asume ligado a una literatura nacional—Fresán define: mi patria es mi biblioteca—y ninguno cree que un escritor latinoamericano debe parecer, aya, latinoamericano" (156).

on.[5]

At the other temporal end, Volpi's "young writers" navigated the late development of post-Washington Consensus Latin America without the responsibility of witnessing the trauma that its incipient phases caused intellectual communities in the Americas. As has been the case with the *Boom* writers, if the young Latin American author lives abroad today, it is to be close to publishing houses in Barcelona or within budget-flight striking distance of London and Berlin, not due to political or economic exile, even by the loosest of definitions. And with the exception of the *novelas de la dictadura* that form part of the late-*Boom* corpus in texts such as Augusto Roa Bastos' *Yo el supremo* (1974) and Elvira Orphée's *La última conquista de El Ángel* (1977) and the occasional use of dictatorships on the wane as a backdrop to Bildungsroman or cyberpunk novels, such as in Alberto Fuguet's *Mala onda* (1991) or Edmundo Paz Soldán's *El delirio de Turing* (2003), a realist rendering of globalization's dark side in the last third of the twentieth century is notably absent from either group. A realist rendering of life in times of terror, shock economics, and forced-exile rests solely on the shoulders of the Generation of '72.

Lived experience has a lot to do with this. When Julio Cortázar moves to Europe during the *Rayuela* years, it is under strikingly different terms than when, two decades later, Peri Rossi will follow suit. When José Donoso and Mario Vargas Llosa go to Princeton it is with a different degree of necessity than when Ricardo Piglia does the same. And when Ariel Dorfman writes *Konfidenz* (2002), a novel set in World War II Paris, fragility and darkness fill the narrative in a way that does not convey in Volpi's attempt at the same genre and setting in *En busca de Klingsor* (1999). There is a marked contrast between the literature produced in times of globalization and that which stems from the duress of acquiesced global citizenship.

Indeed, the Generation of '72 experiences a stark contrast in political realities with their predecessors: less the cultural good will associated with soft power and more the harsh reality associated with global civil war. By the seventies, the international circulation

---

5. In her article, "A Tale of Two Translation Programs: Politics, the Market, and Rockefeller Funding for Latin American Literature in the United States During the 1960s and 1970s." *Latin American Research Review* 41.2 (2006): 139-64, Deborah Cohn goes into detail about the rise of Area Studies and its philanthropic outposts in the United States and the implications that this had for Boom literature.

of knowledge did not so much favor intellectuals and left-leaning writers and artists in Latin America as it did a technocratic elite with authoritarian tendencies. What went global was not literature and cultural artifacts so much as strategies associated with widespread oppression. Myriad quotes have come to light from Henry Kissinger that attest to the disposability of Latin American leftists, their inability to govern themselves, the C.I.A.'s waging of a "campaign of terror" in the sixties in Chile, half a decade before Allende was even elected, along with the clear contradictions of promoting democracy through dictatorships. The United States Government's shift away from the attempt to win hearts and minds through cultural exchange in Latin America can, perhaps, best be summed up by the point-blank vote of confidence that Kissinger gives Pinochet when he meets him at the Organization of American States General Assembly in 1976: "My evaluation is that you are a victim of all left-wing groups around the world and that your greatest sin was that you overthrew a government which was going communist" (56).[6] Contemporary scholarship on the Cold War in Latin America highlights to what extent the transnational and globalized properties associated with authoritarian networks such as Operation Condor usurped former avenues of cultural exchange.[7] In the edited volume, *In from the Cold: Latin America's New Encounter with the Cold War* (2008) Daniela Spenser discusses how globalization played to the favor of oligarchies and autocrats more than democracy promoting cultural institutions, writing in particular about the Argentine Junta's ability to export their tactics to outposts of leftist and right-wing conflict in the rest of Latin America:

> In its crusade to transnationalize the dirty war, the Argentine military exported arms, counterinsurgency doctrine, and expertise in the practice of state terror. To advance its goals, the military counted on a well-constructed network of like-minded Latin American, North American and Asian anti-Communists, and also on conservative domestic civil society. In the process, the military established a wide international network, which included the sharing of logistical information and the ideas and techniques of counterinsurgency war, as well as an illegal trade in arms, drugs,

---

6. This exchange is taken from Gilbert Joseph and Daniela Spenser's *In from the Cold: Latin America's New Encounter with the Cold War* (2008).

7. Lois Hecht Oppenheim's *Politics in Chile: Democracy, Authoritarianism and the Search for Development* (1993) serves as a good source for details on the Chilean "campaign of terror" in the sixties.

and money laundering independent of the United States. (385)

With the River Plate area no longer serving as an exporter of an iconography of Latin American cosmopolitanism, but as a source of tactics of oppression, and with Chile taking a rapid shift from a country associated with internationally lauded idealist poets and committed writers to being a puppet government of the C.I.A., writers that come of age in the seventies in the Southern Cone especially offer a darkening of global and cosmopolitan themes in their work.

To write with allegory based in the sustained residue of melancholic connection to the home space marks a break from the *novela de la dictadura* that is more narrowly concerned with the apparatuses of power and the textual characterization of the cult of dictators on one generational side and the benefit of the literary navigation of the cosmopolitan marketplace from home on the other. The Generation of '72 stands between writers that fall into line with incipient and comparatively benevolent Cold War programs and cultural globalization in terms of the *Boom* and subsequent generations, such as the *McOndo* and *Crack* who come of age after the return to democracy and are unconcerned with the effect that neoliberal globalization has on memory on the other. For the former, the cosmopolitan rite, in keeping with the Latin American tradition, consists of a trip to major European capitals, where one can become universally lettered in the high aesthetic register of nation building. For the latter the same market forces that erode the memory of authoritarian atrocities for the Generation of '72 allow them, for the first time in Latin American history, to be cosmopolitan in the singular and universal sense *from home*, and to earnestly celebrate post-national popular aesthetics. The Generation of '72, by contrast, receives less subsidized translations, world literary prizes, and effortless international communication and travel, and more the fulfillment of a hemispheric paranoia that views ideas and intellectualism with enmity. It is not for nothing that John Beverley marks the de facto end to the *Boom* as September 11, 1973.

A New Idealism

When the characters in the Peri Rossi short story alluded to above travel to a nondescript Spanish city, they do not experience the pride of homeland but are surprised by the barbarian nature of the Spaniards themselves, whose only place for South Americans in their economic and symbolic economy is to paint themselves as caricatures of indigenous subjects and beg for money. The existential low-tide her characters experience exposes fissures in the foundational promises of post-Enlightenment civilization and the binary thinking that has long dictated Latin America and its relationship to cosmopolitan centers. Neither civilized, nor barbarian, Peri Rossi alludes to a generation altogether desensitized to such simplified modes of thought. And she does so in spirited terms. The narrator explains:

> Esta era otra raza, provista de una singular resistencia, y en la matriz original, habían asimilado las enseñanzas de íntimas, oscurísimas derrotas; en el útero materno habían aprendido la tristeza, el fracaso, la desolación, y cuando vieron la luz del mundo, supieron cómo vivir a pesar de todo ello. Concebidos en noches amargas, en noches de pena, persecución, incertidumbre, miseria y terror, concebidos en casas que eran como calabozos o en calabozos que eran tumbas, en camas que eran ataúdes, los sobrevivientes de esas noches de torturas y de dolor, nacían con el signo de la resistencia y de la fortaleza. (59)

The failure of the aesthetic and political promises of the civilizing State are central to the work of both Peri Rossi and her peers. Charged with political meaning, aesthetics and civilization, for them, are not always positively inflected. In Chile, it is the *aesthetic* implication that Allende's government will careen toward chaos, breaking with order that the technocratic elite will discursively use to prop up its neoliberal policies.[8] Colombian governing elites use similar tactics, beginning as early as the nineteenth century and developing into a contemporary semantics of cleanliness versus squalor. And in Argentina, aesthetics have always been invoked in order to philosophically frame violent political projects, including Sarmiento's use of a civilizing hierarchy in which French and English affectations anchor his arguments.

Far from fostering a collective will in the State, aesthetics,

---

8. In Chile, the Catholic Church's tendency to side with progressive and socially inclusive governmental policies in the second half of the twentieth century caused liberal economists and the technocratic elite to use the discourse of chaos and order as a way to frame their policies for a popular audience. For more, see David E. Hojman, *Neoliberalism with a Human Face?* (Liverpool, England: University of Liverpool Press, 1995).

for the Generation of '72, is a double-edged medium. Literature, for it's writers, does not consist of a tool in nation, or even region, building, nor does it offer a clear path to collective catharsis, in a regional literature that has long used its literary archive to work through philosophical problems. By contrast, literature, for the first time as a regional medium, becomes comprised of, on the one hand, what Nelly Richard refers to as "signos que guardarán en su interior una memoria lingüística de los choques nacidos de tantas desarmaduras de sentidos", and on the other, a poetics that balances the novel cultural affect in global popular culture, the depiction and influences of exile, and a second look at universal political projects (17).[9]

In many ways, the Generation of '72 offers a novel poetics of Latin American citizenship, one that is trapped between the codified regionalism of the *Boom* and the privileged navigation of the global market of the *Crack* and *McOndo*. Caught in multiple cultural and economic flows of globalization, they offer a literature that resonates well beyond regional boundaries and speaks to the pushing and pulling, masking and unmasking, lettering and 'unlettering' of globalism, culminating in a new faith in literature, and in turn a new poetics, that is at times unexpectedly hopeful and at others critically poignant. It ties together a literary response from a group of writers that turned to a socially committed literature precisely at a time in which the Latin American aesthetic and political citizen appear to die a simultaneous death. Neither indicative of a swan song nor fresh naiveté, the Generation of '72 works toward a poetics that navigates the labyrinth of globalism and feels out a literary response that resonates increasingly with audiences who experience the ecological, political, and economic hang-ups of cosmopolitan modernity in their own right. And readers can turn to the Generation of '72, as Richard would claim, to navigate the ruinous archives of memory form the regional perspective.

It is an uneasy aesthetics filled with irony that the Generation of '72 produces. They, at once, are the first generation to take popular media seriously, *en masse*, and are presented with the problem of critiquing the largely imperial culture from which popu-

---

9. Nelly Richard goes into depth about the crisis of the arts and the radicalization of poetics both during and after Pinochet's regime is in power in Chile in her book *La insubordinación de los signos: cambio político, transformaciones culturales y poéticas de la crisis* (1994).

lar mediums emanate. They are caught between the publishing effortlessness of the *Boom* and the pop-cultural fluency of those born a decade after them. Neither fully at ease in soirees at the Balcells' nor the blogosphere, the Generation of '72 leaves a telling aesthetic inscription of the not so comfortable phase of incipient globalization. Not indicative of a publishing culture that fosters violent tomes for export, nor young enough for political oppression to act simply as a bildungsroman backdrop, the Generation of '72 marks a group whose collective poetics captures the difficult terms of the movement of the aesthetic and economic border to Latin America for the first time.

Contributors

The theorization of the Generation of '72 began with Brantley Nicholson's doctoral thesis at Duke University and has since developed in conversation with Sophia McClennen. And it is a framework that has benefited from the invaluable consideration this edition's contributors have given it. By poking and prodding the idea, the scholars included in this collection have explored its limits while giving the Generation of '72 the critical attention that they have long been due.

In his chapter, Patrick Dove narrates Ricardo Piglia's intellectual and literary formation in the less than serene Argentine sixties and seventies. Arriving back to his home country from Paris where he had studied with Roland Barthes, Piglia seemed set to carry on the long tradition of transferring cosmopolitan knowledge to the *porteño* capital. And arming an editorial board for the journal *Los libros* with the likes of Héctor Schmucler, Carlos Altamirano, Beatriz Sarlo, Germán García and Miriam Chorne was a good start. But then the political and cultural ground on which he stood underwent a seismic shift, and the local intellectual, following the 1971 "Nixon Shock, had to deal with a local setting in which, according to Dove, "national capitalism and import substitution industrialization [were] supplanted by transnational capitalism and financial speculation." Piglia responds literarily by pulling from popular media, such as the noir novel, and pitting the high rationality of political idealism against the reality of Argentine life. It is in Piglia's recent work, *Blanco nocturno*, for Dove, that we witness the erosion of active political self in the oft futile actions of Piglia's recurring detective, Emilio Renzi.

Global citizenship is at the heart of Leila Lehnen's elucidating study on Osvaldo Soriano's post-national novels, *La hora sin sombra* and *Una sombra ya pronto serás*. Parsing the tension between national and global cultural flows, Lehnen's examination of Soriano addresses one of the more complex themes taken on by the Generation of '72: that of the forced global citizen. National iconographies dark and folkloric spaces, such as the Argentine Pampa, are hollowed out as "liquid modernities" and replace the relative stability of national economies. This reification of spatial symbolic charge acts as a literary analogy for life under both the Junta and Menem, for Lehnen, speaking to the erosion of the basic functions of citizenship and the nation-state.

In his article on Ariel Dorfman's recent novel *Americanos: Los pasos de Murieta*, John Riofrio makes the compelling and innovative argument that in the Generation of '72, and Dorfman's work specifically, we witness a unique form of Latin American realism, one that sidesteps the post-modern naval-gazing and cynicism associated with the generations on either side of them. Neither uninitiated in the cerebral dicta of the post-1968 intellectual world nor the experiential reality of actually lived globalization, the Generation of '72, for Riofrio, writes new foundational fictions, calling on allegory, long a tool in Latin American political collectives, to negotiate the tension between the national and the global, the regional and the Pan-American, the psychologically stabilizing and the traumatic. If the Generation of '72 inherits anything from postmodernism, according to Riofrio, it is an analytical skill set that breaks with meta-narrative—Dorfman claims in *Other Septembers, Many Americas* (2004), for instance, that "one of the prevalent visions in our lands is that of a continent where the past devours the future and forces eternal repetition"—and not the insistence on narcissistic literary games.[10]

Elias Geoffrey Kantaris works through the formal and philosophical tension embedded in Luisa Valenzuela's under-explored novel, *Como en la guerra*, weighing the text against Valenzuela's larger body of works. Skillfully picking up on themes of Sophocles' *Antigone* in *Como en la guerra*, Kantaris uses Lacanian psychoanalysis to address the recurring analogy of the fatherless child. This

---

10. For more see, Ariel Dorfman, *Other Septembers, Many Americas: Selected Provocations 1980-2004*. London: Pluto Press, 2004.

useful revisit to the Oedipal paradigm, for the Generation of '72 *qua* the exilic experience, adds to the formal and sociological analysis of Valenzuela's navigation of the post-*Boom* publishing marketplace. Always already "half-buried," this is a group that seeks epistemological anchors while the in-rush of novel global signifiers reifies national and regional experience.

In her chapter, María Rosa Olivera Williams revisits Cristina Peri Rossi's experimental novel, *La nave de lo locos*, in order to examine the doubly fragile state of the female in exile. Focusing on the inscription of the real and symbolic body during the Operación Condor, and more specifically the Año de la Orientalidad, Olivera Williams weaves a tactful and rich analysis of the exilic body throughout her essay, culminating in what she reads as Peri Rossi's desire to reconstruct imaginaries of the present and future. This mark will be made, she argues using Peri Rossi's own words, "si no en el muro de la catedral, sí en el bastidor de la mente." (21)

José Agustín Pastén's claim that Diamela Eltit is the greatest writer of her generation would feel bold, if not argued with such depth and measure. Opting to write on, perhaps, the Generation of '72's most abstruse writer, Pastén neatly categorizes Eltit's works, pairing her formal evolution with both the political context in which her corpus was written and the publishing cultures and reading publics that she many times antagonized. Spanning Eltit's work with the politically committed avant-garde group, CADA, and her recent novel *Jamás el fuego nunca*, Pastén makes a strong argument that despite the crowded post-dictatorial literary field in Chile Eltit has left a lasting inscription on the Latin American canon that speaks both precisely and abstractly to the existential vicissitudes of the late-20th century Southern Cone.

Randolph Pope uses the collective works of Antonio Skármeta as a metric with which to gauge how the world's perception and expectation of Latin American intellectual subjectivity has evolved, sometimes erratically, since the end of the Cold War. This sociological analysis of Skármeta and his need to morph formally alongside the rapidly shifting Latin American aesthetic landscape traces the Generation of '72's collective unease with World Literary schema and economies of prestige. Imagistically skipping from a young Chilean writer in the sixties that cannot convince his Californian contemporaries that Chile and Argentina are different countries to Skármeta's recent triumphs at the Los Angeles and Paris Opera

Houses, Pope points out that global success, for this generation, is always cut with an undercurrent of irony. And the literature that, early on, was so infused with "a tone that was unmistakingly theirs" has grown increasingly opaque as it has received augmenting international attention.

In her chapter on Fernando Vallejo, Juanita Aristizábal examines the Generation of '72's take on global cultural and political projects. Focusing on the contrast Vallejo strikes between his dandy narrator and the actually lived cityscapes of Medellín, Aristizábal shows how the painter of modern life in Colombia would come to view the modernist destruction with which he is readily associated as quaint. Covering Vallejo's life works, Aristizábal furthers this critical take on universal modernisms in highlighting the plurality of popular voices that Vallejo captures. As the *vox populi* upends the Colombian lettered city, for Aristizábal, we witness a simultaneous trivializing of global cultural standards and a subtly idealist chronicling of life in post-Violencia Colombia.

Lázaro Lima revisits *Antes que anochezca* on the anniversary of its publication twenty years ago in order show why boilerplate political monikers do not stick to this polemical autobiography. Lima proposes that Arenas' autobiography has been too narrowly subjected to left and right readerly expectations that have failed to see the text as Arenas' attempt to fashion his own literary history in relation to the Cuban and the Latin American literature canon. In "The King's Toilet: Cruising Literary History in Reinaldo Arenas' *Before Night Falls*" Lima argues that cruising and "the arts of cruising" for Arenas conforms to a broader history of anti-authoritarian "libertinaje mental" initially posited by Jorge Mañach. For Arenas, Lima argues, both the arts of existence and the literary arts as indispensable to Arenas' aesthetic practice and conditions his insistence on the civic liberties that are required to instantiate it. Insofar as *Antes que anochezca* acts as a guide to Arenas' life and work, the ontological Arenas births the cultural icon Arenas from his deathbed, a finessing of the symbolic economy not out of step with the Generation of '72 and its writers tendency to take up literary rather than real arms.

Postdata

The book version of *The Generation of '72: The Forced Glob-*

al Citizens of Latin America benefits from two addenda chapters that represent a panel dedicated to the topic at the Latin American Studies Association meeting in Washington, D.C. on June 1st 2013. The productive discussion between Olivera Williams, Agustín Pastén, Aristizábal, and Nicholson focused on globalization, urban literature, and feminism in contemporary Latin American literature. We have chosen to add Olivera Williams thoughtful and innovative piece on the masculine shadow cast by the Boom and a response by female members of the Generation of '72 that alludes to a Boom of one's own and Agustín Pastén's exciting exploration of how urban Santiago is persistently reworked and recorded in the '80s and '90s, as much by writers and artists as shock economists.

Works Cited

Avelar, Idelber. *The Untimely Present: Postdictatorial Latin American Fiction and the Task of Mourning*. Durham, NC: Duke University Press, 1999.

Baumgarten, Alexander. *Aesthetica*. Frankfurt: Hildesheim, 1961.

Breckenridge, Carol A. Sheldon Pollock, Homi K. Bhabha, and Dipesh Chakrabarty, ed. *Cosmopolitanism*. Durham, NC: Duke University Press, 2002.

Casanova, Pascale. *The World Republic of Letters*. Cambridge, MA: Harvard University Press, 2004.

Cohn, Deborah. "A Tale of Two Translation Programs: Politics, the Market, and Rockefeller Funding for Latin American Literature in the United States During the 1960s and 1970s." *Latin American Research Review*, 41.2 (2006): 139-64.

Donoso, José. *Historia Personal Del Boom*. Buenos Aires: Sudamericana-Planeta, 1984.

Dorfman, Ariel. *Other Septembers, Many Americas: Selected Provocations 1980-2004*. London: Pluto Press, 2004.

English, James F. *The Economy of Prestige: Prizes, Awards, and Circulation of Cultural Value*. Cambridge, MA: Harvard University Press, 2005.

Felman, Shoshana and Dori Laub. *Testimony: Crises of Witnessing in Literature, Psychoanalysis, and History*. New York:

Routledge, 1992.

Fuguet, Alberto and Sergio Gómez, ed. *McOndo*. Barcelona: Grijalbo Mondadori, 1996.

Goic, Cedomil. *Historia De La Novela Hispanoamericana*. Valparaiso, Chile: Ediciones Universitarias de Valparaiso, Universidad de Chile, 1972.

—. *Mitos Degradados*. Atlanta: Rodopi, 1992.

Manzoni, Celina, ed. *La Fugitiva Contemporaneidad: Narrativa Latinoamericana, 1990-2000*. Buenos Aires: Corregidor, 2003.

Moretti, Franco. *Signs Taken for Wonders: Essays in the Sociology of Literary Forms*. London: Verso, 1988.

Richard, Nelly and Alberto Moreiras, ed. *Pensar en la postdictadura*. Santiago, Chile: Editorial Cuarto Propio, 2001.

Oppenheim, Lois Hecht. *Politics in Chile: Democracy, Authoritarianism, and the Search for Development*. 1993.

Angel Palou, Pedro, Eloy Urroz, Ignacio Padilla, Ricardo Chaez Cstaneda, and Jorge Volpi. "Manifiesto Crack." *Lateral. Revista de Cultura*. 70, 2000.

Rossi, Cristina Peri. *La Tarde Del Dinosaurio*. Letras De Exilio. Barcelona: Terceto, 1984.

Schiller, Friedrich. *On the Aesthetic Education of Man*. New Haven: Yale University Press, 2004.

Shaw, Donald. *Antonio Skarmeta and the Post-Boom*. Nanover, NH: Ediciones del Norte, 1994.

—. *The Post-Boom and Spanish American Fiction*. Saratoga Springs, NY: SUNY Press, 1998.

LITERARY FUTURES: CRIME FICTION, GLOBAL CAPITALISM AND THE HISTORY OF THE PRESENT IN RICARDO PIGLIA

Patrick Dove

Indiana University

> Any attempt to examine the status of potentiality must confront a specific aporia: the fact that, by definition, a potentiality is a possibility that exists.
> —Giorgio Agamben, *Potentialities*.

Through his novels (*Respiración artificial*, 1980; *La ciudad ausente*, 1992; *Plata quemada*, 1997; *Blanco nocturno*, 2010), short story collections (*La invasión/Jaulario*, 1967; *Nombre falso*, 1975; *Prisión perpetua*, 1988; *Cuentos morales*, 1995) and essays (*Crítica y ficción*, 1986; *La Argentina en pedazos*, 1993; *El laboratorio del escritor*, 1994; *Formas breves*, 1999; *Diccionario de la novela de Macedonio Fernández*, 2000; *El último lector*, 2005), as well as his academic presence in Argentine and North American universities such as Universidad de Buenos Aires, UC-Davis, Harvard and Princeton, the Argentine writer Ricardo Piglia (Adrogué, 1941-) has made his mark as one of the most important voices in Latin American letters in the decades following the "Boom." As far as poetics goes, Piglia's writing has little in common with what are now seen as the most recognizable narrative traits of the Boom novel: magical realism, nouveau-roman inspired experimentalism, proliferation of linguistic play, etc. Cultural sensibilities have shifted significantly since the 1960s, and the peculiar mixture of cosmopolitanism and revolution that inspired García Márquez, Cortázar, Fuentes and others would be seen as anachronistic in juxtaposition to Piglia's work. However, there is at least one important way in which Piglia's thought and writing remain adjacent to the concerns of the Boom writers, despite the probability that their respective approaches to these concerns differ significantly. Whatever else it may have been, the Boom novel was always concerned with the problem of Latin American (national or regional) history; the novel was conceived as an allegorical exploration of Latin American modernity and its discontents: the perpetual return of tyranny in *Cien años de soledad*, the question "¿Cuándo se jodió el Perú" that frames *Conversación en la catedral*, the asymptotic identification of personal and national history in *La muerte de Artemio Cruz*, and so on. Piglia's novels are similarly concerned with the relation between past and present, but they also reflect grave doubts about literature's capacity to bring history in its totality into view or to provide the symbolic groundwork for knowledge. The historiographical question "¿Cuándo se jodió el Perú?" is supplanted, in *Respiración artificial*, by a more skeptical but equally persistent primordial question: "¿Hay una historia?"

Piglia's early intellectual trajectory fits somewhat uneasily with the periodization framework of the "Generation of '72" that has been proposed as the unifying thread for this collection, at least insofar as that date implies a rupture with what came before it. Piglia's early work (*La invasión/Jaulario*, the Serie Negra and *Los libros* projects, and up through *Nombre falso* from 1975) is informed very much by what was going on in Argentina in the 1960s: not so much the Boom but the tendency of Left intellectuals to begin reexamining and rewriting the intellectual Left's relation to Peronism, as well as the continuation and deepening of a politicization that was initiated in the late 1950s under the figures of Sartrean "commitment" and the Gramscian organic intellectual, and later continued under figures such as Che Guevara and Maoism's "People's War."[1] While "'72" emphasizes the end of the Boom as well as the imminent demise of the revolutionary imaginary associated with both the Latin American guerrilla movements and Allende's Unidad Popular, it seems to me that in Piglia's case the distinction between "pre 1972" and "post 1972" is less than clean, in large part because his thought

---

1. For discussions of the transformation of the intellectual Left's relation to Peronism in the aftermath of 1955, see José Aricó, *La cola del diablo* and Oscar Terán, *Nuestros años sesentas*. For a brief discussion of Piglia and Maoism see Bruno Bosteels, "In the Shadow of Mao."

and writing pre-1972 was never synonymous with the Boom.

After completing his university studies in history at the Universidad Nacional de La Plata, Piglia moved to Buenos Aires in the late 1960s, where he took up several editorial posts in addition to publishing his first collection of short stories.[2] One project involved a journal, *Los libros* (1969-76), which Piglia co-edited with Héctor Schmucler and Carlos Altamirano (they would later be joined by Beatriz Sarlo, Germán García and Miriam Chorne).[3] Schmucler, who had just returned from a stint in Paris where he studied semiotics with Roland Barthes, envisioned *Los libros* as an Argentine version of *La Quinzaine littéraire*, a Parisian journal founded in 1966 by Maurice Nadeau with the goal of serving as a critical compendium of contemporary French literature. The volumes of *Los libros* included critical essays by an impressive array of well-known and up-and-coming Argentine intellectuals, including José Aricó, Oscar Massota, Juan Carlos Portantiero, Oscar del Barco, Eliseo Verón and Josefina Ludmer as well as Sarlo, Piglia, Altamirano and García. The journal disseminated new developments in Latin American letters (literary critical essays by Benedetti, Roa Bastos, Paz, and others) and European thought (translations of, and commentaries on, the work of Lacan, Althusser, Levi-Strauss, Marcuse, Freud and others). Inaugurated in the aftermath of the Córdoba student and worker rebellions against the Onganía dictatorship in May 1969, however, *Los libros* was never simply a literary or cultural journal; its critical impetus was shaped from the beginning by torsion between literary-cultural and political crosscurrents. While *Los libros* continued to publish until it was shut down definitively following the March 1976 military *coup d'etat*, its editorial board suffered a schism following the death of Perón in 1974—who was succeeded in power by his third wife, Isabel. While Sarlo and Schmucler sided with Left Peronism in its support of Isabel Perón's regime despite its repressive, conservative orientation—because they viewed it as an embattled country's last bulwark against North American imperialism—Piglia and Altamirano, who saw themselves as Maoists

---

2. Published in Cuba under the title of *Jaulario* at the same time it was published in Argentina as *La invasión*, *Jaulario* received special mention in the Casa de las Américas literary competition of 1967.

3. For an informative account of the editorial history of *Los libros* see Somoza and Vinelli's recent interview in *Página/12* with Piglia, Schmucler, Altamirano and García.

rather than Peronist nationalists, rejected any notion of support for a government they viewed as an inevitable precursor to yet another military intervention. Piglia resigned from the *Los libros* editorial board in 1975.[4]

A year prior to *Los libros*, in 1968 Piglia took up the editorial endeavor of directing La serie negra (Editorial Tiempo Contemporáneo), a book series dedicated to publishing Spanish-language translations of novels by North American writers such as Raymond Chandler, Dashiell Hammett, Horace McCoy, David Goodis and others. By then the Anglo-American detective tradition was already familiar in Latin America; the classics of Poe, Chesteron and Doyle had enjoyed popularity among Latin American readerships since at least the 1940s. In Argentina, the genre had an important influence on Jorge Luis Borges and Bioy Casares who, in addition to their own stories, coauthored several volumes of detective stories under the pseudonym Bustos Domecq while also coediting Emecé's Séptimo Círculo series (1946-58), which published Spanish-language translations of Anglo-American detective and mystery novels. Other Argentine writers influenced by the classical detective genre included Silvina Ocampo, the early Rodolfo Walsh (*Variaciones en rojo*), Marco Denevi and Adolfo Pérez Zelaschi. Borges went so far as to assert that Poe's private detective stories inaugurated a new kind of reader, one attuned to the specific codes and sensibility of the detective story: the enigma of the locked room, the paradox of the hidden amidst the visible, the assertion of the superiority of intelligence and deductive reason, the detective's radical skepticism vis-à-vis appearances.

The Serie Negra project played an important role in facilitating a broad reception of the "hard boiled" detective novel in Argentina, whose influence can be seen clearly in the works of later generations of writers who rose to prominence in the 1970s and 80s, including Manuel Puig, Osvaldo Soriano, Mempo Giardinelli, Juan José Saer, Juan Martini, José Pablo Feinmann, Vicente Battista and Martín Capparós. A key distinction between the classical detective story and its 20th century "noir" or "hard boiled" successor can help to shed light on what is at stake in the Latin American appropriation of these traditions. Whereas Poe's and Doyle's detec-

---

4. Three years later, in 1978, Sarlo, Piglia and Altamirano would again join forces to form *Punto de Vista*, in which they began publishing critical essays again under pseudonyms.

tives are literary celebrations of the supremacy of reason over evil in the modern world—intelligence vanquishes not only criminality but uncertainty itself—the post-WWI crime fiction of Hammett and Chandler portrays a drab, sunless world of betrayal and injustice in which the hero is run roughshod by an increasingly impersonal and indifferent society.

What, then, does the Latin American adoption and transformation of this 20th century tradition tell us? Giardinelli asserts that the North American noir novel still retains a vestige of faith in justice and the possibility of fighting back against a corrupted system, whereas the Latin American "translation" of this tradition is generally set in situations in which the promise of modernity has been found empty and justice has been rendered impossible. If Hammett and Chandler's novels reflect the feeling that the system defended by Poe's and Doyle's detectives had become dysfunctional or corrupted, the Latin American appropriation of the noir novel introduces a new diagnosis whose difference is subtle but significant: it is not so much that the system is broken, but rather that the system itself in its ordinary functioning—not only the liberal, capitalist State but also the world-system in which it emerges and which it likewise sustains—produces violence and injustice in the form of perpetual underdevelopment, domination. If Hammett and Chandler's heroes find themselves living in a social system that has begun to break down, their Latin American counterparts reflect the view that the emergence of the modern forms of social organization that have prevailed in Europe and North America since the 19th century was accompanied and buttressed by the asymmetries of colonial and imperial relations between Europe and periphery.

It would be a mistake, however, to conclude that this perspectival shift from a "developed" view of social relations to an "underdeveloped" sensibility occurs all of a sudden with the Latin American reception of the "hard boiled" tradition in the 1960s. As early as his 1946 essay "Nuestro pobre individualismo" we can already see Borges asserting a fundamental distinction between how State ideology functions differently in developed and underdeveloped worlds:

> El argentino, a diferencia de los americanos del Norte y de casi todos los europeos, no se identifica con el Estado. Ello puede atribuirse a la circunstancia de que, en este país, los gobiernos suelen ser pésimos o al hecho general de que el Estado es una inconce-

bible abstracción; lo cierto es que el argentino es un individuo, no un ciudadano. Aforismos como el de Hegel, "el Estado es la realidad de la idea moral," le parecen bromas siniestras. Los films elaborados en Hollywood repetidamente proponen a la admiración el caso de un hombre (generalmente un periodista) que busca la amistad de un criminal para entregarlo después a la policía; el argentino, para quien la amistad es una pasión y la policía una *maffia*, siente que ese "héroe" es un incomprensible canalla. (57-58)

In contrast to the Hollywood character type, whose Kantian ethical heroism is confirmed when he turns in his new friend to the police, in Argentina heroism is conceived according to the model of José Hernández's Tadeo Isidoro Cruz, a conscripted lawman who discards his badge in order to fight side by side with an unjustly accused but valiant outlaw. Giardinelli proposes that the Latin American *novela negra* marks the exhaustion of any residual faith in justice and systematic change; it is thus very much a post-Boom literary form. For Hammett and Chandler, and perhaps Borges too, this hope had resided in the principle of the individual as social monad capable of suffering and resisting the indifference and abuse of society. However, the individual is itself a concept that emerges in a particular time and place, and thus it must in turn be historicized; for Giardinelli the Latin American "translation" of the noir genre precisely initiates this historicizing operation.

> La relación de un estadunidense con el poder es muy distinta de la de un latinoamericano: ambos se resisten, pero el primero está convencido de que puede "hacer algo" para cambiar las cosas, aunque dentro de los márgenes del propio sistema, porque en su conciencia confía en las virtudes del mismo. El estadunidense está educado en la convicción de que el sistema es flexible y amplio; es mutable, se adapta a los tiempos modernos, y si uno se esfuerza y protesta consigue modificarlo. Por esa confianza esencial en el sistema político-social y en su capacidad correctiva, hay la convicción de que las posibilidades son infinitas y están al alcance del esfuerzo y el valor personal, y por eso se valoran tanto la audacia y el individualismo. La rebeldía es individual y puede ser una heroica, fascinante aventura, pero individual. El estadounidense en última instancia siempre se somete al poder y lo acepta porque así fue educado: "la Ley," en abstracto, es sinónimo de referente de conducta. Un policía es "la ley"; y la gente vive "dentro de la ley" o "al margen de la ley"... En América Latina, en cambio, es muy difícil encontrar un escritor que confíe en el sistema de su país. Casi

nadie confía en el poder establecido, más bien se vive en constante sublevación frente a él y, aunque se quisiera modificarlo, es un hecho que se ha ido perdiendo la fe. También estamos llenos de las buenas intenciones y nobles sentimientos, claro está, pero para muchos de nosotros la vida consiste en una constante rebelión. Vivimos en disidencia eterna y además debemos hacer enormes esfuerzos para mantener nuestra fuerza, nuestros ideales y nuestro espíritu de lucha. De hecho hacer cultura, en América Latina es resistir, resistir todo el tiempo. (233-34)

While the conventions of crime fiction and the noir novel are ubiquitous in Piglia's work, their importance is synthesized in his assertion—almost certainly an echo of Borges—that the crime story constitutes a template for modern literature, with the detective embodying the role of a certain reader (the critic) and the author playing the role of the criminal, whose furtive traces and clues are doggedly pursued by the investigator.[5] The importance of detective fiction for modern literature goes beyond analogy or exemplarity; for Piglia, the space of modern literature embodies something akin to a crime scene.[6] This is not to ignore, however, that there are other equally important ways of approaching Piglia's work. Indeed, the question I am interested in pursuing concerns how the detective/noir traditions intersect with or provide a point of departure for Piglia's other literary and extra-literary concerns.

Of course, there can be no substantive exploration of Piglia's novels, short stories and essays that does not also pay attention to a somewhat iconoclastic engagement with the Argentine tradition. While Piglia frequently describes his own writing as attempting to cross Borges with Arlt, his 1992 novel *La ciudad ausente* is one of the first works since that of Borges to proclaim the fundamental

---

5. See in particular "La lectura de la ficción," 20-21.

6. One way of unpacking this enigmatic relation is offered the "Homenaje a Roberto Arlt" portion of *Nombre falso*, where Piglia first begins to develop a thesis concerning literature as plagiarism. See Bruno Bosteels, "In the Shadow of Mao." By the same token, one could argue that, beginning with Sarmiento, the Argentine tradition has repeatedly conceived of the origin of social and political organization as a theft (Rosas as having stolen Facundo's charismatic unifying power, and Sarmiento as aiming to appropriate it for the Unitarian cause, etc.). Or, finally, one could think "crime" in an ontological register, and assert—as Jacques Rancière does—that it is literature which exposes the constitutive gap in the social, the abyssal ground of democracy. See *The Politics of Aesthetics*. I will return to this theme shortly.

status of Macedonio Fernández in Argentine literary history. By the same token, the influence of Brecht and accompanying questions of theatricality, melodrama and gesture in Piglia's writing cannot be ignored. Furthermore, his writing also explores tensions between European and American high modernist prose (Joyce, Kafka, Musil and Faulkner) and questions of orality and testimony raised by Latin American writers such as José Hernández, Juan Rulfo and the later Rodolfo Walsh of *Operación masacre* (whose interest in non-fictive or testimonial literature, it should be noted, was influenced by the work of Truman Capote).

Friction between literary experimentalism and oral tradition is especially notable in Piglia's first novel, *Respiración artificial*, which highlights traumatic ideational-linguistic ruptures in the context of state terror and exile, while also advancing a view of literature as site where an encounter with the limits of what can be said or thought (the "experience" of pain, for instance) might be said to take place. The significance of a given event emerges *Nachträglichkeit*, as Freud says, belatedly and reshaped by the intervening time between occurrence and signification. If the real of history emerges from one or another *missed experience,* narration for Piglia is an attempt to span the gaps that haunt all experience, which voids it proposes to reconstruct as primal scenes. Piglia's long-standing concern with Argentine social history comes forth in *Respiración artificial* through a strange literary juxtaposition: of the 19th century civil war between Unitarians and Federalists on the one hand (seen through the errant letters of an exiled liberal, Enrique Ossorio, as he discursively constructs a utopian future that would finally be free from tyranny), and the political violence of the 1970s on the other hand (seen through the eyes of Renzi as he searches—a kind of private eye—for his disappeared uncle, Marcelo Maggi). Ossorio's brand of Liberal utopianism is construed teleologically as a people's eventual realization of freedom and self-consciousness; he conceives of this gradual but predetermined self-realization as a date [*cita*] with the future... which turns out to be nothing other than the time of El Proceso.

> ¿Qué uso de la crítica hace un escritor?... Un escritor es alguien que traiciona lo que lee, que se desvía y ficcionaliza: hay como un exceso en la lectura que hace Borges de Hernández o en la lectura que hace Olson de Melville o Gombrowicz de Dante; hay cierta desviación en esas lecturas, un uso inesperado del otro texto. La

discusión sobre Shakespeare en el capítulo de la biblioteca en *Ulises*, y ese capítulo es para mí el mejor del libro, es un buen ejemplo de esa lectura un poco excéntrica y siempre renovadora. (*Crítica y ficción*, 17-18)

Deliberately mixing spaces and practices of writing and reading to the point of rendering them nearly indistinguishable, Piglia uses the double temporal structure of the appointment—the initiation through inscription of a new relation between one time and another, a relation which is necessarily promissory in nature but which proves incapable of guaranteeing what it promises—to develop his own anti-teleological understanding of literary "communication" and "expression," an understanding which he elsewhere refers to under the heading of a *relato futuro*.[7] The *relato futuro* designates a constellation of literary traits and tendencies, especially its peculiar forms of temporality or "inactuality." It adapts itself to various literary phenomena at different points in Piglia's writing: his theorization of the enigmatic "secret story" that lurks between the lines of the first, explicit employment in the modern short story; the inference or anticipation of alternative forms of narration—a story that would be told in a language different from the quotidian language in which the prevailing order of things is reproduced—brought about by avant garde breaks with tradition (e.g., Joyce's break with national literature; Macedonio Fernández's unorthodox relation to the Argentine tradition); or literature as ciphering or fictionalization which, by submitting accustomed forms of experience and discourse to strange torsions and displacements, can unexpectedly open up new possibilities for thought. Generally speaking, the *relato futuro* names the internal difference of narrative with respect to itself, a "difference" which is neither actual nor transcendent but which can be theorized as the immanent capacity of literary language to elicit new and unexpected possibilities through reading, possibilities that cannot be controlled or calculated in advance. Neither written nor read, the *relato futuro* is not a property of either the author or the reader. It is not this or that meaning or interpretive relation but the horizontal structure within which sense

---

7. Among other sources see the essay "Tesis sobre el cuento" (*Crítica y ficción*) and the conversation between Piglia and Juan José Saer published under the title *Por un relato futuro*. For critical discussions of the concept of *relato futuro*, see Alberto Moreiras, *Tercer espacio* (389-97) and Gareth Williams, *The Other Side of the Popular* (143-72).

emergences, which *qua* horizon for reading can never itself become legible. *El relato futuro* thus also names the structural incompleteness of every text. Pierre Menard's "rewriting" of the *Quijote* is just one illustration of this internal, unpresentable difference. Literature as *relato futuro* is thus irreducible to any cultural ideology of "national literature" or even "Latin American literature." Moreover, the concept of the *relato futuro* ruins instrumental conceptualizations of language as vehicle for meaning or tool for controlling and administering differences in hegemonic fashion. The *relato futuro* is literature as no-man's land; it has no proper concept and is property of no one.

While echoes of the hard boiled/noir tradition can be found as early as the short story "La loca y el relato del crimen" (*Nombre falso*, 1975), and while the investigatory motif is clearly present in *Respiración artificial* and *La ciudad ausente*, it is not until *Blanco nocturno* that Piglia writes what could be considered—at least by half—as a crime novel. In what follows, I propose a reading of this recent novel that would help to shed light on how Piglia's reflections on literature can be mapped together with concerns about history, and in the case of *Blanco nocturno*, of the history of the present in the context of Argentina's location within the global capitalist system.

Blanco nocturno takes place in 1972, in a small, rural Pampa town in the Province of Buenos Aires. The novel is divided into two parts whose interrelatedness is not readily apparent. A brief synopsis will help clarify my remarks, in which I will indicate one way of thinking the relation between parts. The first half details the investigation into a mysterious murder in the town's Plaza Hotel, where a foreigner—Tony Durán, a native Puerto Rican and resident of New Jersey who recently traveled to Argentina for unexplained reasons—has been found lying dead in his room with a knife deeply embedded in his chest.[8] Working with his assistant Saldías, In-

---

8. Here we see the first of many not-so-subtle allusions to the history of Argentine crime fiction: the scene in the Plaza Hotel unmistakably recalls that of the first murder victim in Borges's "La muerte y la brújula," in which Yarmolinksy is killed in a similar manner by the *compradito* Azevedo. The generic echoes resume at later points in the novel, for example when the lead investigator, Croce, recalls his dealings with a line of fictive inspectors and police officers including "Leoni" (a detective invented by Pérez Zelaschi), "Laurenzi" (Rodolfo Walsh) and "Treviranus" (the pragmatic police commissioner and opposite of the Dupin-like Lönnrot in "La muerte y la brújula."

spector Croce uncovers several important clues. For one, Durán is said to have been involved in a love triangle with Sofía and Ada Belladona, the twin granddaughters of one of the town's founders who recently returned from a trip to the United States. His death is thus clouded by romantic intrigue and the taint of social transgression (the Belladonas belong to a family of the landed elite whereas Durán was a foreigner and a mulatto to boot). By the same token, Durán is said to have been traveling with a suitcase filled with undeclared US currency, a single bill of which is discovered in the hotel's laundry room. However, various witnesses claim to have seen the hotel's effete porter—a Japanese immigrant named Yoshio who is just as much an outsider as Durán in this traditional, rural Argentine setting—leaving the victim's room around the time of the murder. While Croce's intuition is to dismiss the possibility that the meek Yoshio might have killed Durán after a lover's quarrel, faced with the eyewitness reports he is compelled to arrest the porter.

As Croce pursues the investigation, he is joined by Emilio Renzi, an investigative journalist from Buenos Aires and a character who appears in many of Piglia's works. The dialogue between Croce and Renzi serves as a sounding board for Croce's speculations about the murder as well as a forum for expounding on his theory of detection (more about that in a moment). Meanwhile, the sinister local prosecutor, Cueto, dismisses Croce's intuitions and prepares to bring Yoshio to trial, while also convincing Croce's assistant, Saldías, to turn against his mentor. Betrayed by his friend and strategically outplayed by his nemesis, Croce loses his bearings and is finally forced to commit himself to a mental hospital. With the retreat of that interlocutor whose presence helps define the genre, the detective—that modern exemplar of pure reason—becomes symbolically indistinguishable from the specter of madness—in this case, paranoia.[9] In the absence of its other, it would

9. The detective as exemplar of pure reason is of course an allusion to Poe and to Borges's Lönnrot, who sees himself in the line of Dupin as "un puro razonador." In an interview with Silvina Friera, Piglia describes *Blanco nocturno* as belonging to a genre of "paranoiac fiction" characterized, in Croce's case, by the absence of any limit on reason's tendency to forge connections between differences. This same theme of unlimited articulation could also be found in the later descriptions of Luca as "mad inventor." The idea of "paranoiac fiction" is also developed further in the interview with Camilo Hernández-Castellanos and Jeff Lawrence. In Croce's case, meanwhile, his familial history helps to put his immediate situation of abandonment and isolation in another context: Croce's father, he relates to Renzi, was

seem, there is nothing to prevent pure reason from taking flight and abandoning its senses. From there it is Renzi who must take up the investigation into a sordid family history that finally proves to be the story of the locality's incorporation within the network of transnational capital.

Piglia remarks more than once that, in contradistinction to Aristotelian plot-centered poetics, his own poetics is driven by an interest in character. In *Blanco nocturno* there is no doubt that character or *ethos*—Luca in particular, but also Croce, Durán, Sofía and even the gaucho-jockey Chino—is what drives plot and not vice versa. But to this distinction we must add that *ethos* is never encountered in the form of an individuated subject, but rather displays itself as always—already social and relational. Luca's situation, for instance, cannot be understood outside of the complex familial relations in which he is caught up: his largely imaginary relation with a mother who abandoned him at young age, his rivalry with his—now deceased—brother, and his bellicose relation with his father. Moreover, it becomes clear that the family is conceived in *Blanco nocturno* as a privileged site for thinking about narrative. If the question of family is frequently a primary motor for inquiry and storytelling ("Who am I, where do I come from, and what were those who gave me life hoping for?"), family as a constellation of relations is itself also produced and sustained by the telling of stories. *Blanco nocturno* is thus a novel about the Belladona family, which as part of the rural Argentine oligarchic elite is profoundly linked to the history of land tenure. If the novel's focus is influenced by Greek tragedy (the comparison of the daughters to Antigone and Iphigeneia; the theme of the father's sins being visited upon the sons) it also displays a debt to Faulkner's literary considerations of the family in relation to the history of a region that remains caught between tradition and modernity.

The second half of the novel turns away from the detective genre and fashions itself as a pseudo-Arltian story of a mad inventor who is irredeemably ahead of his time, dedicated to bringing

a Peronist who suffered greatly in the aftermath of the 1955 Revolución Libertadora and the subsequent proscription of the Peronist Party. His sense of social belonging was effectively suspended, much as would be the case—one imagines—for someone committed to an asylum. The setting of the novel—which takes place in 1972, the year before Cámpora's election and Perón's return from exile—underscores these symbolic resonances between generations and between the personal and the political.

forth new apparatuses for which contemporary society has yet to develop any practical use. It is Luca—Sofía and Ada's stepbrother and the black sheep of the Belladona family—who emerges as the real protagonist of the novel. The mastermind behind a small, independent but highly innovative automotive factory in the outskirts of the town, he heroically resists the decision of his father and brother to sell the land on which the factory stands in order to resolve the family's debt problems. Cueto, meanwhile, turns out to be acting as member of a hedge fund whose investors plan to buy the land and resell it for development as a shopping mall. The first and second halves of the story are connected by the death of Durán, who has been illegally transporting US currency into the country for Luca's cash-strapped father.[10] Luca, meanwhile, imposes the final seal on the impossibility of justice in the noir novel when he gives in to Cueto's pressure and bears false witness against Yoshio in court—thus ensuring the porter's conviction—in exchange for the return of his father's money, which Luca then uses to liquidate the family debt and retain possession of the factory.

In the remaining part of this essay I want to propose one way of thinking the connectedness between the first and second parts of the novel, a link that could perhaps shed new light on how Piglia's interest in the detective and noir genre(s) is correlated with and informs a broader understanding of literature. Gastón García has observed that Croce's madness in the first half of the novel is mirrored in the second half by Luca's deliriums. This thematic resonance is strengthened by a series of formal anecdotes through which each character in turn describes the perceptual and cognitive basis for their thought. In his first encounter with Renzi (chapter 9), Croce explains his theory of criminal investigation via what at first seems an obtuse pair of analogies with investigatory reason: the optical illusion and the *rastreador*. Gradually it becomes clear, however, that what Croce is really describing are what we might call the a priori or the conditions of possibility for seeing.

¿Ve?—dijo— Éste es un pato, pero si lo mira así, es un conejo. –Di-

---

10. Duran was killed, Croce discovers, by a gaucho-like jockey named Chino who acted as a hired assassin. The question of who hired Chino and with what motive remains an unresolved loose thread, which in turn complicates the matter of generic belonging. Paraphrasing a distinction made by Derrida in the "Law of Genre" essay, we could say that Piglia's novel participates in the hard-boiled detective genre but without belonging to it.

bujó la silueta del pato-conejo—. Qué quiere decir ver algo tal cual es: no es fácil. —Miró el dibujo que había hecho en el mantel—. Un conejo y un pato.

Todo es según lo que sabemos *antes* de ver—Renzi no entendía hacia dónde apuntaba el comisario—Vemos las cosas *según* como las interpretamos. Lo llamamos previsión: saber de antemano, estar prevenidos. Usted en el campo sigue el rastro de un ternero, ve las huellas en la tierra seca, sabe que el animal está cansado porque las marcas son livianas y se orienta porque los pájaros bajan a picotear en el rastro. No puede buscar huellas al voleo, el rastreador debe primero saber lo que persigue: hombre, perro, puma. Y después ver. Lo mismo yo. Hay que tener una base y luego hay que inferir y dedicar. Entonces –concluyó– uno ve lo que sabe y no puede ver si no sabe... Descubrir es ver de otro modo lo que nadie ha percibido. Ése es el asunto. (*Blanco nocturno*, 142-43)

Let us retrace this account in reverse, beginning with the conclusion where we encounter a kind of hermeneutic circle. In order to follow tracks, as the *rastreador* or detective must, it is first necessary to postulate a concept of what one is trying to pursue (man, dog, puma). The endeavor to pursue and locate something by following its traces (trace à being) requires that we begin by postulating the specific being whose traces we seek to follow (being à trace). A trace only become visible *as trace* once we have made a determination as to what it is that could produce the trace in its specificity. In order to see (track), a certain prevision (anticipation, postulation of a subject) is first required. This hermeneutic circle poses a problem when it comes to detective work, which, if it is to lead to a true and just outcome, must be unbiased and open to all possibilities from the outset. The optical illusion—duck or rabbit?—thus harbors a more unsettling truth concerning perception, a truth which cannot be explained away by the supposed distinction between appearance and essence or being. The idea of seeing things "as they really are," according to a certain investigative ideal, is itself already a misnomer, a false problem, since "everything *is* according to what we know beforehand." Investigation and the knowledge it brings to light are shaped silently by a primordial decision that never presents itself for scrutiny and discussion. This sheds new light on the novel's epigraph, taken from the French novelist Louis-Ferdinand Céline: "La experiencia es una lámpara tenue que sólo ilumina a quien la sostiene." But how is what we know beforehand decided? On what basis and on whose authority is this "prevision" carried out?

If Croce does not provide a final answer to these questions he clearly acknowledges the problem when he clarifies that "la experiencia se da en el momento de cambiar del pato al conejo y viceversa. Llamo a este método *ver-como* y su objetivo es cambiar el aspecto bajo el que se ven ciertas cosas. Este *ver-como* no es parte de la percepción. Por un lado, es como ver y también *no* es como ver" (142). Experience is differential in nature, arising with the shift from one form to another, in the original decision for one or another form—a decision which itself never becomes the object of experience, and which logically, therefore, could not be the decision *of a subject*. Croce's investigative "method," meanwhile, seeks to open up the transcendental structure of cognition—the nocturnal target (*blanco nocturno*) of experience—and thus to free thought and perception for other ways of seeing. To offer another analogy, the investigator is to cognition what the philosopher is to history: each endeavor to bracket off the transcendental determination of perception in one or another direction (the "previsión" of the object as "duck" or "rabbit") and thereby to make possible an experience of seeing itself in its historicity. In other words, each seeks to uncover the contingency at the heart of what we ordinarily take to be sheer necessity, inevitability or nature.

Later in the novel (chapter 16) we find a fascinating account of Luca's own "method" of technological innovation. Invention, we are reminded, differs from the forms of production that prevail in the Pampa: unlike agriculture, which cultivates and husbands what are—conceptually speaking—nothing more than natural replicas of pre-existing forms (corn, cattle, etc.), the task of the inventor is to bring into existence something that has never seen the light of day before, something without a model. Seen in this light, invention has to be distinguished from all other forms of production and all other accounts of truth. It constitutes its own modality of truth production, to be distinguished from truth understood as aletheia, adequatio and revelation. Invention, we are told, is akin to the use of metaphor itself.

> Se trata—dijo—, claro, de una metáfora, de un símil, pero también de una *verdad literal*. Porque nosotros trabajamos con metáforas y con analogías, con el concepto de *igual a*, con los mundos posibles, buscamos la igualdad en la diferencia absoluta de lo real. Un orden discontinuo, una forma perfecta. El conocimiento no es el develamiento de una esencia oculta sino un enlace, una relación, un parecido entre objetos visibles. Por eso—y usó nuevamente la primera persona del singular—sólo puedo expresarme con metáforas. (243)

If we think of metaphor as revealing hidden truth we have missed the point. Metaphor is a transfer producing truth through the articulation of a previously unsuspected resemblance. Metaphor is like invention in that, instead of simply revealing what was previously hidden, it brings forth resemblance as having existed only in the mode of potentiality. Let us recall that, for Aristotle, metaphor is the one mode of discourse that cannot be taught. Because metaphor involves discovering sameness or *being* among differences, it can be said to constitute the essence of thought. The always-singular transfer from one word or idea to another is the lightning flash in which language gives us something to think.

The analogy between metaphor and invention is hardly accidental: as Giorgio Agamben puts it, "the historical condition of human beings is inseparable from their condition as speaking beings; it is inscribed in the very mode of their access to language, which is originally marked by a fracture" (*Potentialities*, 51). What Agamben calls "fracture" is a lack or gap haunting being as ground. It is, for instance, Saussure's thesis on the differential nature of language, the inability of any given signifier to account for its own sense, and the consequent need to turn to other signifiers. In Piglia's novel, as I suggested in the earlier discussion of the idea of literature as crime scene, this "fracture," which both gives humans access to language while also delimiting their sovereignty over it, could perhaps be likened to a primordial crime, an originary out-of-jointness toward which all relationality ultimately points.

The reader is hardly surprised to learn that Luca is misunderstood by friends and family, who appear to dismiss his thought as "unreal." What does surprise, however, is when the novel's unnamed editor interjects—in a footnote no less—a contrast between Luca's thought, which seeks to envision and make realizable what previously existed as potentiality rather than actuality, and an emerging global system of financial capitalism which not only threatens the family factory but which also stands poised to displace the sovereignty of national capitalism and to assert itself as the new dominant form of accumulation and wealth production.[11] The ascent of financial speculation is assigned a precise time and place in the aforementioned footnote: the so-called "Nixon shock." In August 1971, a Presidential decree in Washington unilaterally cancelled the direct convertibility of the US dollar into gold, ending an international agreement that had stood since the Bretton Woods pact was signed in 1944. Bretton Woods had served as the foundation for the global financial system since WWII, establishing shared principles for commerce and financial relations while also giving form to the institutional framework (the IMF and World Bank group) for post-war international finance. While a freely floating national currency provides state monetary policy with considerably enhanced flexibility in times of impending recession, as Paul Krugman notes, the end of the gold standard also creates the possibility for intensified uncertainty and leaves investors "free to be irresponsible" in the face of greater unpredictability in flows of investment capital.[12]

---

11. The displacement of national capitalism and import substitution industrialization by transnational capitalism and financial speculation is usually understood in the context of two key moments: the 1976-83 dictatorship and Martínez de Hoz's role as Minister of Economy under Videla, and Menem's privatization reforms of the 1990s. Piglia is thus offering in *Blanco nocturno* an idiosyncratic version of the history of the present.

12. "While a freely floating national money has advantages, however, it also has risks. For one thing, it can create uncertainties for international traders and investors. Over the past five years, the dollar has been worth as much as 120 yen and as little as 80. The costs of this volatility are hard to measure (partly because sophisticated financial markets allow businesses to hedge much of that risk), but they must be significant. Furthermore, a system that leaves monetary managers free to do good also leaves them free to be irresponsible—and, in some countries, they have been quick to take the opportunity. That is why countries with a history of runaway inflation, like Argentina, often come to the conclusion that monetary independence is a poisoned chalice. (Argentine law now requires that one peso be worth exactly one U.S. dollar, and that every peso in circulation be backed by a

In Piglia's novel the Nixon shock synechdochally designates a longer and more diffuse history of transformation in which national capitalism and import substitution industrialization are supplanted by transnational capitalism and financial speculation. At a moment when the national popular was still very much a potent political signifier in Argentina and much of Latin America, the Nixon shock nonetheless constitutes one of the early symptoms of the decline of the modern State form (the Liberal state, the Welfare State, the populist State, and so on) and its displacement by the market under neoliberalism. It likewise helps to shape a new generational sensibility shared throughout much of the hemisphere, one which gives shape to the literary phenomenon that Brantley Nicholson terms the "Generation of '72" in Latin America.

The contrast between Luca's work as inventor on the one hand, and one of the inaugural moments of a new era of accumulation dominated by financial speculation on the other hand, serves two purposes in the novel. First, and most obviously, it comprises a kind of metaphor of the history of the present, of the death of an old form of social organization (import-substitute industrialization and the national popular) and its replacement by a new form (transnational financial speculation and neoliberalism). Second, it juxtaposes the real abstractions of capitalist valuation and social organization with a paradoxical thought that is only confusedly equated with abstraction. The praxis of invention, in which imagination, thought and realization are inextricably linked, compels us to acknowledge the *existence* of what we call potentiality, and thereby to see existence as something more than a mere synonym for the actual. This may provide yet another way of working through Piglia's formulation of the *relato futuro*, which similarly requires us to see in language the paradoxical immanence of the possible. At the same time, it also provides a literary counterpoint to the Liberal philosophy of history, which locates the end of history in the free market and thereby evacuates any possibility of experiencing the historicity of the present.

---

dollar in reserves.)" (67-68). Several years after Krugman's assessment, in 2002, Argentina ended the fixed relation of the peso to the US dollar, which led to the massive depreciation of the peso, severe inflation and all of the well-known ills associated with the Argentine economic crisis.

Works Cited

Agamben, Giorgio. *Potentialities*. Stanford: Stanford UP, 2000.

Borges, Jorge Luis. "Nuestro pobre individualismo." *Otras Inquisiciones*. Buenos Aires: Sur, 1952.

Bosteels, Bruno. "In the Shadow of Mao: Ricardo Piglia's 'Homenaje a Roberto Arlt," *Journal of Latin American Cultural Studies* 12:2 (2003): 229-59.

Derrida, Jacques. "Law of Genre." *Glyph* 7 (1980): 202-32.

Friera, Silvina. "Ricardo Piglia ante la edición de Blanco nocturno." Interview with Ricardo Piglia. *Página/12* Cultura y Espectáculos, 20 September 2010. <http://www.pagina12.com.ar/diario/ suplementos/espectaculos/4-19327-2010-09-20.html>.

García, Gastón. "Entrevista con Ricardo Piglia." *Letras libres*, March 2011. <http://www.letraslibres.com/revista/entrevista/entrevista-ricardo-piglia?page=full>.

Giardinelli, Mempo. *El género negro: Ensayos sobre literatura policial*. Mexico, DF: Universidad Autónoma Metropolitana, 1984.

Hernández-Castellanos, Camilo and Jeff Lawrence. "La ficción paranoica y el nacimiento de la novela policial." Interview with Ricardo Piglia. *Studies in Latin American Popular Culture* 29 (2011): 218-29.

Krugman, Paul. *The Accidental Theorist and Other Dispatches from the Dismal Science*. New York: Norton, 1998.

Moreiras, Alberto. *Tercer espacio: Literatura y duelo en América latina*. Santiago: LOM/Arcis, 1999.

Nicholson, Brantley. A Poetics of Globalism: Fernando Vallejo, the Colombian Urban Novel, and the Generation of '72. Dissertation, Duke University. Ann Arbor: ProQuest/UMI, 2011. (Publication No. AAT 3490351.)

Piglia, Ricardo. "La lectura de la ficción." Interview with Mónica López Ocón. In *Crítica y ficción*. Buenos Aires: Siglo Veinte, nd.

Piglia, Ricardo and Juan José Saer. *Por un relato futuro: diálogo*.

Santa Fe, Arg: Universidad Nacional del Litoral, 1990.

Rancière, Jacques. *The Politics of Aesthetics*. London: Continuum, 2004.

Somoza, Patricia and Elena Vinelli. "Historia oral de los libros." Interview with Ricardo Piglia, Héctor Schmucler, Carlos Altamirano and Germán García. *Página/12* suplemento cultural, 8 April 2012. <http://www.pagina12.com.ar/diario/suplementos/libros/10-4628-2012-04-12.html>.

Williams, Gareth. *The Other Side of the Popular: Neoliberalism and Subalternity in Latin America*. Durham: Duke UP, 2002.

Itinerant Citizens: Imagining Global Citizenship in the Works of Osvaldo Soriano[1]

Leila Lehnen

University of New Mexico

Traditionally citizenship has been conceived as a contractual relationship between a nation-state and its citizens. Derek Heater (2004) defines citizenship as a "form of socio-political identity" (1) among several other models. This contract dictates a covenant of rights and obligations: the citizen pays his/her taxes, obeys the laws and, in exchange, receives services such as security, certain infrastructural amenities and, in some instances, social services, as for example access to health care, public education, social security. Heater postulates that "[g]ood citizens are those who feel an alliance to the state and have a sense of responsibility discharging their duties" (2). The keywords here are "alliance to the state," which constrict the idea of citizenship to a specific geo-political realm. But what happens when the citizen is confronted with the nation-state in crisis? This is to say, what occurs when the state no longer maintains its end of the bargain due to social or political—or both—imperatives, such as authoritarian regimes, the collapse of the national economy, among other events? Under such circumstances, can—and should—the citizen maintain his/hers "alliance to the state?" And how does a national crisis impact another feature of citizenship, namely, sociability?

---

[1]. I would like to thank the editors of this volume, Sophia A. McClennen and Brantley Nicholson not only for including my essay in this collection, but also for their invaluable comments and suggestions. Many of the ideas expressed in this essay are the result of their feedback.

This essay explores the issue of citizenship under duress as it appears in two novels by Argentine writer Osvaldo Soriano. I will analyze two texts that use travel as an allegory to represent the crisis of "territoriality" (Storey 2012) in post-transitional Argentina (Storey 2012). This predicament of territoriality allegorizes the Argentine crisis after its 1983 democratization and the ensuing transformation of the notion of "citizenship" as a pact between the citizen and the nation-state. For David Storey, a territory is not simply a geographical area circumscribed by political boundaries. Rather, a territory is always crisscrossed by the vectors of power and sociability (*Territories* 27). The two novels considered here depict territories where national power (to provide for its citizens, i.e. to maintain its side of the social bargain) is evanescent and where, therefore, sociability is frequently under duress. As such, the two novels by Osvaldo Soriano this articletext discusses are emblematic of some of the preoccupations uttered in the works of Argentina's Generation of '72. The writers that belong to this group reflect on how the factors such as the 1976 military coup de état impacted notions of national belonging (one has to consider that several of the writers in this group went into exile) and hence, of national citizenship (Nicholson 2011).

Both of Soriano's texts examined here,: *Una sombra ya pronto serás* (1990) and *La hora sin sombra* (1995), feature itinerant protagonists that travel towards a continually deferred and, at the same time, unknown destination. Travel in these two novels signifies the crisis of territoriality. The constantly changing landscapes that appear in *Una sombra ya pronto serás* and in *La hora sin sombra* indicate the characters' difficulty in establishing emotional and social attachments.

Though I propose that two novels' scenarios are a deterritorialized landscape, both texts posit their narratives in Argentina, specifically rural Argentina. Nonetheless, despite the specific geopolitical landscape, the two novels portray the nation-state as an entity that has lost its relevance not only politically but also ideologically and culturally. The result is a geo-symbolic vacuum that does not provide social, civil, political or cultural anchors for the characters that roam it. It is nonetheless significant that both texts take place in Argentina's interior regions, in the national space *par excellence* of the *pampa*. By locating his narratives within this territory, Soriano communicates a sense of nostalgia for an idealized nation with its symbolic and material connotations (i.e. community, national identity constructed through national institutions such as the school). In sum, space and dislocation are integral elements in the two novels and contribute to tracing a dystopian cartography of post-transitional Argentina.

The emphasis on spatiality and movement through space in *Una sombra ya pronto serás* and *La hora sin sombra* provides an important commentary on the transformation of citizenship as constructed vis-à-vis national territory. If, as Storey argues, "territory is more than a mere backdrop of the material manifestation of a set of social relations bound into the intersections of power, space and society (Brighenti 2010a),. tThe spatial is not simply the outcome of the social but the two are intrinsically bound up together (Delaney 2009)" (27), then the weakening of territoriality implies a deterioration of the social links that signify this territory. In the case of Soriano's narratives, the decline of the nation-state is the consequence of both past and present socio-political conditions, namely the 1976-1983 dictatorship, the economic crisis that shook the country in the 1980s and the transformation of Argentina's socio-economic make-up in the 1990s.

As indicated in the two texts discussed in this article, Osvaldo Soriano's *oeuvre* mingles political engagement with aesthetic consciousness. His first novel *Triste, solitario y final* (1973) parodies the detective genre and has as two of its main characters both the author, Osvaldo Soriano and one of literature's most famous private eyes, Philip Marlowe.[2] Additionally, the novel is set in Los Angeles, Marlowe's stomping grounds. Metafictionality in Soriano's novels serves as a critical device (in the lines of the Brechtian *Verfremdungseffekt*) that allows the reader to appraise the narrative critically, reflecting upon the power structures that the text comments upon.

This type of meta-fictionality appears in Soriano's last novel, *La hora sin sombra*, which that thematizes the creative process through the lens of a father-son relationship. In the text, a writer in crisis goes on a road trip in searching for his dying father who "había escapado del hospital vestido con la ropa de un roquero al

---

2. Soriano's metafictional play with Raymond Chandler's character is paradigmatic of the interest that the Generation of '72 expressed in mass culture. The noir genre is an integral part of this culture and takes a prominent place in the fictions of this generation.

que habían internado por caerse del escenario" (*La hora* 15). The preposterous image of the aging and terminally sick father clothed in rock star garb inaugurates a narrative in which incongruity is a Leitmotif. Absurdity,—which is also a central theme in *Una sombra pronto serás* and *El ojo de la patria*, allegorizes the Argentine national condition in the aftermath of its 1983 transition to democracy. Humor becomes a tool through which the novels' narrators question prevalent national narratives, such as Argentina's insertion into a cadre of modern nations (Díaz-Zambrana 2005).

As suggested above, the unraveling, or unsettling of traditional social, and, in the case of *La hora sin sombra*, familial order, and the weakening of a body politic is a corollary of socio-economic and political developments in post 1983 Argentina, but also has roots in the country's 1976-1983 dictatorship. Such roots are evident in small hints in each text, such as the redundant and forgotten army outpost that appears in *Una sombra ya pronto serás*, which is commanded by an official with the aspect of a "linyera... Ya no se distinguían los galones y el uniforme era una mezcla de bombacha de paisano y chaqueta desteñida. En el pecho llevaba unas cuantas condecoraciones hechas a mano con pedazos de madera y latas viejas" (*La hora* 234). As in *La hora sin sombra*, the absurdity of the scene typifies the grotesque violence of the authoritarian regime. However, unlike *No habrá más penas ni olvido*, published in 1979—, at the height of the military dictatorship—and *Cuarteles de invierno* (1982), the two above cited novels are not overtly political. Instead, these narratives approach politics circuitously precisely in order to reveal that the political sphere is no longer one of citizenship and that the latter is also largely absent from both the civil and particularly the social realms. As suggested by T.H. Marshall, though the three domains of citizenship have their specificity, they are also interrelated.

In *Citizenship and Social Class* (1952) T.H. Marshall divides citizenship into three categories: the civic (legal recourse), the political (representation, e.g. vote) and the social (access to services such as education and healthcare). To these three ambits one might also add cultural citizenship, namely the right to assert one's identity—be it personal or collective. In other words, "Cultural citizenship is about becoming active producers of meaning and representation and knowledgeable consumers under advanced capitalism" (Isin and Wood 152).

As indicated above, each of the spheres overlaps with the other. Thus, for example, social rights can circumscribe political, civic rights and cultural rights. Frequently, socially disadvantaged citizens have less access to judicial recourse and often these same groups have difficulty in having their demands met by legislative bodies. The degree to which each realm exists within a nation-state varies and is, in part, boundeded to historical circumstances. James Holston (2007) proposes that many recent democracies, as for example those in Southern Cone countries after democratic transitions in the 1980s, evidence a disjuncture in their domains of citizenship. Holston concentrates on the disjointedness between the political and the civil realms, maintaining that in new democracies, "political institutions democratize with considerable success, and although they promulgate constitutions and legal codes based on the rule of law and democratic values, the civil component of citizenship remains impaired, as citizens suffer systematic violations of civil rights and commonly encounter violence, injustice and impunity" ("Citizenship in Disjunctive Democracies" 77). The distinction between different realms of citizenship is not limited to the civil and political ambit. It can also extend to the social sphere realm. Constitutions might thus declare that "Todos los habitantes de la Nación gozan de los siguientes derechos conforme a las leyes que reglamenten su ejercicio, a saber: de trabajar y ejercer toda industria licita…" (Article 14, *Constituición argentina*) but, in Argentina in the 1980s, 1990s and early 2000s saw massive unemployment due to the implementation of neoliberal policies as well as structural adjustment measures, which came on the heels of an economic crisis prompted by Argentina's foreign debt, lack of investor confidence, budget deficit and hyperinflation.

   The Argentine economic crisis began during the dictatorship. In the early 1980s, Argentina underwent near stagnant economic growth combined with an annual inflation rate of over 100%, a deficit of over US$ 4 billion and an external debt of approximately US$ 27 billion. By the end of the dictatorship, approximately 27% of the adult Argentine population was unemployed. This economic scenario, combined with the Malvinas debacle, forced the military out of power ("Inflation" 156). However the democratically elected president, Raúl Alfonsín, inherited the disastrous economic conditions of the previous regime. Attempting to control the damage, he implemented economic packages (Plan Austral in 1985, Plan Austral

II—the Australito in 1987, Plan Primavera in 1987 and Plan Primavera II in 1988) designed to curb inflation and promote job growth, to no avail. In 1987, partly as a result of the ongoing economic crisis, Alfonsín's party the Radical Civil Union (UCR) suffered significant loses in the upper and lower houses. In 1989 Peronist candidate Carlos Saúl Menem replaced Alfonsín, who left the presidency five months before the end of his mandate. Menem promptly adopted a series of market-friendly reforms, in effect fulfilling the dictatorship's economic program (Richards 1997, Klein 2007).

These measures were exacerbated in 1991, when then minister of foreign affairs Domingo Cavallo devised and carried out the *Plan de convertibilidad*, pegging the Argentine peso to the dollar. In addition, responding in part to international pressure, president Menem privatized large sectors of the national industry, including the national airline, telephone and petroleum companies. Menem also slashed public funding, which, together with the privatization of state enterprises led to massive unemployment. The measures were successful in the short term, the Argentine stock market rallied as a response to the policies and the deficit was reduced. However in the long term these policies proved disastrous. Consumer goods became too expensive due to a surplus of imported goods and the newly privatized industries downsized en masse, leading to considerable unemployment (Klein 166-168). Additionally Menem significantly augmented labor flexibility, eroding workers' rights.[3] Labor flexibility had an impact not only on job stability, but also on incomes. The Argentine middle-class was decimated and the country, which had long prided itself on its strong middle class, underwent not only a social, but also an identity crisis.

David Storey links neoliberalization with a transformation of territorial and, by extension, social organization. He maintains that neoliberal policies that privilege private rather than state engagement in social matters put the onus on communitarian rather than governmental (i.e. supra-communal) solutions to socio-eco-

---

3. Menem used executive decree to prohibit "strikes and compulsory, binding arbitration of labour disputes for public employees and others working in industries considered essential" (Inflation 160). Moreover, he allocated significant power to employers who had greater latitude in their employment practices enabling them to hire temporary workers for longer periods of time and who could be dismissed without notice and without cause. These temporary workers were also considered ineligible for the full range of fringe benefits afforded regular full time workers, which further helped to reduce firms' labour costs (Inflation 160).

nomic issues (*Territories* 7). This shift in turn can affect the perception of national belonging and of citizenship. Sociologist Zygmunt Bauman associates the state's drawback from the public sector to a disintegration of citizenship as society becomes increasingly individualized (*Liquid Modernity* 16-17). In this context, one can argue that citizenship rather than vanishing is transformed. The collective sphere is reduced to smaller groups centered on common interests and goals. An example (though not an unproblematic one) is NGOs that address social needs of specific groups.

Specifically in the case of Argentina, Beatriz Sarlo affirms that the dictatorial past, combined with the post-transitional economic crisis promoted a rupture with the idea of a national collectivity. Instead, alternative social identities and projects are privileged. Such identifications are often more localized and respond to specific interest such as security or recreation. Sarlo notes that: "Del estallido de identidades no surgió una nación plural, sino su supervivencia pulsátil. La nación se perdió en el extreme de la pobreza" (*Tiempo presente* 19). *Una sombra ya pronto serás* broaches this loss and the subsequent individualization through the metaphor of the continuous voyage.

Destination Nowhere: Journey and Loss in Una sombra ya pronto serás

Una sombra ya pronto serás follows the anonymous protagonist, a computer engineer, who returns to his native Argentina from a long sojourn abroad. The motives for this return are unclear. In Europe, "tenía una buena situación" (*Una sombra* 22), but his material circumstances in his homeland are more precarious. As the narrative advances, the protagonist's time in Europe fades from the novel, signaling his increased hopelessness. The protagonist's unstable economic—but also psychological—condition, together with the metaphor of the journey, are the threads that weave the narrative together.

The novel's timeframe is unspecified, communicating the idea of a timeless present in which the text's characters are trapped. At the same time, the cast of unemployed and underemployed nomadic characters and the setting of impoverished and ghost towns, shutdown and destitute businesses suggest Argentina during the 1980s. According to Rosana Díaz-Zambrana, Soriano "crea una platea que favorece la presencia de exiliados, desposeídos y la conflictiva espectralidad del regreso a la que debiera vivenciarse como casa. En el caso de Soriano, el elemento cómico sirve para reforzar lo trágico, en el sentido del planteamiento de Ionesco acerca de cómo la desesperación producía la intuición de lo absurdo en lo cómico" (250). In *Una sombra ya pronto serás* the voyage is performed at the social and geographic margins of the nation, as exemplified by the anonymity of the novel's main character and his destitute appearance at the beginning of the narrative ("ya me estaba pareciendo a un linyera" [*Una sombra* 11]).

Una sombra ya pronto serás begins *in media res* with the protagonist stranded in the middle of nowhere without any money: "Nunca me había pasado de andar sin un peso en el bolsillo. No podía comprar nada y no me quedaba nada por vender" (*Una sombra* 9). Beyond squarely locating the reader in a rural landscape—there are no cities in the novel, only desolate small towns—the abrupt *mis-en-scène* introduces us to the prevailing sense of disorientation that pervades the text and which encompasses not only the spatial environment, but also extends to the social and psychological spheres. We find ourselves in a world without any apparent order. It is a parallel universe inhabited by various types of social misfits.

Though apparently already standing at the margins—he hints that he has lost his job (*Una sombra* 10)—the protagonist's penury catapults him further outside the hegemonic socio-economic realm that is governed by monetary exchange. If previously he could use conventional transportation mechanisms (i.e. the train), now his travels are far more precarious. He must either walk or hitchhike. *Una sombra ya pronto serás* oscillates between these two modes of journeying. Whereas walking emphasizes the protagonist's almost complete solitude, hitchhiking creates fleeting companionship, alternative forms of community that last for the time of the journey together. In this sense, the temporary sociability the protagonist encounters evokes the idea of micro communities that form in lieu of a larger national collectivity.

Without money and alone in the midst of a no-man's land, the protagonist begins his wanderings through the Argentine countryside. Initially it appears that he seeks to receive reimbursement for his train ticket (the train in which he was travelling broke down). But his final destination is obscure—though the protagonist mentions that he is *en route* to Neuquén province, he does not seem to make any concrete effort to reach his purported endpoint. During his journey he encounters a colorful array of fellow travellers who also seem to be lost in the desolate landscape that surrounds them.

Similar to the protagonist, his fellow travellers are trickster figures who attempt to survive in an inhospitable environment. Most are, like the protagonist, haunted by a sense of loss and, paradoxically, a hope to recover from this loss that is permeated with the consciousness that this endeavor is impossible. Coluccini, a failed circus owner, the protagonist's first companion, drives a decrepit Gordini[4] and wants to go to Bolivia. The novel thus reverses the established economic migratory pattern in the late twentieth and early twenty-first century whereby Bolivians came to Argentina in search of employment. Coluccini's proposed route thus indirectly highlights the acute state of national crisis. For Coluccini, Bolivia represents the possibility of overcoming a series of losses, not least economic ruin: "En otra época tuve un Buick y también un 505, pero me agarró la tormenta" (*Una sombra* 18). His itinerary, however, does not follow a linear map that would take him from his current location to Bolivia, but seems rather circular. This circularity, an orbit that is described around semi-abandoned travel stations, empty fields, villages and rotundas signifies the voyages' futility. Coluccini, similar to the novel's other characters is literally and metaphorically lost. Spatial markers, reflecting a muddled social order, and the characters' own psyche, serve only to confuse the travellers. When the protagonist asks Coluccini if he recognizes a certain enclosure, the former circus owner responds: "Son todas iguales, Zárate, como los árboles. Hice mil quinientos kilómetros con los curas y nunca supe si iba para el norte o para el sur"[5] (*Una sombra* 178). The confusing cartography transmits the characters' hopelessness—throughout the narrative he repeats the adage: "¡l'avventura è finita!" Coluccini's words indicate his knowledge that he will not reach Bolivia and recuperate his losses, both literal and metaphorical. Nevertheless he continues to nurse this illusion,

---

4. Throughout *Una sombra ya pronto serás* as well as in *La hora sin sombra*, cars are signposts of a past era. Specifically they denote a more affluent Argentina where citizens could afford imported cars and a Fordist (rather than post-Fordist) economic model—with the social implications that these mode of production connotes.

5. Coluccini calls the protagonist by the name of his former associate, who escaped to Australia with the former's family.

stretching it into a non-existent future. After Bolivia, he plans to continue his travels, to Rio de Janeiro or to Miami (*Una sombra* 18). The continual deferment of a destination suspends both Coluccini's failure and repeats it. Rosana Díaz-Zambrana observes that in *Una sombra ya pronto serás* "la circularidad del viaje es la encerrona simbólica del fracaso igualmente insuperable. En este viaje-sin-regreso de la desesperanza sólo la voluntad de aventura y la capacidad de identificación entre los viajeros pueden franquear la omnipresencia de la soledad en las que serán siempre rutas sin salida" (251). Soriano's novel oscillates between the, albeit impermanent, social bonds that are established *en route* and the underlying reality of a crisis of citizenship that impairs longer-term sociability.

Similar to topographical markers, in the novel maps loose their power to orient the traveller. Instead they confirm the sense of disorientation that suffuses the narrative. The characters' bewilderment vis-à-vis these useless documents denotes both their loss/es and their search for new prospects (economic, personal, emotional). As such, maps in *Una sombra ya pronto serás* allude less to an ordered space, created for example by a central administration in order to control the national territory, and more to the crisis of these institutions, the disorder of this territory and the power structures that organize and control the national space.

Doreen Massey states that traditionally maps function as "ordering representations" (*For Space* 106). However, maps can also destabilize order. These are "situationist maps" that attempt to "*dis*orient, to defamiliarise, to provoke a view from an unaccustomed angle. On the other hand…[such maps] sought to expose the incoherences and fragmentations of the spatial itself" (*For Space* 109). Maps reoccur throughout *Una sombra ya pronto serás* but are ineffectual guides. At the beginning of the protagonist's adventure, he consults a map, but ends up doing "a recorrido absurdo, dando vueltas y retrocediendo y ahora me encontraba en el mismo lugar que al principio o en otro idéntico" (*Una sombra* 9). The narrative's imprecise maps create a breach that offers the reader—and the characters—a glimpse into an "unaccustomed angle" of Argentine society. The pampa, symbol of national identity (Ponce 8), becomes a proxy for the entire nation. It is, however an emptied and ghostly space, and not the terrain of the fabled *gauchos* (only two of them appear in the novel, just to disappear quickly). If, in the nineteenth century, the pampa was the frontier to be conquered and "civilized," in Soriano's narrative, it has been abandoned by any ordering venture. Remnants of a former organization, such as damaged and incorrect road signs underscore the contrast between a past order and the present disarray. The defamiliarization provoked by equivocal maps and/or by a confusing landscape connotes the chaotic and constrictive state of social and personal affairs that the novel's characters confront.

Take, for example, Rita and Boris, a young couple that the protagonist meets at one of the several service stations he passes through. They seek to drive to the United States in their old Mercury via the Pan American Highway. Though their motivations are not spelled out in the novel, their desire to go north connotes a lack of perspectives in Argentina (Boris has a degree in physics). The couple's desired migration pattern, similarly to the protagonist's own itinerary, reflects the "brain drain" that the country endured during the 1960s, 70s and 80s. While during the 1960s, Argentine *emigrés* came from mainly the educated, professional classes, in the 1970s and 1980s the migratory population expanded to include unskilled labor as well. The motives for emigration also change. Until 1983, emigrants sought to flee from political violence. In the post-transitional period Argentines have migrated for economic and educational reasons.[6]

Like other characters, Rita and Boris dream of escaping into a different reality. This desire recurs in the novel in the mention of faraway destinations. Beyond Bolivia, Miami and Rio de Janeiro, the characters hope to reach Cleveland and Alaska (Ponce 31) or, as in the case of Coluccini and the protagonist, have estranged family in Australia or in Spain. These locations symbolize adventure (Alaska, Bolivia), excitement (Rio de Janeiro) or economic potential (Miami, Europe), all of which are absent from the bleak landscape that represents Argentina in *Una sombra ya pronto serás*. Rita and Boris cannot, however, find the highway north. Their itinerary, like that of Coluccini, remains circumscribed to the same back roads that the protagonist transverses, suggesting the same circular movement described by the two men.

As indicated above, the characters' itinerary takes them through a ruinous countryside. Coluccini gives the protagonist a

---

6. Adela Pellegrino indicates that an important percentage of Argentines emigrate to pursue post-graduate degrees in the United States and in Europe ("Skilled Labor Migration" 13).

ride to Colonia Vela, the first station in the novel's *via crucis*. For Corina Mathieu (1988) Soriano's fictional town is a microcosm of Argentina. Accordingly, in *Una sombra ya pronto serás*, Colonia Vela evidences the marks of Argentina's national crisis. Whereas a closed-up movie theater alludes to the country's economic breakdown, a monument to the men who fell during the Malvinas conflict in the central square signals the country's recent historic traumas.

The town is generally described as run-down and is dotted by signs that indicate the population's impoverishment. Thus, for example, a well-frequented soup kitchen organized by the local church tends to the needy population, many of which seem to be new to this type of charity. These are people who are uncomfortable with their destitution: "La gente hablaba poco y se lanzaba miradas furtivas" (*Una sombra* 33). The shame encapsulated in the cautious gazes is suggestive of a pauperized middle class that is still grappling with its new socio-economic status. This new social positioning contrasts with the prevalent notion of Argentine national identity. Beatriz Sarlo observes that, by the end of the nineteenth century, the understanding of being an Argentine citizen, "implicaba trabajar, leer y escribir, votar. Ser argentino también significaba un imaginario articulado por principios de orgullo nacional, posibilidades de ascenso social y relativo igualitarismo" (*Tiempo presente* 28). In other words, to be "Argentine" meant that one had access to all four ambits of citizenship: the civil, the political, the social and the cultural. In contrast, Soriano's text describes the weakening of both the social and the civil spheres of citizenship (the political realm is largely and significantly absent from *Una sombra ya pronto serás*). The soup kitchen in Colonia Vela attests to the lack of the basic right to nutrition. And it also indicates the absence of a welfare state that could provide for the essential needs of its population. In its place, private and/or non-profit organizations assume this function. The changed socio-economic panorama profoundly affected Argentines' self-perception, as well as their social relations and political engagement (Grimson and Keller 2005).

The prevalence of a market-oriented logic is a recurrent theme in the novel. It dictates a change not only of living standards, but also of ideology and ethics. Paradigmatic are the characters of Barrante and the priest Salinas. Barrante wears a Perón pin, evoking an era of incremented state intervention. Nonetheless, contradicting this insignia and the state-sponsored economic policies of the Perón era, he believes that private initiative is the salvation to Argentina's woes. In a parody of the neoliberal ethos,[7] Barrante declares that: "Si nos dejan trabajar a los privados vamos a salir adelante. Mire toda la riqueza que tenemos..." (*Una sombra* 108). His words stand in stark opposition not only to the surrounding landscape, but also to his own professional standing.

Though he is a private entrepreneur, Barrante's business represents this economic model and ridicules it. He wanders the *pampa* carrying an onerous contraption with which he bathes *paisanos*. But the enterprise is not lucrative, thus contradicting Barrante's own beliefs in private business. Barrante is a parody of the self-made man proposed by capitalist ideology. His entire figure and the device he carries are "un error y allí, en el descampado, se notaba en enseguida. (...) Movía las piernas como balancines y tenía unos brazos largos que sobresalían de las mangas. El traje era holgado pero le faltaban casi todos los botones y el pantalón tenía unas rodilleras imposibles de planchar" (*Una sombra* 107). The character's shambolic appearance challenges the image of the successful private entrepreneur (which appears in the figure of the banker Lem). In particular the ill fitting and derelict suit comments on Argentina's identification with European cultural models. The suit symbolizes the presence and influence of European culture within the Argentine socio-cultural imaginary. But Barrante's ruinous *traje* signifies the disintegration of such models within a changing social, political and cultural panorama.

Barrante emblematizes the plethora of unorthodox occupations that composes the book's informal economy, and which seems to be the only functional economic sector. Since the 1970s and until recently, the Argentine economy has steadily lost jobs in the formal sector. These have been—partially—replaced by part-time and/or informal employment. In both cases, workers often are deprived of the benefits offered by full-time labor pensions, healthcare, paid leave etc. Members of the working class were, in effect, what sociologist Zygmunt Bauman calls the "collateral damage" of consumer

---

7. David Harvey argues that in neoliberal ethos: "While individual freedom in the marketplace is guaranteed, each individual is held responsible and accountable for his or her own actions and well-being. This principle extends into the realm of welfare, education, health care and even pensions (...). Individual success or failure are interpreted in terms of entrepreneurial virtues or personal failings (...) rather than being attributed to any systemic property (such as the class exclusions usually attributed to capitalism)" (65-66).

society, or what Bauman calls the "underclass" (*Consuming Life* 122). This underclass conjures "an image of an aggregate of people who have been declared off-limits in relation to *all* classes and the *class hierarchy itself*, with little chance and no need of readmission: people without a role, making no useful contribution to the lives of the rest, and in principle beyond redemption" (*Consuming Life* 123, emphasis in the original). Barrante reflects the precarious position occupied by the members of the informal sector, the de facto "underclass" that has no space within the sanctioned national imaginary. Not only is he lost in the territorial margins of the nation, unable to reach its economic and symbolic centers (Buenos Aires for example), but also his professional activity is obsolete. As a result, his earnings are so low that he cannot eat more than twice a week. And, being a widower, he has a son to whom he cannot send money. When Barrante is accidentally killed his social marginalization is exacerbated. He is interred in a nameless grave; near the wire fencing that separates a gas station from the adjourning empty fields. The location is a borderline between the terrain inhabited by fellow travellers and a no-man's land.

In contrast to Barrante, the priest Salinas typifies the successful side of the free market. He has privatized soul saving. Salinas goes from ranch to ranch performing religious duties in exchange for cash. His business is lucrative to the point that he is saving to buy a Renault 12 and has outsourced some of his services to two lay associates. The market-friendly priest offers a re-interpretation of the biblical maxim: "Again I tell you, it is easier for a camel to go through the eye of a needle than for a rich man to enter the kingdom of God" (Matthew 19:24) by making his clients believe that "los ricos pasan por el ojo de la aguja" (*Una sombra* 164). The priest's words signal the prevalence of a market-oriented rationale in all realms of life, including the spiritual one. Within this framework, one can, quite literally, buy an entrance to eternity. Not only does human life become commodified, but also the "soul," i.e. the spiritual life and the institutions that attend to it (Bauman 2007). Not surprisingly, social bonds become part of an economy of exchange.

Exemplary is the relation between the protagonist and his *socio*, Lem. Lem is the "lost banker," searching for the arithmetic formula that will allow him to win a fortune in gambling. Unlike most other characters in the novel, Lem apparently is affluent. In contrast to Barrante, he wears tailored suits, eats imported chocolate and drinks expensive whiskey. But analogously to the book's other characters, Lem is also an eternal wanderer.

Lem and the protagonist engage in an unproductive business relation and their association suggests a disencounter between two strangers. Like the protagonist, Lem is a solitary wanderer simultaneously fleeing for unknown reasons and in search of an elusive goal ("...me perdí en el camino" [*Una sombra* 104]). His ongoing travels connote a cosmopolitan elite that, due to its socio-economic standing, is not constrained to a particular territory. Appropriately, Lem likes to (or must) travel, seemingly without any specific destination, driving a flaming Jaguar.[8] The car is an enclosed territory that contains the banker's life, creating a space mostly detached from any material territory. As he transverses various locations he remains bound to the circumscribed sphere of his car. The Jaguar is paradigmatic of Lem's deterritorialized space: though Lem has driven from Alaska to Kuala Lumpur, the vehicle's papers are from New Jersey.

Lem's car-residence is diametrically opposed to the traditional notion of a home, and, by extension of homeland as a fixed entity, delimited by geo-political boundaries and signified by structures of political and symbolic power. Instead, the Jaguar is both a fragmented space and a non-space (Augé 1995). On the one hand, the car is a fragmented space in that it condenses the character's lived experiences in bits and pieces. These are symbolized by the haphazard collection of items in the vehicle: water bottles, cigarette packs, scraps of paper. The car, with its objects and the memorial slivers that these denote, signals Lem's truncated personal narrative. This notion of truncation is highlighted by the character's demise: he commits suicide without leaving any explanation behind.

On the other hand, while the historicity condensed in the car contradicts the notion of it as a non-space,[9] the Jaguar is nonetheless a non-space in that it is a terrain where relations of contractuality prevail—in this case, the business transactions between him and the protagonist. The non-space is a locale void of affectivity. If territory is an important factor in the formation of self and social

---

8. The car, an English brand, is significant in that it too alludes to British culture as referential for certain social sectors in Argentina.

9. For a discussion of inhabited non-spaces please see Brantley Nicholson's and Lucia Reinaga's "On Pirate Cinema and Crying in Airports: A Conversation with Alberto Fuguet."

identity, the ambulant "territory" of Lem's car proposes that his individual and communitarian identities are unstable or nonexistent. Indeed, more than any of the book's other characters, Lem seems unable to engage in any social relationship. The meetings between his fellow travellers and him are ephemeral, marked by unfinished dialogues and incomplete projects, emblematizing estrangement rather than dialogue and communication. Deterritorialization here signifies the coming apart of a collective sphere, and, by extension, of a collective project.

The combination between Lem's interminable journeys and his profession can be read as metaphoric of the spread of deterritorialized finance capitalism that eschews production and the exchange of material goods. Indeed, finance capitalism was one of the motors of the Argentine economy in the late 1980s and during the 1990s. In an article that Soriano wrote about the state of the Argentine economy, he describes this type of financial transaction:

> En noviembre de 1988, depositar dinero a plazo fijo en cualquier banco, redituaba una ganancia del 8 por ciento mensual en dólares. El fenómeno atrajo capitales que sólo circulaban en el mercado financiero para regresar luego, bien engrosados, a sus seguros refugios de Nueva York o Suiza. Se calcula que 10 mil millones de dólares venidos del extranjero circulaban por los bancos y se multiplicaban con la especulación a costa del Estado. ("Vivir con la inflación" 41)

This speculative game became routine, a means to safeguard the income from galloping inflation. For Bauman, this "free-floating capitalism" (*Liquid Modernity* 149) is both a symptom and the cause of liquefying social relations. In contrast to the "free-floating capitalism" emblematized by Lem is the barter economy that sustains Nadia, a (phony) clairvoyant, who dreams of emigrating to Brazil. In exchange for her services, her clients pay her "pollos, tortas, morcillas, salamines y otras cosas que no supe para qué podían servir" (*Una sombra* 54). Paradoxically this barter economy is related to the globalized capitalism performed by Lem. It represents the underside of deterritorialized finance capitalism. Impoverished by joblessness and by inflation, Nadia's customers cannot but compensate her with non-monetary goods.

Like its itinerant characters, *Una sombra ya pronto serás* describes a circular narrative movement. The novel ends where it began, with the protagonist sitting in an empty train wagon—another space that symbolizes deterritorialization, waiting for it to depart, but not knowing whether this will happen ("La partida estaba prevista para las ocho pero no decía de qué día ni yo sabía en qué fecha estábamos" [*Una sombra* 250]). The scene is ambivalent, leaving open the possibility of a forward movement, toward a goal, or a future, while at the same time accentuating immobility and waiting. Significantly, the protagonist is alone in his wait. The social relations that he established during his trip having all gone their own way, in search of ephemeral opportunities somewhere else. *Una sombra ya pronto serás* thus insinuates that, under crisis, citizenship as a communitarian endeavor becomes brittle. And yet, there is always the chance of reencounters.

A History of Dis-encounters: Family and Nation in La hora sin sombra

In an interview with Verónica Chiaravelli for the newspaper *La Nación*, Osvaldo Soriano synthesizes two main themes of his fiction: loneliness and limit situations with which his characters have to deal. These two reoccurring themes appear in *Una sombra pronto serás* and are also the axes that organize Soriano's last novel, *La hora sin sombra*.

La hora sin sombra has two layers. One the one hand, it is the story of the relationship between father and son. The son, a writer, learns that his hospitalized father is dying, and decides to abandon him—just as the father has abandoned him in the past. He plans a road trip through the Argentine provinces during which he will also write a travel book, something to the effect of a *Guía de las pasiones argentinas* (*La hora* 35). The father, however, takes a trip of his own, escaping the hospital in which he is interned wearing the clothes of a rock star. As a consequence, his son transforms this trip into a search for both the missing parent and himself. In the process, his travel book mutates into a combination of familial history, travel narrative and a belated *Bildungsroman*. It is, probably, the text that we are reading.

On the other hand, the novel thematizes the creative process. The novel that the author-narrator is composing, and for which he received an advance from his editor, is a metafictional commentary on Soriano's own aesthetic formation (Martínez 9). Beyond portraying the trials and tribulations of a writer in crisis, the novel also contains multiple references to Argentine literary luminaries such as José Luis Borges and Adolfo Bioy Casares. For Tomás Eloy Martínez, who wrote the prologue to *La hora sin sombra*, this text is "construido como una reflexión sobre lo que él (Soriano) leyó, escribió y vivió. O, mejor dicho, como una autobiografía encubierta" (9). In other words, in this novel, Soriano creates a parallel between life and art. And, following the line of his previous works, *La hora sin sombra* also centers on solitary characters, confronted with borderline situations, specifically the line between (literary) creation and (parental) death. For Cristian Montes Capó, *Una hora sin sombra* is a narrative of orphanhood. Accordingly, the narrative relates the loneliness that haunts the protagonist to a generalized sense of abandonment that is underscored by solitary routes and that can be read as an allegory for a crisis of the national community. The protagonist, who is at the point of being orphaned, feels that he is an outsider within a larger community: "Ya era tarde para mí; no había participado, no era compinche de la tribu" (*Una sombra* 139).

Similarly to *Una sombra ya pronto serás*, *La hora sin sombra* rotates around journeys, internal as well as physical. However, unlike the former, the latter does have a specific, existential (and artistic) goal. As indicated above, the narrator-protagonist wants to find his father and to write a story in which "de nuevo estuviéramos juntos" (*La hora* 23). By extension, the voyage also serves as an exploration of Argentina, both geographically and socio-culturally—as suggested by the narrator-protagonist's original scheme to write a "story of Argentine passions."

But to reach this target, the narrator-protagonist describes a circular trajectory, interspersed with chance encounters and ephemeral social relations. It is, in short, a journey of discovery in a landscape that is defined by spatial and temporal dimensions. For Doreen Massey, such a space is "the sphere of dynamic simultaneity, constantly disconnected by new arrivals, constantly waiting to be determined (and therefore always undetermined) by the construction of new relations. It is always being made and therefore, in a sense, unfinished (except that 'finishing' is not on the agenda)" (107).

As a result *La hora sin sombra* depicts the national territory envisioned as a moving cartography. In other words, the narrator-protagonist of *La hora sin sombra* describes a terrain where the spatial coordinates are not fixed, but ever changing according to the social and symbolic relations that occur within these coordinates. Consequently, analogous to *Una sombra ya pronto serás*, the idea of the nation as a determinate, fixed territory is destabilized. In this framework, the definition of citizenship, this is to say, belonging to a specific geo-political community, also changes. Community is described by local or individual affinities, ties, interests that often are impermanent.

Whereas *Una sombra ya pronto serás* focuses primarily of marginal/ized characters that physically and symbolically inhabit the nation's frontiers, *La hora sin sombra*, though not eschewing these individuals completely, centers on characters that are not completely socially peripheral but that still allegorize the precarious citizenship on the nation's borderlands.

Soriano relies on memorial discourse to represent the national landscape. Hence, for example, similar to *No habrá ni pena ni olvido*, Peronism is both the symbol of a better time, and a questionable enterprise. In the novel, Juan Domingos Perón appears as a benevolent, but somewhat ingenuous leader who finances the protagonist's father's dream to construct a glass city. In the novel the overly optimistic populist president denotes a fallacious confidence that covers a conflicted reality.

The city is a metaphor for the aspirations of middle-class Argentines during the 1940s and 1950s. Throughout these two decades, the country's bourgeoisie and petit bourgeoisie believed in the establishment of Argentina as a modern nation, where progress and social ascension were viable.

Projected to be built as the new southern capital (in the Antarctica), the glass metropolis represents the fusion between a positivist and a mythical vision of Argentina. Envisioned as an enchanted oasis, a "palacio transparente, que fuera una gigantesca biblioteca llena de jardines y fuentes de aguas termales... [una] metrópolis para iluminados" (*La hora* 44), the city also captures Argentina's economic and political ambitions to become a global power. Ernesto, the protagonist's father believes that nuclear power, which, according to the narrative, is one of Perón's ambitions for Argentina, can power his city (*La hora* 45).[10] Furthermore, the

---

10. According to the narrator-protagonist, "En ese tiempo Perón había traído al país al profesor Richter, un austríaco chiflado que había empezado a trabajar en un laboratorio de Bariloche con el propósito de lograr la fusión nuclear. Ese procedimiento revolucionario, que no tenían ni los rusos ni los norteamericanos, iba a dar

city's anticipated location, in the South Pole, denotes Argentina's aspirations for territorial expansion. Ironically, those ambitions are wrecked in the Falklands conflict, another recurring theme in Soriano's texts.

While the glass metropolis represents a fabled modernity, it also stands as a symbol of the brittleness of these ambitions. In this framework the city's obliteration in 1955 during the coup d'état that deposed Perón hints at the gradual destruction of this vision. Modern Argentina gradually morphs into a dystopia, which will culminate in the 1976-83 dictatorship.

Retracing his father's story and his dreams, the protagonist goes in search of the city. He hopes to find "su piedra filosofal" (*La hora* 47) there. His route passes through an empty and desolate landscape that reaches nightmarish proportions on the isle. The deserted roads that lead to the city and its isolated location suggest its peripheral location, at the borders to the national cartography. This remoteness allegorizes the distance of the utopian national projects to the contemporary reality in which the narrator lives.

The conviction and simultaneous interrogation of Argentina as a modern nation also transpires in the narrator-protagonist's description of his mother's trajectory, from country girl to urban sophisticate and finally to embittered provincial housewife. In pictures of her taken during the 1940s,

> se ve a mi madre reluciente y feliz; parece una chica coqueta y atrevida, aunque las fotos son instantes de la vida que después no encajan en ninguna parte. Posaba para Gath y Chaves y otras casa de moda, aunque el éxito le llegó cuando empezó a hacer propaganda del jabón Palmolive. Todavía tengo una instantánea en la que está subida al pescante de un Packard, que era el coche más famoso de la época. (*La hora* 17)

The luxury vehicle in the photograph highlights the affluence enjoyed by Argentines between 1939-45, when beef and wheat, two of the country's main commodities, were in high demand on the global market. Likewise, both the car and the Palmolive soap, two North American imports, imply the insertion of Argentina into a global economy. While it exports raw materials, the country imports the industrialized products that connote a stylish modernity

energía a todo el continente y convertiría a la Argentina en una potencia mundial" (*La hora* 45).

on a par with nations such as the United States. In this context the Packard, similar to the Torino that the narrator-protagonist drives, epitomizes a sense of nostalgia for the auspicious times during which the photo was taken. That these times are long gone becomes clear when the Torino goes up in flames—together with the snapshots of his mother's glitzy past.

The snapshots transmit both the optimism of a modern and urbane young woman, and by association, of the nation that she represents in the advertisements, and the underlying sense of tragedy that will rupture this cheerful imagery/imaginary. Underlying this sunny imagery, however, the protagonist discovers that Laura, his mother, "despreciaba a la humanidad entera, incluidos mi padre y yo, que fuimos un estorbo en su vida" (*La hora* 17). Her bitterness ensues from her personal disappointments, especially from her aborted affair with Bill Hathaway, a charming African-American basketball player recruited by the Palermo sports club.

Laura's past, similar to the nation's past, is reduced to a handful of photographs, postcards, incomplete memorial vestiges. The protagonist, who seeks to understand who his mother was, is unable to reconstruct her image from these fragments. Likewise, national history is disjointed, pieced together randomly. Recalling a beating he witnessed earlier in his trip, the protagonist reflects: "¿Qué hacer con aquel acto de cobardía? Podría escribirlo, tal vez. Escribirlo sin modelos, sin descripciones, sin emoción. Sería una manera de ponerme a tono con este tiempo, cegar la memoria, borrar el pasado" (*La hora* 139). Here personal memory dialogues with the country's collective memory, with the unsettled mnemonic blanks of the recent (authoritarian) past.

Whereas the protagonist's mother ultimately settles into a mediocre existence and marries a provincial shopkeeper, the nation goes through the 1976-83 *proceso de reorganización nacional*, the Malvinas conflict and the post-transitional socio-economic crisis. This history underlies the narrative that we are reading. We learn *en passé* that the protagonist has just returned from exile and that Ernesto, his father, was a messenger boy of sorts for the Montonero guerrilla, having gone into exile in 1978. Exile alludes not only to Argentina's dictatorial past, that continues to haunt the country, but, as in other texts of the Generation of '72, exile is also a symbol for the coming apart of the national territory, and of the sense of displacement felt by both those who return to the country in the aftermath of the military regime, and those who remained.

La hora sin sombra uses the memorial discourse to map the national territory and the protagonist's own trajectory. For Amalia Ran, "la reconstrucción del pasado privado impulsa la revisión de otro tipo de historia: la oficial argentina y sus símbolos populares. La recuperación del padre desaparecido implica, por ende, otro giro hacia el origen e induce ciertas aclaraciones respecto al modo de ser argentino" (26). Not coincidentally, much of the narrator's itinerary takes him through barren landscapes and small, dying towns. If memory in our contemporary period is associated with specific sites (Nora 1989), then bleak locales, such as the pampa and run-down beach towns that the protagonist transverses signifies an emptiness of memory. The only significant memorial site of *La hora sin sombra* is the rebuilt *Torino* that the protagonist inherits from his father and with which he begins his road trip. Nonetheless, as the car was burned in a fire, his memories also go up in flames—at least temporarily.

Despite the loss, the protagonist must continue his voyage on foot or by public transportation—echoing the journey/s of *Una sombra ya pronto serás*. Dislocation is the only way that he can recuperate his lost novel (that burned down with the car) and, therefore, his past and the national history that is inscribed into the individual storylines that he pursues (that of his progenitors' and his own). *La hora sin sombra* also evokes the *Una sombra ya pronto serás* in the bizarre and fleeting acquaintances that the protagonist makes on his way. Paradigmatic is Walter, who inhabits a storm hole. The character combines strangeness with a quotidian normalcy: he prepares a *mate* for the protagonist who ventured into the storm hole. Upon leaving Walter's abode, the latter hears him repeating "¡Ah, el horror, el horror!" (*La hora* 151). The sentence parodies Kurt's words in Conrad's *Heart of Darkness* and its echoes in Marlon Brando's performance of Kurtz in Francis Ford Coppola's *Apocalypse Now* (1979). In this framework, Walter's words suggest a parallel between Marlowe's and the protagonist's quest. Both transverse a dark(ened) territory punctuated by isolated and, at times, bizarre, interactions.

Space in the text exemplifies Massey's conception of it as a locale where diverse and, at times, divergent trajectories meet up. Random encounters, such as that with Walter or when the protagonist comes across the fugitive Pastor Noriega, establish signifying vectors on the map that the protagonist is tracing while he journeys. Nonetheless, the various paths that coincide with that of the protagonist do not ultimately create a coherent topography. *La hora sin sombra* traces a fragmented map of Argentina.

On the one hand, *La hora sin sombra* articulates writing as a means to counter this disjuncture. It is through writing that the protagonist re-encounters his father and reconciles with him. Nonetheless, on the other hand, the narrative suggests that this project is doomed: "Una novela es como una tormenta en el océano, pasa y no deja huella" (*La hora* 179). However, similar to a storm, the novel also leaves debris, fragments that can be used to assemble an alternate story. *La hora sin sombra* ends with the protagonist finding the buried copy of the burned narrative that he was writing about his parents. The only thing missing is an ending: "Sólo faltaba agregar el final" (*La hora* 288). The ending suggests an ongoing process of constitution, both personal and collective, a mobile mapping of the nation and its communitarian spaces.

The Generation of '72 is one marked by various types of displacements. Beyond the (often forced) geographical dislocations, the writers who belong to this grouping are also in-between political places (between the utopian project of the Cuban Revolution and Salvador Allende's brief presidential term) and between cultural markers (bookended by the success of the *Boom* and their own vision of Latin American culture, which included international pop and mass cultures). Finally, the authors of the Generation of '72 had to navigate different social configurations: pre, during and post-dictatorial. *Una sombra ya pronto serás* and *La hora sin sombra* evidence the imprint of these experiences and moments. Specifically, the idea of fragmentation—individual, social, cultural and territorial—transmits the nostalgia for a lost unity, a communitarian whole. Nonetheless, at the same time Soriano's texts transmit the knowledge that this collectivity is but a shadow.

Works Cited

Augé, Marc. *Non-places: Introduction to an Anthropology of Supermodernity*. London: Verso, 1995. Print.

Bauman, Zygmunt. *Consuming Life*. Cambridge: Polity Press, 2007. Print.

—. *Liquid Modernity*. Cambridge, UK: Polity Press, 2000. Print.

Díaz-Zambrana, R. "'La carretera es la vida:" La ética picaresca en *Una sombra ya pronto serás* de Osvaldo Soriano." *Neophilologus*. 89.2 (2005): 249-259. Print.

Grimson, Alejandro, and Gabriel Kessler. *On Argentina and the Southern Cone: Neoliberalism and National Imaginations*. New York: Routledge, 2005. Print.

Harvey, David. *A Brief History of Neoliberalism*. Oxford: Oxford University Press, 2005. Print.

Heater, Derek B. *A Brief History of Citizenship*. New York: New York University Press, 2004. Print.

Holston, James. "Citizenship in Disjunctive Democracies." Joseph S. Tulchin and Meg Ruthenburg. *Citizenship in Latin America*. Boulder, Colo: Lynne Rienner Publishers, 2007. 75-94, Print.

Isin, Engin F, and Greg M. Nielsen. *Acts of Citizenship*. London: Zed Books Ltd, 2008. Print.

Klein, Naomi. *The Shock Doctrine: The Rise of Disaster Capitalism*. New York: Metropolitan Books/Henry Holt, 2007. Print.

Martínez, Tomás Eloy. "Prólogo. El último piso de la Torre De Babel." *La hora sin sombra*. Buenos Aires: Seix Barral, 2004. 7-11. Print.

Marshall, T H. *Citizenship and Social Class: And Other Essays*. Cambridge [Eng]: University Press, 1950. Print.

Massey, Doreen. *For Space*. London: SAGE, 2005. Print.

Mathieu, Corina S. "La realidad tragicómica de Osvaldo Soriano." *Chasqui*. 17.1 (1988): 85-91. Print.

Montes Capó, Cristian. "Escritura y subjetividad lírica en *La hora sin sombra* de Osvaldo Soriano." *Revista Chilena de Literatura*.62 (2003): 47-63. Print.

Nicholson, Brantley. "A Poetics of Globalism: Fernando Vallejo, the Colombian Urban Novel, and the Generation of '72." Doctoral. Duke, 2011. Print.

Nicholson, B, and L Reinaga. "On Pirate Cinema and Crying in Airports: a Conversation with Alberto Fuguet." *Studies in Latin*

American Popular Culture. 29 (2011): 202-217. Print.

Nora, Pierre. "Between Memory and History: *Les Lieux De Mémoire.*" *Representations.* (1989): 7-24. Print.

Pellegrino, Adela. *Skilled Labour Migration from Developing Countries: Study on Argentina and Uruguay.* Geneva: ILO, 2002. Print.

Ponce, Néstor. "Azar y derrota: El fin de las ilusiones en "*Una sombra ya pronto serás*", De Osvaldo Soriano." *Hispamérica.* 30.89 (2001): 29-41. Print.

Ran, Amalia. "El viaje por la memoria en *La hora sin sombra.*" *Chasqui* 37.1 (2008): 25-35. Print.

Richards, D G. "Inflation, Unemployment and Distributional Conflict in Argentina, 1984-90." *Journal of Development Studies London.* 34.2 (1997): 156-172. Print.

Sarlo, Beatriz. *Tiempo presente: Notas sobre el cambio de una cultura.* Buenos Aires: Siglo Veintiuno Editores Argentina, 2001. Print.

Soriano, Osvaldo. "Vivir con la inflación." *Nueva Sociedad.* 100 (1989): 38-43. Print.

—. *Una sombra ya pronto serás.* Buenos Aires: Editorial Sudamericana, 1990. Print.

—. *La hora sin sombra.* Buenos Aires: Seix Barral, 2004. Print.

Storey, David. *Territories: The Claiming of Space.* New York: Routledge, 2012. Print.

CONNECTING SEPTEMBER 11'S: HEMISPHERIC HISTORICAL
AMBIGUITY IN ARIEL DORFMAN'S *AMERICANOS: LOS PASOS DE MURIETA*

John Riofrio
College of William & Mary

In 2005 Andrés Neuman, the celebrated Argentine author and winner of the 2011 Alfaguara prize for best novel, published a beautiful book of aphorisms entitled, *El equilibrista*. In it, among many similar gems, he writes: "La postmodernidad es onanista"[1] (73). It is a short but scathing condemnation of postmodernism[2] as an endless series of intellectual games and queries meant for the private pleasure of the knowing few. That Neuman's assertion has teeth is due, no doubt, to the fact that the charge holds, to a degree. Like all good aphorisms, however, its strength as polemic lies in

1. [Postmodernity is onanistic.] All translations, unless otherwise noted, are my own.
2. Paula Moya's definition of postmodernism remains one of the clearest, most brilliantly accessible explanations I have thus far encountered. Rather than try to emulate as clear a definition, I will defer here to Moya and quote at length from her book *Learning from Experience*: "Most critics agree that [postmodernism] can be characterized in at least three (analytically separable) ways: (1) as an aesthetic practice; (2) as a historical stage in the development of late capitalism; and (3) as a theoretical and/or critical position... While I will describe the (often implicit) epistemological underpinnings of 'postmodernist' theoretical conceptions of identity, I am aware that postmodernist theory does not constitute a unified intellectual movement. Rather, it embodies a range of theoretical and political practices that emphasize the unstable and contingent nature of discursively produced meaning. Moreover, the arguments of many prominent figures in contemporary feminist, postcolonial, antiracist, and queer theory (some of whom reject the terms I am using to describe them) share important commonalities; they are characterized by a strong epistemological skepticism, a valorization of flux and mobility, and a general suspicion of, or hostility toward, all normative and/or universalist claims" (8).

its overgeneralization. Like many of the brilliant new generation of young Latin American writers—many of whom, like Neuman, were named to the Hay Market Festival's list *Bogotá 39*, a list of the thirty-nine most influential writers in Latin America under the age of forty—Neuman's critique *could* be read as a salvo of sorts aimed at his literary forbearers, whom he charges with having played literary intellectual games at the expense of a concerted engagement with the world around them. I don't think this was the intention of his critique of postmodernism. Regardless, his aphoristic critique reveals, to a subtle degree, Neuman's own relative privilege as a writer of a generation freed from the particular constraints faced by the Generation of '72.

As Brantley Nicholson and Sophia McClennen have argued in the introduction to this volume, the Generation of '72 "is a generation that, for the first time in twentieth-century Latin America, experiences the roundly negative aspects of globalization and whose writers make less voluntary trips to the cosmopolitan center than enter into acquiesced global citizenship through political exile" (4). Moreover, as a generation of writers shaped by particular historical, social and economic forces, Nicholson and McClennen argue that they, as a group, have been "presented with the task of mourning while questioning the very limits of a literature that undergoes a double affront through the strict control of symbolic systems by authoritarian regimes and the influx of new cultural referents that the abrupt liberalization of Latin American economies causes" (5). Contrary to Neuman's assertion that postmodernism is about the playful scattering of one's intellectual seed, for this generation, the incessant questioning and suspicion at the center of postmodernism forms the very center of their efforts to contend with the crisis of interpretation wrought by authoritarian regimes. I would suggest that Ariel Dorfman's novel *Americanos: Los pasos de Murieta* functions as a poetic refutation to Neuman's entertaining, but perhaps heavy-handed, critique of postmodernism. Further, this essay will argue that *Americanos* foregrounds the postmodern sensibility of slipperiness and ambiguity in order to aggressively assert our inability to narrate history in any complete way and to underscore the senseless violence that stems from the construction of multiple, competing, heavily-mediated histories.

Americanos: Los pasos de Murieta, a deeply complex and layered novel that has not received the kind of critical attention it deserves, is the latest novel by the Chilean-American writer Ariel Dorfman.[3] Released in 2009, *Americanos* is set in the wild west of the mid-1800s. The story takes place in California at the precise historical juncture of both the impending US Civil War and the transition of California from a Mexican territory to a possession of the United States. *Americanos* is narrated, primarily, by its hero, Harrison Lynch. Born in the early 1800s in England, Harrison is sent to Chile where he grows up under the tutelage of Bernardo O' Higgins the Chilean hero of the wars of independence. After a series of adventures and tragedies, Lynch assumes the name Harrison Solar and escapes to California where he is eventually employed by the Amador family to tutor the twins Rafael and Pablo Amador. Harrison's narrative recounts his biography as well as the story of the twins and their beloved cousin Marcadia Amador, the youngest of the Amador, born at the precise moment when California is illegally proclaimed a US possession only to revert back some hours later into a Mexican territory.

Rafael and Pablo, who grow up as close as is physically and emotionally possible, are eventually cleaved apart by the alleged death of the *bandido* Joaquín Murieta, a local, mythical figure who in his day was seen as either a plague on the lives of "honest" western businessmen, or a Robin-hood type folk-hero standing up against the Yankee incursions into Mexican California. One of the defining features of both Dorfman and the other writers of the Generation of '72 is their contention that, as Nicholson has put it, "no grand political discourse or stabilizing cultural frame is complete without its negative and antithetical undercurrent." Seen in this light my reading will demonstrate that Dorfman's *Americanos* is both a reflection on the history which divided these two twins and an effort to imagine, against all odds, the reconciliation of America's complex, profoundly bifurcated legacy of hope *and* hypocrisy.

Incredibly, Dorfman's novel was a full thirty-five years in

---

3. As he describes in his memoir *Heading South, Looking North*, Dorfman was born in Chile, lived in the US as a child, was forced to flee back to Chile because of the virulent McCarthyism of the 1950s, and then later forced back into US exile with the violently repressive ascension to power of General Augusto Pinochet in 1973. He has been a professor of Literature at Duke University for over twenty-five years and, although he has written works in every major literary genre including opera, he is most widely recognized for his classic Marxist study of US imperialism, *Para leer al pato Donald* [*How to Read Donald Duck*] and his play *Death and the Maiden*.

the making. It begins with Dorfman's attendance, in 1975, of a play by Neruda entitled *El fulgor de Joaquín Murieta*. The play features a life-size headless marionette that represents Murieta and that Dorfman reads as an emblem of exile. At the time, the image was particularly powerful to Dorfman because he read the decapitated figure of Murieta as an intriguing metaphor for exile: "pensé que atrás de eso había una novela interesante, una manera de hablar del destierro, de la pérdida de lo familiar en el mundo. Y eso era lo que estábamos viviendo nosotros ahí, en ese momento."[4] The image of the headless Murieta from the mid-nineteenth century nags at Dorfman for years and sets him on the path to *Americanos*. In the intervening years between his viewing of Neruda's play and the publication of *Americanos*, Dorfman would, of course, become one of most successful, exiled Southern Cone writers. His work, *Death and the Maiden*, is a classic of exile literature and reflects Dorfman's continuing interest in exile as both a sense of geographic displacement (a byproduct of forced physical movement) and an emotional displacement that stems from "the loss of the familiar." Murieta's transformation, in Dorfman's literary mind, from a symbol of headless exile to a figure of historical ambiguity that functions to symbolically connect the Americas, embodies Dorfman's long trajectory as an intellectual, essayist and novelist. What began as a period novel or a contemplation of exile, morphs into a work that actively seeks to juxtapose 19th century California with contemporary, post 9/11 US society in order to explore larger issues regarding history, identity and the right to interpretive power.

On the surface *Americanos*, written in Spanish, is a novel about the 19th century Mexican territory of California. It tells the stories of the struggles for independence in Chile and the subsequent efforts by the Spaniards to retain their colonies under imperial control. It also, however, tells the story of the rampant US imperialism that would, in the span of a few decades, transform California from a largely quiet Mexican territory into the pulsing center of the United States' hemispheric expansionist efforts. As the novel makes clear, the struggle for California would set the pattern for US incursions throughout the Americas while simultaneously establishing the long-standing antagonism between Mexico and the

---

4. [it occurred to me that behind this there was an interesting novel, a way of talking about exile, of the loss of the familiar in the world. And that this was what we were living there, in that very moment.]

US. *Americanos* tells these stories peripherally while focusing the novel on three generations of the Amador family and their efforts to secure and retain land.

In linking their story of success and eventual decline with the fortunes of Mexico and its territory, Dorfman reengages the long tradition of the Latin American Romance novels of the 19th century. Building on what Doris Sommer has described as "the inextricability of politics from fiction in the history of nation-building" (5-6) Dorfman's novel is an updated version of the Romance novels that Sommer has signaled as intimately connected to the flurry of Latin American nations born in the 19th century.[5] *Americanos* uses the Romance genre as scaffolding upon which to narrate the nation-building of 19th century United States in order to elucidate the process of nation-building he sees taking place, now, in the 21st century. Linking these two principle narratives—the fury and insistence of US 19th century imperialism and the rise and fall of the Mexican land-owning class in the territory of California—is the long-disputed figure of Joaquín Murieta. A well-documented historical subject, Murieta's life and death, however, have been intriguingly hard to confirm. Debates regarding his place of birth—Mexico versus Chile—as well as his death, or not, at the hands of a Texas Ranger, make Murieta a fascinating symbolic axis for Dorfman's sustained examination of post 9/11 US identity.

My argument, moreover, is that Dorfman uses the notion of historical ambiguity—our inability to *know* or even *tell* history in any concrete, culturally neutral way—in order to decry the endless, mobius-like cycles of violence that emerge out of culturally constructed, narrative histories. He sees in this historical ambiguity, a conditioned obsession with narrating history as if it were Truth and then utilizing this "truth" to perpetuate and justify violence and repression.[6] *Americanos* emphasizes Dorfman's point by constructing a subtle rhetorical line that spans generations and geographies

---

5. Sommer's larger argument with regards to the connection between romance novels and 19th century nation-building centers around the idea that the novels played out and performed the supposed "natural" relationships of heterosexual love and their allegorical connections to the presumed natural relationships between creoles and the variegated civil societies of the burgeoning nation-states.

6. Although my focus in this essay is on the novel *Americanos*, Dorfman's concern with the instability of truth and its consistent, material effects on people's lives is a hallmark of his entire *oeuvre* spanning such dramatically different works as *Death and the Maiden* and *Konfidenz*.

in order to connect historical moments throughout the Americas that *seem* isolated both chronologically and geographically. His novel interrogates these connections in order to offer storytelling and narrative as a means to constructing alternate worlds capable of standing in opposition to the consistent, historical perpetuation of violence. Further, I contend that *Americanos* is a novel that intentionally seeks to straddle historical periods in order to explore the profound feelings of disconnect, of emotional and cognitive disembodiedness, which marked the September 11's of both 1973 and 2001.

My argument, that *Americanos: Los Pasos de Murieta*—which ends 110 years before Chile's September 11th and 138 years before our own—is at heart a novel about 9/11, is not a reading that is patently obvious upon first blush. On the surface *Americanos* seems to be more concretely focused on revising and updating the romance novels of 19th century Latin America. It is Dorfman's effort, however, at writing a 19th century Latin American Romance novel with a distinctly postmodern aesthetic sensibility that marks the crux of the matter. Understanding *Americanos* as a postmodern 19th century Latin American Romance hinges upon understanding two key interventions that Dorfman makes in the genre. Building upon Sommer's assessment that the "continent seemed to invite inscriptions" (7) and that this "invitation" remains equally true today as it did 150 years ago, *Americanos* updates the romance genre through the introduction of: 1) postmodernism's penchant for formalistic experimentation—in this case by having several of the novel's chapters narrated by a miraculous bar of soap crafted by indigenous hands—and 2) the postmodern propensity towards ambiguity as an organizing trope.

Historical Ambiguity: The Blunt Force of Doubt

Dorfman himself asserts that his original intention had been to write a traditional, epic Latin American novel that would move chronologically through the upheaval that spanned generations of families across the Americas. He then confesses, however, that the 30+ years that it took him to complete this novel, were decades marked intensely by the influence of postmodernism and what Dorfman describes as the "relativizing of knowledge." He explains that:

"la persona que escribe *Americanos* es la misma que escribió *La muerte y la doncella*, donde no se sabe si el doctor es torturador o no, o si la mujer es loca o no. Me atrajo esta idea de trabajar la incertidumbre de la historia, mirarla con ironía y distancia, en paralelo con el heroísmo y la epopeya" (*Página/12*).[7] The postmodernist irony at the center of Dorfman's novel is that his sincere belief in the power of narrative to construct imagined, more productive worlds is aligned with the task of undermining our collective efforts to narrate histories in any concrete, satisfactory way.

Dorfman places his goal of "[working uncertainty]" at the center of his novel by quietly undermining the notion of narrative and asking implicitly: who bears the right to tell a story? *Americanos* opens with a note from the translator that sets out to detail the difficulty of working with the author, Ariel Dorfman. The translator, Eduardo Vladimiroff, explains the enthusiasm with which he began this project motivated, in part, by the privileged opportunity to discuss, in detail, the content and character of a novel of epic scope with a living author. He is assured by the editor that Dorfman is "[a model of courtesy]" and accepts the job. The sad reality, according to Vladimiroff, is that his repeated letters and intellectual queries go summarily unanswered and that the "famous" Dorfman never bothers to make an appearance.

Vladimiroff utilizes the translator's note to chastise Dorfman for being, "much too busy" to reply to questions about historical events described in the novel, or to suggestions regarding a time-line of historical events or a chart delineating the Amador family genealogy. Vladimiroff's note, dripping with disdain, paints Dorfman as a prima donna of sorts who robs the translator of an opportunity to produce the best possible translation of a difficult novel. The joke, and this would not be immediately apparent to a first-time reader of Dorfman's work or even to the occasional reader not familiar with Dorfman's memoir, is that Eduardo Vladimiroff is actually a play on Dorfman's birth name Vladimiro Ariel Dorfman. In reality the two—author and translator, Dorfman and Vladimiroff,—are one and the same, and the footnotes that riddle the novel exposing the author's missteps, the liberties taken with both his-

---

7. [the person who writes *Americanos* is the same who wrote *Death and the Maiden*, in which we don't know if the doctor is a torturer or not, if the woman is crazy or not. I was attracted to the idea of working the uncertainty of history, observing it at a distance and with irony but also paralleled by heroism and epic storytelling].

tory and fiction, are pointed out by the same man who originally wrote them. The process of undermining narrative accuracy begins on page one.

The notion that History and Narrative are slippery and culturally constructed is not new of course[8], yet Dorfman's interest is in showing how our ideological commitments to particular historical narratives enable and even encourage us to participate in endless cycles of violence. Dorfman uses the figure of Joaquín Murieta to indicate the long history of an intertwined Americas—the case that is being made by scholars of inter-American and Hemispheric Latin@ studies—but also as a means to make a case for the impossibility of narrating history in any complete way.

Murieta is a fascinating character through which to focus on these arguments precisely because his biography not only highlights the concept of an Americas as a unified object of study, but also foregrounds the issue of historical ambiguity. Robert McKee Irwin writes that Murieta is "in many ways a typical borderlands icon, representing no one group, signifying in multiple directions to multiple audiences" (40). For the principle characters of the Amador family, the twins Pablo and Rafael and their cousin Marcadia, Murieta's legend, at least initially, does symbolize in a single direction. For the Amador children, Murieta represents the evocative image of a single, solitary Mexican standing in opposition to Yankee aggression.

Their profound reverence for Murieta signals to the reader the depth of connection between Marcadia and the twins but especially between the two brothers, Rafael and Pablo, who begin the novel as closely allied as is physically and emotionally possible for two separate beings. Jaboncito, the miraculous bar of soap that narrates several of the novel's chapters, describes the moment of bathing the twins for the very first time: "[In the impossible fraternal unanimity of their breath I couldn't detect any variation, so inseparable was the one from the other...each one spoke for the other and for both, the very notion of "I", "mine", "my eyes", did not hold for those twins I bathed]" (127). For Jaboncito, whose magical ability allows him to see the innermost thoughts and experiences of those he bathes and touches, Rafael and Pablo exist as a single entity. This idyllic unity, however, doesn't last and it is Murieta's alleged beheading that eventually separates Rafael and Pablo with the former

---

8. One text that immediately comes to mind is Hayden White's *Metahistory*.

assuring the latter that Murieta is indeed a hero while Pablo insists that Murieta is emblematic of the lawlessness of a less civilized land.

This divergence of opinion over the legacy of Murieta would come to define the split between Rafael and Pablo and becomes the symbolic center of the novel's efforts to understand the burgeoning identity of the United States. I will examine this notion further in a later section of this essay, however, for the moment the key point is that Murieta, in addition to becoming the root of the twins' untimely and unfortunate separation, perfectly embodies the ambiguity that Dorfman finds both troubling and evocative. Dorfman's interest in Murieta is not simply *how* Murieta is represented to, and signified by, multiple cultural constituencies but also the fact that Murieta has, for decades, remained a figure marked deeply by ambiguity. McKee Irwin writes:

> from the early newspaper reports and the first literary representations of Murrieta [sic] to the hundreds of reformulations of the legend in novels, plays, *corridos*, poems, histories, movies, and the like over the past century and a half in California and the United States, France, Spain, Chile, and Mexico by *gringo*, Native American, Chicano, Sonoran, Latin American, and even Russian writers, it seems that no one can agree on the many details of the case. (38)

To Dorfman, the unverifiable truth of Murieta's biography becomes as important as the way in which his story shines light on the ascertainable experiences of ethnic Mexicans whose lives were, and are, *undeniably* dictated by hemispheric events and protagonists and by processes that emerge out of efforts to narrate those lives as historical characters and events.

The Untenable Ambiguity of Murieta's Life, Death and Legacy

Pablo and Rafael—each convinced of their version of the events regarding Murieta's death, or survival—undertake a fevered quest to find out "the truth" about Murieta. As the narrative progresses and they journey further and further from home, they find that the truth remains no less accessible than the rumors they entertained on their own doorstep. After weeks of travel, the only apparent truth is the way in which historical truth frustrates their efforts at certainty. This revelation leads to the following dialog between the two exasperated twins:

> [—Let's say we find him.—His voice was calm, genuinely interested.
> —I'm sure you won't be able to, but let's suppose it happens. Then what?
> —We listen to him. We hear his story, what really happened, directly from the lips of Murieta.
> —And how can you know that it's really him? What was your name in the States, son? Johnson or Thompson or Bates. That song by Eamons. People invent whatever tall tale, construct a fictitious history about themselves, especially if they are far from home, from those who watched them grow. The only thing I am going to believe in, from now on, is that which I've submitted to my own reason.] (285)

Whereas under distinct circumstances Pablo would likely have praised the US for being a place where people can constantly reinvent themselves, in this case, Pablo's discourse belies a growing cynicism with regards to the possibility not only of Murieta's existence but also more deeply with the possibility of truth. Pablo, in this way, begins to sense that historical narrative is a seriously flawed mechanism for conveying historical truth, the reality of people and events.[9]

His words bring to mind what anthropologist Renato Rosaldo, in a different context, points to as the unwitting, "authoritative" arrogance of the ethnographer. Rosaldo, writing of the complexity inherent in ethnographic fieldwork writes that "all interpretations are provisional; they are made by positioned subjects who are prepared to know certain things and not others" (8). What strikes me as important here is the way in which our faith in reason often makes it difficult for us to consider the ways in which our social location influences the wielding of that reason. Like the ethnographers that Rosaldo warns his readers about, Pablo doesn't realize that even his vaunted reason is a culturally constructed artifact of a *particular* social context.

Perhaps the most climactic of moments in regards to the

---

9. Like many of the other writers of the Generation of '72, Dorfman underscores the fact that established narrative truths, like national narratives, are consistently eroded by the public voice or, to use a phrase suggested to me by Nicholson, the "orality of everyday life." Dorfman's novel, like much of his work, does not seek to hierarchize public voice over national narratives, but he is deeply interested in considering the almost constant ebb and flow that exists between them.

ambiguity of Murieta's story comes two-thirds of the way through the novel. The twins meet a cowboy named Henderson who narrates, with stunning detail, the last minutes of Murieta's life. Henderson lays claim to having killed Murieta and condemns the Texas Ranger, Harry Love, for having cheated him out of his part of the reward money. The twins leave the saloon with Pablo convinced of his triumph over his brother. Minutes later, however, they are chased down by the saloon's dishwasher, a Chilean named Ramón Sandoval who refutes Henderson's story by explaining that Love and his group would kill anyone who resembled Murieta, and had the unfortunate name of Joaquín, and then would sell off their horses as a way to make the venture profitable. Sandoval offers two pieces of evidence as proof. 1) Murieta himself appeared at a local saloon in order to look at his own head; 2) shortly thereafter Murieta sent a letter to the local paper asserting that he could assure that it was not his head being exhibited in the glass bottle because "[I have mine, firmly-placed, on my shoulders and these are my hands which are writing this letter of protest]" (298). Sandoval's refutation, however, rests on two shaky foundations: 1) he never actually witnesses Murieta come to see his own head and 2) he never sees Murieta's signature at the bottom of the letter. Both of these acts were witnessed by Sandoval's friend Heraldo Rosales. Pablo, unconvinced by the story, asks Sandoval about his friend Rosales:

—And where is this Heraldo Rosales?
—The dummy went back home, to Quillota, you know, in Chile.
—In other words, if we want to verify if this Rosales is telling the truth, we would have to go to Chile to confirm it, right?
—Why would my friend lie?
—Asked Pablo exasperated—. Why does every person we come across seem to be telling us another lie? (298-299)

Every narrative that seems to confirm or deny Murieta's death is followed closely by an equally (im)plausible narrative that effectively counters the preceding one. Bearing in mind McKee Irwin's assertion vis-à-vis the tendency of multiple audiences to signify Murieta in particular ways, we come to understand the twins' impasse as being one of signification. For the various communities Murieta represents the larger divisions that have marked both America and the Americas. The divisions among Americans and Americanos is focalized through Murieta in such a way that his biography, whether one believes that he was born in Chile or in So-nora, attests to the legacy of a 19th century America that from the outset was a hemispheric destination.

Put another way, while the amnesia with which we've tended to discuss, interpret and understand Latino/a history in the US places their arrival and impact within the last few decades, the figure of Murieta highlights the reality of a burgeoning United States marked by the arrival of Mexican but also waves of South and Central Americans as well as Asians from the "Far East" spanning more than a century. Murieta thus speaks to the centuries-long *hemispheric* history of the United States, one that is, in part, addressed by the US's long history of incursions into Latin America, but that is also marked by the constant immigration of Chileans and Peruvians to the West Coast in search of gold. Given the rampant historical amnesia that marks our educational system[10] we might then suggest that Murieta's history in this novel acts to dispel the notion that the US has always been sharply distinct from the rest of Latin America.

For the twins, Rafael and Pablo, the debate over Murieta's death and his legacy transcends the question of historical veracity and instead points to the fact that Murieta's legacy is, at heart, a living manifestation of Sommer's notion of "writing America." For Rafael and Pablo, establishing the narrative surrounding Murieta is an act of active, engaged construction: what kind of "America" do they want to believe in? Is it Rafael's vision of an Americas united by dreams of revolutionary struggle against imperialism and colonialism, or is it Pablo's vision of an America inspired, but also dictated, by the emerging and overwhelming power of the United States' version of the American Dream? Ultimately, both the history and legacy of Murieta reveal themselves as an inaccessible tangle of fact and fiction, constructs meant to enable preexisting versions of the social world foregrounded by each of the varying social groups invested in Murieta. For his victims and his beneficiaries alike, Murieta becomes simultaneously everything and nothing. In the social context of 19th century California (and beyond) he is *both* a bandit and a hero, and he is *neither*. Murieta's legacy is as ambiguous as his actual history and as such comes to embody the ambiguousness

---

10. For two decidedly distinct, but perhaps equally brilliant, ways of addressing the issue of the US's propensity for historical amnesia see Ali Behdad's *A Forgetful Nation: On Immigration and Cultural Identity in the United States* and Jon Stewart's handling of the 2010 Texas textbook controversy: http://www.thedailyshow.com/watch/wed-march-17-2010/don-t-mess-with-textbooks.

of History *writ large*.

Historical Ambiguity or Birth on the Hyphen

Dorfman furthers the connection between ambiguity and History by introducing the symbolic opposite of Murieta's unverifiable death, the seemingly concrete and verifiable birth of Marcadia Amador, Rafael and Pablo's beloved cousin. Marcadia's birth, unlike Murieta's death, seems patently straightforward to confirm. Debate, however, arises because of the possible symbolism attached to her birth. In this scene, Pedro Amador (the eldest son of the patriarch Álvaro Amador), is trying to determine if Harrison knows anything about the moment in which California passed over, momentarily, into the hands of the US:

> —I thought that you, having been there, might inform us of the exact hour at which the North American flag was raised over Monterrey on the 19th of October, something that is more transcendent than might otherwise seem. Isn't that right, Father?
> —My granddaughter Marcadia—he explained in a voice that was louder and definitely less courteous than that of his son—was born, mind you, the 19th of October at 9:47am. Therefore, what matters is to know if she was born *after* the Yankees raised that piece of shit flag. My son Pedro says yes, I say no. You will tell us who is right. (142)

Verifying Marcadia's birth appears to be a simple matter; however, again like Murieta's death, Marcadia's birth is laden with symbolic import in that the Amador family sits within a territory in transition, at a historical moment of profound crisis and reflection.

As Rosaura Sanchez has noted "this sense of being 'social exiles' and decentered, the outrage, resentment, and disillusionment at being displaced by others within their own terrain, constitutes the sociospatial dominant mapped in the nineteenth-century Californio testimonials" (3). For Álvaro, Marcadia's birth is inescapably connected to the growing sense of "outrage" and "disillusionment," but also condenses symbolically the question of citizenship and belonging inherent in the experiences of *californianos*. To accept Marcadia as an "American" would be in some way to accept the reality of California's transition, its conquest, by the US, what Sanchez has called the "liminal point of passage from market to monopoly capital" (2). Álvaro Amador's cognitive struggle is, therefore, the struggle to hold at bay the military might of the US, but also the insistent temptation of the American Dream that had begun to propagate itself far and wide.

Harrison Solar's rebuttal, however, is instructive in its repudiation of the very terms of the debate. For, although Álvaro Amador has made his wealth and his reputation by always fighting, by always resisting, Harrison's insight is into the futility now inherent in that struggle.

> —I don't see why the hour should matter, sir. The North American flag was taken down two days later, but it remains there, perhaps for the moment invisible to some, but I assure you that it continues to fly. And tomorrow, or the next day, or perhaps in three years, that flag will once again be raised and when that happens, I assure you, it will never again be taken down...What matters, then, if you'll excuse me, isn't knowing the precise hour of anything. What matters is preparing for that inescapable day. (144)

In the moment of sharp, historical disjunct wrought by the growth of the US in the Americas, Marcadia's birth signals that the terms of the debate have shifted. The inclination and the faith, in concrete historical narratives (i.e. she was born under the Mexican flag and is, as such, Mexican) no longer hold and instead give way to the realities which those (hi)stories occlude. In the case of California and the Amador family, the question becomes not whether California remains Mexican, but for how long and at what cost? The question of Marcadia's birth, like the question of Murieta's death, is therefore more revealing of the way in which ambiguity hinders our attempts to understand the world around us, particularly in turbulent times like the transition of the territory of California or like the intervening months and years after September 11, 2001.

For Dorfman, our understanding of categories of thought, like progress and modernity, are as critically suspect as our understanding of historical events and figures in the sense that they are necessarily confined to an ambiguous telling and retelling that serves only to reflect the particular biases of our own time and place. As the dying Harrison recounts his life to the twins, he tells the story of his complicated loyalty to the rebels' struggle for independence and the battle that ended the life of his mortal enemy Ignacio Ibarra. Speaking in regards to Ibarra's dying assertion that the conflict between the Spanish Empire and the Rebels was pointless, Harrison says "Of course he was right. Of course he was wrong" (338). Our efforts to delineate sharply our distinct histories and cultures, like the twins' efforts to trace the solid lines of Murieta's life, are hopelessly ambiguous; neither side is correct, neither side is wrong.

Faced with the hopeless ambiguity of history and narration, Marcadia and the twins, rather than slip into the dead-end of cultural relativism, fall into an equally lamentable state of perpetual conflict. It is through this conflict that we see manifest the consequences of the US's September 11th on our national consciousness. *Americanos* ends with an amorous tryst between Marcadia and her two cousins, one she designs to be purposefully ambiguous. Demanding total darkness and silence, Marcadia makes love to both twins simultaneously, willfully ignorant of which is which, a decision that relieves her, and denies us, of the knowledge of which of the two twins is the father of the child she bears. Marcadia is ambiguously American or *americana*, and the child she bears is either the son of Pablo (and the child of American exceptionalism and progress) or the son of Rafael (and the inheritor of Latin American independence, of revolution and resistance both physical and philosophical). Marcadia is transformed into a revised Malinche figure who bears the future child of cultural and nationalist *mestizaje* (he/she will be both American and Mexican), yet the legacy of that child's conception goes unresolved. Was this child conceived with Pablo turning him/her (and Marcadia) into race "traitors" the way Malinche has been unfairly interpreted by traditional Mexican culture, or is he/she Rafael's child and therefore "true" to the spirit of Latin American independence and autonomy? Dorfman refuses to answer the question and in doing so highlights the profound anxiety of two nations split—*rajados* to use Gloria Anzaldua's term—by their shared inheritance.

Leaping Across Centuries: Historical and Geographical Continuity

For Dorfman, nowhere is the question of historical ambiguity more salient that in the months and years following the events of September 11, 2001. Although Dorfman's dedication to a literature of compassion, humanity and quiet rage has been a trademark of his entire career, *Americanos* represents the continuation of one of the literary and philosophical projects at the center of his moving collection of essays, *Other Septembers*. As one reads through the essays in *Other Septembers* one is struck by the fact that many of the essays written in the late 80s and early 90s remain relevant even now, *especially* now. In the essay, "The Last September 11" Dorfman talks about the haunting need he feels "to understand and extract the hidden meaning of the juxtaposition and coincidence of these two September 11s" (39). Dorfman goes on to argue about the paradoxical opportunity which the pain of the US's September 11 held for its citizens:

> One of the ways for Americans to overcome their trauma and survive the fear and continue to live and thrive in the midst of the insecurity which has suddenly swallowed them is to admit that their suffering is neither unique nor exclusive, that they are connected, as long as they are willing to look at themselves in the vast mirror of our common humanity, to so many other beings who, in apparent faraway zones, have suffered similar situations of unanticipated and often protracted injury and fury. (41)

The opportunity, which Dorfman sees as central to the hope of redemption and healing, is the idea that the US is, indeed, a part of the larger world, that contrary to the outsized notion of exceptionalism, the US too suffers, has suffered, and might well suffer again. Just like the rest of the world. Dorfman is fascinated with these two September 11s for their rhetorical potential, the possibility that inheres in them to tell a story that will join the US to Chile—and the hemisphere—in what is clearly a story of loss, but also of hope. This central paradox of lingering hope braided movingly with aching loss is one that resonates deeply with the Generation of '72. What, then, makes *Americanos* in particular a novel about the trans-American and transhistorical importance of 9/11, both 1973 and 2001?

Early in the novel, Dorfman writes that "History loves certain dates; she repeats them incessantly, intent on finding in them some order hidden amidst the chaos" (43). A short while later in the novel—seven pages later in fact—Dorfman suggests that certain historical moments are more chaotic than others, that History's desire for order, manifest in the curious repetition of dates, is crucial in these moments of total and complete disorder:

> When war arrives at the very doorstep of the city, and the population has no idea who will triumph, if the victors of today will be

in power tomorrow, and no one knows who the hell is really in charge, something strange tends to happen... In these moments, it feels as if there is no solid ground upon which to tread, everything solid seems to melt before our eyes, anything can happen. (50)

The historical setting for the above passage is not New York post 9/11, but it could be. It is not the Chile of 1973, but it could be. Instead it is the Chile of the early 1800s, and although Dorfman is describing the climate of war surrounding the battles for Chile's independence, his discourse emphasizes the idea that during moments of chaos and disillusionment we are ultimately informed and guided by the fact of historical continuity. As Dorfman himself has said in reference to the most recent 9/11, "I have been through this before."

Dorfman's novel takes us back to the precise moment when the notion of what it means to be American vs. *americano* is born and is deeply connected to Dorfman's desire to think through *an* identity for the United States. *Americanos* places us at a crossroads, at the juncture where the twins Pablo and Rafael, the US and Mexico, are at great risk of losing each other, perhaps forever. For me, what is crucial to grasp in order to understand this moving and complex novel is the convergence of two dynamics: 1) the incessant repetition of history, particularly of certain dates and 2) the need to return to a historical crossroads in order to better understand the path we have collectively chosen. *Americanos* emphasizes the fact of historical continuity by repeating "as often as possible" the repetition of dates and events such that the superficial connection of dates emphasizes, more significantly, the connectedness of the *consequences* of each historical moment (September 11, 2001 thus retains the profound *echoes* of September 11, 1973). Linking *Americanos* to *Other Septembers* we can appreciate how, for Dorfman, the two most notorious September 11s are connected because they reveal the US's deeply bifurcated legacy. Literary scholar Teresa Longo makes the following assertion about Dorfman's "Letter to America":

> The hole where the Twin Towers previously stood is not merely an empty space. It is a space that contains the specter of US hegemony in the hemisphere and the globe. Dorfman's work is mindful of this. His "Love Letter" does not ignore the specter in the center of the Manhattan landscape. It unmasks it. And in the unmasking, it envisions another more humane, more peaceful America.

The effort to unmask both the harm and the hope of the US's hemispheric legacy is representative of Dorfman's larger interest in symbols, specifically the fact that they can be read in multiple ways. And yet, as a literary critic, Dorfman would argue that some interpretations are simply better than others. *Americanos* signals Dorfman's intention to address, through the power of narrative, precisely these sorts of struggles over representation. The moment of California's absorption into the US becomes *the* moment of irredeemable fracture for the Amador family in that Pablo comes to believe in the hope of US exceptionalism while Rafael can see nothing but the racist egoism of US capitalism and its constant need for acquisition and gain.

Taking this further, if Rafael and Pablo were to stand at the edge of ground zero and look deep into the gaping wound left by the events of 9/11, if, in other words, his twins were to gaze upon the space left by another set of twins, Pablo would see nothing more than the pain of human suffering, the pain inflicted upon a civilized nation by a jealous, spiteful act of terrorism. Rafael, on the other hand, would see in the crater a reflection of the US's cavernous appetite for wealth and expansion in the Middle East and in the Americas. Dorfman's argument in "Love Letter" and in *Americanos* is that to see one and not the other is to not see at all. *Americanos* goes beyond simply pointing out the ways in which historical events can produce radically different interpretations and instead tries to shape our understanding of those radically divergent positions. As Sophia McClennen argues in her recent book on Dorfman's work, "For Dorfman, the aesthetics of engaged literature offer the reader an opportunity to see the world from a new angle, one that has been lost or forgotten, repressed or silenced, censored or ignored by mainstream worldviews" (x). Moreover; Dorfman's *Americanos* takes us back to Neuman's critique of the self-involved trap of postmodernism by asking us to think about the role that global compassion might play in deciding for ourselves, as Marcadia must, which twin is right, or rather, which twin is more right.

The historical moment where the US absorbs California and splits irrevocably from Mexico functions to divide the world into Americans and Americanos, *ellos y nosotros*; it is a moment echoed sharply in the events of 9/11 when the world, similarly was divided into us versus them. This dynamic, the reduction of complex historical processes to overly simplistic binaries, is one of the sad realities of our present historical moment. One only needs to tune in to any number of "news" programs to see the reduction of issues like immigration, poverty, and terrorism into social dynamics existing only in their present form.

Dorfman's effort in *Americanos* is to resist the type of historical amnesia that produces knee-jerk reactions to events like terrorist attacks. Because Dorfman understands narrative as a powerful tool for unearthing silenced histories, he relies on literature as a means to open up and reveal the historical connections that arc across centuries. Stories, like the myth of Joaquín Murieta, force us to engage the world around us in order to redefine it. Here the act of literary creation is nothing if not the creation of new worlds, worlds functioning in opposition to the realities of oppression and violence. But these are not artifacts of escapism, these are not alternate realities within which we can close our eyes and drift off to a better place. By using the contested figure of Murieta, *Americanos* parallels the contested reading of ground zero such that this story about 19th century California seems to reach out and grasp the present in order to highlight the presence of those rare historical moments when we find ourselves clearly being asked to choose, this path or that one. They oblige us, as the Generation of '72 would, to refuse simplified realities in order to seek solutions that are more honest, more real. In fact, as Ariel Dorfman's work has been telling us all along: in these, our deepest, most troubling moments (and aren't they always such) it is our ability to tell stories—to imagine worlds through our words—that will set us on the right path, one that, rather than divide us into small, hostile factions of "us" versus "them" will turn "us" *towards* "them" and vice versa, not in conflict but in hope, always in hope.

Works Cited

Anzaldua, Gloria. *Borderlands/La Frontera: The New Mestiza*. San Francisco, CA: Aunt Lute Books, 1987.

Behdad Ali. *A Forgetful Nation: On Immigration and Cultural Identity in the United States*. Durham, NC: Duke University Press, 2005.

Berlanga, Angel. "El oro y el barro." *Página 12: Radar*. Domingo, 3 de mayo de 2009. http://www.pagina12.com.ar/diario/

suplementos/radar/9-5269-2009-05-05.html [accessed July 23, 2010].

Dorfman, Ariel. *Americanos: Los Pasos de Murieta*. Buenos Aires, Argentina: Seix Barral, 2009.

—. *Death and the Maiden*. New York: Penguin Books, 1991.

—. *Heading South, Looking North: A Bilingual Journey*. New York: Farrar, Straus and Giroux, 1998.

—. *Konfidenz*. New York: Viking Books, 1996.

—. *Other Septembers, Many Americas: Selected Provocations 1980-2004*. New York: Seven Stories Press, 2004.

Dorfman, Ariel and Armand Mattelart. *Para leer al pato Donald: Comunicación de masa y colonialismo*. Valparaíso: Ediciones Universitarias de Valparaíso, 1971.

Longo, Teresa. *Visible Dissent*. Unpublished manuscript.

McClennen, Sophia A. *Ariel Dorfman: An Aesthetics of Hope*. Durham, NC: Duke University Press, 2010.

McKee Irwin, Robert. *Bandits, Captives, Heroines, and Saints: Cultural Icons of Mexico's Northwest Borderlands*. Minneapolis: University of Minnesota Press, 2007.

Moya, Paula M.L *Learning from Experience: Minority Identities, Multicultural Struggles*. Berkeley, CA: University of California Press, 2002.

Neruda, Pablo. *Fulgor y muerte de Joaquín Murieta*. Madrid: Debolsillo, 2004.

Neuman, Andres. *El equilibrista*. Barcelona: Acantilado, 2005.

Rosaldo, Renato. *Culture and Truth: The Remaking of Social Analysis*. Boston: Beacon Press, 1993.

Sánchez, Rosaura. *Telling Identities: The California Testimonios*. Minneapolis: University of Minnesota Press, 1995.

Sommer, Doris. *Foundational Fictions: The National Romances of Latin America*. Berkeley, CA: University of California Press, 1991.

Stewart, Jon. *The Daily Show with Jon Stewart*. Comedy Central. 17 March 2010. Television.

White, Hayden. *Metahistory: The Historical Imagination in Nineteenth-Century Europe*. Baltimore, MD: The Johns Hopkins University Press, 1975.

THE PSYCHOSOMATIC TEXT: RE-READING PSYCHOANALYSIS AND
SEMIOTICS IN *COMO EN LA GUERRA*, OR, THE SISTER(S) OF OEDIPUS

Geoffrey Kantaris
University of Cambridge

> [Ella] me dijo: estoy hecha para despertar en los otros un amor tan intenso y real que después no pueden con él y me abandonan. Bea sonrió un poco al copiar esta frase, una sonrisa triste, y me preguntó ¿alguna acotación? y yo dije que no porque no tenía ninguna.
> —Valenzuela, *Como en la guerra*, 1st ed., p. 64.

Re-Reading

    Luisa Valenzuela's novel *Como en la guerra* (1977), which appeared improbably amidst the maelstrom of the newly installed military regime in Argentina, has received far less critical attention than her other novels, eclipsed in part due to its problematic publication history, to its extraordinary complexity, and to the brilliance of her posterior and more readily available writings. But *Como en la guerra* is an equally brilliant text, raising complex questions about the relationship between identity, language, sexuality and politics, questions that lie at the core of much of Valenzuela's subsequent writing. I would thus like to give a triple sense to the idea of *re-reading* this highly self-reflexive novel. In the first place, belatedness and displaced reading mark the very structure of *Como en la guerra* as well as its publication history, so that we are in a sense forced into an atemporal reading of the text—something which even its earliest readers could not escape. Secondly, any act of reading and analysis of this novel must be marked by a deep sense of iterability and circularity, because the reader's analysis is always already undercut by the superfluous nature of the protagonist's own displaced acts of analysis within the novel. Through a set of proleptic frames both embedded within the novel and accidentally reproduced in its publication history, we are condemned to re-iterate, even as we disavow it, the role of Professors of Semiotics dabbling in psychoanalytical readings of the body of a text—and the text of a body—which resists any such appropriation. But then every reader, whether a Professor of Semiotics or not, must travel that circuit in the long run, must confront that totemic border formed by signs circulating incessantly around a prohibition, and this is clearly a position which the author and her readers inevitably share.

Indeed, such autotelic processes of re-reading and reformulation are a characteristic more generally of the works of the Generation of '72, where constant reframing insistently reveals the circularity of the exchange of signs, creating a fascinating if unsettling (and for that reason fruitful) short circuit between writer and readers. Moreover, iterative tropes of self-reading and self-rewriting are given a particular weight, and often become a structural feature of many works of these writers: witness Fernando Vallejo's collapse of autobiography into autopoiesis and Laura Restrepo's meta-*testimonio* form in which prosopopoeia is engulfed by a constant diegetic framing of the duplicity of representation. Valenzuela's own work shows compulsive traces of a deep process of reflection on the indeterminacy of writing, along with creative engagement with that slippery interface between the body (with its drives, compulsions and fleshy materiality) and the socio-linguistic systems in which the human body is immersed and which mediate its power of action over other bodies. In the 1970s and '80s, these areas of interest were being actively explored and theorized in the fields of semiotics and poststructuralist psychoanalysis, especially in literature departments in US universities, and it is no accident that Valenzuela's writing, throughout this period, engages with the often contradictory points of encounter between these systems of thought, albeit mischievously, parodying their formalities and confounding their categories. For early in her literary career, in 1969, Valenzuela won a Fulbright Commission scholarship to attend the International Writers Program in the University of Iowa, and subsequently spent time in New York, experiences which fundamentally marked her writing style, rendering it more ludic, non-linear and experimental (as seen in *El gato eficaz* [1972] written during this period). Travelling to Barcelona, Paris and Mexico in the 1970s, she "was reading Jacques Lacan's theories on language and the unconscious" (Valenzuela in Díaz, *Women and Power* 100), reflected in the close engagement with, and parody of, Lacanian theory in *Como en la guerra*. Subsequent books by Valenzuela are marked by her engagement with fervent debates within feminist literary theory of the late 1970s and '80s during her writer's residence at Columbia University and subsequently at CUNY. It is for this reason that, for reader and literary critic alike, a certain autotelic circuit occurs in reading much of Valenzuela's experimental writing, whereby the literary tools one might bring to a reading of her work are already pre-empted and discursively framed in ways that creatively disarm hierarchies of literary creation, secondary elaboration and interpretation. This disarming corresponds to her shuffling of various rhetorical frameworks which uphold (gendered) systems of social power. Hence, my own use of literary theory in this article is prompted by Valenzuela's complex challenge to her readers not to take the imbrication of language, gender and power at face value, while the proleptic structures of (psychoanalytical) interpretation that she *builds into her texts* force her readers, at every step, to reframe their own act of reading, whether theoretical or otherwise.

Yet there is a third sense in which this is a re-reading. Those of us who first read *Como en la guerra* in the 1980s were probably unsettled by a novel that describes itself in the original blurb as a *rompecabezas*, with the veiled violence which that term implies. We noted with discomfort the irony surrounding its male protagonist, the Professor of Semiotics, and his flirtatious interest in Jacques Lacan as we ourselves were perhaps struggling with the appropriation of Lacan by feminist theory of the late 1970s and 1980s. We saw that the novel moved in obscure ways between semiotics, psychoanalysis and politics, and some highly insightful first analyses of these configurations were produced, particularly by Sharon Magnarelli who, in 1988, carefully elucidated the sexual politics of the male protagonist's construction of the woman he "psychoanalyses" as mythical Other.[1] A second wave of interpretation appeared

---

1. Magnarelli, *Reflections/Refractions*. Other interpretations from this first wave include Hicks, "That Which Resists", republished in Hicks, *Border Writing*, which

in the late 1990s, with Avery Gordon's surprise use of this novel at the centre of her theory of ghosts and haunting in the sociological imagination (*Ghostly Matters*), and Emily Tomlinson's sophisticated comparative reading ("Rewriting Fictions of Power"), which put the text into dialogue with Elaine Scarry's *The Body in Pain* and Marta Traba's *Conversación al sur*.[2] For at least a decade, however, there has been a dearth of fresh critical readings of this text and, surprisingly, virtually no critical response to its republication in 2001 by Casa de las Américas. The growing body of critical collections on Valenzuela tended to ignore it as well: Gwendolyn Díaz's and María Inés Lagos-Pope's *La palabra en vilo*, which appeared in 1996, contained no contribution on this novel apart from brief mention of it in Magnarelli's overview essay on Valenzuela's metonymies of "writing the body" ("Luisa Valenzuela: cuerpos que se escriben"), while the later 2002 collection, *Luisa Valenzuela sin máscara* (Díaz), concentrated on her writing from *Simetrías* onwards.

Yet the novel continues to niggle, hovering silently behind Valenzuela's more recent textual production, setting itself up as somehow paradigmatic for understanding her work more generally, as well as the broader concerns of her generation. Indeed Valenzuela said as much, with regard to her own work, at the time of the novel's republication, in a prefatory piece in *Casa de las Américas*:

> Desde mi personal posicionamiento en el mapa del lenguaje, la escritura es una búsqueda. Por eso *Como en la guerra* podría ser considerada mi novela paradigmática, porque encara la búsqueda de frente. No me resultó nada fácil. A cada página me dispuse (sin quererlo) a espiar tras la cortina del Secreto, y fui descubriendo con posterior aterramiento que sólo hay oscuridad del otro lado. (Valenzuela, "Siete aproximaciones al Secreto" 94)

Valenzuela subsequently declared the three novels *Hay*

---

cleverly elucidates the Freudian parodies in the novel together with a series of five other "referential codes"; Cordones-Cook, who explains the text in terms of the dispersion of the monological bourgeois subject articulated and disarticulated around Lacanian psychoanalysis; Hoeppner, who investigates the text's displacement/rewriting of the Lacanian theory of identity; and Martínez, who gives an involved poststructuralist account of the play of writing in the text's specular processes.

2. Gordon's account mixes extensive plot summary and quotation with elucidation of some of the sociological themes that relate the text to psychoanalysis and politics in Argentina. In this second wave, there is also Donald Shaw's quizzical trawl through the novel, written with some scepticism as to its worth.

que sonreír (1966), *Como en la guerra* (1977) and the much commented *Novela negra con argentinos* (1990) to be a "trilogía de los bajos fondos de tres ciudades y de los bajos fondos propios del ser humano" (Díaz & Lagos-Pope 46). Indeed *Trilogía de los bajos fondos*, was the title chosen for the publication of these three novels as a single volume, effectively the third edition of *Como en la guerra*, which appeared in Mexico in 2004. Given this, together with some of the complex ways in which feminist theory's use of psychoanalysis has evolved since the 1980s, it seems necessary now to return to this paradigmatic text in order to confront its displaced, atemporal haunting with the theoretical revenants that populate the temporal gap implied both in its analytical structure and in its displacement of the intimacies of the reading process. To do so, I have chosen here to re-read *Como en la guerra* through Judith Butler's re-reading of Sophocles' Oedipal trilogy, as set out in her book-length essay *Antigone's Claim: Kinship Between Life and Death*. This text roughly coincides with the second Spanish edition of *Como en la guerra* in 2001, and I hope here to draw the parallels between Valenzuela's critique of psychoanalysis and Butler's displacement of the Lacanian symbolic in the switching of circuits between Oedipus and Antigone.

Misreading the Symbolic

The epigraph which I chose for this article points, I think, to a spectacular moment of misreading, of missed analysis and critical blindness by the protagonist of the novel, Professor of Semiotics and part-time analyst, possibly named AZ. The "sonrisa triste" of this passage hints at a shared experience *between women* who are otherwise conventionally figured as "rivals": the unnamed guerrilla-turned-prostitute who is the object of AZ's analytical/sexual attentions, and his homely wife Beatriz. This shared experience of *déréliction* (Irigaray, *Éthique de la différence sexuelle* 70), which underpins (and undercuts) the mythification of woman as Other, goes to the heart of the displacement of symbolic configurations at the centre of the story. If *déréliction* "is a kind of fulsome abandonment, a form of melancholia without an object, a grief that is potentially overwhelming, without parameters, knowledge, or term" (Summers-Bremner 98)—if, in a sense, it is the enforced feminine *embodiment* of lack within the symbolic—, then its trace lingers in all of the specular relationships at work within *Como en la guerra*. For what hangs over this novel, as it hangs over so much of Valenzuela's work, is what we might term the curse of the father, following Butler's careful relay of Lacan through Sophocles:

> The curse of the father is in fact how Lacan defines the symbolic, that obligation of the progeny to carry on in their own aberrant directions his very words. The words of the father, the inaugurating utterances of the symbolic curse connect his children in one stroke. These words become the circuit within which her desire takes form, and though she is entangled in these words, even hopelessly, they do not quite capture her. [...] Is it not precisely the limits of kinship that are registered as the insupportability of [Antigone's] desire, which turns desire towards death? (Butler 54)

Derived from Oedipus, the symbolic order inaugurated by the father's prohibition, by his curse, seems to flounder, as we shall see, in its attempt to capture Antigone, Oedipus' daughter but also, crucially, his sister.

Como en la guerra was written between 1973 and 1975 (Valenzuela, "Siete aproximaciones al Secreto" 91), but like everything else, it got caught up in the maelstrom of the coup d'état of 1976. Abduction, torture and murder had begun well before the *coup* finally settled the political deadlock amongst the Peronists, with José López Rega's clandestine murder squads of the Alianza Anticomunista Argentina operating from at least 1974. Although Valenzuela and her publisher managed to bring the novel out in Buenos Aires in 1977, several changes had to be made to pre-empt censorship. The most drastic of these was the omission of a kind of fictional prologue entitled "Página cero" which graphically recounts the torture of the novel's protagonist and sets up a clear political frame for what may otherwise appear to be "merely" a psychoanalytically inspired story about the lack underpinning desire and the fantasies of fulfilment with which human beings invest desire. The entry for "Página cero" still remained in the index, however, so the discerning reader might have been able to intuit (self-)censorship and interpret the truncated simile of the title in its latent political sense. The suppressed prologue was published two years later in the English translation of the novel, *He Who Searches*,[3] but did not appear in a Spanish-language version of the text for some 24 years until the

---

3. Valenzuela, *Strange Things Happen Here: Twenty-Six Short Stories and a Novel [He Who Searches]*.

2001 Casa de las Américas edition. It radically shifts the metaphorical ground of the novel by creating a frame, which, in hindsight, reverberates throughout the displaced power structures that populate the text's interpersonal relationships:

> —Yo no fui. No sé nada, les juro que nunca tuve nada con ella.
> —Se te vio entrar a altas horas de la noche en su casa. En Barcelona. Dos veces por semana durante varios meses. ¡Cantá!
> Una mano enorme se acerca a su cara para estallar. No, no, no, no en una bofetada, sino en caricia sobre su frente. Eso en épocas de chico, no ahora mientras aprende entre rejas el oficio de adulto. [...]
> Violado por un caño de revólver. Este triste destino parece ser el mío. Y grito de dolor, nunca de miedo. [...] Está muerto mi cuerpo por debajo de las cejas, muerto mucho antes de que el tipo me sacuda el revólver en las tripas y se ría mientras dice ahora aprieto el gatillo. AHORAAPRIETOELGATILLO resuena en todas partes [...]. (*Como en la guerra*, 2nd ed., 9-10)

Although by no means intentional, the broken, displaced reading across time and languages which this publication history imposed on anyone trying to read the text in Spanish, obliged to have recourse to the English translation (if available) to "complete" the sense, in some ways mirrored and performed the thematization of a "broken" political reading of a "senseless" text which the protagonist himself undertakes, perhaps in the instant before his brutal murder at the hands of his torturers. The precarious shuttling between presence and absence of mastery over the text's systems of signification, together with the text's slippage between political and libidinal frames, is aptly represented in the paradoxical absence-presence of a page numbered "zero" which retrospectively generates the rest of the text as temporal flashback or inversion of cause and effect.

The main "events" of the novel can be easily summarized. This Argentine Professor of Semiotics in Barcelona believes that he recognizes a former acquaintance from Argentina in a possible prostitute. He decides that he must investigate the cause of her turn to prostitution "para saber fehacientemente si aquello que la impulsó a hacer la vida que hace y aquello que la obliga a escribir con compulsión (grafomanía) responden a una misma causa o son un mismo efecto" (21).[4] Adopting different disguises including trans-

---

4. All parenthetical references after quotations are from Valenzuela, *Como en la*

vestism, he visits her at 3am every night to try his hand at amateur "Lacanian" psychoanalysis. AZ discovers her aforementioned graphomania, and the analysis gets confounded with occasional sexual acts. His wife, Beatriz, helps him to transcribe the recordings he makes of her conversations, and even helps with his disguises. Abruptly, the woman disappears, leaving AZ to confront his increasing entanglement with her and his fantasy projections of femininity. The novel then enters an hallucinatory world, possibly an extended dream, or perhaps the delirium produced under the torture described in "Página cero". In these sections, AZ travels first to Mexico, undertakes a Mazatec purification ritual which degrades into the counter-cultural icon of María Sabina, the well known Mexican *curandera* who in the 1960s introduced New Age Westerners to the hallucinatory mushrooms used in the Mazatec mushroom ritual known as the *velada* (María Sabina, Wasson, & Rhodes; see also "María Sabina"). AZ then travels south, through Chiapas, which is superimposed onto the 1970s guerrilla hotbeds of Misiones and Tucumán, where he meets a paradoxical group of theatrical revolutionaries who re-enact some displaced form of anthropophagism in their possible eating of a fat Western hippy woman who has brought various stereotypical New Age trinkets and talismans from India to the indigenous population of the area. Finally, AZ ends up in Buenos Aires, where there are endless queues of people waiting to file past the coffin of *la Santa*.[5] AZ makes his way painfully and slowly towards the sarcophagus, but gets caught up with a group of militants who want to blow up the concrete structure surrounding it. He agrees to take part, and under constant machine-gun fire, he manages with great difficulty to insert the sticks of dynamite into the holes around the concrete building (Freudian dream-interpretation definitely intended). The dynamite is finally set off, and the structure explodes to reveal *Ella*—AZ is convinced that it is his *Ella*—suspended in her crystal tomb.

On the question of naming, it should be noted that neither of the principal characters has a stable name. The "name" AZ for the Professor of Semiotics, which is teasingly given us, of course evokes Roland Barthes' *S/Z*, published in 1970, only three years before Valenzuela began to write this novel. But it also suggests a subject who

---

guerra, 1st ed., unless otherwise stated.

5. Most critics speculate that this section of the text bears more than a passing resemblance to the events surrounding the lying-in-state of Eva Perón's body.

exists in a relation of mastery to language, which means one that is both mastered by language and possessing mastery over language, a point which is the subject of much irony in the text. The woman is nameless in the novel, although curiously the 2001 edition named her in the blurb on the back as "Sabina", and one critic goes so far as to call her "María Sabina" throughout his article with no hint of hesitation or irony (Hoeppner 10). The text itself, however, is quite clear in its rejection of the "trap" that the imposition of a name would represent:

> ¿Y si le pusiéramos a ella el nombre de María Sabina? ¿Si se lo transplantáramos, hiciéramos un injerto? Más fácil sería así sabiendo mencionarla, ubicándola en el espacio de estas páginas con la transcripción de un nombre, pero no. Él debe seguir subiendo y no nos deja hacer trampa [...]. (144)

This *antinomic* desire in the text—the desire which counters the Name as Law—can perhaps serve as a useful entry point into the derelict world of Antigone.

Antigone's Claim: Crisis in the Representative Function

Butler's short text is a speculative examination of the puzzle that Antigone represents for philosophy, psychoanalysis and feminism. Antigone is born out of incest to a father, Oedipus, who is also her brother, having a sister, Ismene, who is also her aunt and her niece, and brothers Polyneices and Eteocles who are also uncles and nephews. She thus seems to trouble that boundary where kinship relations become reified as symbolic structures, a symbolic which, for Lacanians, is *not* the same as social norms, but is the rarefaction and idealization of kinship as an "enabling linguistic structure", i.e., the "sphere of norms and law that govern the accession to speech and speakability" (Butler 3). Lacan's structuralist legacy establishes the symbolic as the manifestation of an abstract and unmoveable set of structures which confer cultural intelligibility on certain forms of family and social organization and which disallow or render unintelligible other configurations. As Butler says of Antigone, "She points not to politics as a question of representation but to the political possibility that emerges when the limits to representation and representability are exposed" (2).

Antigone's act of burying her brother Polyneices is a direct challenge to the Law of her uncle and king Creon, but unlike Hegel, Lacan and Irigaray, who in one form or another interpret Antigone's act as the primitive sway of kinship or blood ties—even of incestuous brotherly love—against the social law which must demand allegiance to the father, and hence ultimately as an unsustainable social position, Butler suggests that "Antigone figures the limits of intelligibility exposed at the limits of kinship" (23). Traditionally figured through the very etymology of her name as anti-generative (*anti-goni*), if not in fact degenerate, Antigone, and the death sentence which falls on her, comes to stand, then, for the refusal (of the king, of the state, of the established order) to countenance forms of sociality that do not conform to the standard models by which the (Freudian) Oedipal drama is resolved. While not exactly setting up Antigone as a queer heroine, Butler engages the kinship trouble that surrounds Antigone, the instability of the subject positions available to her, as a way of challenging what she ultimately names as the curse of the symbolic order: "The symbolic might be understood as a certain kind of tomb that does not precisely extinguish that which nevertheless remains living and trapped within its terms" (44).

It seems to me that the terms with which Butler engages Antigone provide a productive way of thinking through the challenges posed by *Como en la guerra* from a contemporary theoretical perspective, but one which also engages with the retrospection which informs, *ex post facto*, the structure of the novel as an investigation into the cultural origins and myths which govern the field of gender relations and underpin the power structures derived from them. By this I do not wish to imply that *Ella* is Antigone in any simple sense; indeed, in many ways she is the reversal of Antigone, as I shall suggest later. But, like Antigone, *Ella* forces a crisis in the representative function at many different levels, one which opens up the contingent and mutable nature of those symbolic structures to which the Law of the Father confers intelligibility. For *Ella*'s subject position is unstably written into the text even as she radically confounds AZ's blundering attempts to analyse her:

> Porque aun teniéndola debidamente calibrada y tabulada y viviseccionada y anotada, clasificada, impresa, de nada serviría porque con ella de ejemplo jamás se podrá deducir una ley que la acompañe. Ella no es la regla, es la excepción que ni siquiera hace el menor esfuerzo para confirmarla sino que la destruye. (97)

What AZ misses until the very end of the novel is the suppressed story of her militant past, her possible betrayal by her militant lover Alfredo Navoni—a character familiar to readers of *Cola de lagartija* and *Cambio de armas*—and her love/hate relationship to her twin sister and double, whom it is tempting, if only in terms of a structural parallel, to call Ismene. Ambiguously subject to the Father's Law in the form of the ambiguous father/brother/lover figure that is Alfredo Navoni, who has perhaps cursed her to a living death through a possible betrayal, and at the very least a subject of *déréliction* in her abandonment in exile, she appears to have turned to that unstable subject/object position, both the margin and the precondition of normative patriarchal femininity, that is represented by prostitution. So, while not quite immersed in the "incestuous legacies that confound [Antigone's] position within kinship" (Butler 2), *Ella*'s unstable subjectivity nevertheless poses a serious challenge to that Lacanian insistence that the symbolic is not the social, even as it *fatally* determines and structures the social. If the symbolic has the effect of reifying and freezing familial and social structures as norms, then it also governs the production of perversion, since the norm and its perversion are instituted as a necessary couple, the norm requiring its perversion in order to maintain and police its boundaries, the boundaries of the polity.

The weight of that fatal determination is perhaps represented enigmatically in the novel by the presence of a paternal genealogy, which, to quote Marx, "weighs like a nightmare on the brains of the living," from the Oedipal-paternal to the military machine. At a key moment of decision for AZ, after he has lost all physical trace of *Ella*, alone in an abandoned room surrounded by photographs of her, he remembers one of her many enigmatic texts, which takes the form of a parable concerning "los padres adoptivos invisibles". While the precise meaning of this remains obscure, in the parable the city's inhabitants are urged in public posters to adopt an invisible father; these "hijos", however, find themselves inhabited and tormented by something nameless which can never be forgotten, something that causes them inhuman levels of suffering. Meanwhile, the "padres invisibles" advance like a military procession that we mortals are powerless to prevent:

> los padres invisibles desfilan marcialmente y nada podemos hacer nosotros los mortales para detener su paso. [... a los hijos de padres adoptivos invisibles] les pesa [...] algo sin nombre y sin nin-

> guna posibilidad de olvido. [...] se niegan para siempre a hablar de sus dolores aunque por la mueca que se les escapa por entre las manos que les tapan la cara sabemos que estos dolores son casi inhumanos. (126)

The anti-generative movement implied by adopting an (invisible/symbolic) father (when it is usually parents who adopt children, not vice versa) signals a destabilization of paternal function in which the symbolic father does not give the name/law to the child, but takes/steals the name, leaving his child in a state of *anomie*. Three paradigmatic "scenes" appear to be being alluded to here. The first is evident from the quotation above, and suggests militarism as a parade of martial fathers who steal the name/law. The second is suggestive of the psychoanalytical scene in which the child must "adopt" the psychoanalyst as a substitute parent (subsequently to be rejected during transference), and this is alluded to as AZ, who has been playing at being the psychoanalyst, asks himself "¿seré yo sin saberlo un padre invisible para ella? ¿la buscaré tan sólo para metérmela bajo un ala y echar vuelo?" (127). And the third scene is suggested by the "dolores casi inhumanos" which take us back to the primal scene which governs the entire text and whose reverberations structure and warp all the interpersonal relationships established in the text:

> siento que están poco a poco rompiéndome por dentro, demoliendo mis escasas defensas. a veces cortan con un bisturí afiladísimo, a veces me desgarran con la mano arrancándome pedazos de carne. sólo me resta retorcerme en esta pieza ignota con el consuelo de saber que si es ella quien lo hace, también ella participa del dolor. cada tirón le duele, cada tajo. la destrucción no puede menos que alcanzarla y estamos juntos mientras pasan las horas y yo lucho contra el sueño aunque el desgarramiento me deja pocos minutos de respiro y a veces hasta pierda la conciencia. (127-28)

Here, AZ has to decide whether to accept the solitude embodying her loss, her dereliction, or whether to seek refuge in the adoption of some "padre invisible", a course of action, which he ultimately rejects.

Displacing Psychoanalysis

The redoubling of the psychoanalytical relation and the

erotic sexual encounter in the scene of torture, mediated by the curse of the invisible fathers who fatally determine the present, powerfully suggests the critique of patriarchal systems, inhabited by these symbolic structures, which this novel is undertaking. Avery Gordon, in her chapter on *Como en la guerra*, gives an in depth sociological discussion of the role that the institutions and practices of psychoanalysis found themselves playing in Argentina during the dictatorship, a role which was keenly felt by the International Psychoanalytic Association in Paris in 1981 at a meeting which convened French and Latin American psychoanalysts, where Jacques Derrida gave the opening address referring to the situation in Argentina:

> The kinds of torture to which I refer sometimes appropriate what we'll call psycho-symbolic techniques, thereby involving the citizen-psychoanalyst, as such, as an active participant either on one side or the other, or perhaps even on both sides at once, of these abuses. In any case, *the psychoanalytic medium is traversed by this violence*. All intra-institutional relations, all clinical activity, and all its dealings with civil society and with the state are marked by it, directly or indirectly. There is no imaginable self-relation of the psychoanalytic there without these marks of internal and external violence. (Derrida, cit. Gordon, "Ghostly Matters" 95, translation also adapted from Derrida 341, my emphasis)

It is little wonder in this context that the psychoanalysis which AZ practises on *Ella* should be "traversed by this violence", in Derrida's words, and specifically the violence of torture, which from the opening of the novel sets the parameters for the *interrogation* of that interface between the body (as sensorium) and its sociality. Of course, Valenzuela was to take up this critique, begun in *Como en la guerra*, and build on it in the well known and widely commented collection of short stories she wrote towards the end of the dictatorship, *Cambio de armas* (1982).

Ella, like Antigone, thus stands at the point of destabilization of psychoanalytical law, and hence the very *structures* of social law. In fact, she unleashes a destabilizing force at the heart of the pseudo-erotic psychoanalytical encounter before "disappearing" within the text, so that it is indeed AZ who finds his subject position radically destabilized by incestuous legacies that seem to be reactivated within his highly symbolic, fantasized relationship to her: "Mañana volveremos a ser Madre. A dejarnos chupar. Convertidos en un Pecho Gigante. Y blanco" (97). Let us remember that one of the etymologies of Antigone's name, according to Robert Graves, is that she stands "in place of the mother" (cit. Butler 22). What does this displacement infer for the investigation into the myths and discourses structuring gender relations in general, and femininity in particular, in the novel? For at this point in the text, the woman disappears, becomes phantasmatic, mythical, perhaps intimating Irigaray's contention that "women are nowhere, touching everything, but never in touch with each other, lost in the air like ghosts. Dissolved, absent, empty, abandoned, gone—gone away from themselves" (Irigaray, "The Poverty of Psychoanalysis" 91). All we are left with, discursively, is the male semiotician-*cum*-psychoanalyst's fantasy of femininity, which grows into mythic proportions as he undertakes a transcontinental journey in search of her essence.

The parodic nature of this quest, both in mythical and psychoanalytical terms, is suggested by Emily Hicks in her brief discussion of two of the explicit psychoanalytical parodies within the text: Navoni's "Wolfman" dream, which *Ella* dreams vicariously on Navoni's behalf; and the totemic meal of the fat woman, both of which take place or originate in the revolutionary hotbed of "Formosa" (Tucumán, transposed onto a Mexican jungle).[6] Here is Hicks' interpretation of the latter scene:

> In the episode involving Fatty [...], Valenzuela parodies Freud's totemic meal, in which the band of sons commemorates the mythic killing of the primal father. In the totemic meal postulated by Freud, taboos are broken: there is the destruction of the totem figure and incest is allowed. [...] In *Como en la guerra*, the semiotician meets a group of men and women keeping a vigil for the death of a revolutionary. This parallels the commemoration of the death of the primal father. The group tells the semiotician about Fatty: in a ritualistic totemic meal, Fatty was covered with food by the group and eaten. By rewriting the totemic meal as the eating of a woman, the mother figure Fatty, Valenzuela has forced a provocative juxtaposition: the destruction of that which is desired. (Hicks, "That Which Resists", *Border Writing* 73)

This episode occurs during "El viaje", and takes the form of a titled inset-story, "La larga noche de los teatrantes" (166) told to AZ by one of this revolutionary group whose dead leader might

---

6. Valenzuela explains the reason for substituting Formosa for Tucumán in "Siete aproximaciones al Secreto".

or might not be (the text tells us) the famous Mexican "Che Guevara", Lucio Cabañas.[7] Hicks' reading of the dead revolutionary as the "primal father" does not, then, easily fit the Freudian story as set out in *Totem and Taboo*, since (whether Lucio Cabañas or not) he can hardly bear the role of the tyrannical father when he is explicitly referred to as "hermano" (165) in a struggle against a higher authority. Nevertheless, the displacement of the totemic meal onto the body of a fat Western hippy (her predilection for eating sandwiches and processed cheese suggests her likely origin, 169), invests this unintentional or disavowed meal with a twin focus: the female body which just "disappears" during the theatrical meal, leaving no trace of its (excessive) materiality (no blood, guts or bones); and the post-colonial struggle (as seen by revolutionary groups of the 1970s in Latin America) for cultural as well as political autonomy. In any case, to return to a quotation from Butler, the episode of the theatrical revolutionaries ("teatrantes") points, like Antigone, "not to politics as a question of representation but to that political possibility that emerges when the limits to representation and representability are exposed" (2).

In the former dream, recounted by the woman to AZ during the psychoanalytical sessions, and attributed to Navoni, "a man eats a wolf, becomes a Wolf Man, and then eats a dog and ducks" (Hicks 73). In the original Wolfman case, Freud, as is well known, initially attributed the Wolfman's psychosis (manifested in his terrified dream of wolves waiting to eat him) to his observance of a primal scene, aged one-and-a-half, of his parents engaged in *coitus a tergo* (Freud, "From the History of an Infantile Neurosis" 235). Further analysis led Freud to deduce a perversion of this fairly common "primal scene" via the (incestuous) seductive attentions with which the Wolfman's older sister had regaled him when he was just over three, while she tormented him with the picture of a wolf from a picture book which would set him screaming furiously, "fearing that the wolf would come and gobble him up" (213). Hicks attributes the neurosis in the dream to AZ, hinting that it might explain his passive fantasies as expressed in his transvestism (*Border Writing* 74). However, the role of the (twin) sister(s) as a latent content underlying the dream of the revolutionary (if we read Navoni's dream

---

7. Lucio Cabañas Barrientos (1938-74), a Mexican schoolteacher who became a revolutionary (non-Marxist), subsequently iconized as a hero for the Mexican left ("Lucio Cabañas").

through Freud's analysis), and his ultimate rejection/betrayal of the sister(s), leads us back to the suppressed political text which in fact frames the two dreams that are recounted:

> los soñó en Formosa con delirio y fiebre, cumpliendo una misión que no tuvo éxito y que llevó a varios compañeros a la muerte (75)
>
> [...] recuerdos remotos [...] de tiempos cuando ella y su hermana gemela, o ella-ella como quieran llamarlas (las dos tan idénticas [...]) peleaban por una misma causa [...] y hasta encontraban la forma de tener esperanzas. Después no, ya no, atadas de pies y manos y humilladas. [...] La necesidad de olvidar para poder re-componerse. [... O]lvidarse del amor de ese Alfredo Navoni sin preguntarse más si había sido o no el traidor que finalmente acabó delatándolos [...]. (82)

The Sister(s) of Oedipus

If, according to Claude Lévi Strauss, the incest taboo is not exclusively biological, nor exclusively cultural, but exists "at the threshold of culture" (cit. Butler 15-16), then Valenzuela's disturbance of the "primary" symbolic structures which derive from it—in the dreams and episodes recounted above, but more fundamentally her account of their abuse by the terrorist state, as well as the battle for representability amongst those who would alter these sedimented and immutable "laws"—raises the same set of questions which Butler asks of Antigone, who is both the offspring and sister of Oedipus:

> what will come of the inheritance of Oedipus when the rules that Oedipus blindly defies and institutes no longer carry the stability accorded to them by Lévi-Strauss and structural psychoanalysis? In other words, Antigone is one for whom symbolic positions have become incoherent, confounding as she does brother and father, emerging as she does not as a mother but [...] "in place of the mother." [...] If the stability of the maternal place cannot be secured, and neither can the stability of the paternal, what happens to Oedipus and the interdiction for which he stands? What has Oedipus engendered? (22)

In a seminal passage placed between sections I and II of the novel, the narrator, whose voice appears at certain points in italics, indicates the pathos that AZ's torture and death are rendered senseless by his inability to interpret the political dimensions of the psyche:

> *Claro que se cuidó muy bien de hablar de Navoni, de su hermana la capitana [...] o de la Organización. Si AZ conociera estos detalles podría interpretar los símbolos, descifrar el significado de los compañeros en la cárcel, conocer los secretos. Habría interpretado los odios de ella hacia su hermana mítica, su doble, y quizá habría sacado conclusiones. [... S]u posterior tortura (y posterior es la palabra) y hasta quizá su muerte, habrían tenido para él una razón de ser y eso es lo intolerable: la causa que justifica los efectos, la explicación racional infiltrándose en medio de toda la irracionalidad que implica la conducta humana.* (92-93).

What then of *Ella*'s—and Antigone's—relationship to the polis, to polity, and ultimately to the political, especially "in time of war"?[8] For to inhabit that liminal state, along with Ismene, of being Oedipus' sister as well as his daughter, is to inhabit the threshold of the social. To disobey the king's law directly, and to do so twice, is to interrogate fatefully the point where questions of kinship become questions of politics.

Antigone, of course, became a potent political symbol in the Argentina of the dictatorship and its aftermath. Her enactment of a burial for her brother Polyneices in the face of a state edict that the body should be ignored had obvious political overtones which allied her to the *Madres de la Plaza de Mayo* with their claim for justice and for the bodies of their disappeared relatives to be returned and publicly accounted for. Several cultural texts subsequently drew on this parallel, from the film *La amiga* (dir. Meerapfel) to Griselda Gambaro's play *Antígona furiosa*.[9] It is of course Antigone's fate herself to be buried (alive), at least symbolically, in Sophocles' version: walled up in her cave, a living tomb, she takes her own life before Creon can reverse his order: "The symbolic might be understood as a certain kind of tomb that does not precisely extinguish that which nevertheless remains entrapped within its terms, a site

---

8. W.H. Auden's coding of (gay) love and politics as civil strife *In Time of War* would make for a fascinating triangulation of Valenzuela's and Butler's concerns. However, Valenzuela's decoy reference in the title of *Como en la guerra* is to a sonnet by Quevedo and a *"copla anónima"* (in fact penned by Aníbal Ford). The "sources" are given in the novel's epigraphs, and allow Valenzuela to mask a war story as a love story, arguably inverting Auden's procedure.

9. See also Diana Taylor's *Disappearing Acts* (207ff), for a discussion of the significance of Antigone in this play and more generally in the period.

where Antigone, already half-dead within the intelligible, is bound not to survive" (Butler 44). Curiously, it had also been Oedipus' fate to meet his death by being swallowed into the earth at Hippeios Colonus. Do Oedipus and his progeny, unstably sited at some shifting border between the omphalic realm of the chthonic gods, and the phallic realm of the polis, throw into crisis the very order they found? Indeed, this shift from the phallic to the omphalic is one which *Como en la guerra* engages explicitly, and can perhaps stand as the sign governing the text's movement from Lacanian psychoanalysis to the chthonic realms of mythical and cultural origins in "El viaje": "todos estamos así lacónicos de búsqueda, y yo prefiero concentrarme en ella, sacudir mis largos bigotes e irme husmeando en cuatro patas hasta dar con esa latitud que es su guarida. la zona onfálica" (107).

Finally, to state that the daughter of Oedipus is also the sister of Oedipus, is radically to disinvest the position of the feminine within the Oedipus complex, allowing perhaps, for experimental writers such as Valenzuela, different imaginative solutions to its conundrum. For, as Valenzuela says, "[Todos t]enemos poderes inimaginables. Sólo que ese saber nos atemoriza. Una tradición milenaria nos detiene y nos sugiere que ese saber se paga: más que el incesto, Edipo paga el haber develado el enigma" (Satinosky). If Antigone is the conundrum which loosens the knot of Oedipus, then maybe one solution is in fact, at the end of this novel, her reversal, the projection from the position of *Anti-goni*, the anti-generative, of a hypothetical *Anti-Anti-goni*. As Oedipus and then Antigone are swallowed into the earth, symbolically returning the Phallus to the Omphalos, our Anti-Anti-goni, *Ella*, is, in a reverse but parallel movement to Antigone's political act of burial, *unburied* in a final, climactic explosion:

> Las paredes de la fortaleza revientan como una gran cáscara y emerge brillante el corazón del fruto. [...] Y él cree volverla a ver después de tanto tiempo, allá arriba en lo alto sobre una tarima blanca, toda resplandeciente, irradiando una luz sorda pero intensísima, majestuosa en su ataúd de vidrio que es como un diamante. (195)

Valenzuela's self-avowedly "paradigmatic" text within her *oeuvre* can, perhaps, also be seen as paradigmatic for the Generation of '72 more broadly. While a number of Boom motifs remain—whether it be the invocation of absent symbolic fathers and the structures of meaning rendered spectral by the crisis in the paternal function (Rulfo), the ironic mythic/anthropological quest for origins (Carpentier), or the disturbance of (Freudian/Lévi-Straussian) taboos and nightmarishly self-replicating symbolic/social structures (Paz/García Márquez)—these are all now framed as the proleptic delirium of a Lacanian semiotician suffering the most unimaginable of acts of torture. Where García Márquez had both paid homage to and ironized structuralist anthropology and linguistics, Valenzuela does the same to their bastard Lacanian progeny while at the same time framing her texts' relationship to the generational dynamics of the Boom. The complex, half-buried, anti-generational figure of Antigone—postulated, twisted and inverted in Valenzuela's *Ella*— comes in some sense, then, to stand for the complexities of a new generation of writers in whose work politics and representation no longer simply frame each other but become intertwined in fractal patterns which render fatally unstable the structural labyrinths of their forebears.

Works Cited

Barthes, Roland. *S/Z*. Paris: Éditions du Seuil, 1970.

Butler, Judith. *Antigone's Claim: Kinship Between Life and Death*. New York: Columbia University Press, 2000.

Cordones-Cook, Juanamaría. *Poética de transgresión en la novelística de Luisa Valenzuela*. New York: Peter Lang, 1991.

Derrida, Jacques. *Psyche: Inventions of the Other*. Ed. Peggy Kamuf & Elizabeth Rottenberg. Stanford: Stanford University Press, 2007.

Díaz, Gwendolyn. *Luisa Valenzuela sin máscara*. Buenos Aires: Feminaria Editora, 2002.

—. *Women and Power in Argentine Literature: Stories, Interviews and Critical Essays*. Texas Pan American Literature in Translation Series. Austin: University of Texas Press, 2007.

Díaz, Gwendolyn, and María-Inés Lagos-Pope, eds. *La palabra en vilo: narrativa de Luisa Valenzuela*. Santiago de Chile: Editorial Cuarto Propio, 1996.

Freud, Sigmund. "From the History of an Infantile Neurosis". *The*

"Wolfman" and Other Cases. Ed. Louise Adey Huish. New York: Penguin Books, 2003.

—. *Totem and Taboo and Other Works: (1913-1914)*. Ed. James Strachey. London: Vintage, 2001.

Gambaro, Griselda. "Antígona furiosa". *Teatro*. Buenos Aires: Ediciones de la Flor, 1984.

Gordon, Avery F. *Ghostly Matters: Haunting and the Sociological Imagination*. Minneapolis: University of Minnesota Press, 1996.

Hicks, D. Emily. "That Which Resists: The Code of the Real in Luisa Valenzuela's *He Who Searches*". *The Review of Contemporary Fiction* 6.3 (1986): 55-61.

—. "That Which Resists: The Code of the Real in Luisa Valenzuela's *Como en la guerra*". *Border Writing: The Multidimensional Text*. Minneapolis: University of Minnesota Press, 1991. 68-75.

Hoeppner, Edward Haworth. "The Hand that Mirrors Us: Luisa Valenzuela's Re-writing of Lacan's Theory of Identity". *Latin American Literary Review* 20.39 (1992): 9-17. 29 Mar 2009 <http://www.jstor.org/stable/20111370>.

Irigaray, Luce. *Éthique de la différence sexuelle*. Paris: Éditions de Minuit, 1984.

—. "The Poverty of Psychoanalysis". *The Irigaray Reader*. Ed. Margaret Whitford. Oxford: Wiley-Blackwell, 1991. 79-104.

"Lucio Cabañas". *Wikipedia: The Free Encyclopedia* 19 Sep 2008. 6 Abr 2009 <http://en.wikipedia.org/wiki/Lucio_Cabañas>.

Magnarelli, Sharon. "Luisa Valenzuela: cuerpos que escriben (metonímicamente hablando) y la metáfora peligrosa". *La palabra en vilo: narrativa de Luisa Valenzuela*. Ed. Gwendolyn Díaz & María-Inés Lagos-Pope. Santiago de Chile: Editorial Cuarto Propio, 1996. 53-77.

—. *Reflections/Refractions: Reading Luisa Valenzuela*. New York: Peter Lang, 1988.

"María Sabina". *Wikipedia: The Free Encyclopedia* 10 Dic 2008. 30 Mar 2009 <http://en.wikipedia.org/wiki/María_Sabina>.

María Sabina, R. Gordon Wasson, y Willard Rhodes, eds. *María*

Sabina and Her Mazatec Mushroom Velada. New York: Harcourt Brace Jovanovich, 1974.

Martínez, Zulma Nelly. *El silencio que habla: aproximación a la obra de Luisa Valenzuela*. Buenos Aires: Corregidor, 1994.

Meerapfel, Jeanine. *La amiga*. Alma Film, 1988. 6 Abr 2009 <http://www.imdb.com/title/tt0094646/>.

Satinosky, Óscar. "*Como en la guerra* de Luisa Valenzuela". *La opinión* 1977. 16 May 2008 <http://www.luisavalenzuela.com/images/Guerra6,2.jpg>.

Scarry, Elaine. *The Body in Pain: The Making and Unmaking of the World*. New York: Oxford University Press, 1985.

Shaw, Donald Leslie. *The Post-boom in Spanish American Fiction*. Saratoga Springs: State University of New York, 1998.

Sophocles. *Antigone*. Trad. Andrew Brown. Warminster: Aris & Phillips, 1987.

Summers-Bremner, Eluned. "Reading Irigaray, Dancing". *Hypatia* 15.1 (2000): 90-124. 31 Mar 2009 <http://muse.jhu.edu/journals/hypatia/v015/15.1summers-bremner.html>.

Taylor, Diana. *Disappearing Acts: Spectacles of Gender and Nationalism in Argentina's "Dirty War"*. Durham: Duke University Press, 1997.

Tomlinson, Emily. "Rewriting Fictions of Power: The Texts of Luisa Valenzuela and Marta Traba". *The Modern Language Review* 93.3 (1998): 695-709. 14 May 2008 <http://www.jstor.org/stable/3736491>.

Traba, Marta. *Conversación al sur*. 1st ed. México D.F.: Siglo Veintiuno Editores, 1981.

Valenzuela, Luisa. *Cambio de armas*. Hanover NH: Ediciones del Norte, 1982.

—. *Cola de lagartija*. Buenos Aires: Bruguera, 1983.

—. *Como en la guerra*. 1st ed. Buenos Aires: Sudamericana, 1977.

—. *Como en la guerra*. 2nd ed. La Habana: Casa de las Américas, 2001.

—. *El gato eficaz*. Nueva narrativa hispánica. Mexico: Joaquín Mortiz, 1972.

—. "Siete aproximaciones al Secreto". *Casa de las Américas* 42.226 (2002): 90-95. 27 May 2008 <http://www.casadelasamericas.com/publicaciones/revistacasa/226/luisa.htm>.

—. *Simetrías*. Buenos Aires: Editorial Sudamericana, 1993.

—. *Strange Things Happen Here: Twenty-Six Short Stories and a Novel [He Who Searches]*. Trad. Helen Lane. New York: Harcourt Brace Jovanovich, 1979.

—. *Trilogía de los bajos fondos [Hay que sonreír, Como en la guerra, Novela negra con argentinos]*. México, D.F.: Fondo de Cultura Económica, 2004.

El legado del exilio de Cristina Peri Rossi:
un mapa para géneros e identidades[1]

María Rosa Olivera-Williams
University of Notre Dame

Cuando en 1984 Cristina Peri Rossi (1941-) publicó, en la editorial Seix Barral de Barcelona, *La nave de los locos*, la crítica reconoció casi de inmediato en esta novela la madurez narrativa de su autora. La precoz uruguaya, había sido galardonada desde temprano con importantes premios nacionales, que legitimaban la originalidad revolucionaria de su voz. En 1963 publicó la colección de cuentos *Viviendo*; en 1968, *Los museos abandonados*, libro de relatos reconocido con el Premio de los Jóvenes de Arca; en 1969, la novela *El libro de mis primos*, que recibe el Premio de Novela Biblioteca de Marcha, siendo la primera vez que el semanario que reunía a los intelectuales y escritores más importantes del país organizaba un concurso en dicha categoría. Peri Rossi nacía al mundo de las letras con la fuerza e innovación de la juventud, pero con el dominio de la madurez en el arte de la escritura. Con los relatos de *Indicios pánicos* (1970), Peri Rossi plasma el horror ante la inminencia de un mundo que se desmorona. La violencia política de Uruguay y el Cono Sur de esos años se alegoriza en textos que subrayan tanto el poder de las palabras como el peligro que el poder de aludir y simbolizar de las mismas presentaba para el Estado que, gobernando

---

[1]. Este artículo se basa en el capítulo ocho de mi libro de reciente aparición, *El arte de crear lo femenino: ficción, género e historia del Cono Sur* (2012). El libro es un estudio teórico y analítico de los movimientos sociales de mujeres y de la ficción femenina durante la segunda mitad del siglo veinte en el Cono Sur, enfocándose en los periodos del pos-sufragio, de las dictaduras militares de los 70 y 80, y de la pos-dictadura.

de manera absolutista, se había adjudicado la función de censurar todo lo que se publicaba y transmitía a la población. Esta característica marcará a una generación de escritores cono-sureños que vivieron la violencia de la historia que intentó marginarlos de la política, de lo social e inclusive del ámbito simbólico, tanto los que fueron forzados a abandonar la nación, como los que se quedaron dentro de las fronteras nacionales en situación de insilio. En 1971 se publica el último libro de la producción uruguaya de la autora, *Evohé*, poemario de amor, donde el deseo erótico lesbiano crea desde múltiples perspectivas el cuerpo de una mujer. La mujer se nombra en los poemas y surge nueva y enriquecida porque esa mujer, como la palabra que la nombra, es la proyección del deseo de la hablante. La obra de esta autora que se autodefine como "escritora total", ya que los géneros literarios no le imponen barreras al poder y la libertad de su escritura, y que se destaca tanto en la ficción como en el ensayo y la poesía, continuó, en su producción en España, país en el cual se exilió en 1972 y tomó la ciudadanía española en 1975, indagando las pasiones humanas dentro de un contexto histórico que si bien orienta su performance no las determina. Asimismo, continuó experimentando con el lenguaje como único campo de batalla desde el que participa en el debate intelectual, académico y político sobre las maneras en que nos vamos identificando como nación, como individuos que pertenecemos a determinado sexo o género, religión, etnia, cultura, en un presente de radicales dislocaciones. Poemarios tan importantes como *Descripción de un naufragio* (1974), *Diáspora* (1976), y *Lingüística general* (1979) y los libros de relatos: *La tarde del dinosaurio*, con prólogo de Julio Cortázar (1976), *La rebelión de los niños* (1980), y *El museo de los esfuerzos inútiles* (1983) antecedieron e hicieron posible *La nave de los locos*. Esta novela que coloca a su autora entre los mejores novelistas del siglo veinte, originando una abundante producción crítica, es la que propongo analizar en este trabajo ya que presenta la fuerza de los proyectos políticos de la juventud uruguaya y conosureña de los 60 y 70, los que fueron abortados con el fracaso de las revoluciones de las izquierdas aún antes de la asunción de la dictadura militar (1973-1985). Esta novela asimismo plasma la dinámica entre el deseo de pertenencia, lo que podría traducirse como el deseo utópico y nunca creído de una ciudadanía global, y el constante estado de exilio de quienes no se ajustan a las arbitrariedades del poder. La querella simbólica, existencial e histórica entre el arraigo y el desarraigo lleva a cuestionar todo, especialmente el lenguaje.[2] Peri Rossi seguirá profundizando en estos temas a lo largo de su extensa obra.[3]

La juventud y su rebelión contra los valores, costumbres y moral de la hegemonía burguesa se encarnó en un año, 1968, y en las imágenes de jóvenes, estudiantes y obreros, que ocuparon los espacios públicos y tomaron las armas contra el Estado como metonimia de esa hegemonía. La política que se unía a la violencia de las pedradas y los tiros, exteriorizando la urgencia de sus demandas, no se había visto en el escenario uruguayo desde los comienzos del siglo veinte con el último levantamiento del caudillo blanco Aparicio Saravia en 1904. Sin embargo, la militarización y consecuente jerarquización de los cuadros revolucionarios que replicaron la organización de las Fuerzas Armadas que los reprimían,[4] así como "la zona gris" del colaboracionismo hizo que una de las propuestas más subversivas de esa juventud quedara sin efecto. Esa propuesta que podría haber realizado una verdadera revolución era la destrucción

---

2. En uno de sus grandes cuentos "La influencia de Edgar A. Poe en la poesía de Raimundo Arias", se subraya la falsedad de todo lo que se dice y se ve como lo real. Falsedad y fracaso parecen marcar a una generación víctima de múltiples violencias. Sin embargo, en el desfase entre lo simbólico y lo real palpita la mirada crítica de esa generación, como lo indica el parlamento final del relato en las palabras de la protagonista niña : "Estoy segura de que lo que piensas acerca de nuestra generación es completamente falso" (Peri Rossi 52).

3. Después de *La nave de los locos*, publica las colecciones de cuentos: *Una pasión prohibida* (1986), *Cosmoagonías* (1988), *La ciudad de Luzbel y otros relatos* (1993), *Desastres íntimos* (1997), *Por fin solos* (2004), *Cuentos reunidos* (2007), volumen en que los cuentos editados cobran significados diferentes por la nueva estructura interna del mismo, *Habitaciones privadas*, al salir y ganador del premio "Mario Vargas Llosa NH" de relatos inéditos de 2010; los poemarios: *Europa después de la lluvia* (1987), donde la mirada melancólica de una extranjera hace surgir la ciudad de Berlín, *Babel bárbara* (1990), *Otra vez Eros* (1994), *Aquella noche* (1996), *Inmovilidad de los barcos* (1997), *Poemas de amor y de desamor* (1998), *Las musas inquietantes* (1999), *Estado de exilio* (2003), *Estrategias del deseo* (2004), *Poesía reunida* (2005) y *Habitación de hotel* (2007); las novelas: *Solitario de amor* (1988), *La última noche de Dostoievski* (1992), y *El amor es una droga dura* (1999); y los libros de ensayo: *Fantasías eróticas* (1990), *Julio Cortázar* (2000), y *Cuando fumar era un placer* (2002). La cosmovisión literaria de Peri Rossi plasma todas las pasiones humanas.

4. Este fenómeno se dio también en Argentina y Chile. Para el caso argentino, Calveiro explica cómo la militarización se enfocó en aptitudes bélicas y disciplinarias, y en "el desinterés por el militante en tanto individuo... La guerrilla había comenzado a reproducir en su seno las formas y las técnicas del poder establecido, antes que generar su cuestionamiento y desarrollar variantes alternativas de práctica y participación política" (Calveiro 2005: 134-135).

del monopolio del poder patriarcal, proyectado en la hegemonía del poder heterosexual, en la que se continuaba con el concepto de una identidad fuerte basada en las coordenadas de nación, cultura y sexo.[5] Es precisamente el deseo de esa otra manera de relacionarse, de ver y sentir al otro, lo que narra esta novela desde el no-lugar del exilio, desde el no-lugar del constante movimiento, que es desde el no-lugar del narrador que "siempre piensa *desde afuera* de la experiencia" (Sarlo 166).

¿Cómo se leyó *La nave de los locos*? La riqueza y complejidad tanto de la historia como del discurso de esta novela que construyen una alegoría de múltiples y ambiguos significados de la vida contemporánea como un viaje marítimo circular y "ya leído" (Peri Rossi 11), por medio de la fragmentación, la intertextualidad, la yuxtaposición de sueños con descripciones detalladas de *El tapiz de la creación* de la Catedral de Gerona, recortes de diario, programas de actividades de un barco que lleva a personajes marginales a lugares indefinidos, notas al pie de página, fue estudiado por un temprano trabajo de mi autoría.[6] Mi lectura de la relación entre el protagonista Equis, el hilo conductor de la historia, y el tapiz como espejo que *por momentos* le permite a Equis creer encontrar la imagen unificada de su identidad dentro de un sistema cósmico completo pero cercenado, cuya original armonía sólo se percibe en el ámbito del deseo de Equis, encontró inteligente recepción en los

---

5. Es interesante notar el uso de la bandera nacional para los Tupamaros en los años de militancia y guerra sucia y en posdictadura, cuando ex-integrantes del movimiento paulatinamente ocupan puestos de importancia en la administración del país hasta que el 1ero. de marzo de 2010 José Mujica asume la presidencia, habiendo ganado las elecciones con el 52.39% de los votos. En un país donde los símbolos nacionales tienen valor sagrado, los Tupamaros desde muy temprano se opusieron a reconocer la bandera bicolor uruguaya como símbolo de la patria, ya que según ellos esta bandera reconocía el triunfo de los intereses económicos del imperio británico en la creación de la república independiente de Uruguay. En la guerra de símbolos, los Tupamaros optaron por las banderas tricolores (azul, blanca y roja) tanto la de los Treinta y Tres Orientales como la de José G. Artigas, las que les sirvieron de modelo para su propia bandera. Desde la posición marginal de revolucionarios no se sentían representados en los símbolos dados de la nación. Tampoco ellos eran aceptados por el Estado que les quitó su posición de ciudadanos y adversarios políticos al identificarlos como "subversivos". Sin embargo, cuando Mujica asumió la presidencia de Uruguay, la bandera nacional bicolor más grande que se haya hecho sirvió para representar a la patria. Cabe preguntarse si se trata de un cambio en el concepto de nación e identidades o un compromiso con la antigua identidad nacional representada en la bandera bicolor.

6. Ver "*La nave de los locos* de Cristina Peri Rossi" de 1986 (81-89).

trabajos de Elia Geoffrey Kantaris (1989; 1995), dando origen a lo que se podría llamar la crítica lacaniana de la novela. Asimismo la originalidad narrativa de *La nave de los locos* permitió que se la leyera en el contexto de los debates del posmodernismo en América Latina, en su carril de "resistencia" (Foster xii), cuestionadora de las formas de "representación sociales, políticas y estéticas engendradas en el seno de la tradición humanística", tal como lo plantea Raúl Rodríguez Hernández (122). Dentro de estos mismos debates y atendiendo a los postulados teóricos que de ellos se originaron, cabe destacar el trabajo de Gabriela Mora, quien encuentra el concepto de "rizoma" de Deleuze y Guattari esclarecedor para la novela de Peri Rossi. Mora explica la estructura de la misma "como un tubérculo capaz de producir numerosos e inesperados brotes" (Mora 343), donde lo erótico, lo histórico, lo lúdico, lo político pasan a tener múltiples significados, representando la realidad en su condición inestable y móvil. Finalmente en un período en que el estado de exilio pasó a ser una condición generalizada para un amplio sector de conosureños, los trabajos que se enfocan en el exilio como metáfora de la condición humana y de la historia latinoamericana contemporánea tal como se presenta en la novela son numerosos. Entre ellos importa señalar el de Sophia A. McClennen así como el de Parizad Tamara Dejbord, quien da un panorama amplio del tratamiento del exilio por críticos y teóricos, así como de los debates y aproximaciones sobre la producción literaria que se da durante los procesos militares rioplatenses, tanto dentro de fronteras nacionales como en el extranjero, para luego analizarlo en la obra de Peri Rossi (Dejbord 1997; 1998). ¿Por qué volver entonces después de más de dos décadas a *La nave de los locos*?

Podría responder parafraseando el comentario de Equis personaje frente al *Tapiz de la creación*, que en esta novela el lector que siente el placer de la lectura como impacto que lo lleva a reaccionar y actuar sobre los desafíos que la misma ofrece en su representación de la realidad, "podría vivir [en ella], si se tuviera la suficiente perseverancia" (Peri Rossi 20). Asimismo, una gran novela, y *La nave de los locos* lo es, nunca agota sus posibilidades de significación. En un momento en que, como Elizabeth Jelin argumenta, el mundo occidental vive una explosión memorialista, "cultura de la memoria" de acuerdo a Andreas Huyssen, volver al pasado remoto y al contemporáneo que recrea Peri Rossi como cuestionamiento de certezas internalizadas y naturalizadas será útil para pensar en nuevos espacios para la memoria (Jelin 9).

Estar fuera de lugar

Linda McDowell en *Gender, Identity and Place* (1999), desde la perspectiva de una geógrafa feminista, explica que uno de los temas centrales que absorbe el interés de su disciplina es el estudio de distintos tipos de lugares, diferenciados por las relaciones de poder que construyen fronteras entre ellos. Uno de esos lugares es el cuerpo. El cuerpo no sólo tiene materialidad y ocupa un espacio, sino, en palabras de McDowell, es: "the place, the location or site… of the individual, with more or less impermeable boundaries between one body and another" (34). El cuerpo como lugar en contacto con otros cuerpos, o sea otros espacios, lo que crea sus límites, es una construcción social y cultural que origina diferencias así como los significados de los géneros. Las diferencias que se inscriben en el cuerpo más allá de lo femenino / masculino incluyen entre otras, raza, edad, peso, capacidades físicas, clase social, todo lo que hace posible ciertas opresiones sociales e imposiciones culturales (McDowell 40). El cuerpo, como argumenta Foucault, es un mapa que se va inscribiendo. Y Elizabeth Grosz complementa este argumento proponiendo que el mismo cuerpo es también una construcción cultural, que no existe como una página en blanco antes de su inscripción. Para Grosz: "Bodies are not inert; they function interactively and productively. They act and react" (xi).[7]

Estas aproximaciones teóricas sobre el cuerpo como espacio y sus relaciones de poder con otros cuerpos a través del tiempo y el espacio incitan a nuevas lecturas de *La nave de los locos* de Peri Rossi, en el contexto de una ficción que desde la perspectiva del exilio y del fracaso de un proyecto político cuestiona los valores del mundo occidental. Esta tendencia de la obra de Peri Rossi: su cuestionamiento profundo de valores occidentales que habían llegado a naturalizarse, desde el espacio cosmopolita, desde Europa, es una característica que comparten los integrantes de la generación del 72 y que los distingue de la generación del boom, quienes nunca fueron tan críticos de los idilios cosmopolitas.

---

7. Aquí Grosz no piensa el cuerpo en el sentido foucaultiano de "cuerpo dócil", sino un cuerpo que responde a sus propias proclividades, como queda demostrado en los recientes informes de la neurociencia.

Los personajes de esta novela como los orates medievales abandonados en alta mar en una nave sin capitán ni destino, de acuerdo a la alegoría medieval que sirvió de marco al libro de Sebastian Brant y éste a la famosa pintura de Bosch "La nave de los locos" son cuerpos fuera de lugar. En el segundo capítulo de la novela, "Equis: el viaje II", se califica al protagonista como "extranjero", el que por definición está fuera de lugar:

> Extranjero. Ex. Extrañamiento. Fuera de las entrañas de la tierra. Desentrañado: vuelto a parir. No angustiarás al extranjero. Pues. Vosotros. Vosotros. Vosotros. Los que no lo sois. Sabéis. Vosotros sabéis. Nosotros empezamos a saber. Cómo se halla. Cómo el alma del extranjero. Del extraño. Del introducido. Del intruso. Del huido. Del errante. ¿Alguien lo sabía? ¿Alguien, acaso, sabía cómo se encontraba el alma del extranjero? ¿El alma del extranjero estaba dolorida? ¿Estaba resentida? ¿Tenía alma el extranjero? *Ya que extranjero fuisteis en la tierra de Egipto*. (Peri Rossi 10)

Equis, en el relato, se hace extranjero. Renace (ha sido parido nuevamente por el exilio que lo expulsó de su círculo) en un viaje sin destino a través de la cultura occidental, la cual por ser hombre le había dado las posibilidades de un rey (Rex). El personaje sin nombre, previo a adquirir el nombre indeterminado de una incógnita en una fórmula matemática, la "x" (equis), aparece como un asiduo cliente del destartalado cine Rex donde experimenta el placer de ver la imagen de Julie Christie en la película de 1977 *Demon Seed* del director escocés Donald Cammell. Como argumenta Kantaris, el deseo de Equis de salvar a Julie Christie, en su papel de Susan Harris, de la poderosa computadora que la viola para poder reproducirse y el secreto placer de observar esa violación dejan al descubierto cómo dos códigos aparentemente disímiles (la caballerosidad y el poder de la posesión) están íntimamente unidos (Kantaris 1995: 62). Si bien es cierto, como anota Kantaris, que Equis se siente "uncomfortable whenever he is put in the traditional role of the powerful male" (61), su incomodidad y conocimiento gradual de cómo su posición masculina hegemónica afecta a los otros comienza justamente cuando se convierta en Equis, en "ex", en "extranjero" que "empieza a saber" las angustias de quien está a punto de ser violado, como Julie Christie por una "máquina brutal", cuyo poder invisible y omnipresente reproduce el de "las dictaduras", como observa el amigo de Equis, Vercingetórix, o como "Leda por el cisne", metonimia del poder masculino (Peri Rossi 23-24).

Equis comienza a poder mirar el mundo desde una perspectiva más libre a la reglada por el centrismo occidental (universal) que en la novela se representa en la metrópolis del "Gran Ombligo" cuando encuentra en un baldío la letra "x" del rótulo lumínico del antiguo cine "Rex". La "x", como valor cambiante y dependiente de otros valores, es lo único que Equis rescata de las ruinas de la masculinidad tradicional representada en el título de rey, el nombre en latín del cine (Rex), donde sentía el placer del gran falo omnipotente en su ataque a la atrayente Julie Christie así como el llamado al deber caballeresco de proteger o salvar a los débiles (Susan Harris/ Julie Christie). Es el acto simbólico de no aceptar un "nombre" lo que hará posible su performance de una masculinidad más amplia que la dominada por las reglas genéricas de la heterosexualidad. El descubrimiento de la "x" aparece en una nota de página, contribuyendo al proyecto de Peri Rossi de desjerarquizar todos los conceptos que aceptamos como naturales:

> Años después—cuando Julie Christie ya se había convertido en monja de una congregación de Hermanas Descalzas—Equis descubrió, en el baldío cercano, el resto del rótulo luminoso del cine, precisamente la letra "X". Todavía conservaba algunas lamparitas y alambres, los cables se habían desflecado y era inútil pensar que iluminara nada, pero *se abrazó a ella como a un rencor*, y la arrastró hasta su apartamento. (Peri Rossi 26; el énfasis me corresponde)

El ex rey en sus dos códigos (el poder de la posesión y la caballerosidad de la defensa) abraza otra forma de devenir masculino. Es interesante que Peri Rossi introduzca la famosa línea del tango de 1930 de Antonio Miguel Podestá con música de Rafael Rossi, "Como abrazado a un rencor", ya que los primeros versos de este tango presentan las limitaciones del ser "varón". Las comadres, mujeres que asistían como parteras cuando una mujer iba a dar a luz y, por lo tanto, anunciaban luego del nacimiento el sexo de la criatura, yuxtaponen sus funciones con las mujeres que preparan el cuerpo de un difunto. El varón, este "varón" del tango de Podestá y Rossi, perteneciente a una clase social baja ("una infancia sin juguetes, un pasado sin honor, / el dolor de unas cadenas que me queman las muñecas, / y una mina que arrodilla mis arrestos de varón"), vivió su vida prisionero a las performances de la masculinidad de su clase y época. Tales performances se presentan desde su nacimiento como un destino funesto, anticipando el legado existencial que deja al morir:

> "Está listo", sentenciaron las comadres y el varón, / ya difunto en el presagio, en el último momento / de su pobre vida rea, dejó al mundo el testamento / de estas amargas palabras, pintadas de su rencor...
> (Podestá y Rossi)

La "x" final de la palabra "Rex" a la que se abraza Equis, como se abrazara el varón que canta al rencor de una vida infructuosa: la vida del varón, es metonimia de la muerte de esa vida, de esa performance de lo masculino.[8] La extranjería de Equis es salirse de las imposiciones culturales a su género. Esta condición se presenta como una actitud ética que trata de "entender" la otredad en sus múltiples versiones. Son los "Vosotros" que saben cómo se siente el extranjero porque ellos, como dice el Éxodo bíblico, fueron también extranjeros y ahora hay un "Nosotros" que empieza a saber cómo se siente ser extranjero porque comienzan a serlo. Este estar "fuera de lugar" hace posible que Equis encuentre la respuesta correcta al acertijo medieval que se le aparece en el sueño: "¿Cuál es el tributo mayor, el homenaje que un hombre puede hacer a la mujer que ama?" (Peri Rossi 195), al final de la novela.

Poder político / violencia sexual: Vercingetórix y Equis

Cuando Vercingetórix, el amigo de Equis, ve en el cine Rex la escena de la violación de Susan Harris/Julie Christie por la poderosa computadora compara el poder silencioso y omnipresente de la máquina con el de las dictaduras. Ante el horror de la escena, horror que anticipa el de su propia desaparición en una fábrica de cemento, donde el poder concentracionista uruguayo, al igual que el de las dictaduras en Argentina y Chile, hacía desaparecer a todos los que se le oponían, abandona la sala: "—No la aguanto más. Me voy. Ya tuve bastante" (Peri Rossi 23). Los dos hombres sienten el poder como la violencia que en el caso que se proyecta en la pantalla se ejerce sobre el cuerpo de la mujer. Sin embargo, mientras Vercingetórix entiende ese poder como violencia política, sin prestar aten-

---

8. Amanda Holmes, sin mucho argumento, relaciona la "x" con el signo usado por los analfabetos como firma. Esto ciertamente es cuestionable ya que Equis subraya siempre su acervo cultural. "Los locos de Babel o la ciudad imaginada de *La nave de los locos* de Cristina Peri Rossi": 180.

ción a que esa violencia sea una violencia sexual, Equis se siente atado a los dos códigos del poder heterosexual patriarcal. Dicho de otra manera, su atracción al cuerpo palpitante de Julie Christie ante el poder agresor del gran falo mecánico le hace prestar atención al aspecto sexual.

Equis y Vercingetórix podrían leerse como dos aspectos de la masculinidad revolucionaria. Peri Rossi en esta gran alegoría que es *La nave de los locos* da importancia a los nombres. De Equis dijimos que su nombre o la ausencia del mismo marca simbólicamente la muerte de un tipo de masculinidad, la que se basa en el poder binario de la posesión, en cualquiera de sus formas: la brutal o la caballeresca. Por otro lado, Vercingetórix evoca la fuerza del rey de los galos, su valor que le sirvió para unirlos y atacar al imperio romano. El Gran Rey Guerrero de los galos se enfrentó al ejército de Julio César y fue vencido por éste en la Batalla de Alesia (52 AC), entregándose al gobernador de la provincia de Gallia Narbonensis, Julio César, quien lo hizo prisionero y finalmente ordenó su muerte. El Vercingetórix de Peri Rossi, quien quiere un mundo de libertades,[9] también fue vencido y obligado a exilarse por las Fuerzas Armadas en el poder. Vercingetórix quiere reformas y también busca justicia pero desde una estructura de poder que no cuestiona la violencia entre los sexos. Su idea de justicia sigue obedeciendo a una estructura patriarcal de poder.

Al lado del cine Rex, en un edificio público unas mujeres habían colgado un cartel que en letras mayúsculas leía: "EL HOMBRE ES EL PASADO DE LA MUJER" (Peri Rossi 24). Vercingetórix que no soportó la escena de violación y se retiró de la sala cinematográfica antes que la película finalizara, después de haberse emborrachado en un bar cercano, con la conciencia turbada por el alcohol, deshace el cartel. El ambiguo mensaje, ya que parecería indicar un devenir histórico lineal a la manera hegeliana, en que el presente siguiendo la ideología del progreso tiene que ser mejor que el pasado, devenir que niega la narración en su insistencia por los tiempos

---

9. En un episodio paródico en que Equis es multado por un guardia al haberse quedado dormido en un banco de una plaza pública y él pretende instruir al guardia y a la gente que aprueba el comportamiento del representante de la autoridad sobre "las libertades, el individualismo, los derechos humanos y la noción de autoridad", Vercingetórix, rescatando a Equis con su fuerza física (lo levanta en vilo por un brazo), le dice: "—A mí me parece que también el agua, la luz, los autobuses y los cines deberían ser gratis" (Peri Rossi 66-67). El equilibrio de poder será un tema que se cuestiona constantemente a lo largo de la novela.

circulares y saltos que mueven la historia tanto hacia atrás, como hacia adelante y los lados, se carga de significados cuando se compara los efectos que el mismo tuvo en los dos hombres. Para Equis, seducido por la escena de la violación en la pantalla, el mensaje le hace reflexionar sobre las relaciones de poder basadas en la violencia de una fuerza superior sobre un individuo inerme: "*el hombre es el pasado de la mujer*, un pasado tosco, anterior a la conciencia, deplorable como todos los pasados" (Peri Rossi 24). La hegemonía del poder heterosexual, la virilidad como poder privilegiado en las sociedades occidentales,[10] todo lo que está simbolizado en el poder absoluto del gran falo mecánico debe cambiar. Mientras la descripción de la escena en la que Vercingetórix destroza el cartel parecería indicar un deseo de no tener que atender las relaciones de poder basadas en diferencias sexuales y de género:

> Vercingetórix estaba medio borracho, en la puerta del bar. Se había empeñado en destruir el cartel golpeándolo con sus grandes manazas de orangután. Mojado y todo, el cartel resistía, a pesar de que Vercingetórix había conseguido perforar la H de hombre y la S de pasado.
> —Pero, ¿qué estás haciendo?—le reprochó Equis, cuando lo vio, el brazo derecho amarrado a una A y una D al hombro, como un disfraz de payaso.
> —Estoy haciendo pedazos el futuro del hombre—dijo Vercingetórix, con esa rapidez que caracteriza al borracho con un largo ejercicio en rescatar palabras del lago del alcohol. (Peri Rossi 25)

Retirarse del cine Rex para Vercingetórix no es abandonar la casa del "rey patriarca" buscando otro tipo de masculinidad. En verdad, la abandona para "hacer pedazos" el proyecto de un cambio social que destruyera las bases del sistema falocéntrico. Vercingetórix bufonescamente y no del todo consciente de su accionar destruye el cartel que proponía un futuro diferente, impensado para él como líder de los oprimidos. Hay que recordar que el personaje histórico Vercingetórix a quien el personaje de Peri Rossi integra en la historia por medio de su nombre, organizó un ejército de pobres después de haber sido expulsado de Arvernia, su ciudad natal, por los nobles e incluso su tío, y debido a sus dotes de mando fue acla-

---

10. Aunque como observa McDowell, no todas las sociedades occidentales basan su poder en la hegemonía heterosexual. Ver: "In and Out of Place: Bodies and Embodiment" (34-70).

mado rey.[11]

El dejar de lado la dominación masculina en la revolución de una generación, la uruguaya, que en un principio quería luchar contra todas las maneras que el Estado—dirigido en los 70 por la dictadura militar—ejercía el poder se critica por medio de Vercingetórix. Este personaje que se caracteriza por su fuerza física y código caballeresco para con las mujeres: una enana de circo, pequeña y delicada como una muñeca y niñas, representa al militante. Vercingetórix había entendido el poder "monstruoso, invisible y omnipresente" de la máquina violadora, como el poder "de las dictaduras", indicando de esta manera la fuerza de un poder feroz contra todo aquél que se le opusiera. La mujer, representada por Julie Christie, es metonimia de los grupos subyugados y no necesariamente una representación de la violencia contra un sexo y género determinados. En la militarización revolucionaria que se dio en el Cono Sur y de la que el Uruguay no fue excepción, las cuestiones de género y sexo fueron abandonadas. Por eso Vercingetórix representa a un desaparecido, a un posible revolucionario.

Este personaje, como Sophia A. McClennen indica, le sirve a Peri Rossi para denunciar las desapariciones y los campos de concentración donde se torturaban y mataban prisioneros sin que el resto de la población supiera o viera lo que allí pasaba (104). La existencia de los campos de concentración en una ciudad, así como en sus suburbios y el campo de un país que en el mes de agosto es muy frío, alude a Uruguay. Cárceles y cuarteles se convirtieron en centros concentracionistas en el caso uruguayo. En la novela, una fábrica de cemento representa el campo de concentración a donde llega Vercingetórix. El relato en tercera persona, en estilo indirecto libre, del impacto de la fábrica de cemento y del mecanismo desaparecedor del Estado en Vercingetórix le permite al lector entender la expansión y perversidad con la que el poder dictatorial hizo, simbólicamente, prisioneros a la totalidad de la población. Se podría hablar de la expansión de la "zona gris", fenómeno sobre el cual reflexionó Primo Levi en *I sommersi e i salvatti* (1986). Levi se enfoca en los prisioneros-funcionarios del Lager, los campos de concentración nazi, quienes movidos por el terror de su situación, la presencia del "musulmán", prisioneros con la apariencia de muertos en vida, que en cierta manera ya habían dejado su calidad

---

11. Julio César escribió sobre este episodio en el Libro VII de *Commentarii de Bello Gallico*, sección 4ta.

de humanos por la inanición, el hacinamiento y las torturas, y que devenían en un recordatorio constante y tortuoso de lo que les esperaba al resto de los prisioneros, comenzaban a colaborar con los oficiales nazis en un programa que tenía por fin exterminar a los judíos, o sea exterminarlos a ellos también. Esa colaboración que Levi llama, sin hacer ningún juicio de valor, "la zona gris" o área de colaboración surge, de acuerdo al químico y escritor judío italiano y prisionero por un año en el campo de concentración nazi en Auschwitz, de: "multiple roots. In the first place, the more the area of power is restricted the more it needs external auxiliaries" (27). Esa zona de colaboración, cuyos límites son borrosos, se expande en *La nave de los locos* a la gran mayoría de la población, que teme ser desaparecida y como los prisioneros del Lager que cerraban los ojos para no ver al "musulmán" y cerraban los ojos para no ver que la cámara de gases también los esperaba a ellos, cierran los ojos, las puertas y las ventanas, para no ver "la fábrica de cemento" ni los desaparecidos:

> Vercingetórix no sabía si la fábrica de cemento existía antes de que ellos llegaran, o fue construida después cuando los primeros desaparecidos ya habían sido desplazados allí... Nadie conocía la existencia de la fábrica de cemento que volvía cenicientos y esperpénticos los árboles del lugar, que cubría de polvo amarillo las ropas, los ojos, que tapaba las montañas como si fueran de cartón. Nadie conocía, tampoco, la existencia de los desaparecidos, en ese lugar, atrapados entre el polvo del olvido y el polvo de la muerte... (Peri Rossi 58)

La creación de la zona gris, la colaboración consciente o inconsciente con un régimen desaparicionista, (campos de concentración, exilio, muerte), movida por el deseo de sobrevivir, lleva a que existan dos mundos paralelos, dos ciudades que funcionan independientemente la una de la otra: "Había gente que iba al cine y otros a las fábricas, y las mujeres preparaban la comida o leían...y sin embargo, hombres y mujeres desaparecían, un día de la ciudad, en la casa vacía quedaba el perro rumiando su soledad...mientras el polvo de cemento los iba ahogando, los debilitaba, los aturdía" (Peri Rossi 60).

Estos mundos paralelos que se ignoran mutuamente tienen un nexo en la retórica patriotera dictatorial. En un pasaje paródico, Vercingetórix observa que los oficiales y soldados que controlan la fábrica de cemento tienen "predisposición a la poesía y al relato", con temas que hablan del "amor a la patria, la belleza de la bandera, el honor de las Fuerzas Armadas, la encarnizada lucha contra los Oscuros Enemigos...las buenas costumbres y el espíritu cristiano" (Peri Rossi 62). Estos temas, típicos de todas las dictaduras que se asignan la tarea de restaurar el orden basado en una estructura de corte patriarcal, debían inculcarse en todos los ámbitos de la nación. Los sobrevivientes de los campos de concentración, como los prisioneros-funcionarios de los campos nazis, tenían que pasar por esta reeducación nacional si es que salían con vida del campo. Los que estaban afuera, en el mundo donde aparentemente la cotidianidad seguía su curso sin mayores obstáculos, tenían que saber que la única manera de escaparse del caos era permitiendo que el discurso oficial "pro patria", aunque vacío de los valores fundacionales de la misma, obliterara cualquier reclamo de justicia.

En 1975, en Uruguay, la dictadura cívico-militar celebró el "Año de la Orientalidad", donde en medio de discursos que recuerdan la crítica paródica de la "predisposición poética" de los militares de la fábrica de cemento se definió la ética patriótica e impulsó el desarrollo del cuerpo por medio de un régimen militarista de educación física. La Comisión Nacional de Educación Física hizo varias publicaciones sobre la importancia del control del cuerpo en la juventud. Así, en 1976, declaraba que: "La práctica organizada y sistemática de la educación física se inserta en el proceso del país forjando una juventud físicamente apta, moralmente sana y mentalmente capaz, protagonizando con su patriótico esfuerzo la afirmación de una vida mejor para todos los orientales" (CNEF 2). El poder, como estudió Foucault a lo largo de toda su obra, no es verticalista ni aún en los sistemas más centralizados, como las dictaduras. El poder es una red de poderes. De esta manera, el poder sobre el cuerpo para fortalecerlo, limpiarlo, hacerlo sano, ocupó los espacios de la polis suspendida uruguaya. La dictadura cívico-militar había prohibido todo tipo de reunión en su afán por aniquilar la revolución y el espíritu "subversivo" de los jóvenes militantes. Sin embargo, en el año del sesquicentenario de la Cruzada Libertadora de 1825, las competencias deportivas ocuparon todos los espacios públicos del país. La disciplina sobre cuerpo y mente en un intento de "naturalizar"/"orientalizar" a sus ciudadanos, erradicando toda traza de extranjerismo que sería cualquier idea y acción que los moviera a quebrar el orden establecido salvaría a la nación y aseguraría el poder a la dictadura. Esta política así como una crítica a la misma aparecen en *La nave de los locos* en ese lazo que indica que los aparentemente paralelos y autónomos mundos de la cotidianidad y la desaparición estaban unidos por las redes del poder que los hacían posibles. Esta extensa "zona gris" de la complicidad explica también el fracaso revolucionario, ya que como Foucault argumenta no puede triunfar una revolución en que persistan las mismas relaciones del poder anterior.

El último comentario de Vercingetórix sobre el campo de concentración que lo despareció por dos años es el relato de su mirada al exterior del lugar, umbral donde precisamente la política del control del cuerpo y la mente se hace explícita, uniendo el afuera y el adentro en una inamovilidad de piedra. Esta inamovilidad será quebrada por Equis en su viaje de exilio el que como viaje soñado, leído, circular por un mapa sin coordenadas de espacio ni de tiempo es un viaje por la microfísica del poder. Aquí la mirada de Vercingetórix:

> Vercingetórix señala que a la entrada del campo, había un cartel, en grandes caracteres de imprenta: CUERPO SANO EN MENTE SANA. El polvo amarillo de la fábrica de cemento cubría los escasos árboles, la plataforma de madera donde eran atados los prisioneros, la base de la montaña y tapaba las letras del cartel. Una desaparecida estaba encargada de limpiarlo. Como el polvo se extendía rápidamente y era imposible detenerlo, la desaparecida no podía moverse de allí, porque las letras eran continuamente tapadas por el polvo. (Peri Rossi 63)

La leyenda que proclama que en un cuerpo sano habita una mente sana, hace desaparecer a todos aquéllos que se oponen al régimen dictatorial que se enfoca en los trabajos del cuerpo para que la mente quede inerme. La "desaparecida", como un Sísifo del siglo veinte, está condenada a limpiar el cartel, desapareciendo ella así como la memoria de las catorce jornadas y competencias de atletismo que se llevaron a cabo en distintos lugares del país entre 1975, el Año de la Orientalidad, y 1976,[12] a las cuales las palabras del cartel

---

12. En 1975 se realizaron los siguientes eventos: Jornadas Docentes de integración en todas las Regiones; Juegos Atléticos Deportivos Estudiantiles del Sesquicentenario de los Hechos Históricos de 1825, donde se obliga a participar a 50.000 estudiantes; Campeonato Atlético Escolar Nacional del Sesquicentenario de los Hechos Históricos de 1825, que contó con un total de 80.000 estudiantes; Certamen Nacional de Danzas; Campeonato Nacional Interplazas de Deportes de Fútbol de Salón del Sesquicentenario de los Hechos Históricos de 1825, con 1.200 estudiantes; Festival Gimnástico-Atlético en el Estado Centenario; Juegos Atlético Depor-

en sus grandes letras mayúsculas aluden. La "Desaparecida" y el cartel son borrados por el polvo amarillento de un programa educativo que considera al individuo, especialmente a los niños y los jóvenes, como piezas que se deben amoldar para que sirvan dentro de las redes del poder. A los inadaptables se les desaparecen, pero al hacerlo, la meta de construir una nación fuerte física e intelectualmente también desaparece. Si bien las competencias deportivas (la preparación del cuerpo) abundaron bajo dictadura asimismo lo hicieron las publicaciones y competencias literarias (la preparación de la mente) corriendo con la misma suerte.[13] La imposición de un programa mecánico cuyo verdadero fin es anular la libertad intelectual del individuo, libertad de reflexionar, de cuestionar, de disentir, no podía tener éxito ni larga duración. La novela se refiere a este intento de desarrollo literario de los miembros de las Fuerzas Armadas de manera paródica en una nota al pie de página:

> La afición [a la literatura] se extendió tanto que las Fuerzas Armadas crearon, al poco tiempo, una pequeña editorial destinada a publicar los poemas de los esforzados servidores del orden. *Como nadie compraba sus libros*, obligaron a los diarios del país a publicar, en los suplementos del domingo, selecciones de poesía militar, *con lo cual la venta de periódicos disminuyó sensiblemente.* (Peri Rossi 62; el énfasis me pertenece)

Nueva mirada al Tapiz de la Creación de Gerona

La originalidad con la que Peri Rossi intercala las descripciones y reflexiones del *Tapiz de la Creación* de la catedral de Ge-

---

tivos de Instituciones Militares. En 1976: Jornadas Docentes de integración a nivel Preescolar; Campeonato Atlético Escolar Nacional de los 250 años de la Ciudad de Montevideo, con 90.000 estudiantes; Festival de Multiactividad en Explanada de la Intendencia Municipal de Montevideo en adhesión a los 250 a "los del Proceso Fundacional de Montevideo, con la participación de 2.400 estudiantes; Festival Nacional de Educación Física en el Estadio Centenario, con una participación de 90.000 estudiantes; Campeonato de Baby Fútbol; Campeonato del 40 aniversario de PLUNA (la compañía de líneas áreas uruguayas) y Campeonato Nacional Interplazas de Deporte de Fútbol de Salón. Comisión Nacional de Educación Física, 1976.

13. Esta crítica al poder de corte eurocéntrico puede enriquecerse con la lectura del estudio sociológico de Aníbal Quijano, "Coloniality of Power, Eurocentrism, and Latin America."

rona en la estructura fragmentada de *La nave de los locos* ha hecho que todos los trabajos críticos sobre la misma se detengan en el simbolismo del bordado de tema religioso más importante e impresionante del arte románico que se conserva. La simetría, la representación del cosmos, siguiendo la doctrina del teocentrismo medieval, con figuras abstractas y simbólicas que buscaban impactar al espectador por medio de su expresividad y no por la belleza, de la que generalmente las figuras del arte románico carecían, cumplían en los siglos once y doce, fecha que se atribuye a la creación del famoso tapiz anónimo, una función esencialmente didáctica. En un mundo en que la mayoría de la población era analfabeta, las imágenes planas, ingenuas y desproporcionadas, bordadas con vivos colores de lana enseñaban a los fieles los dogmas y principios del Cristianismo. Dos concepciones estéticas diferentes se yuxtaponen en la novela. Por un lado está la medieval del tapiz que muestra, como su nombre indica, la iconografía del Génesis, donde todas las figuras están fijas y jerárquicamente posicionadas, ya que el centro del tapiz está ocupado por el Pantócrator, Jesús como Dios joven y creador que bendice con una mano y en la otra tiene abierto el libro de la creación, donde aparecen las letras griegas alfa y omega, lo que indica que Él es el principio y el fin de todas las cosas. Por la otra, se presenta la alegoría fragmentada e inestable del viaje de exilio en la historia de la novela. Son dos estéticas que reclaman dos perspectivas narrativas diferentes. La primera persona del plural gobierna la descripción del tapiz, ya que la función didáctica del mismo tiene que impactar a todos de la misma manera. El mensaje de la omnipotencia divina mostrada en su poder creador del Cosmos y la Tierra así como el de la salvación tienen que ser sentidos por todos los que miran el tapiz sin equívocos. La creación totalizadora "convincente, placentera y dichosa" de "una sola mente" (Peri Rossi 21) parecería no aceptar lecturas plurales de la misma. De esta manera, el nosotros que reproduce en palabras el tapiz aparece como pronombre de objeto indirecto, es el sujeto, transformado en objeto, sobre el que recae el mensaje teocrático medieval: "Lo que *nos* asombra y *nos* asombrará siempre..." (Peri Rossi 21, el énfasis me pertenece). Por otra parte, la otra estética que se opone a la medieval, la del viaje constante, en la que el individuo carece de un lugar en el espacio y el tiempo, se narra por una tercera persona que en el estilo indirecto libre se mete con fluidez dentro del protagonista, narrando desde su interior sin dejar la tercera persona. En una nota al pie se nos indica que los fragmentos del *Tapiz de la Creación de Gerona* son relatos del recuerdo de Equis, quien en uno de sus viajes vio la obra medieval que lo "conmovió" y dejó "fascinado" (20).

Orden y caos parecen ser las coordenadas que rigen la estructura de la novela. El protagonista, así como los personajes que conoce a lo largo del viaje, son fruto del caos que niega la posibilidad del orden absoluto. Equis, un exiliado, como los orates medievales, los desaparecidos del Cono Sur, los judíos en el régimen nazi y todos los que se oponen a cualquier tipo de poder absolutista, el que no admite disidencias, son metáforas del caos y dentro de la ideología del centralismo jerárquico tienen que eliminarse. Sin embargo, esto no impide que quien se halla en el vórtice del caos no desee sentirse en algún momento "en perfecta armonía" e "integrado al universo" (20). Equis que debe cumplir con el mandato reiterativo de sus sueños: describir las ciudades donde llegue, así como resolver un ambiguo y anacrónico acertijo que liberaría "a la mujer que ama" (195) del poder de un padre-rey, quien está enamorado de su hija, no puede menos que sentir, al observar el tapiz, el impacto de la ordenada estructura del mismo. El primer afecto de Equis hacia la obra es la atracción por su armonía integradora. Como explica Benedictus de Spinoza en su obra monumental *La ética* (1677), la única manera de conocernos y conocer los cuerpos y eventos externos a nosotros es por medio de los afectos o impactos que estos últimos producen en nuestros propios cuerpos. Esta afección o impacto es, de acuerdo al filósofo holandés, la manera más primitiva del conocimiento, ya que conocemos al azar. Sin embargo, es este primer impacto el que lleva a conocimientos más profundos tanto del individuo y de su propio potencial de ser impactado como del exterior. No sorprende que la fascinación de Equis por el orden que lo invita a formar parte de una representación compleja y armónica del universo, casi de inmediato lo mueva a reflexionar críticamente sobre "la destrucción de los elementos reales" (Peri Rossi 20) que se oponen a la armonía. Este nuevo impacto como conocimiento más profundo resulta del conocimiento de Equis de su propio potencial de ser afectado, todo lo que se exterioriza alegóricamente en los mandatos que aparecen en sus sueños. La manera en que los mandatos se articulan, especialmente el acertijo del rey enamorado de su hija a los pretendientes de ésta, los relacionan con el período medieval del tapiz, con una ideología centralista y teocrática.

La primera persona del plural que describe el tapiz, el "nosotros" donde Equis y todos los lectores de la novela se integran, parecería indicar la imposibilidad de no sentirse atraído por la estructura de la obra: "Lo que admiramos en la obra...es una estructura, una estructura tan perfecta y geométrica, tan verificable que aún habiendo desaparecido casi su mitad, es posible reconstruir el todo, si no en el muro de la catedral, sí en el bastidor de la mente" (Peri Rossi 21). En esta estructura tan perfecta se podría vivir porque todas las figuras tienen un lugar asignado por el Gran Creador, el "Rex Fortis", como indica el tapiz en el espacio que sirve de fondo a la figura del Pantocrátor. Equis, desde afuera del tapiz, puede proyectar su imagen en el espejo de la creación, y allí, por medio del tramado que existe "en el bastidor de la mente", encontrar su lugar en la representación del Cosmos y la Tierra. La repetición del mensaje del orden teocrático patriarcal es precisamente la que por siglos imprimió una manera determinada de ejercer el poder, de comportarse y relacionarse, de entender sistemas jerárquicos y concebir la idea de justicia, de la que depende la felicidad y el dolor, "el ángel de la luz" y "el ángel de las tinieblas" en el tapiz. Equis puede proyectarse y verse en la obra medieval porque el mensaje plasmado en lana de colores, a través de los años y el espacio, adquirió el ritmo de "una vieja leyenda" que "nos fascina, pero que no provoca nostalgia" (20). Se trata de una leyenda que puso a todo el mundo en su sitio y la que no puede provocar nostalgia, ya que hay que perder mucho para tener un lugar en ese orden. Foucault se refirió al espacio medieval de la siguiente manera:

> ...in the Middle Ages there was a hierarchic ensemble of places: sacred places and profane places; protected places and open, exposed places; urban places and rural places (all of these concern the real life of men). In cosmological theory, there were the supercelestial places, as opposed to the celestial, and the celestial was in its turn opposed to the terrestrial place. There were places where things had been put because they had been violently displaced, and then on the contrary places where things found their natural ground and stability. It was this complete hierarchy, this opposition, this intersection of places that constituted what could very roughly be called medieval space: the place of emplacement. (Foucault: "Of Other Spaces" 22)

¿Qué tipo de lectura invita a hacer este tapiz/espejo? ¿Se trata del espejo lacaniano donde el individuo encuentra su subjetividad? O ¿estamos ante el tapiz/espejo que apunta a un espacio otro, el espacio de una heterotopia foucaultiana, donde el individuo se encuentra y desencuentra?

Antes de responder a estas preguntas hay que subrayar, como lo hace McClennen, que tanto el tapiz como la novela son representaciones (106). Son metáforas que responden a una ideología y sensibilidad determinadas. El enfrentamiento de ambas deja ver y sentir las perversiones de las redes del poder. En el caso medieval, la estética del orden jerárquico perfecto había sucumbido cuando en el siglo diecisiete Galileo quiebra los conceptos de la estabilidad y del espacio concreto de las cosas con sus descubrimientos de un espacio infinitamente abierto y el eterno movimiento de todas las cosas, como subraya Foucault ("Of Other Spaces" 23). La vulnerabilidad del concepto medieval de un espacio estable y concreto ya parece hacerse sentir en la creación del tapiz de Gerona. Pese a que en la novela se dice que los fragmentos que le faltan al tapiz debido a la destrucción del tiempo se podrían fácilmente reconstruir, los estudiosos de la obra de finales del siglo once o comienzos del doce no se ponen de acuerdo sobre qué relatos iconográficos lo completarían.[14] Paradójicamente, el espacio geométricamente organizado y armonioso del Cosmos y la Tierra de acuerdo a la creación medieval del tapiz se abre por la destrucción fortuita de casi la mitad del bordado, anticipando en su presente estado de obra fragmentada el descubrimiento de Galileo. Sin embargo, lo que persevera es el ritmo de leyenda de la historia representada en el tapiz. Persevera la historia de un poder que necesita de la estabilidad y la polarización, que necesita la aceptación absoluta de la relación amo/esclavo. La fuerza de esta historia que carece de argumentos teóricos contundentes radica en la repetición de la misma, la que la transforma en leyenda. No se sabe qué historias bíblicas habría concebido el anónimo artista medieval, cuya obra al sufrir la desaparición de una parte considerable de su estructura anticipa involuntariamente una nueva concepción espacial. Sin embargo, en el espacio de la memoria, como un paño fuertemente marcado por la hegemonía del poder centralista y patriarcal, las historias desaparecidas del tapiz original pueden volver a emplazarse.

Equis entra al *Tapiz de la Creación* como a un espacio otro, donde está y no está porque su entrada en el esquema trazado por un poder hegemónico está condicionada por los mandatos del sue-

---

14. Para un mejor conocimiento del *Tapiz de la Creación* de Gerona, leer "*Tapiz de la Creación*" de Pere de Palol.

ño. Tiene que describir las ciudades donde llegue sin la preconcepción de qué es principal y secundario. Asimismo tiene que descubrir por qué las relaciones de lo masculino/femenino son relaciones que reproducen la subyugación de un grupo (las mujeres representadas en Eva) a otro que se asigna la herencia directa del Rex Fortis/Dios (los hombres representados en Adán). El *Tapiz de la Creación* es para Equis una heterotopia, el espejo que describe Foucault:

> In the mirror, I see myself there where I am not, in an unreal, virtual space that opens up behind the surface; I am over there, there where I am not, a sort of shadow that gives my own visibility to myself, that enables me to see myself there where I am absent: such is the utopia of the mirror. But it is also a heterotopia in so far as the mirror does exist in reality, where it exerts a sort of counteraction on the position that I occupy. From the standpoint of the mirror I discover my absence from the place where I am since I see myself over there. Starting from this gaze that is, as it were, directed toward me, from the ground of this virtual space that is on the other side of the glass, I come back toward myself; I begin again to direct my eyes toward myself and to reconstitute myself there where I am. (Foucault: "Of Other Spaces" 24)

Equis entra a la representación del esquema medieval del poder como "x", como la ruina del "Rex", la posición establecida por el sistema para los hombres. Es indudable que este concepto de ruina de lo masculino asumida por Equis se origine en las consecuencias que dejaron las dictaduras del Cono Sur,[15] hecho histórico que mueve al personaje a considerar todos los hechos ruinosos y trágicos del mundo occidental, asimismo frutos de la centralización del poder, el cual en la ficción de Peri Rossi queda emplazado en la metrópoli, el "Gran Ombligo" (Peri Rossi 115). La asociación del nombre de la metrópoli, sitio en que se criticará con humor e ironía las falencias del centralismo del poder, a la que uno de los personajes que conoce Equis en su odisea, el excéntrico escritor Morris debe viajar, con la concepción medievalista de Jerusalén como *umbilicum mundi* es innegable. Jerusalén, la ciudad sagrada del judaísmo y cristianismo, era concebida como el centro del mundo.

---

15. Mabel Moraña en "La nave de los locos", de 1986, también hace referencia a las múltiples alusiones a la historia uruguaya de la dictadura en la novela: "Múltiples indicios marcan a lo largo del texto, la referencia al clima de violencia y represión del Uruguay posterior al golpe de estado de 1973, y confieren al texto anclaje en una realidad cercana y acotada, de modo que la fantasía, la ironía, la parodia, aparezcan como modalidades de la reflexión histórica y existencial" (206).

Esta concepción espiritual del lugar sagrado de todos los eventos del dios humano, Jesús Cristo, se yuxtapuso con una concepción centralista y patriarcal del poder, justificando con el aspecto espiritual y evangelista, las violencias de ese poder. La entrada de Equis al tapiz medieval desde las ruinas del presente le permite desmadejar el acertijo sobre las redes de poder entre los sexos.

Desde el espacio irreal del tapiz/espejo, Equis comienza a entender su relacionamiento con los otros. Lucía, una de las jóvenes mujeres que Equis había llevado a hacerse un aborto en una clínica londinense cuando trabajaba como conductor de la clínica, lo que permite la reflexión crítica al abuso sobre los cuerpos de las mujeres en el mundo contemporáneo occidental, sirve de catalizador para la cruzada de Equis. Cuando éste la ve haciendo una parodia lésbica en un espectáculo "porno-sexy" (189), descubre la solución al viejo enigma: "El tributo mayor, el homenaje que un hombre puede hacer a la mujer que ama, es su virilidad" (196). La yuxtaposición de papeles de lo femenino/masculino en el personaje de Lucía no sería suficiente para llegar a la solución dada. Como Kantaris argumenta, siguiendo a Judith Butler, la parodia de por sí no es subversiva; para serlo tiene que contar con cierta recepción (Kantaris: 1995 77). La performance de Lucía, quien asume una cadena de papeles que subrayan la transexualidad de sus personajes: Charlotte Rampling, Helmut Berger y Marlene Dietrich, así como la performatividad de los géneros: "Charlotte Rampling en *Portero de noche*, quien imitaba a Helmut Berger en *La caída de los dioses*, quien imitaba a Marlene Dietrich en *El ángel azul* " (191), ponen de manifiesto la circense parodia de asumir un poder en la cual las relaciones que lo constituyen no cambian. El espectáculo pornográfico ante un público de hombres excitados por la escena representada por una Lucía que como Marlene Dietrich actuaba de hombre sin dejar de ser mujer y una Dolores del Río, que podría ser un hombre que actuaba sus fantasías sexuales como mujer no encuentra la recepción adecuada para volverse subversivo. Sin embargo, para Equis que entró al tapiz de la representación de un poder donde todo debía ocupar un lugar preciso y fijo para que la armonía se cumpliera y que puede mirar el espectáculo de su entrada al mismo desde afuera del tapiz/espejo, la representación de Lucía, como parodia lésbica que parodia la heterosexualidad, y su hermoso rostro ambiguo de efebo son la parodia subversiva al poder patriarcal. Equis es el receptor ideal para diseminar el cambio básico entre las relaciones de poder entre los sexos. La ofrenda de su virilidad, poder dado como natural a los hombres en el sistema patriarcal, termina, en el sueño, con los abusos del mismo. Finalmente, la figura del rey, con el simbolismo argumentado en este capítulo y que desde el comienzo de la novela se estuvo cuestionando, cae. En el sueño se hace visible y audible el deseo de Equis para un futuro:

> ...Equis se yergue, en el sueño sus ojos brillan triunfadores, se aproxima, sigiloso, al viejo rey y le grita a la cara, le anuncia, lentamente: "El tributo mayor, el homenaje que un hombre puede hacer a la mujer que ama, es su virilidad"...y el rey, súbitamente disminuido, el rey, como un caballito de juguete, el rey, como un muñequito de pasta, el reyecito de chocolate, cae de bruces, vencido, el reyecito se hunde en el barro, el reyecito, derrotado, desparece. Gime antes de morir. (196-197)

El mapa trazado por Cristina Peri Rossi en *La nave de los locos* se opone al mapa trazado por *El tapiz de la creación* al haber borrado su centro (la eliminación del rey), interrumpiendo de esta manera el ritmo de leyenda con que se impuso por milenios la hegemonía del poder patriarcal. El mapa que se crea en la ficción alegórica de Peri Rossi depende de las relaciones múltiples y heterogéneas entre los individuos, relaciones que no sólo determinan distintos sitios, sino también la posibilidad de salirse de ellos, cuando sea necesario tomar una distancia crítica. En este mapa todo lo "desaparecido" por el poder centralista de corte patriarcal ocupa un espacio, aunque sea transitorio, y puede ser visto, abriendo nuevas posibilidades de ser y de actuar.

Breves palabras sobre la Generación del 72

Podría decirse, parafraseando a Bertolt Brecht, quien hablaba de los "procesos de producción de los clásicos", que hablar de generaciones literarias es el resultado de procesos de producción, especialmente cuando las generaciones no resultan de un evento particular que reúne las sensibilidades artísticas de un grupo en determinado tiempo y lugar, como ser, la Generación del '98 o del '27 en España, o la Generación del '45 en Uruguay, por dar tres ejemplos ampliamente conocidos. La Generación del *boom* fue, sin duda, el exitoso resultado de un proceso de producción, que puso a América Latina como creación ficcional dentro de las coordenadas cosmopolitas de la cultura.

El crítico chileno Cedomil Goic, por otra parte, hizo una obra monumental al estudiar la ficción latinoamericana siguiendo una división generacional. Su fin no fue solo didáctico, sino que impulsó a que obras y autores de distintos países latinoamericanos conversaran entre sí, mostrando semejanzas, diferencias, así como fragmentaciones en el entramado cultural de nuestra América. Sin embargo, el exhaustivo trabajo de Goic, basado en un concepto estructuralista de la novela, fue paulatinamente abandonado no sólo por las limitaciones de la teoría estructuralista, sino porque aproximarse a la narrativa desde una perspectiva generacional parecía asimismo limitante. Cabe, entonces, preguntarnos sobre la necesidad de entrar en el proceso de producción de una generación literaria latinoamericana: la Generación del '72. ¿Qué ventajas tiene estudiar la obra de una gran escritora como Cristina Peri Rossi desde el enfoque generacional del '72?

Para responder a esta pregunta, propongo que reflexionemos sobre este presente de globalización, de imposiciones de la economía neoliberal del mercado, de avances tecnológicos que hacen impensables los conceptos tradicionales de tiempo y espacio, al tiempo que nuestras sociedades en el Cono Sur continúan entregadas a nuevos y renovados trabajos de la memoria para rescatar la historia de violencia de las guerras sucias de los 70 y 80. Este presente es estudiado por Josefina Ludmer en su libro más reciente, *Aquí América Latina. Una especulación* (2010), como temporalidades y territorios: la ciudad como "isla urbana", la nación, y el territorio de la lengua, donde la ficción reciente es leída como realidad. Para Ludmer, la realidad de que trata la ficción publicada a partir de 2000, la realidad cotidiana, es "una realidad producida y construida por los medios, las tecnologías y las ciencias"; es pura representación. Hay una fusión entre realidad ficción que lleva a leer con otras coordenadas la literatura. De acuerdo a Ludmer, estamos presenciando un fenómeno que nos lleva a eliminar los conceptos conocidos con que se leía la literatura: "autor, obra, texto, estilo, valor literario, e incluso ficción".[16] Esta nueva ficción que da cuenta de una realidad que es pura representación pierde para Ludmer la autonomía de lo literario y, por eso le da el nombre de "literatura postautónoma".

En este contexto, la literatura de una generación que se vio

---

16. Entrevista de Hugo Fontana a Josefina Ludmer.

violentada por la historia, que experimentó de primera mano las desilusiones de los proyectos políticos de la militancia, los horrores de la represión estatal, las diferentes marginaciones de la globalización, que vivió los cambios tecnológicos con respecto a la escritura que los llevó de escribir a máquina, a las computadoras y a los blogs, puede ser leída como faro de posibilidades de lo simbólico. Como propone Beatriz Sarlo en *Tiempo pasado: cultura de la memoria (una discusión)*, es en la literatura donde se encuentran: "las imágenes más precisas del horror del pasado reciente y de su textura de ideas y experiencia" (163). Es en la literatura, con su autonomía simbólica y la textura del lenguaje, donde el presente de la lectura y el presente del texto dan prueba de su existencia. Es en el mapa alegórico creado por Cristina Peri Rossi en *La nave de los locos* donde el futuro se divisa por medio del foco epistémico del exiliado, del extranjero, de un náufrago por el mundo de la cultura occidental, un personaje llamado Equis, y esta esperanza en lo literario desde los márgenes es característica de un grupo de grandes escritores latinoamericanos entre los que se encuentran además de Peri Rossi: Marta Traba, Tomás Eloy Martínez, Juan José Saer, Luisa Valenzuela, Antonio Skármeta, Ricardo Piglia, Fernando Vallejo, Ariel Dorfman, Osvaldo Soriano, Reinaldo Arenas, Héctor Aguilar Camín, Diamela Eltit, César Aira, Laura Restrepo: la generación del '72.

Obras citadas

Caesar, Julius. *Commentaries on the Gallic War*, con notas, vocabulario y mapas de G. K. Bartholomew. Cincinatti: Van Antwerp, Bragg & co, 1877. Impreso.

Calveiro, Pilar. *Poder y/o violencia. Una aproximación a la guerrilla de los años 70*. Buenos Aires: Norma, 2005. Impreso.

Cammell, Donald, director. *Demon Seed*. Act. Julie Christie. Metro Goldwyn Mayer, 1977. Filme.

Comisión Nacional de Educación Física. Educación Física y Deporte. *Revista de Educación Física y Deporte* 1(1976): 1-100. Impreso.

—. Educación Física y Deporte. *Revista de Educación Física y Deporte* 2 (1981):1-37. Impreso.

—. Educación Física y Deporte. *Revista de Educación Física y Deporte* 3 (1982): 1-7. Impreso.

Dejbord, Parizad Tamara. "Nuevas configuraciones del exilio en *La nave de los locos, Solitario de amor* y *Babel bárbara* de Cristina Peri Rossi". *Revista Hispánica Moderna* 2 (Diciembre 1997): 347-362. Impreso.

Fontana, Hugo. "'La isla urbana': entrevista a Josefina Ludmer". *El País* (Montevideo) 9 de octubre de 2009. En línea. Internet 16 de mayo 2012. Disponible: http://www.josefinaludmer.com/Josefina_Ludmer/entrevistas.html

Foster, Hal. "Postmodernism: A Preface." *The Anti-Aesthetic: Essays on Postmodern Culture*. Ed. Foster. Seattle: Bay Press, 1989. ix-xvi. Impreso.

Foucault, Michel. "Of Other Spaces." *Diacritics* 16 (Spring 1986): 22-27. Impreso.

Grosz, Elizabeth. *Volatile Bodies: Toward a Corporeal Feminism*. Bloomington: Indiana UP, 1994. Impreso.

Holmes, Amanda. "Los locos de Babel o la ciudad imaginada de *La nave de los locos* de Cristina Peri Rossi". *Escritos, Revista del Centro del Lenguaje* 25 (enero-junio 2002): 175-197. Impreso.

Huyssen, Andreas. *Present Pasts: Urban Palimpsests and the Politics of Memory*. Stanford, California: Stanford UP, 2003. Impreso.

Jelin, Elizabeth. *Los trabajos de la memoria*. Madrid: Siglo XXI de España Editores: Social Research Council, 2002. Impreso.

Kantaris, Elia Geoffrey. *The Subversive Psyche: Contemporary Women's Narrative from Argentina and Uruguay*. Oxford: Clarendon Press; Oxford UP, 1995. Impreso.

—. "The Politics of Desire: Alienation and Identity in the Work of Marta Traba and Cristina Peri Rossi". *Forum for Modern Literature Studies* 25:3 (Julio 1989): 248-264. Impreso.

Lacan, Jacques. *Ecrits: A Selection*. Trad. Alan Sheridan. New York: Norton, 1977. Impreso.

Levi, Primo. *The Drowned and the Saved*, traducido por Raymond Rosenthal. Londres: Abacus, 1989. Impreso.

Ludmer, Josefina. *Aquí América Latina. Una especulación*. Buenos Aires: Eterna Cadencia, 2010.

McClennen, Sophia A. *The Dialectics of Exile: Nation, Time, Language and Space in Hispanic Literature*. West Lafayette: Purdue UP, 2004. Impreso.

McDowell, Linda. *Gender, Identity and Place: Understanding Feminist Geographies*. Minneapolis: U of Minnesota P, 1999. Impreso.

Mora, Gabriela. "Peri Rossi, *La nave de los locos* y la búsqueda de la armonía". *Nuevo Texto Crítico* 1.2 (2do. Semestre 1988): 343-352. Impreso.

Moraña, Mabel. "*La nave de los locos* de Cristina Peri Rossi". *Texto Crítico* 34-35 (1986): 201-213. Impreso.

Olivera-Williams, María Rosa. *El arte de crear lo femenino: ficción, género e historia del Cono Sur*. Santiago, Chile: Editorial Cuarto Propio, 2012. Impreso.

—. "*La nave de los locos* de Cristina Peri Rossi". *Revista de Crítica Literaria Latinoamericana* 12.23 (1986): 81-89. Impreso.

Palol, Pere de. *Catalunya románica*. Vol. XXIII. Barcelona: Generalitat de Catalunya, 1988. 188-189. Impreso.

Peri Rossi, Cristina. *Viviendo*: Montevideo: Alfa, 1963. Impreso.

—. *Los museos abandonados*. Barcelona: Lumen, 1984. Impreso.

—. *El libro de mis primos*. Barcelona: Grijalbo, 1989. Impreso.

—. *Indicios pánicos*. Barcelona: Bruguera, 1980. Impreso.

—. *Evohé*. Montevideo: Girón, 1971. Impreso.

—. *Descripción de un naufragio*. Barcelona: Lumen, 1975. Impreso.

—. *Diáspora*. Barcelona: Lumen, 2002. Impreso.

—. *Lingüística general*. Valencia: Prometeo, 1979. Impreso.

—. *La tarde del dinosaurio*. Barcelona: Plaza y Janés, 1980. Impreso.

—. *La rebelión de los niños*. Barcelona: Seix Barral, 1980. Impreso.

—. *El museo de los esfuerzos inútiles*. Barcelona: Seix Barral, 1983. Impreso.

—. *La nave de los locos*. Barcelona: Seix Barral, 1984. Impreso.

—. "La influencia de Edgar A. Poe en la poesía de Raimundo Arias" (1976). *Cristina Peri Rossi. Cuentos reunidos*. Barcelona: Lumen, 2007. 38-52. Impreso.

Podestá, Antonio Miguel y Rafael Rossi. "Como abrazado a un rencor". 1930. Odeón. *Todo Tango. The Library*. Web. 2 agosto 2011.

Quijano, Aníbal. "Coloniality of Power, Eurocentrism, and Latin America." *Neplanta:Views from South* 1.3 (2000): 533-580. Impreso.

Rodríguez Hernández, Raúl. "Posmodernismo de resistencia y alteridad en *La nave de los locos*, de Cristina Peri Rossi". *Revista Canadiense de Estudios Hispánicos* 19.1 (Otoño 1994): 121-135. Impreso.

Sarlo, Beatriz. *Tiempo pasado. Cultura de la memoria y giro subjetivo. Una discusión*. Buenos Aires: Siglo Veintiuno Editores, 2005. Impreso.

Spinoza, Benedictus de. *Ethics*, editado y traducido por G.H.R. Parkinson. New York: Oxford UP, 2000. Impreso.

Radiografía de un pueblo enfermo:
la narrativa de Diamela Eltit

J. Agustín Pastén B.
North Carolina State University

Este artículo sobre la obra de la novelista y crítica[1] chilena Diamela Eltit, la más lúcida e inteligente voz en el panorama literario de los últimos treinta años en Chile, consiste de cuatro apartados. En el primero, a fin de situar su producción literaria dentro de los parámetros de la violencia, el trauma, la política, y la poética—cuatro de los posibles parámetros alrededor de los cuales gira la novelística de los miembros de la "Generación del '72"—, se ofrece un repaso parcial pero necesario de la crítica especializada en su obra. En el segundo y tercer apartados se efectúa un análisis de *Jamás el fuego nunca* (2007) e *Impuesto a la carne* (2010), respectivamente, por ser las novelas de Eltit que menos atención crítica han recibido hasta la fecha. En el último apartado ofrezco una conclusión.

Diamela Eltit ante la crítica

Quien conozca la obra de Eltit sabe muy bien que sus primeras novelas, y muy en particular *Lumpérica* (1983) y *Por la patria* (1986), recibieron no sólo escasa atención crítica sino también juicios negativos derivados de la miopía y la consabida envidia chilena. "¿Y ésta quién era?," se preguntaban los críticos machistas, "¿cómo

---

1. Eltit reúne sus ensayos de crítica literaria, política y de arte escritos antes de la década del 2000, en *Emergencias: escritos sobre literatura, arte y política* (2000).

se le ocurría escribir así, quién se creía, cómo podía *una mujer*, más encima, escribir de ese modo, qué diablos quería decir, dónde estaba la trama de sus novelas?"[2] No es de sorprender, por tanto, que inicialmente los asedios críticos a su producción narrativa fueran mínimos. Entre los más ampliamente conocidos durante algún tiempo, estuvieron los de Eugenia Brito en la sección sobre Eltit de su *Campos minados (literatura post-golpe en Chile)* (1990), y los de la antología crítica *Una poética de literatura menor: la narrativa de Diamela Eltit* (1993), de Juan Carlos Lértora. Sin embargo, como ha rectificado recientemente la chilena Raquel Olea—otra conocida crítica de su producción literaria—, la recepción de la obra de Eltit en Chile se realizó también en sitios no académicos que, mediante la teoría feminista, el psicoanálisis y el postestructuralismo, intentaron establecer lazos entre su obra narrativa y su participación como artista de *performance* en el grupo CADA y en la llamada *escena de avanzada* (92).[3] Con el tiempo, y especialmente en la academia norteamericana, la obra de Eltit empezó a recibir el reconocimiento de la crítica.[4] Además de los numerosos artículos consagrados a su obra, hoy ya hay secciones de libros sobre su novelística[5] así como también libros enteros.[6] En Chile también la autora se ha ido haciendo un mayor espacio gracias a los estudios de María Inés Lagos,[7] Leonidas Morales, Bernardita Llanos y, especialmente,

2. En cuanto a *Lumpérica*, por ejemplo, Olea señala que se la condenó como "críptica, experimental o ambiguamente ubicada en las fronteras de lo lírico, con lo cual se operó un primer momento de aislamiento y confinación de los textos al reducto de lo elitista o lo marginal" ("El cuerpo" 83). Cánovas, por su parte, afirma que el lenguaje de las primeras novelas de Eltit se calificó de "letal, catastrófico, obsesivo, obtuso, enervante, lumpen" ("Diamela" 26).

3. Entre los críticos tempranos pero más o menos ignorados de la obra de Eltit que Olea menciona, se encuentran Marta Contreras, Ivette Malverde, Agata Gligo, Soledad Bianchi, y Marcela Prado ("El deseo" 92).

4. Entre quienes han contribuido al conocimiento y difusión de la obra de Eltit en Estados Unidos, están el peruano Julio Ortega, Gwen Kirkpatrick, la chilena María Inés Lagos-Pope, y Francine Masiello.

5. En los estudios de Tierney-Tello, Avelar, y Kulawik.

6. Por ejemplo el lúcido estudio de Norat así como el excelente estudio de Green. También el de Silvia Tafra, *Diamela Eltit: el rito de pasaje como estrategia textual* (Santiago: RiL-Red Internacional del libro 1998), aunque no he tenido la oportunidad de cotejarlo.

7. Sobre Lagos, además de la publicación de varios artículos sobre la obra de Eltit, en 2000 ella editó un número monográfico de la revista *Nomadías* titulado, *Creación y resistencia: la narrativa de Diamela Eltit, 1983-1998* (Santiago: Edi-

merced a Rubí Carreño Bolívar, quien el 2006 organizó el "Coloquio Internacional de Escritores y Críticos: Homenaje a Diamela Eltit."[8] ¿Podría afirmarse entonces que, finalmente, este feliz aguijón en la carne del ambiente literario-cultural chileno se ha consagrado y que sus novelas serán tan leídas como las de Isabel Allende, Marcela Serrano, Hernán Rivera Letelier, Ramón Díaz Eterovic, Pablo Simonetti o algún otro novelista chileno? Yo albergo mis dudas.

Para empezar, y como dijo uno de los exponentes del coloquio en Santiago, "leer a Diamela Eltit cuesta" (Hozven 79). Sí, es cierto que *Mano de obra* (2002) es significativamente más asequible que *Lumpérica* y que desde *El cuarto mundo* (1988) en adelante, o bien desde *Los vigilantes* (1994) en adelante, la factura textual de sus novelas, siguiendo a Barthes, se hace más *lisible* que *scriptible*.[9] Aun así, la ficción de Eltit sigue exigiendo un lector activo, como tendremos la oportunidad de apreciar en el análisis de su última novela. No es por acaso, consecuentemente, que en algún momento de sus apreciaciones críticas sobre las novelas de la escritora chilena, sobre todo en referencia a *Lumpérica*, *Por la patria*, *El cuarto mundo*, y *Vaca sagrada* (1991), los críticos hablen de la resistencia que el lenguaje de éstas presenta, de su, por qué no decirlo, dificultad y reflexividad. Las definiciones, por supuesto, abundan, y hay una conciencia de que, efectivamente, para escribir en dictadura y engañar a los censores no quedaba otra alternativa sino hacer lo menos transparente posible el texto. Vivir en dictadura, en otras palabras, condiciona inevitablemente la escritura. Pero ello no explica del todo el uso de este tipo de lenguaje en sus primeros textos. Incide asimismo en esta práctica de ciertas formas posestructuralistas el estudio de diversos aspectos del postestructuralismo que los miembros del grupo CADA llevan a cabo en los primeros años y que de alguna forma calzan perfectamente con la sensibilidad estética de Eltit. Además, coincidentemente según Brito, en dictadura se produce en Chile un nuevo paradigma de la literatura que llevará

---

torial Cuarto Propio); Morales, además de escribir el prólogo de *Emergencias*, ha publicado también *Conversaciones con Diamela Eltit* (Santiago: Editorial Cuarto Propio, 1998); Llanos es editora de *Letras y proclamas. La estética literaria de Diamela Eltit* (Santiago: Editorial Cuarto Propio, 2006).

8. Este coloquio tuvo lugar en la Facultad de Letras de la Pontificia Universidad Católica de Chile entre el 17 y el 19 de octubre. Las distintas ponencias del coloquio fueron publicadas posteriormente en *Diamela Eltit: redes locales, redes globales* (2009), editado por Carreño.

9. Barthes establece una distinción entre estos dos tipos de texto en *S/Z*.

a lo que denomina "'una escena de la escritura' [caracterizada por un lenguaje] cifrado y vuelto a cifrar" (11).[10] Ella alude a la permanente "sospecha del significado" en *Lumpérica* (113) y al hecho de que esta primera novela de Eltit crea "un modo nuevo de pensar el género novela, en particular y la escritura, en general" (116). Asimismo, se refiere a la "torsión del género novelesco en la escritura de *Por la patria*" (140). Lértora, por su parte, caracteriza el discurso eltitiano en general como un discurso esencialmente "fragmentario" pero al mismo tiempo integrador de un "verdadero mestizaje de voces" así como de una "heteroglosa desenfadada" ("Presentación" 11). Sara Castro-Klarén destaca la autoconciencia y autorreflexividad de *Lumpérica* (98) y afirma que diferentes secciones de este texto, desde frases a párrafos completos, pueden leerse como "acertijos" (102). Guillermo García Corales llama la atención sobre cómo en *Lumpérica* existe la clara intención de alejarse del lenguaje realista, de eliminar la anécdota, a fin de priorizar "la textualidad de su producción" (112). Finalmente, Gisela Norat se refiere a la "Joycean quality" del lenguaje de las novelas de Eltit (15). Todos estos juicios críticos relacionados de alguna manera a la naturaleza "scriptible" del discurso eltitiano convergen en la caracterización de su obra como una obra esencialmente vanguardista (Cánovas, *Novela* 60; Cánovas, "Diamela" 31), neovanguardista (Kulawik 54) o bien neobarroca y cuyos principales antecedentes serían los cubanos Severo Sarduy y Lezama Lima (Brito 117; Cánovas, *Novela* 61). Curiosamente desde mi punto de vista, varios críticos definen la producción narrativa de Eltit como postmoderna aunque sin extenderse demasiado acerca de si Eltit es postmoderna desde una óptica filosófica (Lyotard), cultural (Hassan), económico-cultural (Jameson), puramente económica (Harvey), o estilística (Hutcheon): (Sklodowska 158 [en lo tocante a *Lumpérica*]; Kulawik 21; Williams 211; Lagos 135-36 [en relación a *El cuarto mundo*]; y Norat 17, 24).[11]

Tal vez pudiera decirse que, estilísticamente hablando, las primeras novelas de Eltit son más postmodernas que las más recientes (que *Mano de obra* o *Jamás el fuego nunca*, por ejemplo). Pero éstas son más postmodernas por la intensa reflexividad que las

---

10. El contraste con Dorfman y Skármeta, que sí escribieron desde el exilio, no podía ser más evidente.

11. Norat está consciente, no obstante, que el postmodernismo latinoamericano carece de los elementos apolíticos y ahistóricos que caracterizan la mayor parte del postmodernismo norteamericano (156).

caracteriza y no en el sentido de imitación, simulacro o pastiche de Jameson, ni tampoco en el sentido de "historiographic metafiction" de Hutcheon, cuyo propósito final consistiría en problematizar la historia a través de una ironía permanente y juguetona. Además, lo que los textos no ficticios de Eltit—*El padre mío* (1989), *El infarto del alma* (1995), y *Puño y letra* (2005)—anhelan, es, más que parodiar o ironizar la historia, inscribirla, fijarla, rescatar un testimonio antes de que se pierda en el primer caso, celebrar a un grupo de personas abandonadas en el segundo caso, y servir de testigo de cómo el estado dictatorial se deshizo de personas indeseables en el tercer caso. Ahora bien, volviendo al carácter "scriptible" de sus primeros textos, en particular, éste se manifiesta de las siguientes formas: inestabilidad de una voz narrativa que, siguiendo los planteamientos de Wayne Booth, podríamos calificar de "dramatized" o "dramática" en la mayor parte de los casos (Onega 147-48);[12] lenguaje marcadamente anti-mimético; experimentación lingüística constante mediante modificaciones de la sintaxis, el uso de neologismos, diversos juegos de palabras, y ambigüedad; inclusión de hablas regularmente excluidas de discursos oficiales, incluidos modismos y garabatos; fragmentación en todo sentido. Desde este punto de vista, no hay que olvidar que los miembros de la Generación del '72 son los primeros en hacer uso de la cultura popular de manera seria y consistente. Temáticamente, los estudiosos de la obra de Eltit han explorado la relación cuerpo femenino/escritura en sus novelas así como también la relación entre el cuerpo y el poder. También se ha abordado la representación del sujeto subalterno, primero en el contexto de la dictadura y más tarde en el contexto de Chile como "nación-mercado."[13] Han sido tratados igualmente el tema del incesto, la sexualidad de la mujer, la maternidad, y la familia en su condición disfuncional. A continuación, para ver en qué sentido *Jamás el fuego nunca* e *Impuesto a la carne* representan una nueva dirección en la trayectoria estética de Eltit, se ofrece un brevísimo compendio de cómo algunos críticos han visto su corpus narrativo precedente.

---

12. El "dramatized narrator," de acuerdo a Booth, se distingue del "undramatized narrator" por su participación en la fábula, ora como "mere observer," ora como "narrator-agent" (en Onega 148-49). Ver también "Types of Narration," el capítulo seis de su famoso libro dedicado a la narrativa, *The Rhetoric of Fiction* (149-64).

13. Tomo esta expresión del artículo de Luis E. Cárcamo-Huechante sobre Lemebel (99).

Sin lugar a dudas, las novelas que más atención crítica han recibido son *Lumpérica* y *Por la patria*; a éstas les siguen *Mano de obra*, *Los vigilantes*, y *El cuarto mundo*. Dejando de lado tanto *Vaca sagrada* como las novelas que se analizarán inmediatamente después de este resumen crítico, *Los trabajadores de la muerte* (1998) es la novela de Eltit que menos reflexión crítica ha suscitado. En cuanto a *Lumpérica*, no debiera sorprender que sea el texto de Eltit sobre el cual más se ha reflexionado. Es, desde todos los ángulos—lingüístico, genérico, temático, político, social, cultural—, el más fascinante de todos. Y, junto a *Por la patria*, el que más desafíos formales presenta. Jaime Donoso la llama incluso una "antinovela" (245) en el sentido de que resulta prácticamente imposible seguir una línea argumental, aunque aclarando que ello tiene que ver con "el estado interrumpido en el cual se encontraba el régimen de producción de la lengua pública" durante la dictadura (246). Como se dijo anteriormente, de acuerdo a Brito *Lumpérica* constituye una verdadera renovación de la novela. Tanto Ortega ("Diamela" 55, 63) como Olea ("El cuerpo" 90) han señalado asimismo la importancia que tienen la inscripción y la puesta en escena del cuerpo femenino en la plaza pública, plaza pública, abría que agregar, donde fuera de producirse la *performance* de una nueva identidad femenina emerge también una comunidad otra, la de los "pálidos," metáfora no sólo de los marginados sino también de los detenido-desaparecidos. Uno de los aspectos más originales de *Lumpérica* es el título, obviamente. La conexión con "lumpen" y "América" es evidente, pero, como advierte Idelber Avelar en su análisis de la obra, está presente también la conexión con "lumen" (169), particularmente si se toma en cuenta la ubicua presencia de la figura panóptica del "luminoso" que vigila a L. Iluminada y a los pálidos.

Pues bien, si al final de la diégesis de *Lumpérica* se produce el triunfo del poder autoritario encarnado en el luminoso, en *Por la patria* ocurre todo lo contrario; triunfa el sujeto subalterno y concretamente la mujer o, mejor dicho, la comunidad de mujeres guiadas por Coya devenida en Coa. Prácticamente todas las aserciones críticas sobre este texto característicamente polifónico, se refieren a su naturaleza épica: "canto épico" (Lértora, "Presentación" 14); "relato neo-épico" o "épica de resistencia" (Ortega, "Diamela" 53 y 68); "national epic" (Norat 119); "novela épica" (Arrate 147); "épica de una marginalidad social" (Olea, "El deseo" 95). Y ¿por qué es un texto épico? Porque en *Por la patria* Eltit propone la refundación de

Chile o, al decir de Brito, "la reescritura de la patria" (141). "La novela traza el proceso de una épica popular femenina desde su propia indagación como escritura... y como espacio," afirma Ortega ("Diamela" 68). Ya no estamos en ese "choreographed" o "phantom space" (184, 185) que es la plaza en *Lumpérica*, al decir de Djelal Kadir, sino en el barrio y en el bar (y también en la cárcel). Es justamente en estos sitios donde, según Nelly Richard, se produce "una gesta fundacional" que tiene como rasgo central un proceso interesantísimo: el triunfo del sujeto se realiza a la inversa, es decir, de Coya, princesa Inca, se desciende a Coa, subvirtiendo totalmente el movimiento ascendente triunfalista del héroe (masculino) y el padre (47).[14] Específicamente, la victoria de Coya/Coa, la protagonista del texto, sobre Juan, amante y carcelero a la vez—"reflejo degradado del padre" (Brito 138); "figura *contra-épica*" (Richard 40); "Coya's counter-memory" (Tierney-Tello 94)—, sería la victoria no sólo de la mujer sino de la oralidad sobre la historia oficial, del mundo indígena[15] y mestizo sobre el mundo blanco, de la ciudad real sobre la ciudad letrada. Pero sin olvidar, como nos recuerda Marina Arrate, que es un triunfo desde "la validación de las mujeres" que busca Coya/Coa (144). Desde este punto de vista, tiene razón Mary Beth Tierney-Tello cuando se refiere al intento de confeccionar una memoria colectiva de parte de Coya (80), así como del hecho de que, en gran medida—y como no debiera sorprender a ningún lector de Eltit, habría que agregar—, en *Por la patria* existe un claro esfuerzo por repensar lo materno (110-18), esfuerzo cuyo análisis realiza brillantemente Mary Green en su estudio *Diamela Eltit: Reading the Mother*. Finalmente, y antes de pasar a lo que se ha escrito sobre las subsecuentes novelas de Eltit, pienso que Carreño da en el blanco cuando señala que en este texto épico Eltit hace públicos y políticos los planteamientos más o menos privados de los textos narrativos

---

14. Olea lo dice de la siguiente manera: "*Por la patria* re-marca el cuerpo como espacio político que escabulle la heroicidad mítica, al re-armar un espacio antiheroico en la épica colectiva de mujeres" ("El cuerpo" 91-92).

15. De acuerdo a Norat, en *Por la patria* Eltit confecciona "a literary space for representing the indigenous peoples of Chile" (52), grupo que, como señala más adelante en su estudio, queda simplemente fuera de la construcción de la nación (85). En *Por la patria*, según ella, Eltit "attempts to narrate a nation of multilingual/cultural/social realities, thus demythologizing a false homogeneity that inculcates in Chileans the myth that they are the English of South America"; de este modo, sigue la autora, Coya no es sino "a symbolic figure that incarnates marginalized Chileans, including the mestiza, the Indian, the witch, the poor, and the persecuted" (85).

de Marta Brunet y José Donoso (*Memorias* 88).

En *El cuarto mundo*, la tercera novela de Eltit, el espacio público de la plaza y el barrio son reemplazados por el útero, espacio desde donde dos narradores dramáticos u homodiegéticos (Gérard Genette)[16] relatan la historia de su concepción. Al igual que en *Por la patria*, aquí también se encuentra presente el tema del incesto, salvo que son hermanos y no padre e hija quienes se involucran sexualmente. Si en *L'enfant méduse* (1991) la novelista francesa Sylvie Germain presenta el más certero retrato de las negativas repercusiones de la violación de una niña por su hermano mayor, en el texto de Eltit se describe, analípticamente y desde el punto de vista del feto masculino, la violación misma de la madre por parte del padre, violación a la que la voz dramática femenina de *Los trabajadores de la muerte* volverá una y otra vez. Como dice Ortega, "la familia es aquí la escena primaria transgredida" ("Diamela" 77). Lagos, por su parte, subrayando la naturaleza "metaficticia" (136) del texto, establece una relación entre el título de la novela y el hecho de que, lo mismo que en sus narraciones anteriores, los personajes habitan una zona periférica alejada de los centros del poder, o sea, una especie de "cuarto mundo." Norat ve en *El cuarto mundo* el desarrollo del tema de la vocación literaria desde una perspectiva feminista (27) pero destaca que aun cuando es la melliza quien narra el nacimiento, es el mellizo quien inscribe la autoridad al ser él quien formula las primeras palabras (124). Debe recordarse, al respecto, el "jostling for space" que se lleva a cabo en el interior mismo del útero (Maloof 107). En su propio juicio de la novela, Lértora pareciera reunir las opiniones críticas de Ortega y Lagos al afirmar respecto de los mellizos: "a partir de la degradación realizan todo un periplo anti épico: reverso de la metáfora de la unidad familiar, y manifestación de una falta de identidad que rebasa la experiencia individual para ser el signo de la condición de toda una comunidad: la sudaca" ("Diamela" 34).

Como se puede apreciar hasta aquí, trabajar, elaborar, inscribir, pensar y re-pensar la diferencia en toda su plenitud es lo que más distingue el proyecto literario de Eltit. Desde esta óptica, me parece acertadísimo que Lértora haya reunido bajo el título de *Una poética de literatura menor* la primera antología crítica sobre su obra. Apoyándose sobre todo en *Kafka: hacia una literatura me-*

---

16. En *Narrative Discourse. An Essay in Method* (Ithaca: Cornell U P, 1980), en la sección consagrada al concepto de "person" (243-52).

nor, de G. Deleuze y F. Guattari—aunque reconociendo el ensayo precursor de T.S. Eliot "What is Minor Poetry?"—, Lértora argumenta que la narrativa de Eltit tiene todas las características de la literatura menor. Empezando por el lenguaje, la autora hace uso de las prácticas discursivas del lenguaje mayor o predominante pero con el único propósito de subvertirlo y cuestionarlo ("Diamela" 29).[17] Este aspecto atraviesa toda la obra de Eltit, y muy particularmente sus primeras cuatro novelas, y no es un accidente que algunos críticos hayan encontrado un paralelo con la poesía de Vallejo, en particular con *Trilce* (por ejemplo Kirkpatrick 63). Política y culturalmente, a su vez, hay un máximo distanciamiento de los valores estéticos e ideológicos del momento, lo que lleva a Eltit a la construcción de textos fragmentarios pero habitados por hablas colectivas surgidas de los márgenes, como ocurre en *Por la patria* ("Diamela" 30). Finalmente, en la literatura menor se da espacio a "manifestaciones neuróticas o esquizofrénicas" ("Diamela" 31), como puede verse específicamente en *El padre mío*,[18] donde la autora transcribe el "habla" de "El Padre Mío," grabado en tres ocasiones diferentes (en 1983, 1984 y 1985) pero sin la intervención editorial que ocurre, verbigracia, en *Hasta no verte, Jesús mío* (1969), de Elena Poniatowska, o *Me llamo Rigoberta Menchú y así me nació la conciencia* (1983), ¿de Rigoberta Menchú?

En nuestras propias palabras, diríamos que la literatura menor de Eltit se manifiesta en la revelación de aquello que no se ve, en lo que, a pesar de su existencia real y cotidiana, se rechaza o se disfraza, simple y permanentemente; es ahí, en ese "erial," donde elabora la autora su poética. No existe un texto que más gráficamente ilustre esta práctica de visibilizar lo invisible que *Vaca sagrada*, su

---

17. En última instancia, en contraste con los demás escritores de la Generación del '72, Eltit persiste en la práctica de una literatura menor. Pero este mantenerse al margen ha de entenderse no sólo como una práctica lingüística o estilística sino, además, como una postura eminentemente política: impedir que sus textos entren en el circuito mercantil con la misma velocidad con la que entran textos novelísticos no solamente "populares" sino, de alguna manera, "hechos para el mercado" (mis comillas). Insisto, la literatura de Eltit es para pensar y reflexionar, no para consumir y engullir.

18. Sí, es verdad que *El padre mío* no es una novela, pero indudablemente forma parte de la literatura menor a la cual Eltit se suscribe. Es más, según Leonidas Morales, en este texto "parecieran confluir todas sus novelas" (23). Richard lo califica de "relato fronterizo" (50) mientras que Ivette Malverde se refiere a su "discurso esquizofrénico" (156), agregando que "lo recuperado y transcrito en este relato es la memoria colectiva chilena" (164).

cuarta novela. En gran medida, el protagonista de la novela es el cuerpo, específicamente el cuerpo de la mujer y sus funciones fisiológicas. En una entrevista que le hace Ana María Larraín en 1992, dice Eltit: "me sigue pareciendo que el cuerpo es un territorio moral donde ensayan su eficacia o su fracaso los sistemas de poder" (4). De acuerdo a Olea, en *Vaca sagrada* se manufactura una nueva identidad mujer mediante "la resignificación de signos femeninos desprestigiados culturalmente" ("El cuerpo" 93) y, además, a través de la plena capacidad de la mujer para el aprovechamiento máximo de sus deseos. La representación gráfica de la menstruación en el texto constituiría una suerte de celebración de esta nueva identidad. Para Green, quien culpa a los discursos oficiales sobre la maternidad por la opresión de la mujer, *Vaca sagrada* representa el primer esfuerzo de parte de Eltit por retratar abiertamente un movimiento feminista (103). Así, el motivo de la sangre menstrual en la novela, conectado tanto al deseo como a la memoria, le otorgaría a la sangre de la mujer un valor que trasciende la reproducción (97). Formalmente, aun cuando a primera vista es un texto que, como asevera Fernando Moreno, "semeja un objeto discursivo de factura tradicional" (170), la crítica concuerda en que dicha "factura" es sólo una ilusión (Norat 46).

Estructuralmente, la siguiente novela de Eltit, *Los trabajadores de la muerte*, es particularmente interesante pues, además de su conexión con el teatro—empieza con un prólogo que semeja un entremés ("A las puertas del albergue") y termina con un epílogo ("Los príncipes de las calles"), y hay también un oráculo[19]—, ofrece varias voces narrativas, la mayoría de ellas dramáticas. Al igual que en *Vaca sagrada*, aquí también los personajes circulan entre Santiago y el sur. Pero si en la primera el sur representa el lugar de la tortura, tortura de Manuel, en la segunda éste es el lugar de la venganza, venganza de la madre, quien envía a su hijo a Concepción para que, tras hacer el amor con la hija del esposo que la ha abusado y abandonado, le dé muerte. En este sentido, y como afirma Norat, hénos en *Los trabajadores de la muerte* ante la distorsión del mito de Edipo (211). Específicamente, y como señala Green, "the myth of Medea [quien para Eltit representa la figura materna más radical] functions in the novel as a counter-myth to Oedipus, in this way stripping the Oedipal narrative of its primary prestige and allow-

---

19. Francine Masiello centra su análisis justamente en estas secciones de la novela (207-17).

ing Eltit to write the mother into the Oedipal story" (136). Escrita durante la transición[20]—aunque la fecha de publicación coincide con el año en que Pinochet fue arrestado en Londres (1998)—, es claramente menos política que las novelas anteriores. Lo cual no quiere decir que no sea política, obviamente. En efecto, pienso que de todas las novelas de Eltit, ésta es la más radical en su propuesta de que, a fin de cuentas, la maternidad, el acto y el proceso de ser madre, constituye el peor enemigo de la mujer en el proceso de su liberación.

La relación madre/hijo está particularmente presente en la sexta novela de Eltit, *Los vigilantes*, pero, eso sí, el hijo aquí no es el ángel exterminador que tendrá que matar sino la manzana de la discordia que se disputan madre y padre. Hasta cierto punto un regreso a su novelística anterior—si bien para Norat el texto podría marcar un *turning point* en la escritura de Eltit (28)—, la mirada autoritaria del luminoso de *Lumpérica* se convierte en esta novela en la vigilia constante del padre. Pero también la vigilia de la madre del padre, así como la de los vecinos del barrio, quienes vigilan y espían los quehaceres diarios de madre e hijo. Y, como si no fuera poco, el hijo que no sólo vigila sino que también condena a la madre por escribir sin prestarle la atención que requiere, a pesar de que ella no escribe por placer sino para defenderse de las acusaciones del padre. Sea como fuere, sigue presente en Eltit el tema de la disfuncionalidad de la familia, pero producto esta vez de un nuevo tipo de economía, la economía neoliberal,[21] impuesta durante la dictadura y, como ha mostrado inteligentemente Tomás Moulian en su ya clásico *Chile. Anatomía de un mito* (1997), perfeccionada durante la transición. En este contexto de la "disintegration of family ties in the neoliberal age", donde el mito de la familia latinoamericana es subvertido (Masiello 136-137), el hijo, más que una bendición, representa una amenaza para el arte de la madre. "Numbers, cor-

---

20. Aun cuando no exista un consenso respecto de cuándo termina la "transición" en Chile, es un período que se extiende desde el fin de la dictadura, en 1990, hasta la llegada al poder del gobierno de derecha de Sebastián Piñera (2010). Durante este período de "democracia vigilada" o "consensuada," hubo dos gobiernos del partido de La Democracia Cristiana (Aylwin y Frei) y dos gobiernos de El Partido Socialista (Lagos y Bachelet).

21. Hasta el momento, el más concienzudo estudio sobre el neoliberalismo es el de David Harvey, *A Brief History of Neoliberalism* (2005), el cual presta cuidadosa atención a los primeros y más emblemáticos gobiernos neoliberales en la historia del neoliberalismo: los de Pinochet, Margaret Thatcher, y Ronald Reagan.

poreality, and oral expression prevail over writing: the child's presence dominates the mother's discourse and vision" (Masiello 137). Significativamente, como apunta Green apoyándose en Foucault, el poder ya no se ejerce desde arriba sino que está repartido en todo el cuerpo social (119).

Ahora bien, si existe un texto donde la colonización de las mentes y del cuerpo por parte del mercado se ejerce de manera despiadada, ese texto es *Mano de obra* (2002), el último que tendremos la ocasión de examinar antes de pasar al análisis de *Jamás el fuego nunca*. Aquí ya no estamos en la plaza sitiada ni en el bar ni en el erial ni el barrio sino en el territorio público-privado de "el súper." Sin embargo, el control sigue ejerciendo su poderío, esta vez no sobre la mujer sino sobre los trabajadores en general, quienes son constantemente asediados por cámaras, supervisores, clientes y la luz, la omnipresente luz que no se apaga nunca. "... templo panóptico del poder del consumo y de la supervisión del capital," llama al "súper" Olea ("El deseo" 99). "El súper es como mi segunda casa" (*Mano de obra* 71), señala la voz narrativa dramática que sufre una "enfermedad horaria" (*Mano* 48) y que no puede ir al baño por miedo a perder su trabajo. Aunque no estoy enteramente de acuerdo con Carreño cuando afirma que "el artista es un joven explotable" en esta novela (*Memorias* 55), sí concuerdo con ella cuando dice que *Mano de obra* constituye, por un lado, "una reflexión sobre cómo hacer una novela social luego de la caída del muro en el contexto del hipercapitalismo globalizado" (*Memorias* 82-83), y por otro, la cristalización de la "disolución de la clase trabajadora" (134). Cánovas ve la novela como la "alegoría de una sociedad de entes cosificados bajo le ley neoliberal" ("Diamela" 30), pero la entiende como una alegoría teológica donde se produce no sólo la caída del sentido del lenguaje sino también la caída del grupo en la barbarie. Estaríamos, según Olea, no sólo ante un "sujeto sin pertenencia" ("El deseo" 97) sino ante un "trabajador post sindical, post movimiento social, post proyecto político de justicia" ("El deseo" 98). *Mano de obra* daría cuenta de dos procesos: por una parte, la demonización de la "'pauperización'" del sujeto, y por otra, la "desagregación discursiva" y la consecuente "alienación psíquica" diaria de los trabajadores explotados en Chile (Blanco 129). Ortega resume así el trayecto eltitiano hasta *Mano de obra*: "En sus libros anteriores, la plaza se abría en el performance, el barrio en la protesta, el cuerpo en sus gestaciones y flujos, el orden patriarcal en el lenguaje.

Ahora, se trata de la puesta en página del eje de estas versiones: el mercado como un sueño de la razón civilizatoria" ("El polisistema" 57). No obstante, para no finalizar este compendio crítico sobre la obra de Eltit de un modo negativo, quizá haya que tener en consideración las palabras de Michael Lazzara en su análisis de las acciones de robo y pillaje por los llamados "malos clientes" en el texto: "... *Mano de obra* parece sugerir que un desafío al poder biopolítico del neoliberalismo no reside en los grandes gestos redentoristas o revolucionarios, sino en los microespacios y en las esferas minoritarias de resistencia... Es decir, la poética de Eltit... permite intuir algunas líneas de resistencia posible *desde dentro*" (163-64). Pasemos a continuación al análisis de *Jamás el fuego nunca*.[22]

Crítica de la célula

"Unidad fundamental de los organismos vivos, generalmente de tamaño microscópico, capaz de reproducción independiente y formada por un citoplasma y un núcleo rodeados por una membrana." Así define el diccionario de la Real Academia la palabra "célula" en su sentido biológico. También la define como "un grupo reducido de personas que funciona de modo independiente dentro de una organización política, religiosa, etc." Finalmente, en su tercera definición del término, se refiere a una "célula" como "una pequeña celda, cavidad o seno." En *Jamás*, el vocablo "célula," especialmente en las dos últimas acepciones aquí consignadas, constituye el corazón mismo del texto. En esencia, es la historia de una pareja de ex miembros de una organización de izquierda que, aun después de la dictadura militar, permanece en la clandestinidad en un estado de absoluta decadencia y reducida a la más abyecta pobreza. "Esta es una novela del derrumbe," señalaba Eltit en una entrevista de 2007. Curiosamente, no obstante, cuando en la misma entrevista Álvaro Matus le pregunta si acaso ésta representa "una crítica a las opciones políticas radicales," la autora responde, "No, en ningún caso me anima una crítica general. Sólo funciona para este caso, para este libro," si bien más adelante concuerda con Matus en que es evidente en el texto "el paralelo entre estas ruinas humanas y el fracaso del proyecto revolucionario." Claramente, se percibe cierta

---

22. *Jamás* desde aquí en adelante. Además, cuando se cite textualmente de esta novela, sólo se incluirá el número de página entre paréntesis.

ambigüedad en las palabras de Eltit. Es como si no hubiese querido que la acusaran de haber abandonado su postura tradicionalmente contestataria. Además, generalmente no asociamos a Eltit con un posicionamiento crítico del desempeño de los partidos políticos de izquierda en Chile. Todo lo contrario. En plena dictadura, fue una de las intelectuales que a fines de los setenta y principio de los ochenta, a través de *performances* artísticas de todo tipo, comenzó a desestabilizar el reprimido ambiente cultural chileno.[23]

Sin lugar a dudas, *Jamás* representa una nueva arista crítica del estado de cosas en el Chile actual. Lo más novedoso de su factura, a mi juicio, es que, en un contexto político-cultural que ha estado marcado por múltiples ataques tanto contra los militares como contra los civiles que colaboraron con el régimen de Pinochet, Eltit ofrece, aunque no pareciera admitirlo plenamente en la entrevista arriba mencionada, uno de los más mordaces asedios críticos contra la izquierda más extrema en Chile. Saludable y valiente gesto el suyo en círculos literarios e intelectuales donde aún resultan inmensamente escasos, si no inexistentes, las aproximaciones críticas a la izquierda tradicional.[24] En efecto, en *Jamás*, a través de una voz narrativa femenina dramática que interpela incansablemente a un tú masculino que básicamente rehúsa el diálogo, lo que se busca es escudriñar detenida y analíticamente el dogmatismo de la célula, el inherente machismo de sus miembros y, finalmente, las razones por las cuales quedaron fatalmente marginados de la historia. Este texto, en suma, constituye un tipo de memoria política a la inversa, a saber, no los acostumbrados actos de memoria típicos de la izquierda en Chile, o, en el más común de los casos, los ataques contra el blanqueamiento del pasado dictatorial, sino más bien la interrogación, desde la célula misma, sobre por qué, como sugiere

---

23. Eltit es, de hecho, una de las fundadoras del grupo de arte colectivo CADA, que, en plena dictadura y a través de múltiples actos artísticos—exposiciones de fotografía, obras de teatro, laceración del cuerpo, instalaciones, visitas a sitios marginales tales como prostíbulos y clínicas psiquiátricas, entre otros—comenzó a criticar y desafiar el ambiente político-cultural de la época. Para una visión crítica bastante completa del contexto cultural en Chile desde que se impuso la dictadura de Pinochet hasta mediados de los años ochenta, consúltese la nueva edición de *Márgenes e instituciones. Arte en Chile desde 1973* (2007), publicado por primera vez en 1986 por Richard. Consúltese también el artículo de Donoso.

24. Una excepción sería Ariel Dorfman, también miembro de la Generación del '72, quien recientemente, en *Feeding on Dreams. Confessions of an Unrepentant Exile* (2011), critica a la izquierda. A lo contrario de Eltit, no obstante, sus juicios son mucho más personales.

Matus, fracasó la revolución. Desde este ángulo, más que un mea culpa, *Jamás* viene a ser una autocrítica y sobre todo una autoevaluación que, por cierto, todavía no tiene su contrapartida ni entre quienes participaron directamente en el régimen de Pinochet ni entre los actuales líderes de la derecha. Resulta muy interesante, asimismo, que esta novela haya aparecido justo en el momento en que empezaba a sentirse en Chile un cierto cansancio con los gobiernos de la Concertación.[25]

Pero en *Jamás*, en contraste con *Mano de obra*, la atención no se centra en la actualidad sino en el pasado, específicamente en el lapso de tiempo que transcurre entre el primer encuentro de los protagonistas, anónimos en la novela, y el reencuentro de los mismos después de haber sido brutalmente torturados; cronológicamente, el período de tiempo que va desde el gobierno de Allende a probablemente las primeras semanas o los primeros meses después del golpe. La narración misma, empero, se efectúa en los primeros años del siglo en curso. El título de la novela proviene de un verso del conocido poema de César Vallejo sobre el dolor humano, "Los nueve monstruos," de *Poemas humanos*, el cual, junto con un segundo verso, aparece como epígrafe: "jamás el fuego nunca / jugó mejor su rol de frío muerto." La obra está dividida en secciones sin nombre ni número. La diégesis consiste principalmente de dos partes. La más importante, y a la vez la más extensa, es aquélla en la cual se lleva a cabo una especie de diálogo-monólogo entre una mujer y su compañero en una cama, una pieza y un comedor pequeño. La otra parte consiste de las visitas que hace la mujer a varias casas de la ciudad con el fin de limpiar y bañar a ancianos enfermos que están al borde de la muerte. Una cierta ambigüedad e incertidumbre recorre todo el texto, ya que no queda claro, en especial hacia el final del mismo, si lo que lee el lector son los sueños o pesadillas de la primera persona, o si, como en *Pedro Páramo*, la narración tiene lugar desde ultratumba, tras haber sido eliminados los diez miembros de la célula, incluyendo a la pareja de ex militantes. A continuación, veamos en qué sentido *Jamás* constituye no sólo "el obituario de una esperanza muerta," al decir de Javier Edwards, sino la crítica por excelencia de la célula y, en gran medida, el aná-

---

25. La llamada "Concertación de Partidos por la Democracia" se refiere a una coalición de partidos de izquierda, centroizquierda y centro que gobernó durante la transición (1990-2010): (Patricio Aylwin [1990-1994], Eduardo Frei Ruiz-Tagle [1994-2000], Ricardo Lagos [2000-2006], y Michelle Bachelet [2006-2010]).

lisis del derrumbe ideológico de la izquierda más intransigente en general. A fin de probar mi tesis, centro mi atención en los siguientes aspectos del texto: a) la difícil relación entre el yo femenino y el tú masculino, sin lugar a dudas la espina dorsal del texto; b) la búsqueda de un cuarto propio existencial de parte del yo dentro de la célula misma; y c) la conexión entre el espacio físico de la pareja y la ciudad.

Así alude al estado de la relación el yo: "Estamos en un estado de paz cercano a la armonía, tú ovillado en la cama, cubierto por la manta, con los ojos cerrados o entreabiertos, yo en la silla, ordenando con parsimonia y lucidez los números que nos sostienen" (17). En contraposición a cuando eran miembros activos de la célula, el yo femenino aquí, una voz narrativa plenamente dramática, tiene todo el poder. De hecho, en el transcurso de la narración éste interpela, pregunta, analiza, calcula, indaga, cuida y trabaja. El tú, en cambio, "bulto acurrucado" (35), apenas responde, duerme con los pantalones puestos, y no sale casi nunca a la calle. El yo anhela dilucidar el pasado, averiguar especialmente qué es lo que falló en la célula; al tú, encarnación viva de la derrota de la izquierda, no le interesa el pasado y tampoco entiende el presente. Acaso con el propósito de subrayar la absoluta intrascendencia de una ideología que no tiene ya relevancia en el presente, pero a la que sus más ardientes defensores siguen aferrados sin cuestionar, en el curso del texto la voz narrativa describe el estado de la relación de múltiples formas: "célula clandestina enclaustrada en la pieza" (28), "célula muerta" (79), "una célula de otro siglo o de otro milenio" (123), etc. Físicamente, aun cuando comparten el mismo "colchón ínfimo" (104), evitan tocarse a toda costa: "Libero así un pequeño espacio para mi pierna, lucho contigo para establecer la competencia en torno al ínfimo territorio que poseemos" (65). Paralelamente al derrumbe de la izquierda que se ficcionaliza en *Jamás*, destaca asimismo, como no podía ser de otro modo en una novela de Eltit, el triunfo de la mujer sobre el hombre: "Pareces, no sé, un perro" (73), "Prácticamente no te mueves. Ya no" (79). La pregunta más recurrente que le hace el yo al tú, pero que éste niega contestar, es por qué no llevaron al niño al hospital. En términos de la fábula, la muerte del hijo—al que no llevaron al hospital porque, según deduce el yo, ponía en riesgo "la totalidad de las células" (66) y quien para el tú constituía un "error de cálculo" (105)—marca, por una parte, la génesis del proceso de deterioro de la relación, y, por otra, uno de los factores que simplemente no tenía cabida en la lógica perfecta de la célula. El otro factor, aunque menos vital no menos significativo para la liberación del yo, es un vestido rojo del cual se enamora a primera vista: "de pronto experimenté el impacto ante ese vestido que... me enfrentó a la vitrina y, súbitamente, lo quise, lo quise, lo amé... Luché por sacarme los pantalones desorbitados, la blusa amorfa, el chaleco, quemarlos, aniquilarlos... y acudir ciega o virginalmente hacia el vestido para renacer o resurgir... fue lo único espontáneo" (110-11, 115).

Esto nos lleva al segundo apartado de esta sección, vale decir, a la paulatina confección de un cuarto propio al interior mismo de la célula. En su recorrido por el pasado mientras ejercía la función de analista del grupo, la voz narrativa dramática hace un recuento de cómo, por medio de preguntas y críticas, fue haciendo tambalear las certezas del tú. Uno de los aspectos de éste que más censura es el empleo de cierta retórica conceptual no para comprender sino tergiversar la realidad: "Una palabra máscara que intimidaba... Saqué mis propias conclusiones, me aferré a los términos más sencillos para distanciarme de tu hábito, la manía de apoyarte en una densidad con la que dramatizabas cada una de tus intervenciones" (26). Desde ese momento, afirma la voz narrativa, empieza a producirse al interior de las células una "crisis celular" (61, 64). Tanto al tú como a los demás miembros masculinos de la célula les resultaba difícil aceptar que una mujer pudiera poner en tela de juicio sus procedimientos, de ahí que la tildaran de "muñeca" (84), "aristocratizante" (108), y "burguesa" (108). Consciente de que las circunstancias cambian, en un discurso que yo definiría como caótico pero certero, el yo narrativo femenino pasa revista a una serie de instantes del pasado en el que fue ofreciendo sus propias aserciones críticas respecto de qué es lo que debía cambiar en la célula para que ésta pudiera seguir siendo vigente. Después de todo, señala, "Nos habíamos convertido en una célula sin destino, perdidos, desconectados, conducidos laxamente por un conjunto de palabras selectas y convincentes pero despojadas de realidad" (27). En ningún momento de la trama, por cierto, se menciona un grupo o país específico, lo cual hace posible que *Jamás* pueda leerse como una censura no solamente de las células de izquierda en Chile, tales como el MIR o el Frente Patriótico Manuel Rodríguez, por ejemplo, sino de todos los movimientos revolucionarios radicales en general. En concreto, apela a lo que denomina la "acción directa" (27) y a la necesidad urgente de "ligarnos a las bases" (59) y de "comprometer a las bases" (60). El desmantelamiento posterior de las células, efectivamente, responde en parte a la inmensa brecha que se produce entre sus miembros, y particularmente los líderes de la misma, incluido el tú, y la historia de carne y hueso: "Hoy puedo constatar que el aislamiento y la fuerte compartimentación celular nos expuso a un espacio demasiado vacío, donde las referencias terminaron por desaparecer" (82). Más aun, tal vez para hacer hincapié en el dogmatismo del grupo, y puesto que, como ya dije, el argumento del texto se sitúa en una atmósfera confusa, a través de toda la novela, tal un acusatorio coro griego, los miembros muertos de la célula se presentan en la habitación de la pareja frecuentemente: "se pasean malhumorados, tensos, nos observan con irritación... figuras... heladas y lúcidas y aún supremas en sus errores" (109, 120).

Finalmente, pasemos al tercer apartado de esta sección: la conexión entre el espacio físico de la pareja y la ciudad. A lo contrario de lo que pudiera pensarse, la ciudad no ofrece una salida a la situación claustrofóbica en la que se halla la pareja. De hecho, aun cuando no tan apocalíptica como en *Los vigilantes* pero sí tan hostil como en la tercera sección de *Los trabajadores de la muerte*, en *Jamás* la ciudad se presenta como un sitio peligroso y violento. Esta representación del espacio urbano, presente también en algunas crónicas urbanas de Pedro Lemebel y las novelas de Ramón Díaz Eterovic si bien ausentes en la narrativa de Alberto Fuguet (salvo *Tinta roja*),[26] concuerda con el cuadro desalentador de las localidades urbanas que proveen varios estudios recientes sobre la violencia en las ciudades latinoamericanas. Aunque seguramente sería injusto proveer un retrato uniforme de la ciudad latinoamericana de hoy, no cabe duda, como afirma Andrés Duany, que muchas ciudades del continente han experimentado una "pérdida de su fantástica ca-

---

26. Eltit (en *Jamás*) y Fuguet (en *Mala onda* y *Por favor, rebobinar*, por ejemplo) ofrecen un cuadro bastante diferente de la ciudad. En parte, ello responde a la diferencia generacional. Pero lo que podría llamarse el retrato positivo (Fuguet) y el retrato negativo (Eltit) de la ciudad también está estrechamente relacionado con la ideología de cada uno de estos autores. La metrópolis de Eltit, aun durante los tiempos de la transición, guarda las huellas imborrables de la violencia de Estado durante la dictadura y recoge los pedazos del desastre. Los adolescentes de *Mala onda* y los adultos jóvenes de *Por favor, rebobinar* celebran la llegada de una nueva cultura y una nueva economía—la neoliberal—y quieren hacer borrón y cuenta nueva. Consúltese mi estudio "Ni *g*robalizado ni *g*localizado: ¿la metrópolis de Fuguet o la metrópolis de Lemebel?" (2009) para un análisis de la representación de la ciudad en Fuguet.

lidad cívica" (82) como consecuencia directa de múltiples políticas neoliberales que paulatinamente han socavado el rol protector del Estado. De acuerdo al recientemente fallecido Carlos Monsiváis, la metrópolis moderna se ha convertido en el lugar donde diariamente se celebran los "rituales del caos."[27] Mabel Moraña[28] y Beatriz Sarlo,[29] por su parte, destacan el miedo como uno de los rasgos más sobresalientes en los espacios públicos hoy en día. En *Jamás* únicamente el yo narrativo tiene acceso directo a la urbe moderna; el tú, salvo muy infrecuentes salidas alrededor de la cuadra, sólo accede al mundo externo a través del periódico. Es ahí, por ejemplo, donde se encuentra con las fotos de ex militantes que ahora son grandes empresarios. En cualquier caso, tanto para el tú como para el yo, "la calle nos resulta un jeroglífico" (62), recalcando de esta manera la total desconexión entre la célula clandestina y el tiempo presente, tiempo que se presenta en el texto como "siempre colapsado" (45). La voz narrativa dramática se refiere a "una ciudad verdaderamente moderna y colapsada" (154) donde abundan los asaltos y la desconfianza entre los "anónimos ciudadanos" (147). Pero el espacio que habita la pareja no es mucho mejor tampoco. Además de carecer de ventanas, sólo tiene una "ampolleta de 25 vatios" (68). Su rutina diaria se reduce a tomar té, comer arroz o pan, e ir al baño. En resumidas cuentas, el "estábamos esperando la llegada ineludible de la historia" (36) que marca el tiempo de la militancia, se contrasta con el presente de la narración cuando, al referirse al ojo, escribe el yo, "nuestra atención se centra en la disgregación de sus partes" (55). La última novela de Eltit también podría entenderse como la representación de una cierta "disgregación," la disgregación del cuerpo y la patria, como veremos a continuación.

Radiografía de un pueblo enfermo

Impuesto a la carne[30] es la crónica de un país enfermo.[31] En

---

27. Véase su colección del mismo nombre, *Los rituales del caos* (1995, 2001).
28. En *Espacio urbano, comunicación y violencia en América Latina*.
29. En "Violencia en las ciudades. Una reflexión sobre el caso argentino."
30. *Impuesto* desde aquí en adelante.
31. La idea de concebir la nación como organismo no es nueva, lógicamente. Desde fines del siglo XIX hasta las primeras décadas del siglo XX, resultaba común, en los discursos políticos y ensayísticos en general, hacer diagnósticos de los males y

las antípodas de la obra de Bolaño, desde una perspectiva diametralmente opuesta a la de Fuguet, y al margen, muy al margen de los vaivenes del mercado editorial, la narrativa de Eltit sigue aferrada a lo local, a lo "patrio," si se quiere, reacia a escribir sobre otro tema que no sea Chile. Sí, es cierto que Bolaño trata magistralmente el tema en *Estrella distante* y *Nocturno de Chile*, y que *Mala onda*, de Fuguet, también lo hace aunque desde una óptica distinta. Pero Bolaño es un escritor "extra-territorial"—para utilizar la expresión de Ignacio Echevarría (piénsese tan sólo en *Los detectives salvajes* y, en particular, en *2666*)—y Fuguet, tanto en *Las películas de mi vida* como en *Missing (Una investigación)*, trasciende con creces la temática propiamente chilena. Ello pudiera explicarse parcialmente por el hecho de que Bolaño dejó Chile a los quince años y Fuguet vivió en Estados Unidos hasta los trece. Sea como fuere, el caso es que Eltit, porfiada, testaruda, obstinadamente vuelve al problema de Chile, vuelve a su enfermedad, sin querer ocuparse de otra cosa, en el preciso momento—¿o en los varios momentos históricos de los últimos treinta años de historia nacional?—en que éste, con bombos y platillos, se presenta a sí mismo como el país más económicamente pujante de América Latina. Sin lugar a dudas, la autora no ha podido superar el trauma de Chile. Al echar un vistazo rápido a su producción novelística, da la impresión que, independientemente de los discursos triunfalistas tanto de derecha como de izquierda, Chile será siempre un territorio enfermo. Primero fue la enfermedad de la dictadura, después la del olvido de los marginados de todo tipo y, más recientemente, la enfermedad neoliberal. Ahora, en *Impuesto*, Eltit nos ofrece nada menos que la radiografía de un pueblo enfermo. Específicamente, Chile no tanto como "nación-mercado" sino Chile-hospital o "patria médica" (83) donde, en el transcurso de lo que podría llamarse la diégesis, una hija y una madre, ésta dentro de aquella, literalmente, esperan ser curadas ansiosamente

---

las enfermedades que sufrían las naciones. La Generación del '98 en España, por ejemplo, enfocó su atención en la búsqueda de un remedio para curar España. En América Latina, el ensayista boliviano Alcides Argueda escribió *Pueblo enfermo*. El argentino Ezequiel Martínez Estrada tituló su más famoso ensayo nada menos que *Radiografía de la pampa*. Más recientemente, y como ha mostrado ejemplarmente Luis Cárcamo-Huechante en *Tramas del mercado*, justo antes de la imposición del neoliberalismo en Chile surge un discurso que, apoyado por Milton Friedman y los Chicago Boys, ve el país como un país enfermo cuya única panacea era la venta de las instituciones públicas a sectores privados y la privatización de la educación y la salud, entre otros posibles "remedios."

al mismo tiempo que entretienen la idea de vender sus riñones o su piel. Insertas en una sala de espera común donde los médicos, las enfermeras, y los "fans" las amenazan y vigilan constantemente, estas mujeres, hija y "madre bicentenaria" (74, 163), esperan a su vez la llegada de la conmemoración del Bicentenario. Como no podía ser de otra manera en Eltit, estas mujeres enfermas y "organodependientes" (127), nacidas hace "doscientos años," constituyen por así decirlo la última esperanza de la nación, una nación que les ha hecho históricamente la guerra y de la que, como dice la voz narrativa femenina dramática, hay que escribir la crónica y dejar testimonio. En ésta su última novela Eltit nos dice que no, que en Chile, aunque les pese a políticos y tecnócratas, la modernidad sigue siendo un proyecto incompleto y la postmodernidad una vaga ilusión.

Tras una breve descripción de la novela, abordaré los siguientes puntos: a) la naturaleza alegórica del texto; b) la necesidad de dar testimonio; c) la relación hija/madre; y d) la representación del tiempo. Hasta cierto punto, *Impuesto* constituye una vuelta a los temas más representativos de la obra de Eltit (desde esta perspectiva, *Mano de obra* y *Jamás* representarían más bien una excepción): la mujer como el sujeto subalterno por excelencia; el cuerpo como el *locus* donde se libra la batalla por el poder; el cuestionamiento de la historia, entre otros temas. Al igual que *Jamás*, el texto está dividido en secciones sin título, y, aun cuando consiste de un diálogo entre una hija y una madre, es la hija quien, como narradora homodiegética o "dramatized" en un nivel intradiegético, siguiendo a Genette, reproduce el discurso de la madre las pocas veces que ésta habla. Eltit sustituye aquí la plaza o el súper por el hospital. Lingüísticamente, *Impuesto* es una novela plenamente "lisible." Eso sí, hay dos aspectos estilísticos de su discurso que lo caracterizan. Por un lado, la presencia, a lo largo del texto, de partes de oraciones que repiten, secuencialmente, la misma palabra: "... un dolor inimaginable en cada segundo, en cada segundo, en cada segundo" (154); "... los escalofriantes años que ya siento cómo se vienen en picada en contra de nosotras decididos a acuchillarnos, a acuchillarnos, a acuchillarnos" (174). Por otro, oraciones que, por su disposición en el texto, semejan poemas: "Ella. / Mi madre. / Viva. / Sí. / Furiosa. / Respirando adentro de mí" (128), además de otras (129, 144, 167, 175). Aunque profundizaré en ello en la sección correspondiente, cabe señalar que, temáticamente, hay cuatro rasgos de la novela que de alguna manera marcan su ritmo. En primer lugar, la insistencia de parte de la voz narrativa que su madre habita dentro de su cuerpo:[32] "Mi mamá está absolutamente callada adentro de mi pecho, pequeñita, encogida como un retazo antropológico mi madre" (47). En segundo lugar, la insistencia de que ella y su madre están solas en el mundo:[33] "entiende que somos dos ancianas solas en el mundo" (60). En tercer lugar, y aun más persistentemente, la referencia, casi siempre en forma de pregunta, a la indeterminación del tiempo en el cual sucedió tal o cual evento:[34] "¿Cuántos?, ¿doscientos años?, ¿o más?, no lo sé, mi madre tampoco" (33). El número que más se repite es el doscientos, como no podía ser de otro modo en un texto cuyo tiempo de la narración coincide con el tiempo de la historia, tiempo que marca la conmemoración del nacimiento de la patria en la trama. En cuarto lugar, la repetición, a lo largo del texto, de la frase "la nación o la patria o el país" (10) con variantes tales como "La patria o el país o el territorio o el hospital" (18), o bien "una nación o un país o una patria médica" (31).[35] Finalmente, como para despejar cualquier duda sobre dónde se realizan los acontecimientos, se utiliza el adjetivo "chileno/a" varias veces. Por ejemplo, refiriéndose a su madre, dice la voz narrativa, "había sobrevivido a una de las hemorragias más radicales de la historia chilena" (29). Asimismo, "Hemos pasado, ¿cuánto?, ¿dos siglos?, en suelo chileno, sí, dos siglos conectados entre sí por la sensación indestructible de la angustia" (116); "este médico nos mira con su cara rara, curiosa, una cara chilena fuera de sí porque está preocupado" (124); "La enferma y yo tenemos un físico, una forma de hablar y de mover los ojos y la mandíbula que nos confirma a las dos como chilenas" (165).

Análogamente a casi todas las novelas de Eltit, *Impuesto* tiene que leerse como un texto eminentemente alegórico. En concreto, es la alegoría de Chile no sólo como país enfermo sino también como país explotado y ultrajado. Esta idea se ilustra sobre todo al final de la diégesis, cuando se produce la fusión madre/hija y territorio físico:

> Ya es tarde para nosotras. El territorio puso en marcha un ope-

---

32. (47, 88, 91, 95, 107, 111, 114, 121, 127, 128, 131, 149, y 165, 181, 182, 184, y 185).
33. (24, 33, 41, 60, 77, 82, 103, 106, 115 y 152).
34. (22, 28, 29, 31, 33, 37, 46, 51, 57, 58, 79, 89, 94, 100, 107, 116, 121, 130, 135, 142, 144, 146, 148, 156, 171, 173, 174, 176, 181, y 185).
35. Ver también 35, 50, 57, 67, 104, 105, 107, 108, 113, 116-17, 121, 129, 139, 155, 164, 166, 180, 181, 186, y 187.

rativo para decretar la demolición y la expatriación de nuestros cuerpos. Minas. Minerales. Nuestros huesos cupríferos serán molidos en la infernal máquina chancadora. El polvo cobre del último estadio de nuestros huesos terminará fertilizando el subsuelo de un remoto cementerio chino. (187)

Si *Mano de obra* retrata los efectos devastadores del sistema neoliberal en la clase trabajadora, aquí en *Impuesto* se muestra el *non plus ultra* del capitalismo tardío, cuando ya nada está fuera del circuito del mercado. Alegóricamente, hija y madre simbolizan la patria misma que se desangra. "El castigo interminable de un territorio que me saca sangre, me saca sangre, me saca sangre, me saca sangre. Que me saca sangre" (80). Los médicos representan la clase adinerada o dirigente que desde la misma fundación del nación explota la sangre de la patria: "[los médicos] Nos han sacado mucha sangre y este hecho es el que obliga a mi mamá a pensar en el principio de nosotras: en su hemorragia y en nuestro nacimiento" (24). Las alusiones a la sangre recorren todo el texto, en efecto: la madre que sangra incontrolablemente (115-18); la madre que quiere vender su sangre (124); los médicos que codician la sangre de los enfermos (153). Pero en esta alegoría donde todo está a la venta, donde, efectivamente, el cuerpo de la patria está a la venta, se rifan también la piel y los riñones (132-33) y se venden igualmente los dientes y los dedos (138) además de apostarse las córneas (173). No queda muy claro en el texto qué podrían simbolizar tanto las llamadas "barras futboleras" como los "fans," a quienes se menciona repetidas veces como presencias amenazantes y peligrosas en la novela.[36] Las "barras" podrían simbolizar los miembros de la clase política en un momento postpolítico y los "fans" podrían representar a la gente común y corriente que simplemente pasa de lo político y se adhiere al sistema sin cuestionarlo. Sea como fuere, en cualquier caso, hay que decir que aunque *Impuesto* sea una novela predominantemente alegórica tiene un origen bastante real. Por un lado, una posible crítica al sistema privado de salud en Chile y, por otro, la condena de una clase política que permite la explotación a ultranza de su territorio sin tomar en cuenta los costos a largo plazo.

Además de ser una alegoría de Chile, *Impuesto* es también un testimonio, o al menos quiere ser un testimonio. ¿No tienen acaso un carácter testimonial, por otro lado, los textos de miem-

---

36. Ver 74, 76-77, 87, 89, 100, 106, 109,113, 117, 121, 125, 129, 131, 140, 152, 164, y 182.

bros de la Generación del '72 tales como Luisa Valenzuela, Cristina Peri Rossi, Dorfman (en particular) y Fernando Vallejo? En efecto, como en muchos textos coloniales—y particularmente en *Historia verdadera de la conquista de México*, de Bernal Díaz del Castillo, por ejemplo—, el yo narrativo dramático de *Impuesto* insiste en dar cuenta, en dejar constancia, en hacer público, en impedir que su historia caiga en el olvido. Desde este punto de vista, podría pensarse como texto épico al igual que *Por la patria*. No se trata aquí de la escritura como actividad individual—como, verbigracia, la madre que escribe frenéticamente en *Los vigilantes*—sino como empresa colectiva que busca la erección de una memoria. A lo largo de la novela se emplean diversos términos para referirse al texto que servirá para recoger los recuerdos de la historia: "relato" (31), "crónica" (31), "testimonio" (32), "escritos" (61), "documento" (61), "confesión" (128) y, finalmente, "la historia de los huesos" (174). En cierta medida, el libro que el lector tiene en sus manos es justamente el documento o testimonio al que se alude en *Impuesto*. Pero, ¿de qué quiere dejar constancia la voz narrativa dramática? Ésta, hablando también por su madre, lo dice de tres formas. Primero, "... clarificar cuándo y cómo se gestó nuestra postergación" (34); segundo, "Vamos a generar el gran manual histórico del maltrato y la postergación" (82); y, tercero, "Sólo intentamos, de manera pausada o solapada, escribir la crónica más ardiente de la postergación" (172). Lo que se anhela, en última instancia, es la creación de una comunidad, la comunidad de los marginados. Significativamente, en un contexto en que el Estado brilla por su ausencia y los partidos políticos tradicionales ya no tienen el poder de antaño, hacia el final del texto se convoca a la lucha particular de la "comuna," una clara alusión no sólo a la Guerra de los Comuneros en España en el siglo XVI sino a múltiples movimientos revolucionarios a través de la historia: "Mi madre y yo acordamos, una vez que nuestras esperanzas de acceder a los porvenires nacionales se han pulverizado, hablar sólo de nuestra comuna, de todas y cada una de las comunas por las que hemos pasado… Sólo en la comuna radica la única posibilidad de poner en marcha la primera gran mutual del cuerpo" (182). Lo curioso, no obstante, es que aun cuando la narradora dramática alude a ella y a su madre como "las más confiables historiadoras inorgánicas de nuestro extenso tiempo" (33), la madre no quiere que la hija hable bajo ningún motivo. "Cállate" (79, 95), le dice cada vez que la hija quiere relatar algún aspecto negativo de la historia, o bien cuando menciona específicamente las palabras "tortura" (72) o "hambre" (160-161). "Mi madre se queja adentro de mí, gruñe y gruñe y me dice no, no, no lo digas, no lo sigas diciendo, no... Está asustada mi mamá y me implora" (182). Irónicamente, hacia el final de la trama, en la ceremonia de celebración del Bicentenario, a hija y madre sólo se les da tres segundos para hablar ante las cámaras, y sólo para decir "gracias": "Mami, nosotras no podemos hablar de la historia, sólo estamos autorizadas para decir gracias o muchas gracias" (113).

Uno de los aspectos más enigmáticos y originales de *Impuesto*, a mi parecer, es precisamente la relación hija/madre. Y me refiero, por supuesto, al hecho concreto de que la madre viva dentro de la hija. Indudablemente, en esta imagen se cristalizan dos temas fundamentales en el ideario eltitiano: el cuerpo y la mujer. A través de toda la trama, la voz narrativa hace frecuentes alusiones al hecho de que ella y su madre son "bajas," "feas," "ancianas," y "morenas".[37] Los médicos, por el contrario, son "altos," "blancos," y "rubios" (13, 27). Teniendo en cuenta que ésta es una alegoría, se critica aquí la incontrovertible verdad de que en Chile el color de la piel y la altura determinan hasta cierto punto la posición social: "Todavía busco una fórmula para hacerme visible," dice la narradora. "Yo soy baja. Baja en todo sentido. Habito en los escalafones más insignificantes del tendedero social... Soy baja. Y mi estatura marcó y marca aún todos los niveles de mi existencia" (130). "... ese aire bajo, bajo, bajo, bajo que los médicos advierten y desprecian" (140). En una clara señal de la permanente tensión que caracteriza la relación hija/madre, la hija hace referencia a "las fantasías nacionales de altura" (29) de parte de su madre. Sin embargo, así como condena su complejo de inferioridad, recalca también que su madre es una "madre anarquista" (98, 127, 140, 145). Así, el diálogo-monólogo hija/madre está lleno de tensiones que se traducen, por un lado, en la presencia de conflictos, y, por otro, en actos de reconocimiento. Producto de un aborto fallido, la voz narrativa está consciente de que, con su nacimiento, "arruinó [los] planes" de su madre (24) y de que la maternidad es un peso enorme (103-04). A su vez, hija y madre discrepan sobre la realidad de los hechos (27, 54, 141) y se acusan mutuamente de mentir (133). Pero por sobre todas estas cosas, lo que distingue la relación es su naturaleza íntima e incondicional. "Alianza indisoluble" es la expresión que utiliza

---

37. Ver 25, 44, 56, 72, 130, 140, 157, 166, y 171.

la narradora para referirse a la relación con su madre (79).

En la penúltima sección de este artículo, quisiera referirme al tema del tiempo en la novela. Aunque queda más o menos claro que la voz narrativa narra desde un tiempo presente, es una narración que por así decir existe en una suerte de no-tiempo, puesto que, a nivel de la fábula, se sugieren eventos que cronológicamente van desde la fundación de la nación hasta la celebración de sus doscientos años de existencia. Para enfatizar el hecho de que la voz que relata y su madre representan a todas las hijas y madres a lo largo de la historia chilena, así como el hecho de que, durante este largo período, su situación en la esfera político-social no ha mejorado sustancialmente, la cantidad de años que más frecuentemente aparece en el texto, los "doscientos años," figura casi siempre como pregunta: "¿doscientos años?" Esto no significa, empero, que no se marque el paso del tiempo en la novela. Todo lo contrario, se utilizan diferentes expresiones para consignarlo: "hasta ese día" (23); "fans del primer tiempo" (44); "la nación que nos maltrataba" (50); "ahora estamos sentadas" (81); "Hoy nos notificaron que" (107); "Estoy agotada" (112); "más adelante me describiré apropiadamente" (116); "no me interrumpas" (117); "Ahora mismo entra" (153), etc. No hay que olvidar, como ya se ha dicho, que *Impuesto* es la crónica de un pueblo enfermo y, más específicamente, el testimonio de la mujer: "mi mamá y yo somos anarquistas y tenemos la obligación histórica de redactar las memorias de la angustia y del desvalor" (156). Y más adelante, "sí[,] doscientos años en que estamos siempre, siempre, siempre en el mismo lugar, en el infinito e incomprensible lugar de madres e hijas esperando su turno, cualquiera, esperando una hora, cualquiera, y esperando ser invitadas a un festejo, cualquiera" (148-49). Ahora bien, aun cuando la meta consiste en "redactar las memorias de la angustia y del desvalor," más que elaborarse detalladamente en el texto los eventos históricos que constituyen dichas memorias, éstos se sugieren solamente, como dije arriba. La fundación de la nación, por ejemplo, coincide con el nacimiento de la madre y de la hija. La alusión a "un cabildo de médicos" (30) así como a "un médico considerado un verdadero héroe o un prócer" (38), remite obviamente al período colonial. Para marcar el período histórico que va desde los últimos decenios del siglo XIX hasta las primeras décadas del siglo XX, la voz narrativa dramática menciona tanto "la insurrección del norte" (79) como "la larga marcha del norte" (95), una clarísima referencia no sólo a la marcha de mineros del salitre que culminará en la famosa matanza en la escuela Domingo Santa María el año 1907 en la ciudad de Iquique, sino también a las múltiples huelgas y manifestaciones de trabajadores a lo largo de la historia chilena. Significativamente, el norte, donde histórica y actualmente se genera la mayor cantidad de ingresos para Chile—aunque sin que por ello se beneficie económicamente como debiera esta región—se convierte en *Impuesto* en un símbolo que define el lugar de la lucha y la esperanza: "Piensa en el norte," le dice la hija a su madre, "en la marcha que iniciaremos de manera reiterativa en el norte" (161). Y, más tarde, "nosotras viajaremos al norte. A buscar nuestra comuna" (168). A pesar de que no se menciona directamente el derrocamiento de Salvador Allende el once de septiembre de 1973, sí se menciona "el desastre" (160) y, a través de todo el texto, se establece una clara relación entre el sistema médico y el régimen militar, sugiriendo que los médicos, en vez de representar a la clase adinerada y dirigente, como se dijo arriba, representan más bien todos los poderes que, históricamente, han oprimido a la mujer. Fuera de que se habla de "médico general" (115), se habla también, en conexión con los médicos del hospital, de "El conjunto de generales" (53), de "los generales (54), y de "Un general" (90) y "su cargo nacional (o patriótico)" (112). Finalmente, el acontecimiento histórico que marca el tiempo presente de la narración, recibe nombres tales como "conmemoración" (118, 122, 143), "conmemoración nacional" (12), y "celebración" (120, 168).

Conclusión

En términos amplios, no existe una transformación sustancial entre *Impuesto* y las novelas de Eltit publicadas anteriormente. Aunque los temas que se tratan en cada una de ellas no sean idénticos, todos forman parte de una misma temática general: el tema de Chile como país enfermo donde, a pesar de las exitosas cifras macroeconómicas, siguen existiendo problemas.[38] De ahí que la literatura de Eltit, aunque a primera vista no lo parezca, sea una literatura esencialmente comprometida. En sus primeras cuatro

---

38. Pese a que, en términos macroeconómicos, Chile sigue figurando como uno de los países más productivos de América Latina, no dejan de aparecer estudios que hablan de la gran desigualdad que existe en el país. Véanse, por ejemplo, el reciente artículo de *The Economist* (sin autor), "Progress and its Discontents" (http://www.economist.com/node/21552566), así como los artículos de Viñas y Diaz.

novelas, el tema de la marginación de la mujer en particular y de los marginados en general, va unido de una u otra forma a la crítica de la dictadura (este aspecto netamente feminista de Eltit la acerca mucho más a Peri Rossi y Valenzuela que a Mistral y Bombal, por ejemplo). En las siguientes novelas, sigue presente la preocupación por la condición subalterna de la mujer así como la de los sujetos marginales de toda laya, pero conectado ahora a la crítica de un sistema económico—el neoliberal—implantado a la fuerza durante el régimen de Pinochet y perfeccionado durante los gobiernos de la Concertación. En cuanto a la forma, es obvio que, desde *Los trabajadores de la muerte* en adelante, los textos de Eltit son mucho más *lisible* que *scriptible*. En contraste con la mayoría de los autores de la "Generación del '72," Eltit no es una escritora "global." Todo lo contrario, es una autora local interesada sobre todo en los problemas nacionales (al igual que, por ejemplo, autores de la "Generación del '72" tales como Luisa Valenzuela, Fernando Vallejo, y Reinaldo Arenas en algunas de sus obras). Su pariente más próximo en la literatura chilena actual en este sentido sería indudablemente Lemebel. Ahora bien, las preguntas que habría que hacerse, y que se hacen quienes conocen la obra de ambos escritores, son: ¿Está Chile tan mal, es que acaso no ha mejorado la situación de la mujer en Chile, no existe ahora, finalmente, la ley del divorcio, no bajaron de manera sustancial los índices de pobreza durante los gobiernos de la Concertación, no existe acaso una mayor aceptación de los homosexuales? Paradójicamente, a pesar de que Chile es uno de los países más desiguales del planeta, hay que responder positivamente a estas preguntas. Es evidente que el país está mucho mejor que cuando Eltit publicó *Lumpérica* en 1983. Pero no hay que olvidar que ella escribe sobre los problemas, no sobre los triunfos, como en cierto sentido lo hace Fuguet, y que detrás de los triunfos hay siempre residuos problemáticos. La última pregunta que habría que hacerse para concluir entonces, es: si ya escribió sobre la plaza, el erial, el barrio, el bar, la casa, el súper, y el hospital, ¿en qué lugar de la sociedad chilena encontrará la enfermedad esta brillante doctora de las letras chilenas en su próxima novela? En vista de las actuales circunstancias tocantes a los severos problemas que afectan a la educación en Chile, no debiera sorprendernos que ese lugar sea la escuela.

Obras citadas

Arrate P., Marina. "Los significados de la escritura y su relación con la identidad femenina latinoamericana en *Por la patria*, de Diamela Eltit." En *Una poética de literatura menor: la narrativa de Diamela Eltit*. Ed. Juan Carlos Lértora. Santiago: Editorial Cuarto Propio, 1993. 141-54.

Avelar, Idelber. *The Untimely Present. Postdictatorial Latin American Fiction and the Task of Mourning*. Durham: Duke U P, 1999.

Blanco, Fernando A. "Poéticas y prácticas de la alienación." En *Diamela Eltit: redes locales, redes globales*. Ed. Rubí Carreño Bolívar. Madrid/Santiago: Iberoamericana/Vervuert/Pontificia Universidad Católica de Chile, 2009. 125-32.

Booth, Wayne C. *The Rhetoric of Fiction*. Chicago: University of Chicago Press, 1961.

Brito, Eugenia. *Campos minados (literatura post-golpe en Chile)*. Santiago: Editorial Cuarto Propio, 1990.

Cánovas E., Rodrigo. *Novela Chilena. Nuevas generaciones. El abordaje de los húerfanos*. Santiago: Ediciones Universidad Católica de Chile, 1997.

—. "Diamela Eltit. Algunos años antes, algunos años después." En *Diamela Eltit: redes locales, redes globales*. Ed. Rubí Carreño Bolívar. Madrid/Santiago: Iberoamericana/Vervuert/ Pontificia Universidad Católica de Chile, 2009. 25-32.

Cárcamo-Huechante, Luis E. "Hacia una trama *localizada* del mercado: Crónica urbana y economía barrial en Pedro Lemebel." En *Más allá de la ciudad letrada. Crónicas y espacios urbanos*. Eds. Boris Muñoz y Silvia Spitta. Pittsburgh: Instituto Internacional de Literatura Iberoamericana, 2003: 99-115.

—. *Tramas del mercado. Imaginación económica, cultura pública y literatura en el Chile de fines del siglo veinte*. Santiago: Editorial Cuarto Propio, 2007.

Carreño Bolívar, Rubí. *Diamela Eltit: redes locales, redes globales*. Madrid/Santiago: Iberoamericana/Vervuert/Pontificia Universidad Católica de Chile, 2009.

—. *Memorias del nuevo siglo: jóvenes, trabajadores y artistas en la novela chilena reciente*. Santiago: Editorial Cuarto Propio, 2009.

Castro-Klarén, Sara. "Escritura y cuerpo en *Lumpérica*." En *Una poética de literatura menor: la narrativa de Diamela Eltit*. Ed. Juan Carlos Lértora. Santiago: Editorial Cuarto Propio, 1993. 97-110.

Diccionario de la lengua española. Vigésima segunda edición. http://buscon.rae.es/draeI/SrvltConsulta?TIPO_BUS=3&LEMA=c%C3%A9lula [consultado el 14 de octubre de 2010]

Diaz, Rodolfo. "Socioeconomic Inequality in Chile." *Harvard International Review* (December 22, 2010): http://hir.harvard.edu/pressing-change/socioeconomic-inequality-in-chile-0

Donoso, Jaime. "Práctica de la Avanzada: *Lumpérica* y la figuración de la escritura como fin de la representación burguesa de la literatura y el arte." En *Diamela Eltit: redes locales, redes globales*. Ed. Rubí Carreño Bolívar. Madrid/Santiago: Iberoamericana-Vervuert/Pontificia Universidad Católica de Chile, 2009. 239-60.

Dorfman, Ariel. *Feeding on Dreams. Confessions of an Unrepentant Exile*. New York: Houghton Mifflin Harcourt Publishing Company, 2011.

Duany, Andrés. "New Urbanism's Latin Connection/La conexión latinoamericana del nuevo urbanismo/Interview with/Entrevista con: Andrés Duany." En *Aula: Architecture and Urbanism in las Américas* 3 (2002): 82-83.

Echevarría, Ignacio. "Bolaño extraterritorial." En *Bolaño salvaje*. Eds. Edmundo Paz Soldán y Gustavo Faverón Patriau. Barcelona: Editorial Candaya, 2008. 431-45.

Edwards, Javier. "Obituario para una esperanza muerta." *Revista de libros* de *El Mercurio* (domingo 15 de Julio de 2007). http://www.letras.s5.com/de1607071.htm [consultado el 14 de octubre de 2010].

Eltit, Diamela. *El cuarto mundo*. Santiago: Seix Barral, 1988, 1996.

—. Entrevista. "El cuerpo femenino es un territorio moral." Por Ana María Larraín. *Revista de libros* de *El Mercurio* (domingo 5

de enero de 1992): 3-5.
—. *El infarto del alma*. Santiago: F. Zegers, 1994.
—. *El Padre Mío*. Santiago: LOM Ediciones, 1989, 2003.
—. *Emergencias. Escritos sobre literatura, arte y política*. Santiago: Planeta, 2000.
—. Entrevista. "Esta es una novela del derrumbe." Por Álvaro Matus. *Revista de Libros* de *El Mercurio* (domingo 15 de Julio de 2007). http://www.letras.s5.com/de160707.htm [consultado el 20 de octubre de 2010].
—. *Impuesto a la carne*. Santiago: Seix Barral, 2010.
—. *Jamás el fuego nunca*. Santiago: Seix Barral, 2007.
—. *Los trabajadores de la muerte*. Santiago: Seix Barral, 1998.
—. *Los vigilantes*. Santiago: Editorial Sudamericana, 1994.
—. *Lumpérica*. Santiago: Seix Barral, 1983, 1998.
—. *Mano de obra*. Santiago: Planeta, 2002.
—. *Por la patria*. Santiago: Editorial Cuarto Propio, 1986, 1995.
—. *Puño y letra*. Santiago: Seix Barral, 2005.
—. *Vaca sagrada*. Buenos Aires: Planeta, 1991.
García Corales, Guillermo. "La desconstrucción en *Lumpérica*." En *Una poética de literatura menor: la narrativa de Diamela Eltit*. Ed. Juan Carlos Lértora. Santiago: Editorial Cuarto Propio, 1993. 111-25.
Genette, Gérard. *Narrative Discourse. An Essay in Method*. Trad. Jane E. Lewin. Ithaca: Cornell U P, 1980.
Germain, Sylvie. *L'enfant méduse*. Paris: Gallimard, 1991.
Green, Mary. *Diamela Eltit. Reading the Mother*. London: Tamesis, 2007.
Harvey, David. *A Brief History of Neoliberalism*. Oxford: Oxford University Press, 2005.
Hozven, Roberto. "La escritura disidente de Diamela Eltit." En *Diamela Eltit: redes locales, redes globales*. Ed. Rubí Carreño Bolívar. Madrid/Santiago: Iberoamericana-Vervuert/Pontificia Universidad Católica de Chile, 2009. 75-90.

Hutcheon, Linda. *A Poetics of Postmodernism. History, Theory, Fiction.* New York: Routledge, 1988.

Jameson, Fredric. *Postmodernism, or, the Cultural Logic of Late Capitalism.* Durham: Duke U P, 1991.

Kadir, Djelal. *The Other Writing. Postcolonial Essays in Latin America's Writing Culture.* West Lafayette: Purdue U P, 1993.

Kirkpatrick, Gwen. "La materialidad del lenguaje en la narrativa de Diamela Eltit." En *Diamela Eltit: redes locales, redes globales.* Ed. Rubí Carreño Bolívar. Madrid/Santiago: Iberoamericana-Vervuert/Pontificia Universidad Católica de Chile, 2009. 61-73.

Kulawik, Krzyztof. *Travestismo lingüístico. El enmascaramiento de la identidad sexual en la narrativa latinoamericana barroca.* Madrid: Iberoamericana, 2009.

Lagos, María Inés. "Reflexiones sobre la representación del sujeto en dos textos de Diamela Eltit: *Lumpérica* y *El cuarto mundo*." En *Una poética de literatura menor: la narrativa de Diamela Eltit.* Ed. Juan Carlos Lértora. Santiago: Editorial Cuarto Propio, 1993. 127-40.

Lazzara, Michael J. "Estrategias de dominación y resistencia corporales: las biopolíticas del mercado en *Mano de obra*, de Diamela Eltit." En *Diamela Eltit: redes locales, redes globales.* Ed. Rubí Carreño Bolívar. Madrid/Santiago: Iberoamericana-Vervuert/Pontificia Universidad Católica de Chile, 2009. 155-64.

Lértora, Juan Carlos. "Diamela Eltit: Hacia una poética de literatura menor." En *Una poética de literatura menor: la narrativa de Diamela Eltit.* Ed. Juan Carlos Lértora. Santiago: Editorial Cuarto Propio, 1993. 27-35.

—. "Presentación." En *Una poética de literatura menor: la narrativa de Diamela Eltit.* Ed. Juan Carlos Lértora. Santiago: Editorial Cuarto Propio, 1993. 11-15.

—. *Una poética de literatura menor: la narrativa de Diamela Eltit.* Santiago: Editorial Cuarto Propio, 1993.

Maloof, Judy. "Alienation, Incest and Metafictional Discourse in Diamela Eltit's *El cuarto mundo*." *Revista hispánica mo-*

derna 1 (1996): 107-20.

Malverde Disselkoen, Ivette. "Esquizofrenia y literatura: la obsesión discursiva en *El padre mío*, de Diamela Eltit." En *Una poética de literatura menor: la narrativa de Diamela Eltit*. Ed. Juan Carlos Lértora. Santiago: Editorial Cuarto Propio, 1993. 155-66.

Masiello, Francine. *The Art of Transition. Latin American Culture and Neoliberal Crisis*. Durham: Duke U P, 2001.

Monsiváis, Carlos. *Los rituales del caos*. México: Ediciones Era, 1995, 2001.

Morales T., Leonidas. *De muertos y sobrevivientes. Narración chilena moderna*. Santiago: Editorial Cuarto Propio, 2008.

Moraña, Mabel. "Introducción." En *Espacio urbano, comunicación y violencia en América Latina*. Ed. Mabel Moraña. Pittsburg: Instituto Internacional de Literatura Iberoamericana, 2002: 9-15.

Moreno T., Fernando. "*Vaca sagrada*: goce y transgresión." En *Una poética de literatura menor: la narrativa de Diamela Eltit*. Ed. Juan Carlos Lértora. Santiago: Editorial Cuarto Propio, 1993. 167-83.

Moulian, Tomás. *Chile actual. Anatomía de un mito*. Santiago: LOM-ARCIS, 1997.

Norat, Gisela. *Marginalities. Diamela Eltit and the Subversion of Mainstream Literature in Chile*. Newark: U of Delaware P, 2002.

Olea, Raquel. "El cuerpo-mujer. Un recorte de lectura en la narrativa de Diamela Eltit." En *Una poética de literatura menor: la narrativa de Diamela Eltit*. Ed. Juan Carlos Lértora. Santiago: Editorial Cuarto Propio, 1993. 83-95.

—. "El deseo de los condenados: constitución y disolución del sujeto popular en dos novelas de Diamela Eltit, *Por la patria* y *Mano de obra*." En *Diamela Eltit: redes locales, redes globales*. Ed. Rubí Carreño Bolívar. Madrid/Santiago: Iberoamericana-Vervuert/Pontificia Universidad Católica de Chile, 2009. 91-102.

Onega, Susana, y José Ángel García Landa, eds. *Narratology*. London: Longman, 1996.

Ortega, Julio. "Diamela Eltit y el imaginario de la virtualidad." En *Una poética de literatura menor: la narrativa de Diamela Eltit*. Ed. Juan Carlos Lértora. Santiago: Editorial Cuarto Propio, 1993. 53-81.

—. "El polisistema narrativo de Diamela Eltit." En *Diamela Eltit: redes locales, redes globales*. Ed. Rubí Carreño Bolívar. Madrid/Santiago: Iberoamericana-Vervuert/Pontificia Universidad Católica de Chile, 2009. 49-59.

Pastén, Agustín. "Ni *gr*obalizado ni *gl*ocalizado: ¿la metrópolis de Fuguet o la metrópolis de Lemebel? *Diseño urbano y paisaje* (Universidad Central, Chile) 17 (2009): 1-35. http://www.ucentral.cl/dup/pdf/17_ni_grobalizado_ni_glocalizado_ed.pdf

Richard, Nelly. *Márgenes e instituciones. Arte en Chile desde 1973*. Santiago: Ediciones Metales Pesados, 2007.

Sarlo, Beatriz. "Violencia en las ciudades. Una reflexión sobre el caso argentino." En *Espacio urbano, comunicación y violencia en América Latina*. Ed. Mabel Moraña. Pittsburg: Instituto Internacional de Literatura Iberoamericana, 2002: 205-14.

Sklodowska, Elzbieta. *La parodia en la nueva novela hispanoamericana*. Purdue U Monographs in Romance Languages 34. Amsterdam: Benjamins, 1990.

Tierney-Tello, Mary Beth. *Allegories of Transgression and Transformation. Experimental Fiction by Women Writing Under Dictatorship*. Albany: State U of New York P, 1996.

Viñas, Silvia. "The Inequality Behind Chile's Prosperity." *Council on Hemispheric Affairs* (November 23, 2011). http://www.coha.org/the-inequality-behind-chiles-prosperity/.

Williams, Raymond Leslie. *The Twentieth-Century Spanish American Novel*. Austin: U of Texas P, 2003.

Antonio Skármeta's Uniqueness
Randolph D. Pope
University of Virginia

I. "Juntos pero no mezclados" [Together, but not mixed]

What makes a writer unique? Why should we care about Antonio Skármeta (b. 1940) and wonder about his international success? So much is shared among writers—language, historical circumstances, methods of production and distribution, gender, a similar bone structure—that one can easily lift away from the particular and get a bird's eye view of a general framework that includes Skármeta as well as thousands of other writers. And yet there is a resilience that prevents his exchange for another male Chilean writer who participated in the political events that branded so many in his generation: Allende's election, Pinochet's coup, and exile.[1] We are not searching for a single factor that accounts for distinction. The uniqueness of an author is diverse from case to case, subtle, faint, a tinge more than a full color, and blended into a vast amount of shared experiences, topics, concerns, traditions, and all that goes into writing. As cities share elements, such as streets, stores, sewage treatment, traffic rules, mail distribution, and so on, ultimately constituting synergistically very different Cochabamba, Mendoza, Santiago, or Paris, so writers are a constellation, a wide system rooted in time and space, collective and personal memory,

---

1. For the impact of exile and diaspora in recent decades, see Amy K. Kaminsky's thoughtful and informative *After Exile: Writing the Latin American Diaspora*.

main language systems and slang, with millennia of literature at their disposal, and a creative capacity which manifests itself differently. As there are many cities, there are innumerable producers of literature, among them some essential providers for the entertainment industry, others modestly typing ephemeral instant messages, all with their own merit. And yet a few stories or novels gain for themselves at least a temporary widespread presence and are reiterated in numerous editions, pinned into anthologies, encrusted in curricula, mentioned at conferences and morphed for television or movies. Skármeta's "La Cenicienta en San Francisco," "El ciclista del San Cristóbal," "La composición," *No pasó nada* and *Ardiente paciencia* are examples of survivals in the hunger games of literary distribution.[2]

There is one more step to consider beyond becoming particularly recognizable in the original language and in the area of its circulation. Very few writers acclaimed in their country and language actually become international bestsellers and surface in translations with real success. There are of course numerous translations that never take flight, yet do serve to add glow to writers' profiles and receptions at embassies. They await to be discovered, and perhaps find unexpected readers in Helsinki or Budapest, but I am pointing here to those that take residence in many other literatures. As paragons, Cervantes and Goethe, Rumi and Ibsen, Balzac and Dostoevsky are familiar, nested and prolific in numerous and simultaneous languages and traditions. They are commodities, satisfying needs in vastly different markets without it mattering, to

2. For an excellent overview of Skármeta's work one can consult Grínor Rojo's "Celebración de Antonio Skármeta," and, for an earlier period, Donald L. Shaw's *Antonio Skármeta and the Post Boom*. "El ciclista del San Cristóbal," beyond its original publication in Santiago by Quimantú in 1973, is included in *Cuentos hispanoamericanos*, edited by Mario Rodríguez Fernández and published in Santiago in 1994, reprinted in 2003; *16 cuentos latinoamericanos: Antología para jóvenes*, published in 1992 (with a Brazilian translation including "O ciclista do San Cristóbal," published in São Paulo); Poli Délano's *1996 Cuento chileno contemporáneo: Breve antología* "The Cyclist of San Cristóbal Hill," for example, is included in *The Vintage Book of Latin American Stories*, edited by Julio Ortega and Carlos Fuentes in the year 2000. It was translated into German as *Radfahrer vom San Cristóbal by Willi Zurbrüggen* and published in München in Piper, 1986, reprinted in 1991; a French translation, *Le cyclist de San Cristobal* appears in Éditions du Seuil in 1984 and is reprinted in 2002. It was made into a movie, directed by Peter Lillienthal, in 1987. Today, of course, it is available in several sites of the internet such as http://www.literatura.us/skarmeta/ciclista.html [6/1/2012], and http://www.letras.s5.com/skarmeta030303.htm [6/1/2012].

non-expert consumers, who produced them. Some of these international writers are pushed by metropolitan centers and strong publishing conglomerates, and often possess only a meteoric existence. A minuscule minority endures and receives the rare acclaim both of general readers and the attention of specialized literary critics. Of previous generations, to provide examples, among those who justly excel locally but fade abroad one finds Carlos Droguett (1912–1996), Elena Garro (1920-1998), Eduardo Mallea (1903-1982), and Héctor A. Murena (1923-1975), to name randomly a few notable figures, and among the few Latin American writers with deep and ample international presence we find Borges (1899-1986), García Márquez (b. 1927), and Vargas Llosa (b. 1936). From Spain, García Lorca (1898-1936) belongs in this rarefied group. To provide parallel examples from another languages, we will consider later in this essay the Japanese Haruki Murakami (b. 1949), who presents some similarities to Skármeta. Let me stress that this is not an allocation of quotients of quality, but the acknowledgment of a diversity of modes of circulation. For the purposes of Chilean literature, Alberto Blest Gana, María Luisa Bombal, and Manuel Rojas are irreplaceable, yet not particularly well known abroad. Stephen King is entertaining and may top the charts the world over, but leaves nary a trace.

Skármeta's novels and short stories have been translated into tens of languages, receiving significant honors: the Boccacio International Prize of Literature for the Italian translation of *No pasó nada* in 1996; the Medicis Prize for best foreign book published in French in 2001 for *La boda del poeta,* which also received the Grinzane Cavour prize in Italy that same year, the UNESCO Prize of 2003 for *La redacción*, and the Ennio Flaiano International Prize in 2006 for his work in general, but especially for *El baile de la Victoria*, prizes in addition to the ones he has received in Spanish: Premio Casa de las Américas in 1968 for *Desnudo en el tejado*; Premio Altazor in 1999 for *La boda del poeta*; Premio Planeta 2003 for *El baile de la Victoria*, which also received the Premio Municipal de Literatura de Santiago de Chile in 2004, and finally, up to this writing, the 2011 Premio Planeta-Casa de América for *Los días del arcoíris*. This recitation is not an idle exercise in commemoration, but the reaffirmation of the validity of the question we pursue here: What makes Skármeta an internationally successful writer? The variety and importance of the prizes demonstrate he has attained that category, but do little to explain why.[3]

II. Visionary Writing

The printed page, the text, made Borges, García Márquez and Vargas Llosa into world-renowned writers. There is something solid, recognizable as their imprint, which does not quite melt into the air as it transmutes to various languages. As with Kafka, Faulkner, or Flaubert, when asked about them we must point to their unique way of crafting a story, mapping a world with words, completing a sentence with a *mot juste*, that is, creating a page which cannot be abstracted or stated differently, explicated, without betrayal of its unique power of fascination. While some of their pages inspired movies and operas, the result has been far from memorable.[4] The writers who followed, though, have struggled to have an equal recognition. As Juan Armando Epple noted in a pioneering and perceptive effort to trace a profile of what he called "Estos novísimos narradores hispanoamericanos," those writers who were starting to publish around 1960 have "un afán de renovación" (144). Since Epple is too close to the phenomenon he is trying to describe, he

3. Skármeta's excellent "página oficial" in the internet has a comprehensive list of translations: http://www.clubcultura.com/clubliteratura/clubescritores/skarmeta/index.htm

4. A sharp and witty contribution by Lulu de la Nausée, which I assume is a penname, to Opera-L Archives states: "Faulkner novels would of course provide much drama for an opera! All those secrets, all that sweat and grime and faded glamour...," but continues wisely, considering *Absalom, Absalom*: "This novel is as much...or more...about how one constructs a story as about what the story itself is, and I would be offended were an opera to present just the 'Thomas Sutpen story'." http://listserv.bccls.org/cgi-bin/wa?A2=ind0002C&L=OPERA-L&P=158215 [May 29, 2012] Offense is worth meditating upon. An opera libretto by Laura Jehn Menides exists for *As I Lay Dying*. Opera Memphis has produced a one-act operatic version of the first chapter of Light in August, and a project for an opera based on *As I Lay Dying* was not completed, both written and composed by David Olney, Tom House, Karren Pell, and Tommy Goldsmith (Kartiganer xxv–xxvi). Daniel Catán second opera, *Florencia en el Amazonas*, was inspired by *Love in the Time of Cholera*. The libretto is by Marcela Fuentes-Berain. It was premiered in Houston on October 25, 1996. Matthew Welch has composed an opera based on Borges and which has received its first performance on May 2012. http://roulette.org/events/experiments-in-opera-borges-and-the-other-with-music-by-matthew-welch-and-a-text-adapted-from-jorge-luis-borge/ The Ecuatorian composer Mesías Maiguashca composed *Los enemigos*, premiered in Karlsruhe, Germany, in 1997, based on Borges' "El milagro secreto."

justifiably fails to give a precise diagnostic.[5] Looking back it is clear that there were many different ways in which this renovation occurred, but for Skármeta we can indicate a new vocabulary and a new attitude, in addition to the fact that he knew how to tell a story without becoming trapped in the whirls and ostentations of literary language. (Nothing wrong, of course, with Pedro Prado or the masterful Lezama Lima or Carpentier, but Skármeta is not competing with them.)

Remembering Skármeta's short stories, at least in my case, is not being haunted by a happy phrase or a bunch of words to treasure, but to keep memories of having inhabited a world and shared an experience. I believe, as I am sure many readers do, I pedaled my way up the San Cristóbal with his prodigious cyclist. I almost remember being such a penniless foreign student in New York that I sold my blood, spending then the proceeds, ashamed and defiant, to hear Ella Fitzgerald sing live. I seem to have known the Chilean adolescent in Argentina and Germany who earned his friendships with fistfights. And wasn't I there when one of my former students, now a policeman, came to greet me in what seemed a coded warning? And so on. His description of a terrorist shooting in the Fiumicino airport of Rome (in "De la sangre al petróleo") is so vivid, it so much put me in place, that I asked Skármeta in jest if he had been there during the incident. He had, truly. As a storyteller, then, he creates the illusion of transparency, attaining the most difficult appearance of ease. The traces of labor have been wiped away, leaving only the incandescent, three-dimensional event.

When approaching a period of the past and its creative production, they seem givens, but are the result of inertia from the

---

5. "Los rasgos básicos que, a primera vista, los han ido distinguiendo frente a la tradición anterior, conforman una articulación muy especial: por una parte, demuestran un conocimiento atento de la literatura precedente y una apropiación libre de todos los valores que ha gestado (concepción de la literatura, procedimientos narrativos, etc.), y por otra, hacen gala de una desenfadada capacidad para subvertir los modelos consagrados por esa tradición y tentar nuevas vías de apropiación y organización de esa experiencia vital, vías que van fundándose como una aventura lingüística en que el ludismo y la imaginación desacralizan constantemente lo estatuído poniendo al desnudo las constantes precarias de la realidad" (145). This is a good description of what any generation does to distinguish itself from the previous one. From close to seventy writers he mentions among these novísimos, only five are women, missing one of the most important and lasting revolutions of the period, as women authors went from marginal in the canon to essential and even of predominant interest.

many and of an enormous creative effort by the few. Antonio Machado in his autobiographical poem "Retrato" noted that "a distinguir me paro las voces de los ecos," describing not just the poet's quest, but also the task of critics. Skármeta arrives with a creator's voice, an imaginative voice, hardly an echo. There is much more to it, but the starting point must be to recognize him as a creator, a visionary of sorts. To avoid misunderstandings, the claim is that this is one of the factors of Skármeta's irreplaceable nature, not the only one, and there are other writers of this generation who share this admirable talent. Ariel Dorfman's (b. 1942) *Death and the Maiden* and Luisa Valenzuela's "Cambio de armas," for example, also excel by creating a complex, believable, emblematic—yet not bloodless—situation that is then seen both as newly minted and apparently existing beyond the page, a sort of unforgettable literary trompe l'oeil.

As is always the case in any generation, beyond the general similarities, the writers who excel have their own very particular voices, different among them and markedly distinct from their predecessors. In what follows I attempt to describe Skármeta's unique intervention in a wider conversation, where topics are shared (repression, social concerns, diverse media, and so on), but no one would mistake a text by Luisa Valenzuela, Diamela Eltit, or César Aira with one by Skármeta. The depth and variety of this generation is impressive, especially when considered, as in this collection of essays, as a cohort of very diverse individual creators.

III. The Choice of Words

There is, evidently, the language of this voice. The first time I saw Skármeta, he was on a TV screen, being interviewed by José Promis on the occasion of the publication of *El entusiasmo*, a short stories collection published by Zig Zag in Santiago in 1967. He did not look or sound at all as any of the writers then in vogue in Chile, who usually were correct, diplomatic, anxious to show their literary sophistication, and boring for young university students in Valparaíso as I was then. Skármeta read part of "La Cenicienta en San Francisco." The adventures of Chileans who had gone to California were well known: Neruda recalls one in *Fulgor y muerte de Joaquín Murieta*, which was published in 1967 by Zig-Zag and Fernando Alegría's *Caballo de copas* (1957, also published by Zig-Zag) had been successful. But Skármeta's story was very different. It was not only that it corresponded to the shift of the cool from Paris to London, New York and California, but the tone was unmistakably ours, with guitars and beer, an irreverent mix of Stevenson's *Treasure Island* and Saint-John Perse (still alive then [1887–1975]), Goethe and Cinderella, and casual sex in a bramble of cities connected by the inscrutable wanderings of a youthful quest: San Francisco, Rio de Janeiro, Puerto Montt, New York, and Santiago.[6] The protagonist even peed on the fire escape and on the bus... Irreverent indeed, uncouth, shocking.[7]

These early stories and his first two novels incorporated numerous words that were colloquial and yet seemed perfectly in place, not just snippets of local color sprinkled in italics. Ariel Dorfman noted, writing about *La insurrección*, that "toda la obra de Skármeta ha sido una búsqueda de renovación del lenguaje, intentando refrescarlo, desabrocharlo, desnudarlo, volverlo a vestir como para una boda" (*Hacia la liberación* 166). The 1975 edition in Editorial Planeta in Barcelona of *Soñé que la nieve ardía* brings just the text, daringly expecting Peninsular Spanish speakers to work out the meaning of Chilean references and words, but the second edition appeared six years later in LAR containing a glossary, prepared by Soledad Bianchi, entitled "Mínimas explicaciones (en el orden de la novela)," with data about proper names, places, and expressions. These fourteen pages are the scars of the travel, of the text's errancy, the result of deterritorialization, of becoming foreign. Bianchi affirms in her prologue that "la maestría en el uso del lenguaje es uno de los mayores logros de esta novela" (6), indicating the variety of registers used by the characters, including at times a "buscada cursilería" (6), which is part of the faithful reproduction of the period's linguistic energy. Skármeta, as he becomes an inter-

---

6. It is fortunately hard to even remember now how impossibly wild and improbable it seemed then in a very conservative Chile to make love in an attic to a woman whom the character had just met and would leave a few hours later. Ah, San Francisco! That some change has occurred since then, but not too much, can be seen in Pía Rajecić's *El libro abierto del amor y el sexo en Chile*, who writes: "en plena transición el escenario había cambiado y era un secreto a voces que se había tendido un manto de silencio sobre ciertos temas, entre los que curiosamente se encontraban la sexualidad y distintos aspectos de la vida amorosa" (17).

7. Rita Felski in her wise *Uses of Literature* suggests four categories towards a positive phenomenology of reading, including recognition, enchantment, knowledge, and shock, the last one rooted in perceptions about the storyteller made famous by Walter Benjamin. All these categories work well to understand Skarmeta's effectiveness as a writer.

national writer, at times will bleach out the traces of the local. In his 2001 *La chica del trombón*, a novel with many pages of lively dialogue and engaging characters, one can find nevertheless paragraphs that seem airbrushed of all personal flavor:

> Cuánta más bella era la muerte en la pantalla que en la mediocre vida. En el cine los hombres horadaban la dulce tierra con palas y picos, transpiraban gruesas gotas de sudor verdadero, los empleados de las funerarias se ubicaban en un semicírculo como en un coro solemne, el cura, siempre un pariente del difunto, oraba con gesto hierático y el responso final incluía alguna cita poética que intentaba darle sentido al dolor de todos los deudos y de nosotros, los espectadores.
>
> Los parientes vestían de espeso e impecable luto, y a viuda arrojaba con dignidad, superando en última instancia los vértigos de un desmayo, la simple flor sobre el féretro antes que cayera la tierra final sobre su lustrosa madera. (63)

These correct yet very standard sentences conceal many choices: *bella/hermosa/bonita* or any other term young people would use today for this term, *pantalla/telón, horadar/cavar, transpirar/sudar, funerarias/pompas fúnebres, oraba/rezaba, gesto hierático/solemne, espeso/grueso, arrojaba/tiraba, féretro/ ataúd, lustrosa/brillante/pulida*, and so on. In each case the choice decides in favor of the more international and traditionally literary term, defanging the prose, writing in that international "depurated" Spanish to which we are used in academic conferences.

In this temporary claudication for a broader audience he is not alone. A comparison between early Vargas Llosa and his recent publications is disheartening, since much of the spark is gone. In his 1967 *Los cachorros,* for example, one finds crisp and lively youthful expressions: "... los estudios comenzaron a importarle menos. Y se comprendía, ni tonto que fuera, ya no le hacía falta chancar: se presentaba a los exámenes con promedios muy bajos y los Hermanos lo pasaban, malos ejercicios y óptimo, pésimas tareas y aprobado. Desde el accidente te soban, le decíamos, no sabías nada de quebrados y, qué tal raza, te pusieron dieciséis" (63). In his introduction to the first edition of *Los cachorros,* Carlos Barral recounts meeting Vargas Llosa and being struck by his pattern of speech: "Construye con precisión, como en la lengua escrita, en una prosa complicada, a menudo salpicada, como sus textos, de locuciones que no deben ser ni peruanismos, que deben pertenecer a un habla de grupo, que deben ser localismos atesorados con sensualidad" (43). José Miguel Oviedo writes in the introduction to *Los cachorros*:

> La intimidad (o complicidad) con el lector está asegurada también por el uso copioso de expresiones de la jerga colegial y por la insinuante captación de los timbres orales (un poco cariñosos, un poco pícaros) del lenguaje limeño. La jerga y los usos locales no son una novedad para los que han pasado por las novelas de Vargas Llosa, pero su frecuencia es aquí mucho más alta que en cualquiera de sus otras obras, y hasta puede temerse que los menos familiarizados con esos giros perderán muchos matices importantes de la historia. (33)

In contrast, Vargas Llosa's 2010 *El sueño del celta* is so decaffeinated and stilted that my first expectation as a reader was that I would soon discover the first chapters, as in the case of many in his masterful *La tía Julia y el escribidor*, would be dead-on parodies of an alien literary style. A characteristic example:

> El prefecto recibió a la Comisión en su despacho y les ofreció vasos de cerveza, jugos de frutas y tazas de café. Había hecho traer sillas y les repartió unos abanicos de paja para que se airearan. Seguía con el pantalón de montar y las botas que lucía la víspera, pero ya no llevaba el chaleco bordado, sino una chaqueta blanca de lino y una camisa cerrada hasta el cuello, como los blusones rusos. Tenía un aire distinguido con sus sienes nevadas y sus maneras elegantes. (165)

Amazing

As literary critics it is far too easy to discount the importance of the marketplace and the price a writer pays when she or he becomes mired in local slang and local problems to the point readers can no longer follow. This is not just a concern for Spanish speaking writers, as excellent as Vargas Llosa and Skármeta are. The most successful Japanese writer today in the US is Haruki Murakami (b. 1949). Some of his novels, such as *Norwegian Wood*, which propelled him to international fame in 1987, and *Kafka on the Shore* (2002), are about young rebellious, dissatisfied, loners, familiar with rock music and suffering various forms of frustrated love. A translator into Japanese of Raymond Carver, Murakami's short stories have the quirkiness and rapid trace that characterize also Skármeta's. In my opinion his most complex and fascinating novel is *The Wind-Up Bird Chronicle*, which starts out with an unemployed lawyer cooking spaghetti, moves on to the search of a lost cat, and then slashes away onto brutal events of the Japanese past, while spending time in dry magical wells trying to reconnect with the protagonist's wife.[8] What surprises many readers, though, is that this novel, written mostly while Murakami was a writer in residence at Princeton, seems so familiar in its references. It is only when one reads the very small print that one realizes that it was "translated and adapted from the Japanese by Jay Rubin with the participation of the author." A citizen of Tokyo can of course boil a potful of spaghetti "while whistling along with an FM broadcast of the overture to Rossini's *The Thieving Magpie*" (5), conducted by Claudio Abbado. "A well without water. A bird that can't fly. An alley with no exit" (66), the basic elements in the set of the novel's action, could be anywhere. And it is possible that the owner of the cleaner's is listening to "an Andy Williams tape" (80), but this is Japanese-light, adapted for the market. An amusing piece by Sam Anderson in *The New York Times* of 21 October 2011, "The Fierce Imagination of Haruki Murakami," started out as follows:

> I prepared for my first-ever trip to Japan, this summer, almost entirely by immersing myself in the work of Haruki Murakami. This turned out to be a horrible idea. Under the influence of Murakami, I arrived in Tokyo expecting Barcelona or Paris or Berlin—a cosmopolitan world capital whose straight-talking citizens were fluent not only in English but also in all the nooks and crannies of Western culture: jazz, theater, literature, sitcoms, film noir, opera, rock n' roll. But this, as really anyone else in the world could have told you, is not what Japan is like at all. Japan—real, actual, visitable Japan—turned out to be intensely, inflexibly, unapologetically Japanese.

---

8. I believe Michiko Kakutani missed the point in her negative review in *The New York Times*: "While Mr. Murakami seems to have tried to write a book with the esthetic heft and vision of, say, Don DeLillo's *Underworld* or Salman Rushdie's *The Moor's Last Sight*, he is only intermittently successful. Wind-Up Bird has some powerful scenes of antic comedy and some shattering scenes of historical power, but such moments do not add up to a satisfying, fully fashioned novel. In trying to depict a fragmented, chaotic and ultimately unknowable world, Mr. Murakami has written a fragmentary and chaotic book." Why should an internationally successful novel be "fully fashioned"? Fragmentary and chaotic, how delightful! If I bring this comparison into play is because often Skármeta is placed in the wrong context and misjudged.

Indeed, one critic, Myles Chilton, has spoken of Murakami's invented Tokyo.⁹ Adalberto Bolaño Sandoval in a study of *Kafka on the Shore*, which he finds develops "un concepto de ficción más atractivo, más acorde con las necesidades de un tipo determinado de lectores—y con la globalización" (1), indicates correctly that

> a Murakami lo ha seguido una caterva de insobornables lectores, pero al mismo tiempo el desdén de críticos y colegas de su propio país y de otras latitudes, pues consideran de poco valor una narrativa que apela—señalan—a lo popular, a las viejas y socorridas temática del amor, la soledad, el sexo y la música, a lo extranjerizante, pero, por sobre todo, por retomar lo fantástico como elemento constante de su narrativa. (2)¹⁰

Skármeta succumbed to the temptation of the purely international in *Match-Ball*, which in spite of being a clever, intertextual novel which involves a Harvard-educated doctor and a fifteen-year old German tennis player, has not found much favor among his critics. Marcelo Coddou started an interview with Skármeta stating, "Extraña novela ésta dentro de tu producción narrativa" ("Entrevista" 579), but also wrote a very encomiastic review in which he stressed its "humor a todo dar" and predicted that "la novela hará el deleite de quienes ven a un escritor en total posesión de su oficio, multivalente, con proyecciones amplias y diversas, dueño y señor de un lenguaje propio, desenfadado, irreverente" ("*Match Ball*,

---

9. Susan Fisher in "An Allegory of Return: Murakami Haruki's The Wind-Up Bird Chronicle" describes well the tension in Murakami between Western models ("He even claims to have developed his distinctive style by writing first in English, and then translating into Japanese" [155]), and his embracing of Japanese tradition. Postcolonial theory has analyzed extensively the difficulties of writing in languages controlled by a metropolitan center. For the realities of the distribution of literary texts, Pascale Casanova' s *The World Republic of Letters* is invaluable, in spite of her natural overvaluing of Paris as most important center up to the seventies of the past century.

10. Bolaño Sandoval gives a perfect description of Murakami's craft, one that in many ways could also apply to Skármeta: "Lo que hace atractiva la lectura de Murakami es la conjugación de diversos motivos y temáticas: la tragedia convertida en susurro cotidiano, la nostalgia de una pasado que no se cumplió y el presente no puede redimir, una escritura envolvente e hipnótica, los personajes perdidos en medio de la resignación, la soledad y la confusión en esas experiencias, la profusión de elementos oníricos y mágicos que muestran a los personajes con sus inseguridades y miedos, transformándose la literatura en un arcano de lo inexplicable pero cotidiano, y al mismo tiempo una estrategia de Sherezada para crear historias dentro de la historia y manejar la tensión o expectativas"(2).

novela de Antonio Skármeta"). But this topic, which still allowed his playful language, had unmoored him from his other strengths, connected to the middle class and Chilean history. European aristocracy and jetsetters had many other writers to sing their critical rhapsodies. Skármeta saw himself lucidly: "I am a writer who derives pleasure from framing his characters within the problems of his own lifetime, and as a citizen it is my vocation not to accept the repressed language that society prescribes. I am a naïve believer in literature as praxis not only of fantasy but also of freedom" ("The Book Show" 49). As Antaeus, he remains strong as long as he is in contact with the ground. The whole point of this section has been to suggest that even among towering writers an amazing skill with words cannot sustain their work by itself. As I will indicate next, the topic matters.

IV. An Engaging Dialogue

A moment in the "La Cenicienta en San Francisco" can help us highlight another characteristic that defines Skármeta: the smiling humor of many of his dialogues. He is seldom sarcastic or drastically ironic, his approach being more compassionate and nibbling, rather than mordant. The protagonist, named Antonio, which serves to stress the autobiographical aura of the story, attempts to explain to Abby, his partner for the night, where Chile is, spreading out a map of Latin America he keeps folded within a pocket book. After Antonio points out the representation of the Andes, which he has told Abby he sees in Santiago every morning as he goes to the university, she concludes Chile must run parallel to the mountain range and misidentifies Argentina as Chile. Later historical events and the easier access to information about the world have made Chile today a well-known player, but the experience of invisibility we Chileans experimented abroad in the sixties (similar to what today many citizens of African countries must encounter in Latin America) is superbly captured in the following lines:

> —Mira, Antonio, si ahí está el mar—indicó con un dedo el azul del Pacífico—y aquí la cordillera de los Andes, que tú ves todas las mañanas cuando caminas, emputecido por Santiago, y aquí está la Argentina, entonces Chile está en la Argentina y tiene que ser esto que está aquí.

—No—repliqué—. Lo que estás mostrando es Mendoza. Una ciudad de Argentina.
—¿Has estado allí?—preguntó.
—Sí—dije.
—¿Y aquí?—señaló Salta.
—No—contesté.
—¿Por qué?
—No sé. Fíjate bien ahora.
Puse la uña del dedo central en el punto del mapa que decía Arica,[11] y la tiré hacia abajo dejando una frágil hendidura en el papel ajado por tantos ajetreos.
—¿Ves eso?—pregunté.
—Sí—dijo.
—Chile.
—¡Eso! (32–33)

Much of Skármeta's work has continued this early, seminal scene, with the writer responding to the gasp of surprise from Abby, who can hardly believe a thin line of territory can be a real country.[12] In 1960 California had 15,850,000 inhabitants, almost double Chile's eight million. What Skármeta highlights in this story, and later in many of his works, is that while people are not happy in Chile, they are far from crushed: "están empezando" (34). This should remind us that happiness, a state of mind exalted as an ideal and attached as a supposed byproduct of objects (cars, shoes), activities (travel, vacations), accomplishments (admission to a university, attainment of tenure), is, as Schopenhauer exactly saw, transient, disappointing, and enervating. The true energy comes from a healthy dissatisfaction, a longing for a better future, as superbly described by Ernst Bloch in his *Dass Prinzip Hoffnung* and a fact well known on Madison Avenue. Skármeta's writing is seeped in enthusiasm, attentive to harshness, injustice, and frustration, but never defeatist or dejected. There is a surprising definition of Antonio's (the character in the story) conception of being a writer:

—¿Qué haces? —dijo.

---

11. Oddly the translation of this story in from *Watch Where the Wolf is Going* is "the point of the map that said America," but the original reads "en el punto del mapa que decía Arica" (El entusiasmo 33). This erasure of Arica under America is amusing or distressing, or both.

12. Chile has been intriguing to Chilean writers themselves, as the examples of Isabel Allende's 2003 *Mi país inventado* and the much earlier *Chile o una loca geografía* (1940) by Benjamín Subercaseaux (1902–1973).

> —Qué quieres decir?
> —¿A qué te dedicas? ¿Qué haces en Chile?
> —Quiero ser escritor—dije.
> —¿No lo eres ya?—preguntó.
> —Me gusta la vida—respondí.
> —¿Toda la vida?
> —Toda.
> —Las enfermedades y las guerras, y el dolor y la soledad, ¿también?
> —En cierto sentido, sí. (26)

This *sí* is enormously powerful and reminds me of Molly Bloom's final *yes* in Joyce's *Ulysses*. In spite of everything, of the humility of one day, only faintly connected to the great epic by resonance and echoes, Antonio and Molly affirm the worth of living. Liking life would hardly be an appropriate characteristic to describe the writers of the boom and their predecessors. They may have loved the land, great literary works (especially European), travel and the fireworks of language, but life was too contaminated by centuries-long injustice, widespread corruption, racism, economic exploitation, and senseless violence to make it more than the subject of criticism and denunciation. Too much celebration risked being naïve, reactionary, and even a form of betrayal of the writers' responsibility to their continent. This mantle of reasonable gloom—there is much in our history, as in most other regions of the world, to repudiate and not let slide into comfortable oblivion—has continued in most other writers of Skármeta's generation, feeding the general tendency, especially in the US, to concentrate teaching and research on the Latin American dismal: dictators, poverty, dirty wars, corruption, and so on. (This is not too different from the fact that one of the most frequently offered seminars about Spain is on the Spanish Civil War.) With copper, fruit, flowers, cellulose pulp, and coffee, Spanish-speaking countries have provided the United States another valuable commodity, a steady flow of reasons to feel good about the US and its exceptionalism, only disrupted by tornadoes or a heavy snow storm. A rather longish but I hope justifiable quote from Ariel Dorfman's *Los sueños nucleares de Reagan*, the start of a section entitled "Nuestra nieve invisible," brilliant in its formulation of a pedagogical comparison, exemplifies this tendency to decant the great variety of daily life in Latin America to its faults and shortcomings:

> Después de casi diez años de exilio, sólo tengo que mirar por la ventana para sentirme de vuelta en mi país. Este invierno norteamericano, el peor del siglo, ha transformado el paisaje en algo tristemente familiar.
> No es la nieve, le digo yo a mis amigos. Al sur, la nieve es algo que adorna los falsos árboles de Navidad, las remotas cordilleras, los ventisqueros antárticos. Lo que resulta familiar es más bien el desastre que ha traído esta nieve.
> Basta con mirar por la ventana o mirar por esa ventana menos amplia que es el televisor con sus noticias inmisericordes, y heme ahí, de nuevo en el Tercer Mundo, como si nunca hubiera tenido que salir de mis propias tierras.
> Millones de niños sin escuela; gente muriéndose en las calles; un transporte atestado, que no respeta horarios; incontables hogares que carecen de agua o electricidad; fábricas funcionando a medio vapor; un panorama que he visto, y sufrido, antes. Hasta el ritmo de la vida rememora la lentitud de otras latitudes, como si la nieve nos hubiera atrapado en una cámara que apenas anda. La famosa eficiencia norteamericana se ha convertido en un pantano.
> Así son las cosas siempre, todos los días, en nuestros países, les explico a amigos y a conocidos, absurdamente feliz de haber hallado una imagen que comunique y esclarezca nuestra infamante situación. (221-22)

Dorfman's perception is partly accurate, but his insight has also the proverbial blindness rolled into it. On the one side, dreadful schools and unemployed workers do not magically stop north of the Río Grande. On the other, a visit to contemporary Santiago, Buenos Aires, or Mexico City (and countless other cities—I mention only those I know relatively well) reveals that they easily dwarf most cities in the US not only in development, but also in opportunity and sophistication. The rich intellectual vigor of writers of the generation of '72 emerges from a strong city culture, be it Bogotá, Buenos Aires, Havana, México City, Montevideo, or Santiago. If they become exiles instead of expatriates or *transplantados*, it is because their roots are deep in societies which incorporate European and United States' cultural elements (not always to their liking), but have their own very specific, and valuable, irreplaceable life. The accomplishments of Latin American industry, education, and art are immense, yet I have found myself often defending them in front of administrators who wish to internationalize the university by establishing centers in Hungary (where few in my institution speak the language) or in the Far East, instead of the more reasonable and familiar Latin America. Few of my undergraduate students are interested in researching the amazingly resilient creative aspects of a prosperous economy, but their eyes light up with dictatorship and torture. The constant stream of negative information—exact, well-meaning, but partial—does little to provide a broader picture of contemporary Latin America, where the situation is not wholly *infamante*. A recent article in the 2012 *Latin American Research Review*, "Satisfacción de vida en Costa Rica," by Mariano Rojas and Maikol Elizondo-Lara, starts out from the puzzling, even scandalous result of a 2008 Gallup poll of 140 nations which concluded Costa Ricans have the highest level of life satisfaction in the world, even if their per capita income is relatively low, a point worth mulling over. This is a Scylla and Charybdis situation: each generation must remember anew and dispel its own surrounding darkness (and risk being swallowed up by the past in bitter darkness), but also must find its own ray of hope to travel forward (and risk faulty maps, treasonable illusions, and complicit silences).

Skármeta, I would claim, has found a wise middle road. His first novel, *Soñé que la nieve ardía* (snow again, but this time on fire with enthusiasm), starts out with individual hope, provincial Arturo's pursuit of soccer success in the capital. He will be swept away into a larger wave of hope, the movement that resulted in the election of a socialist president opening the way to move from utopian thought to its implementation. Grínor Rojo observes that the displacement from margin to center, from private dream to shared project, from superficial to profound, is frequently found in Skármeta's work. His choice of words is most insightful:

> Estoy aludiendo a su frecuente trabajo sobre un asunto que no por estar cargado de tradición es menos suyo; que no tenía antes y que mucho menos tiene ahora para él nada de imaginario; que se halla inscrito en su biografía y que desde ella se abstrae e influye en la composición de un gran número de sus relatos haciendo que éstos articulen sus fábulas en torno al desplazamiento del protagonista desde un *habitat* conocido a otro desconocido. ("Notas" 100)

The topic of transitioning to a different environment and facing a reconfiguration of the self is indeed old and frequent, and Skármeta himself went from Antofagasta, in the North of Chile, to Santiago, from there to Buenos Aires, back to Santiago, and then to an exile that would lead him to many years in Berlin. What needs to be stressed, though, is that these successive uprootings could have led to chaos and destruction. The predominant definition of the novel at the time of Skármeta's early writing was Georg Lukács', who claimed that the great model was Balzac, who had created "the novel of disillusionment, which shows how the conception of life of those living in a *bourgeois* society... is shattered by the brute forces of capitalism" (*Studies in European Realism* 47). In consequence there was no space for personal fulfillment, and "only those who have given up or must give up their personal happiness can pursue social, non-selfish aims" (52). This is an accurate description of what happens to Arturo, who only by renouncing his personal pursuit and blending into a social aim attains friendship and love.

The inner form of the novel has been understood as the process of the problematic individual's journeying towards himself, the road from dull captivity within a merely present reality—a reality that is heterogeneous in itself and meaningless to the individual—towards clear self-recognition. After such self-recognition has been attained, the ideal thus formed irradiates the individual's life as its immanent meaning; but the conflict between what is and what should be has not been abolished and cannot be abolished in the sphere wherein these events take place—the life sphere of the novel; only a maximum conciliation—the profound and intensive irradiation of a man by his life's meaning—is attainable. The immanence of meaning which the form of the novel requires lies in the hero's finding out through experience that a mere glimpse of meaning is the highest that life has to offer, and that this glimpse is the only thing worth the commitment of an entire life, the only thing by which the struggle will have been justified. The process of finding out extends over a lifetime, and its direction and scope are given with its normative content, the way towards a man's recognition of himself. (*The Theory of the Novel* 80)

One may be puzzled today, in a time of ironic skepticism, about how such a description was so meaningful for our generation, when the belief in the effectivity of communal action still was dogma and the images of Fidel's entry into Havana were deeply engraved in social discourse.[13] There had been enough problematic individu-

---

13. It is worth noting that the postmodern skepticism is limited outside academia (in a sense, unfortunately), where conviction drives stark contests in politics and the law. A recent article by Alan Kirby in *Philosophy Now*, "The Death of Postmodernism and Beyond," claims that "the terms by which authority, knowledge, selfhood, reality and time are conceived have been altered, suddenly and forever," noting the most of the novels taught in courses about postmodern literature were

als, falling into nausea, caught in no exit rooms or cast as outsiders, circulating gloomily in black and white Nordic landscapes, perhaps playing chess with Death, or hearing that outside the Church there was no salvation as a cold eclipse swallowed up the neon lights of aseptic new cities, so that new voices were necessary. Skármeta once and again presented the radically uncomplicated belief in the value of solidarity, political action for justice and a better world, intermingled with good sex, laughter and even sports. While *Ardiente paciencia* ends tragically and a bitter taste, Skármeta affirms that "expresa la alegría del crecimiento humano, la expansión de la democracia en Chile. Es todo el pasado democrático chileno el que yo celebro en mi literatura" (Figueroa 27). While celebration prevails, he adds that "también expreso el dolor de la convivencia perdida." In *Soñé que la nieve ardía*, *La chica del trombón*, and *Ardiente paciencia* one of the protagonists is the political transformation that is encompassing all private concerns and moving the country to the socialist government. More than expressed ideologically, it is represented as an energy tide that has a transformational effect. If in two of the novels we can see the end of the dream—*La chica del trombón* ends with a young boy, the future generation, sounding the claxon in celebration—the main focus is a radiant activity that touches and improves people. *La insurrección* pursues the same topic in Nicaragua. Finally, in his most recent novel, *Los días del arcoíris*, he presents the publicists' improbable feat of tipping the balance towards a negative vote in the 1988 national plebiscite that proposed that Pinochet continue for another eight years. (*La boda del poeta* and *El baile de la Victoria* have other main topics.)

Each one of these novels about Chilean politics would merit a detailed analysis, but for our present purposes we need just to state that Skármeta has found here a subject with international resonance for which he cares deeply and for which he has shown a unique angle, still imbued with enthusiasm in spite of the difficul-

written before most students were born. Skármeta cannot be described as postmodern and this may make him more contemporary. Another obituary concerns postcolonial theory, discussed by Robert JC Young in "Postcolonial Remains." He notes that "the desire to pronounce postcolonial theory dead on both sides of the Atlantic suggests its presence continues to disturb and provoke anxiety: the real problem lies in the fact that the postcolonial remains. Why does it continue to unsettle people so much?" (19). I believe a reading of Skármeta's work as in part postcolonial and unsettling would be useful, since he exemplifies that the oppressed will not be silenced or ultimately defeated.

ties of an obstinate classist society and strong, unbridled capitalism. But, in addition, there is a relatively infrequent factor to take into consideration: the morphing of his narrative.

A disconcerting phenomenon associated with Skármeta's novels is that they surface under a variety of names. While it is customary to find short stories reshuffled and packaged under different titles, the same is not usual with novels. *Ardiente paciencia* is translated as *Burning Patience,* but then becomes *The Postman (Il Postino)* in English, and *El cartero de Neruda* in Spanish; *Match ball* is *Love-fifteen* and then *La velocidad del amor;* *El baile de la Victoria* becomes *The Dancer and the Thief.* Clearly some of these changes are due to the great success of the 1994 movie *Il Postino,* directed by Michael Radford, others to making the title more marketable. But beyond the softness of the original title there is in several cases a great variety of approximations to the topic which decenter or reframe the novel as part of a continuing creative process. Yanis Gordils, who studies some of these variations, calls them "metáforas en espejos repetidos" ("El mundo como metáfora" 331), but they seem to me more as jazz melodies implemented always with some difference in various media.

With the German film director Peter Lilienthal he collaborates in *La Victoria* ([a reference to the victory of socialism and to a poor neighborhood in Santiago] 1973), *Es herrscht Ruhe im Land* (En el país reina la calma [the Chilean coup recreated in Portugal] 1976) and *Der Aufstand* (La insurrección [on Nicaragua and the triumph of Sandinismo] 1980). The novel *La insurrección* was then preceded by the movie. Similarly *Ardiente paciencia* will migrate in different incarnations, including a radioplay, a play on the stage, a film directed by Skármeta himself in Portugal in 1983, a novel in 1985, the movie *Il Postino* in 1994, a musical *The postman and the Poet*, performed in London in June 2011, and the opera *Il Postino* with music by Daniel Catán from 2010, in which Plácido Domingo sung the role of Neruda both at the LA Opera House and in Paris. The movie deviated significantly from the novel, changing the time period, moving the action from Isla Negra to Capri, and removing most of the political implications of the action.[14] Equally, his writing

---

14. Irene B. Hodgson in "The De-Chilenization of Neruda in *Il postino*" does a detailed and perceptive analysis of the differences between novel and movie. Skármeta was in St Louis as a Distinguished Visiting Professor at Washington University when Radford came to discuss with him the final details of the script. Skármeta

about the 1988 referendum began with a play which received a few presentations, one of them in Madrid during the Semana de Autor dedicated to Skármeta in the Casa de América in April of 2009, which served as the basis to the script for the movie *No*, directed by Pablo Larraín and with the protagonism of Gael García Bernal, premiered in Cannes. The film received the Art Cinema Award in the Directors' Fortnight section and will be distributed by Sony Pictures Classics, which promises a repeat of the success enjoyed by *Il Postino*. The novel *Los días del arcoíris* (2011) also focuses on the referendum, but with a larger number of characters and a slightly different story. One can imagine that eventually it will be retitled *No*... Several of Skármeta's novels appeared first in translation and then in Spanish, among them *No pasó nada* (also titled *Chileno!*) and *La insurrección*, and there are in this later case several differences between versions. Speaking about the different outlets for his narrations, he recently wrote in "Elogio del papel":

> Para mí el problema de la literatura no es el tipo de soporte sino la falta de lectores. Si hago el elogio del libro de papel con entusiasmo es porque hasta ahora éste ha sido el vehículo que me ha permitido contactarme con lectores en más de treinta lenguas. Pero también lo han conseguido los filmes hechos sobre mis novelas y las óperas que las han cantado. No temo a las transformaciones: al contrario, las aliento. Trabajo con ellas. Sé que cualquiera que sea el soporte de las cartas que le lleva mi cartero a Pablo Neruda la emoción que tendrá el lector del libro, del i-pad, del e-book, o de la pantalla de cine, o de los escenarios teatrales, será la misma. Un discurso que convivirá entre marejadas de otros para ocupar en el alma de su gente un espacio inmaterial.

As I argued at the beginning of this essay, Skármeta is first and foremost a visionary who then pursues in different ways to bring what he has imagined to the theater, movies, and the printed page. His work, then, has to be understood in this ample range of creation, and not just as the written text. His inspired creation of a dialogue between a postman and Neruda has the same sort of life as Don Quixote, they have left the text. They are sure to reappear in even newer versions, true to a deeper self that has connected them with spectators and readers all over the world. Equally, the story told in *No* of a country voting peacefully to send a dictator home, facing impossible odds and winning with good humor, cheer and

argued strenuously to bring the film closer to the novel, but to no avail.

youthful spirit is the sort of inspirational story that will become the standard definition of the power of creative imagination over oppression. When the film was shown in Cannes on May 18 of this year, it received a long ovation which may stand for now as the most recent evidence of Skármeta's unique way of creating a story that is meaningful, moving, and important, a story that will cross borders and find a home in different languages, and endure.

Works Cited

Anderson, Sam. "The Fierce Imagination of Haruki Murakami." *The New York Times Magazine* October 21, 2011. Web. 15 May 2012.

Bianchi, Soledad. "En el fondo la realidad tiene un sabor a verdadero," and "Mínimas Explicaciones (en el orden de la novela)." In Antonio Skármeta, *Soñé que la nieve ardía*. 2nd ed., Madrid: Ediciones LAR, 1981. 3-7 and 229-42. Print.

Bolaño Sandoval, Adalberto. "Paraíso perdido y contracultura de la imaginación en Haruki Murakami." *Espéculo: Revista de Estudios Literarios* 14, 44 (2010). Web. June 2, 2012.

Casanova, Pascale. *The World Republic of Letters*. Trans. DeBevoise, M. B. Cambridge, MA: Harvard UP, 2004. Print.

Chilton, Myles. "Realist Magic and the Invented Tokyos of Murakami Haruki and Yoshimoto Banana." *Journal of Narrative Theory* 39.3 (2009): 391-415. Print.

Coddou, Marcelo. "Entrevista a Antonio Skármeta de *Match Ball*. *Revista Iberoamericana* 56 (1990): 579–82. Print.

—. "*Match Ball*, novela de Antonio Skármeta." *El Sur*, September 17, 1989, p. vii. Web. June 2, 2012.

Dorfman, Ariel. *Hacia la liberación del lector latinoamericano*. Hanover, N.H.: Ediciones del Norte, 1984. Print.

—. *Los sueños nucleares de Reagan*. Buenos Aires: Editorial Legasa, 1986. Print.

Epple, Juan Armando. "Estos novísimos narradores hispanoamericanos." *Texto Crítico* 4.9 (1978): 143-64. Print.

Felski, Rita. *Uses of Literature*. Blackwell Manifestos. Malden, MA

; Oxford: Blackwell Pub., 2008. Print.

Figueroa, Gabriel. "Fantasías y ternuras de Skármeta." *Hoy* (15-21 September, 1986): 26-28. Print.

Fisher, Susan. "An Allegory of Return: Murakami Haruki's *the Wind-up Bird Chronicle.*" *Comparative Literature Studies* 37.2 (2000): 155-70. Print.

Gordils, Yanis. "El mundo como metáfora en *El Cartero De Neruda* o *Ardiente Paciencia* y en *Il Postino.*" *Torre: Revista de la Universidad de Puerto Rico* 6.20-21 (2001): 331-79. Print.

Hodgson, Irene B. "The De-Chileanization of Neruda in *Il Postino.*" *Pablo Neruda and the U.S. Culture Industry*. Ed. Longo, Teresa. New York and London: Routledge, 2002. 97-113. Print.

Kakutani, Michiko. "Books of the Times; On a Nightmarish Trek through History's Web," *The New York Times, Arts* October 31, 1997. Web. June 1, 2012.

Kaminsky, Amy K. *After Exile: Writing the Latin American Diaspora*. Minneapolis, MN: U of Minnesota Press, 1999. Print.

Kirby, Alan. "The Death of Postmodernism and Beyond." *Philosophy Now*. May/June (2012). May 25 2012.

Lukács, Georg. *Studies in European Realism*. New York: Grosset & Dunlap, 1964. Print.

—. *The Theory of the Novel*. 1971. Whistable, Kent: The Merlin Press Ltd., 1988. Print.

Murakami, Haruki. *The Wind-up Bird Chronicle*. Trans. Jay Rubin. New York: Vintage International, 1998. Print.

Rajecić, Pía. *El libro abierto del amor y el sexo en Chile*. Santiago: Planeta, 2000. Print.

Rojas, Mariano, and Maikol Elizondo-Lara. "Satisfacción de vida en Costa Rica: Un enfoque de dominios de vida." *Latin American Research Review* 47 (2012): 78-94. Print.

Rojo, Grínor. "Notas sobre *Chileno!* de Antonio Skármeta." *Texto Crítico* 7.22-23 (1981): 96-108. Print.

—. "Celebración de Antonio Skármeta." *Anales de Literatura Chilena* 3 (2002): 139-50. Print.

Shaw, Donald L. *Antonio Skármeta and the Post Boom.* Hanover, N.H.: Ediciones del Norte, 1994. Print.

Skármeta, Antonio. *El Entusiasmo.* Santiago: Zig-Zag, 1967. Print.

—. "La Cenicienta en San Francisco." *El Entusiasmo.* Santiago de Chile: Zig-Zag, 1967. 9-41. Print.

—. *El ciclista del San Cristóbal.* Santiago de Chile: Quimantú, 1973. Print.

—. *No pasó nada.* Barcelona: Editorial Pomaire, 1980. Print.

—. *Watch Where the Wolf Is Going: Stories.* Columbia, LA, USA: Readers International, 1991. Print.

—. "The Book Show," in *The Writer in Politics*, edited by William H. Gass and Lorin Cuoco. Carbondale and Edwardsville: Southern Illinois UP, 1996. 39–51.

—. *La chica del trombón.* Madrid: Areté, 2001. Print.

—. *Los días del arcoíris.* Santiago de Chile: Editorial Planeta, 2011.

—. "Elogio del papel." *Clarín, Revista de Cultura*, April 4, 2012. Web. May 20, 2012.

Skármeta, Antonio, and Alfonso Ruano. *La composición.* Madrid: Ediciones SM : Ediciones Ekaré, 2000. Print.

Vargas Llosa, Mario. *Los cachorros.* Barcelona: Editorial Lumen, 1974. Print.

Vargas Llosa, Mario. *El sueño del celta.* Madrid: Alfaguara, 2010. Print.

Young, Robert JC. "Postcolonial Remains." *New Literary History* 43 (2012): 19-42. Print.

GAZING BACKWARDS IN FERNANDO VALLEJO

Juanita Cristina Aristizábal
The Catholic University of America

Fernando Vallejo is one of Latin America's most acclaimed writers, and also one of its most polemical. Vallejo, who was born in Medellín and has been living and writing in Mexico since the 1970's, has become an important presence in Latin American fiction. In addition to 11 novels, he has also written three biographies, numerous eccentric essays on topics ranging from religion to physics, edited several volumes of poetry and correspondence, and published a treatise on what he calls literature's grammar.[1] He has also become a popular speaker, appearing at literary conferences and book fairs—often accompanied by a pack of street dogs—to accept prestigious awards or to give controversial speeches in which he advocates for animal rights and rants about the failures of the Catholic Church, the horrors of overpopulation and the stupidity of soccer matches.

The narrator that Vallejo has created for his novels is just as peculiar as the public authorial persona that he has devised for himself. The narrator is a nostalgic old man that aimlessly strolls

1. Vallejo has published the following novels. *El fuego secreto* (1986), *Los caminos a Roma* (1988), *Años de indulgencia* (1989) and *Entre fantasmas* (1993) were published in a volume entitled *El río del tiempo* (1998). *La Virgen de los sicarios* (1994), *El desbarrancadero* (2001), *La rambla paralela* (2002), *Mi hermano el alcalde* (2004) and *El don de la vida* (2010). The titles of his biographies of Porfirio Barba Jacob, José Asunción Silva and Rufino José Cuervo are: *El Mensajero* (1984), *Almas en pena, chapolas negras* (1985) and *El cuervo blanco* (2012). His treatise on literature's grammar is entitled *Logoi. Una gramática del lenguaje literario* (1983).

European and Latin American cities and small towns, bearing witness to the geopolitical transformations that have radically transformed the idealized notion he holds of his country and hometown.

A writer himself named Fernando, the narrator is caught in a set of interactions with late 20th century decaying urban landscapes. Fernando responds to these interactions with harsh and oftentimes inappropriate diatribes against politicians, religious institutions, democracy, mass media and popular culture, among many others.[2] A jaded old man, Fernando indulges in misogynistic, elitist and at times even racist discourse, including rants against modern egalitarian values. This aggressive discourse is so candid and shocking as to make Vallejo seem an odd presence among the generation of '72. Vallejo seems far from being one of his contemporaries who often reacted to oppressive regimes and the rise of neoliberalism in late 20th century Latin America by turning to a socially committed literature.

In a time marked by a return to the concern for ethics in the arts, in which we are the beneficiaries of half a century of feminist discourse questioning patriarchy, and in which we discuss and rightly celebrate the culture of minorities and other traditionally marginalized groups, what are we to make of Vallejo's display of a discourse that can easily be labeled as anti-modern? And more problematic perhaps, of his commitment to this discourse through a seemingly autobiographical narrator?[3]

In *Entre fantasmas* (1993), the narrator suggests an angle

---

2. This type of discourse is, of course, disconcerting in and of itself, but it is particularly challenging because of the uncanny resemblances that exist between author and narrator. Although the resonances between Vallejo and Fernando suggest an autobiographical connection, Vallejo affirms the fictional nature of his narrator. The author has often declared that the many traits he shares with Fernando—they were both born and raised in Medellín, both are gay, failed filmmakers, animal lovers, obsessed with grammatical correctness, exiles in Mexico and highly disdainful, cynical and at the same time nostalgic about everything Colombian—are irrelevant. He further distances himself from Fernando by killing him off, not once but twice. For a recent interview where Vallejo discusses his narrator see Brantley Nicholson, "Entrevista a Fernando Vallejo." *Chasqui* 40.2 (2011).

3. As Jean Franco pointed out, while it may be evident that irony cuts across the misogynistic and at times even racist comments articulated by Fernando as a *letrado*, confronting the narrator's aggressive and polemic rhetoric in *La Virgen de los sicarios* is an unsettling experience for the reader: "As a letrado, he is 'our' ally 'mon semblable, mon frère.' The question is whether he is deliberately forcing us to face the 'fascist within' or whether he expects our complicity" (Franco 225).

from which to approach Vallejo's writings when he proudly declares his own outdated preferences: "Anacrónico como siempre he sido, siempre a la trasantepenúltima moda, añorando un tango, muero como un jacobino. De heterodoxia"(587). This relentless return to previous times and spaces is characteristic of Vallejo's narrative, which looks back with particular insistence to the discourses that shaped cultural production at the turn of the 20th century such as secularization, individualism, commoditization, urbanization and democratization. The dialogue that Vallejo establishes with these discourses throughout his writing points to his links to the Spanish American *modernistas*, a generation of writers between the 1880's and the 1920's considered foundational to Spanish American literature and culture. Vallejo's dialogue with this generation signals his affinity with decadence, a polemical discourse within the *modernista* movement and one tightly embraced by his narrator. Fernando is, in fact, shaped in the fashion of a contemporary decadent dandy, a nostalgic iconoclast in constant despair because of the state in which he finds his hometown and his country at the turn of the 21st century.

Fixing his gaze backwards often puts Vallejo's dandy at odds with the present, his insistent anachronism necessarily making him a contentious figure. My approach to Vallejo will show how his gaze backwards to preceding cultural and literary traditions makes him an odd figure in the Generation of '72. His recurring dandy narrator, a heterodox, overpowering and erudite authorial voice, highly disdainful of popular culture and imbued with longing for the nation, clearly sets Vallejo's work against the grain of late 20th century Latin American cultural production. At the same time, through his ironic adaptation of this caricaturized *fin de siècle* character, Vallejo's literary project articulates one of the most intriguing testimonies of the unease with which, as Brantley Nicholson and Sophia McClennen argue in the Introduction, the generation of Latin America's forced global citizens experienced the failures of cosmopolitan modernity at the turn of the 21st century.

I

Vallejo's backwards gaze is perhaps most superficially apparent in his narrator's incessant dialogue with images and discourses rooted in Latin America's cultural traditions. In addition to weaving into almost every patch of his writing words and images from the Catholic tradition, Vallejo's writing has a strong relationship with a discourse that dates to the arrival of the Spanish in the Americas: grammar.

Language is one of the many elements in contemporary society that Vallejo identifies as facing corruption and decay. "El hombre", his narrator states in *Entre fantasmas*, "descubrió en la palabra lo más noble que tenía ...lo que lo distinguía de los animales... y la devaluó, la volvió mierda. Por eso yo digo tantas palabrotas... La palabra se ha vaciado de sentido y explota como una pompa de jabón." (*Entre fantasmas* 586)[4] As can be seen from this passage, Fernando laments the devaluation and corruption of Spanish, marking himself as heir to that tradition of grammarians to which the Chilean Andrés Bello belonged, along with the Colombians Rufino José Cuervo and Miguel Antonio Caro. Indeed, he often calls himself "Colombia's last grammarian."[5]

Indicative of the importance that looking backwards has in Vallejo's literary project is the fact that his heterodox and iconoclastic narrator declares himself the last representative of an old tradition instead of the pioneer of a new one. The mere act of looking back makes Vallejo an atypical writer. Julio Ortega has referred to the impossibility of reading contemporary Latin American fiction retrospectively because of what he called its loss of its "estatuto normativo, su índole disciplinaria prefijada, su familia de imágenes retrazable" (30). But Vallejo's work is constituted from the retrospective point of view; under his persistent backwards gaze, the limits of Ortega's proscription are clear. Echoing Ortega, Josefina Ludmer talks about the task of approaching contemporary culture as an operation of "reading the mystery of the present." According to Ludmer, "para poder especular hoy desde aquí necesitamos un aparato diferente al que usábamos antes. Otras palabras y categorías para pensar los regímenes de significación y las políticas de la ciudad naturalizada de América Latina." (138) Mary Louise Pratt has also

---

4. Vallejo frequently comments on his preoccupation with language and animal rights. In one of his eccentric speeches entitled "El lejano país de Rufino José Cuervo" he stated: "El idioma está tan indefenso como los animales. Todos los atropellan con impunidad. Y esas dos causas perdidas son las que he tomado como mías, por el gusto de perder" (5).

5. His most recent book entitled *El cuervo blanco* is a biography of Rufino José Cuervo, Colombia's most renowned 19th century grammarian, admired by Vallejo and whose life and work he had been studying for many years.

referred to that elusive present as generating what she calls a trope in Latin American literature of the global era: "imágenes alegóricas de sistemas epistemológicos que el protagonista reconoce, pero que es incapaz de descifrar" (Pratt 272).

Vallejo's narrator, however, refuses to abandon familiar words, categories and epistemological systems in favor of something new and unique to the present. An obvious example is his obsession with the nation, an obsession that may be symptomatic of his belonging to a generation described by the editors of this issue as one forced into global citizenship at the not so comfortable phase of incipient globalization.

One of the characteristic aspects of the global era is the emergence of identities and literatures detached from the boundaries traced by the nations that were imagined and imposed in the 19th century. José Joaquín Brunner has referred to an "international character," and a "deterritorialization," as the cultural tendencies in a context in which the nation state can no longer mobilize or organize the cultural field (64). According to Román de la Campa, in the society of global capitalism, collective identities opposed to the expansionist drive of free global markets—such as the nation—are anachronistic (305). De la Campa speaks of "indeterminacy" as a global condition that shapes cultural production, and that is characteristic of what he calls "a crisis of the national." Along the same lines, Ludmer states that literature is no longer the manifestation of a national identity but a locus for other subjectivities and politics. And Sergio Echevarría speaks about "internationalism" as a trait of late 19th century cultural and literary vision.

It is common to see young Latin American writers, and also writers from the Generation of '72, setting their novels in foreign countries. This internationalism is mostly a characteristic of the writers that proclaim themselves as members of the *McOndo* generation. In the prologue to the collection that serves as that generation's manifesto, Alberto Fuguet and Sergio Gómez declare that: "… lo que se escribe hoy en el gran país McOndo, con temas y estilos variados, [es] mucho más cercano al concepto de aldea global o mega red" (15). According to Fuguet and Gómez, in the context of the global world Latin American writers do not feel they are the representatives of any ideology or even of their own countries: instead they have broken their ties with Macondo and exchanged the topic of the Latin American identity for the topic of personal identity (13). More recently Jorge Volpi spoke about what he calls the "universality" of the new generation of Latin American writers. According to Volpi they are not striving to preserve the parameters of national literature and they do not hesitate to find foreign settings and stories. These writers, Volpi says, are "universal" and approach the idea of Latin America without "el tono salvífico o politizado de algunos de sus predecesores... sin resabios de romanticismo o de compromiso político, sin esperanzas ni planes de futuro" (170).

Yet Vallejo's fixation with Colombia is in clear opposition to this shift. In Vallejo's writing the tension between the local and the global, always at play in a generation working between national and post-national aesthetics, results in an obsessive return to his homeland.

Colombia is deeply embedded in his work even when he is writing from exile in Mexico and narrating Fernando's strolls through streets of cosmopolitan centers such as Barcelona, Rome, New York, London or Paris. Vallejo laments the fate of his beloved Colombia, which he describes as a languid country that has fallen victim to bloodshed, and has been sacked by oil barons and politicians, bribed by drug lords and blown up by guerrillas. At other times he is outraged by his nation, calling it the land of a "iraza tarada" con "alma de periferia!" and identifying it as a poor country rich in hate, a nation of assassins where mini-Uzis have replaced machetes. Fernando's obsession with Colombia, an obsession that is also pervasive in Vallejo's own speeches and public appearances, appears out of place in today's globalized world.

Vallejo's work is also in conflict with some of the important characteristics of the literature of the postboom that literary scholars and critics have identified, characteristics that mark precisely the break between the writers discussed in this issue and the boom authors that precede them. One such characteristic is the predominance of personal and everyday narratives in contemporary literature. These narratives left behind the *grand récits* articulated by the "total novels" of the boom that intended to provide keys for the interpretation of national and continental realities and identities in Latin America. A second feature of the novels of the postboom is that they seek to erode the notion of the author or the narrator as a godlike or demiurgical figure in total control of his or her text.[6] These characteristics of course hardly describe Vallejo's work.

6. In his *The Voice of the Masters: Writing and Authority in Modern Latin Amer-*

Far from providing keys for interpreting Colombia, Vallejo's sole purpose in his novels seems to be to attack it. Nevertheless, one of the most quoted passages of *La Virgen de los sicarios* suggests that Vallejo's writing does aspire to transcend the level of personal memory and reach the collective: "Yo soy la memoria de Colombia y su conciencia y después de mí no sigue nada" (21).

And if what his narrative purports to be is the memory of Colombia, then it is a memory trapped almost entirely in Fernando's monologue, a discourse in which the reader will only occasionally hear other voices. In opposition to the contemporary notion of the erosion of the control of the authorial figure, Fernando dominates Vallejo's novels in an overarching way. The narrator often claims ownership and domain over the world that he creates in his text and that, very much in the fashion of a decadent dandy, he dominates from a high tower. As he puts it in the following passage of *El fuego secreto* (1987): "Desde mi alta torre, mi atalaya viendo pasar las nubes domino el tiempo, domino el mundo... Sepan tan sólo que si se me antoja y quiero rompo la reja y salgo por la ventana y dejo este encierro y bajo por un lazo que me hago con hilos de recuerdos." (276)

Fernando is determined to dominate his text and at times reveals himself to be much closer to the *modernista* search for linguistic transcendence or to the boom's "totalizing" perspective than to the everyday narratives of his generation. In the following fragment, for instance, he goes as far as to declare himself the only "truth" and "reason", an almighty voice that does and undoes arbitrarily:

> ¿Qué me dicen? ¿Qué me niegan? Yo soy la única verdad, la única razón. Y la suave brisa se fue volviendo viento y el viento huracán y se lo fue llevando todo, los sombreros de los transeúntes, los paraguas de las señoras, las mitras de los obispos, el solideo del cardenal y las torres de las iglesias y los techos de las casas y, ratas, perros cerdos, hijos de la gran puta, el protagonista de mi propia vida empecé a ser yo. (*El fuego secreto* 181)

As "the protagonist of his own life," the old man's tales

---

ican Literature and *La ruta de Severo Sarduy*, Roberto González Echevarría refers to the post-boom's deconstruction of "the power of the self." According to this critic this "power" supported the literary ideology behind the novels of the boom, which aspired to be "total" and assumed that "a certain knowledge of Latin America must be sought through its literature" (*The Voice* 84).

jump erratically following his memory-string. In accordance with the strong self-affirmation expressed in this passage, the old man fashions himself in ways that resemble that cult of personality characteristic of the pose of the decadent dandy. This is a feature of his narrative related to his transgression of another postboom trend: the democratization of literary discourse. Aníbal González has identified this phenomenon as the result of the rapid growth of the reading public in Latin America starting in the late 1970's, and writers' concomitant desire to produce more accessible and readable works (*Love and politics* 5).

Readability and accessibility are not necessarily traits embraced by Vallejo. In addition to his lack of chapters and erratic and abrupt jumps in space and time, Vallejo's narrator is extremely, almost comically, erudite, full of eclectic and at times quite arcane references to science, history, literature, art and music. He presents himself as a polyglot who wants to know everything that there is to know—from the Icelandic and ural-altaic languages to the glucose-cycle, atomic orbits and the mechanics of the magnetron (*Los días azules* 130).

All this erudition is typical of the dandy's desire to distance himself from the "rest." It also marks a clear connection between Vallejo and the turn of the 20th century when, for both Latin American and European writers, a penchant for the erudite and the arcane was related to a desire to make art both a medium for the creation of a new aristocracy outside the social conventions of money and labor, and a substitute for religion in response to secularization and positivism.[7] Vallejo's erudition may not make his work accessible only to a small reading public, but it does maintain a level of discourses and codes that are shared by a restricted elite of readers, negating today's democratization of literature and culture.

This erudition is only one of the antediluvian aspects of Vallejo's narrator that appears to draw on *modernista* discourses and images. Many other connections between his writing and the *modernistas*, such as Fernando's dialogue with secularization and

---

7. Many critics have studied the peculiarities of this process in the *modernista* context. See for example Ángel Rama, *Las máscaras democráticas del modernismo* (Montevideo: Fundación Ángel Rama, 1985); Graciela Montaldo, *Sensibilidad amenazada: Tendencias del modernismo latinoamericano* (Caracas: Planeta/Fundacion CELARG, 1995) and Gerald Aching, *Politics of Spanish American Modernismo: By Exquisite Design* (Cambridge/New York: Cambridge University Press, 1997).

the death of God through a sacrilegious proliferation of religious topics and imagery, attest to what critics have recognized as *modernismo's* lasting impact in Spanish America in the 20th century.[8] But, ever the dandy, Vallejo invokes the *modernista* tradition in ways that break with the dialogue with *modernismo* undertaken by other writers from the mid 20th century to the present. For instance, as Aníbal González has argued, *modernismo* reappears in the writing of Miguel Barnett, Guillermo Cabrera Infante, Severo Sarduy or Luis Rafael Sánchez through the filter of popular culture, in particular through the genres of popular music, such as bolero, on which the movement had a significant and lasting impact (137).

The issue of popular culture is fundamental to understating the work of writers from the Generation of '72, as they are pioneers in incorporating this realm into literature. It is also an issue that also puts Vallejo against the grain. Popular culture has an undeniable presence in his novels; especially in *El fuego secreto,* in which Fernando remembers the time he spent in gay clubs and bars in Medellín in the 1960's when boleros and tangos by Leo Marini, Daniel Santos and Carlos Gardel were ubiquitous. Disseminated throughout Vallejo's novels are melodramatic evocations of lyrics from bolero, a musical genre considered to be an expression of the entrance of the masses into modernity in Latin America starting in the 40's and 50's. In *El fuego secreto* the old man even declares that his life is written in its lyrics: "[y]o tengo la vida mía apuntalada en canciones: me quitan una y se inclina hacia un lado, me quitan otra y se inclina hacia el otro, me quitan otra y se desploma en el aire" (205). In passages like this one the narrator distances himself from what is other wise a forceful rejection of popular culture. Even in the passage previously quoted, while allowing his elitism to lapse for a moment, Fernando remains self-consciously archaic, indulging in the popular culture of a vanished era. Yet he is more

---

8. See Aníbal González, "Modernismo's Legacy," *A Companion to Spanish American Modernismo* (Woodbridge y Rochester: Tamesis, 2007); Iván Schulman, *El proyecto inconcluso: Vigencia del modernismo* (México: Siglo Veintiuno editores, 2002); Cathy Jrade, "Modernismo's Lasting Impact," *Modernismo, Modernity and the Development of Spanish American Literature* (Austin: University of Texas Press, 1998). For an analysis of this topic and its links with Rubén Darío and Vargas Vila in *El desbarrancadero* see my article "Telología literaria en *El desbarrancadero* de Fernando Vallejo," en *Literatura: teoría, historia, crítica.* Número monográfico: Literatura colombiana entre milenios: balance crítico de dos décadas 1990-2010 (June 2012): 14.

often almost entirely disdainful of modern mass media and trumpets his hatred for soccer, television, samba, jazz and rock and roll. Fernando laments that Colombia used to be a country plagued by poets and is now a nation obsessed with soccer, which according to him is the most antipoetic thing that could ever exist. "La vida me ha castigado con un siglo de jazz y estrépito rock, que me revientan el hígado y la cabeza" he says in *Los días azules* (109).

II

Declarations by Fernando, such as his claim that a century of jazz and rock music has made his head explode, call attention to how the nature of his experience of modernity shapes his behavior and self-expression. The experience of modernity is not detachable from the *modernistas*, being as they were the first generation of writers to have reacted to the changes modernity brought to the recently independent Latin American nations in the 19th century. These changes were linked to some of the ideals of the project of modernity, such as secularization, positivism, industrialization, urbanization, democratization and capitalism. *Modernista* writers conveyed an ambivalent reaction to the experience of modernity in growing urban centers such as Mexico City, Buenos Aires, Havana, Santiago and Bogotá. While figures like Silva, Casal, Darío, Martí and Gutierrez Nájera expressed discomfort with the uncertain place of the poet in societies increasingly guided by utilitarian and scientific values, they were also fascinated by the transformative power of money or electricity and expressed this fascination by actively publishing in newspapers and journals chronicles devoted to capturing the spirit of modernity.[9]

9. The ways in which Latin American countries—as former colonies of Spain and Portugal—would have experienced modernity is the subject of much controversy, an ubiquitous debate that exceeds the scope of this text. It is important to clarify that by modernity I am referring to the project of modernization that started with the changes brought by the Industrial Revolution and the consolidation of the nation states in the 19th century. The recently published study on the topic by Alejandro Mejías-López provides valuable insights to these debates and their relevance and implications for the study of the *modernistas*. According to Mejías-López if the experience of modernity in the 19th century is related to the variety of processes that constitute what we call modernization, then there should be no doubt that "there was nothing vicarious or ghostly in the Spanish American experience so forcefully and insightfully described by modernista writing from Martí to

A century later, when the failures of cosmopolitan modernity in Colombia are evident in its narco-infused society flooded by poverty and violence and trapped in an ongoing civil war, the experience of modernity is equally central to Vallejo's narrator. This becomes clear in his depiction of a character living at the dawn of the 20th century. Tonino Dávila appears several times in Vallejo's novels. According to the narrator this peculiar character died of a most unusual rage. Dávila is the first victim of the "shock del futuro" when the first car arrives in Medellín by mule:

> Por allá a principios del siglo veinte, en los confines del tiempo, trajeron a Medellín, a lomo de mula, el primer carro, y lo pusieron a circular por el parque de Berrío, a darle vueltas y vueltas. Tonino que vivía "en el marco de la plaza", empezó a desvariar, y mientras el carro echaba humo y alegremente resoplaba afuera, el pobre viejo se iba enloqueciendo, se iba desintegrando de rabia. Con cera se taponaba los oídos para no oír el traqueteo infernal pero en vano, el motor le taladraba los huesos de los sesos. No resistió lo que se le venía encima, el alud del futuro que me ha tocado a mí... (662)

The avalanche the narrator claims he has had to endure is essentially the onslaught of modern life at the turn of the 21st century. Vallejo's stance towards this avalanche attests to the parallels that can be drawn between the *modernistas*' cultural production and that of the members of the Generation of '72. Both generations write in the midst of periods of significant transition. A century after the *modernistas*, Vallejo's generation is forced to confront the failures of democracy in the continent as well as to come to terms with the rapid changes brought by the rise of neoliberal politics in the region. In Vallejo's narrative, with his homecoming in novels like *La Virgen de los sicarios* and *El desbarrancadero*, Fernando faces the ultimate failure of the project of modernity begun at the end of the 19th century. This is obvious in his constant evocation of figures like José Asunción Silva, Rufino José Cuervo, and Porfirio Barba Jacob and his declaration that he is "descendiente rabioso de los liberales radicales colombianos como Vargas Vila y Diógenes

---

Rodó. That these processes in Latin America differed from those in Europe and the United States (which also differed from each other) may be true, but in the 19th century (at the very least) 'different' becomes an almost empty signifier; modernization was ultimately different *everywhere from everywhere else* and without fixed directionality." (33)

Arrieta" in *El desbarrancadero* (176). In line with this claim, the old man focuses many of his diatribes on the *Regeneración*, that 19th century project which sought to "redeem" Colombia from the rule of liberal ideas by resolutely declaring that the nation should be built on the pillars of Catholicism and Hispanism, and building these into the new constitution of 1886.

But it is mostly through his accounts of aimless wanderings through decaying landscapes where he encounters beggars, stray dogs, rats, trash, muggers, rapists and stabbers that the narrator confronts the every-day signs of the failure of the modern project in Colombia. According to him, living in Medellín can be compared to bouncing through life like a dead person: "así vamos por sus calles los muertos vivos hablando de robos, de atracos, de otros muertos… sumidos en el desastre" (*La Virgen* 76).

These interactions often lead to the narrator's iconic diatribes tinted by despair and an obsessive nostalgia. He longs for pristine churches now frequented by criminals; crystal-clear rivers now turned into sewers that carry corpses downstream and for Santa Anita, his grandparents' hacienda now vanished into a neighborhood built for the poor. This gaze backwards to a space and time forever lost causes the narrator to see the present as decay rather than progress, rot rather than ripening, and allows him to declare Colombia a total failure.

But the crude realities described by the narrator do not cause only despair. Fernando often finds fascination and joy in his dealings with the underbelly of the city and in his confrontations with an almost catastrophic modernity. One of the more striking examples of this joy is the homoerotic desire that he experiences for the teenage assassins in the slums of Medellín in *La Virgen de los sicarios* (1994). Ever since *El fuego secreto* Fernando had recognized that he felt a "fascinación fascinada por el hampa" (269). In *Años de Indulgencia* (1989), he refers to his search for images in marginal neighborhoods during his years as a filmmaker as a quest that puts him in a delusional state:

> … voy por estos barrios sin agua, sin ley, sin luz, sin alcantarillas, filmando con excitación rabiosa lo que encuentro: niños barrigones, viejos borrachines, perros sarnosos, charcos con moscas, putas preñadas, gallinas, basura, cerdos. Y para acabar de ajustar, para rematar, en la estación del ferrocarril campesinos llegando a la ciudad … Entonces a mí se me enciende el foco, la imaginación: ya sé lo que debo hacer, lo que debo filmar: un tugurio en llamas.

Un tugurio incendiándose en la noche. ¡Qué delirio! ¡Qué poema! (512)

His encounter with landscapes as grim as the one described above excites the narrator's imagination and powers Vallejo's writing. In Vallejo's novels images of poverty and decay are unquestionably invested with an aesthetic value. Like Baudelaire's painter of modern life, Vallejo's narrator is capable of finding beauty in the utmost decay. The *comunas*, he says explicitly, "a fuerza de tan feas son hasta hermosas." (85) He describes them as: "casas y casas y casas de dos pisos a medio terminar, con el segundo piso siempre en veremos, amontonadas, apeñuscadas, de las que salen niños y niños como brota agua de la roca por la varita de Moisés. De súbito, sobre las risas infantiles cantan las ráfagas de una metralleta. Ta-ta-ta-ta-tá..." (85)

Decay is what the narrator claims to find when he returns to Medellín or Bogotá. As he states in *Entre fantasmas*: "Por última y definitiva vez he vuelto al barrio de mi niñez a constatar la inexorable decadencia que nos espera a todos: hombres, perros, gatos, naciones" (707). The narrator's fascination with this inexorable decay underscores how his use of words like disaster and decay should not be taken lightly. In *El desbarrancadero* (2001), the narrator asserts that we live under laws of thermodynamics that stipulate that: "todo lo que está bien se daña y lo que está mal se empeora" (105). This notion of the imminence of decay in Vallejo's narrative is also evident in the narrator's age (Fernando is merely forty). He is somber and aged because, as he puts it in *Entre fantasmas*: "poquito a poco, pasito a paso había dejado de vivir en el presente para vivir en el pasado, y mientras más pasado ese pasado y más lejano, más espléndido" (564).

One of those strong links that Fernando has with the past is his return to decadence. Passages like the ones above point to the obvious relationship between Vallejo's writing and this discourse that was the subject of much controversy for the *modernistas* in Spanish America at the turn of the 20th century.[10] Vallejo's refor-

---

10. As Sylvia Molloy has argued, decadence was seen as nothing more than a European trend that had little to do with a young and promising continent that stood in stark contrast to a decaying Old World. One of the fiercest critics of the use of decadence in Spanish America at the time was a *modernista* himself, José Enrique Rodó. Rodó referred to decadence as a tendency that lead to triviality and frivolity, a "prurito enteramente pueril de retorcer la frase y de jugar con las palabras"

mulation of a decadent aesthetic in response to modernity at the end of the 20th century is one of the most reasons for his referencing of the *modernistas*.[11] Decadent topics and images abound in Vallejo's novels. The narrator's fascination with young men and his association with violence and eroticism, most evident in *La Virgen de los sicarios*, are among the attitudes through which he evokes the tradition of decadence. Among the "perversions" that link him to what critics have called an "erotismo fin de siglo" are some as cliché as the imagery of decadence as necrophilia—confessed in *Años de indulgencia* (562)—and as disconcerting as the narrator's daydream of engaging in sexual contact with a younger version of himself in *El fuego secreto* (241). Other decadent traits present in Vallejo's writing worth mentioning are his narrator's misogyny, which, as David Weir has explained, is associated with the decadents' despising reproduction and their cult of the artificial, and their attacks on democracy—seen as a threat to artistic sensibility and despised by figures like Baudelaire and Barbey D'Aurevilly.

Essential to understanding Vallejo's decadent aesthetic is the irony behind some of Fernando's nostalgic declarations. Take his complaint about the loss of the traditions of "las musas, la misa y el chocolate" or his suggestion that the only way to counterbalance the rule of death in Colombia is through Catholicism and what he terms the reproductive mania of its adherents. These ideas do not fit straightforwardly into the discourse of a narrator who is a furious enemy of the Catholic church and a detractor of human reproduction. Resorting to such assertions underscores the irony that cuts across Vallejo's discourse. Vallejo's acid critiques of the political and religious orders, his inappropriate comments charged with misogyny and disdain for the masses, and, at times, even tainted by

(Rodó 84). According to Rodó this style went against the necessities of the time.

11. Matei Calinescu called decadence one of the "five faces of modernity," one of the discourses that flourished in Europe in the late 19th century as a critique of modernity's "myth of progress." Those artists known as decadents (such as Baudelaire, Verlaine, Wilde and D'Annunzio) experienced modernity as catastrophe. This sense of impending catastrophe sprang from uncertainty about the place of art and literature in a world dominated by the dynamics of the global market economy. The decadent artist's response to this impending catastrophe was to distance himself from the increasingly uniform masses by isolating himself from the rest of society, and finding ways to shock the bourgeois—and to seek pleasure in that distance and shock. The decadent artists found solace in the artificial, the arcane and the exotic and cultivated an ornate and eccentric style with which they sought to make poetry and art a hermetic realm for an initiated few.

racism are, on one level, marked by irony—another decadent trait present in his writing. Irony is essential to the character of the decadent dandy that he uses to fashion his narrator and to articulate, as I will show, a peculiar critique of Colombia's failed project of modernity.

III

One of decadence's traits was a nearly obsessive focus on individualism, a trait expressed in the dandy's cult of personality. The dandy is shaped by his pose. Constantly displaying himself and wishing to be seen by others, he nevertheless remains a character marked by an air of uncertainty, hidden under successive masks (Coblence 178). In his essay entitled "The Painter of Modern Life" (1863), Baudelaire presents the dandy as one of the masks worn by the artist that "seeks modernity" and acts as the interpreter of its beauty, even when this beauty is linked to perverse realities. Baudelaire refers to the dandy's joy in his ability to shock others and his satisfaction with the fact that he is never shocked.

Vallejo's narrator resembles the dandy because he is a figure that is constantly confronting modernity as catastrophe. The old man created by Vallejo is mostly nostalgic about the past, echoing Baudelaire's comparison of the dandy to a declining star full of melancholy. Fernando yearns for a past forever lost: Medellín before there where so many factories, cars, thieves and a subway; Santa Anita, his grandparent's vanished hacienda; and even José Asunción Silva's Bogotá, plagued by poets and obsessed grammarians. Fernando constantly declares himself nostalgic for Silva's cultured and sophisticated Bogotá, for the times when charming and classy young women still knew how to play the piano. The *modernista* poet is, in fact, a point of reference for the unease with which he experiences modernity. Silva stands for what is forever lost in the past, a Colombia where the highest ideal was poetry and not soccer (Chapolas 554). According to Fernando, the decline began with a crucial episode that divides Colombia's history in two: the assassination of the liberal caudillo and then presidential candidate Jorge Eliécer Gaitán in 1948. During the riots that followed the crime--he explains to his readers in *Chapolas negras* (1995) (Vallejo's biography of Silva)—the notes of the poet's autopsy disappeared along with a very special edition of one of his books of poetry. The narrator blames the multitude for its profanation of Silva's body and for its attack on the order that he represented.

Fernando is resentful, even angry at the crowds, and, consequently, goes on to assert that the rise of this multitude marked the beginning of Colombia's inevitable decadence and collapse. He is particularly abhorred by the country's obsession with soccer and asserts that the spectacle of the crowds cheering and screaming in front of the television as they watch twenty-two "idiots" following a ball around, reveals that Colombia is no longer the country of Silva's poetry but a coconut that is emptier than a soccer ball (554).

The narrator's despair is therefore directed towards what could be considered the entrance of the masses into the cultural realm in Latin America, a process that according to critics like José Joaquín Brunner and Jesús Martín Barbero started precisely in the forties with the rise of mass media in the region. The grumpy narrator often declares himself an enemy of popular media and culture. As I have quoted above, he declares that life has punished him with a century of jazz and rock and roll.

The narrator's unease can be compared to what Barbero has called the intellectual's despair in times of "cultural disorder." According to Barbero, a world where the masses have not been entering modernity through books and the lettered culture, but rather through the opportunities and cultural models offered by the mass media, has made intellectuals weary. Barbero criticizes this weariness and considers that intellectuals should redefine their role and embrace the challenges and possibilities opened by this very same "disorder" (123). While many of the writers from his generation were among the first to embrace the challenges presented by popular media and culture, at first glance Vallejo's dandy seems to be not at all interested in these challenges and possibilities. He is constantly complaining about what he perceives as the decay in the present and is constantly longing for Silva's Colombia.

Silva is also the creator of a character who is, in many ways, an antecedent to Vallejo's own narrator: José Fernández, the caricaturized decadent hero of *De Sobremesa*, a novel written by Silva around 1886. Vallejo's work abounds with passages containing self-portraits in which the narrator depicts himself as a sort of descendant of Fernández, a decadent hero isolated from the outside world and surrounded by cosmopolitan objects and luxuries characteristic of the interiors described by Latin American and European novels from the turn of the 20th century.

This image of Fernando secluded from the world in Santa Anita—like *Des Esseintes* in Huysman's *Against the grain*—is nevertheless ironic. The anachronistic portrait of the aristocrat "hacendado" surrounded by luxuries is one in a series of portraits of the narrator as a caricaturized dandy. Those anachronistic portraits often appear intertwined with the narrator's equally anachronistic heterodoxies, with the contents that guarantee that, like a dandy, he will shock his readers in the context of the end of the 20th century. Such is the case in the following fragment of *El fuego secreto*, in which a declaration of a hatred of poverty is accompanied by an image of the narrator as a refined dandy:

> Odio la pobreza. Por ruin y roñosa, indolente y perezosa, altanera y servil. Y por ignorante además. El pobre no lee, no estudia, no progresa, no se quiere superar. Viven en bidonviles, tugurios, vecindales, favelas, y el trabajo les causa horror. Todo lo esperan del patrón o el gobierno, o de usted o de mí... Por eso no quiero al pobre. ¿Que pinte una pared? Empuerca la alfombra. ¿Que limpie la alfombra? Empuerca la pared. Deja sobre mi tapiz fino y caro, el gobelino, sus dedos pegajosos, pringosos, huellas digitales de criminal. ¿Por qué serán así? Su paladar no detecta el caviar, el salmón las trufas; sólo sabores burdos: arroz y frijoles. En cuanto al tacto no distinguen ni el algodón: el lino y la seda se les hacen fibras sintéticas. (*El fuego secreto* 251)

Fernando's exaggerated attacks on and insults of the poor lead to complaints about their lack of taste for refinements as cliché as caviar, salmon, truffles, linen and silk. Vallejo's return to decadence and the figure of the dandy appears to be at least partly parody and caricature. This is confirmed in another series of self-portraits in which he is far from appearing as that refined aristocrat secluded in an "ivory tower." In *Años de indulgencia* Fernando declares that he is closer to his "true self" when in contact with the underbelly of the city, sleeping under its bridges, covered by its filth. In passages that he calls his "baños de tinieblas," he describes his own body as a reflection of the soul of a miserable homeless woman, as a reflection of the decaying urban landscape. In communion with the underbelly of the city Fernando confronts the many faces of the failure of the project of modernity in Colombia, and invites the reader to question his rejection of popular culture, his despair for Silva's Colombia, the sincerity of all those heterodoxies formulated from an ivory tower.

IV

Just as this instability in the self-fashioning of the narrator throughout Vallejo's narrative seems like an invitation to question his sincerity, the passages in which he displays a politically incorrect misogynistic or a racist discourse guaranteed to shock his readers, make it almost too easy to label him as an anti-modern dandy. But the polemical, aggressive and seemingly anti-modern rhetoric with which Vallejo seems to be constantly seeking to shock us is not necessarily shocking or anti-modern purely for its own sake. Seen from the angle of the pose of the decadent dandy that Vallejo recycles to create his narrator, this rhetoric appears to be a peculiar critique not of all modernity or progress, but of what could be regarded as Colombia's failed attempts at modernity.

The politics of posing is an aspect of dandysim that has been addressed by critics like François Coblence and Molloy. According to Coblence, the dandy invites others to question their identity by making his pose a reflection and a projection of a given society. According to Molloy, posing has a destabilizing energy. The poser is constantly seeking visibility and controlling his exaggerations as a strategy of provocation, a challenge forcing a gaze, a reading, a framing (Molloy 142).

Within this framework, the image that Vallejo's dandy reflects and projects and towards which he forces the reader's gaze is of a project of modernity that has proven a failure in the context of the turn of the 21st century. Vallejo confronts this failure by exposing the crude realities of poverty and extreme violence in the slums of Medellín, realities that he frequently traces back to that period of rising political violence of the 1950's known as La Violencia.

What makes his own pose all the more relevant and powerful is that his anti-modern dandy reflects negatively the simulation and posing involved in Colombia's own project of modernity. Concepts like posing, simulation, artifice and masking, cloaking or costuming are frequently found in studies of the peculiarities of the projects of modernity in Latin America. According to Beatriz González-Stephan, modernity in Latin America is marked by an abyss between essence and appearance, a superimposition of structures of the past and the present that were "covered" but never reconciled. Consuelo Corredor approaches Colombian modernity as a project in which an emphasis on the material and economic modernization of the country concealed the lack of a "real" development of modern values like the democratization of education and culture (38). William Ospina also elaborates this idea of modernity as an appearance by referring to Colombian society as one characterized by what he calls "rituals of simulation." According to Ospina, the belief that Colombia inherited the ideals of the French Revolution is a sham. For Ospina, disguised under the values of a liberal republic, Colombia isn't far from being an anti-modern society, still determined by colonial structures and relations and built on the principles of exclusion.

By creating a dandy with an anti-modern pose—a heterodox narrator seemingly opposed to modern egalitarian and democratic values—Vallejo highlights the fraudulent pose in Colombia's own project of modernity. A good example is the truncation of liberal values is the 1886 constitution, which bound national identity to the Catholic and Spanish tradition. The fact that this constitution remained in effect until 1991, and consequently that freedom of religion and the rights of minorities were not recognized until that time and remain an ongoing struggle, demonstrates the stark truncation of Colombia's project of modernity. Perpetual violence and lasting poverty and squalor too mark its limits, and the lack of substance at its core.

To see simulation and posing as concepts that describe the very base of the project of modernity in Colombia suggests that Vallejo's return to decadence and to the figure of the dandy has dimensions that go beyond the merely aesthetic. This return, as I have suggested, has a political dimension through which Vallejo proves to be a meaningful voice in the Generation of '72's questioning of Latin American modernity at the turn of the 21st century. Vallejo's use of the dandy carries an irritating insistence about the way things really are in Colombia; according to the narrator in *Chapolas negras*: "el pecado del escándalo no está en el que escandaliza sino en el que se deja escandalizar. Éste es el que se debe atar la piedra de molino al cuello y echarse al agua" (272).

Works Cited

Barbero, Jesún Martín. "Nuestra excéntrica y heterogénea modernidad". *Estudios Políticos* 25 (2004): 115-134.

Baudelaire, Charles. "Le peintre de la vie moderne". *Sur le dandysme*. París: Union générale d'éditions, 1971. 189-245.

Brunner, José Joaquín. *América Latina: Cultura y modernidad*. Buenos Aires: Editorial Grijalbo, 1992.

Calinescu, Mateu. *Cinco caras de la modernidad*. Madrid: Alianza Editorial, 2003.

Carrasquilla, Tomás. "Homilía No 1". *Obra completa*. Medellín: Bedout, 1958. 664-672.

Casal, Julián del. *Poesía completa y prosa selecta*. Salvador, Álvaro, ed. Madrid: Verbum, 2001.

Coblence, Françoise. *Dandysme obligation d'incertitude*. Paris: Presses universitaires de France, 1988.

Constable, Liz; Dennis Denisoff y Matthew Potolsky, eds. *Perennial Decay: on the Aesthetics and Politics of Decadence*. Philadelphia: University of Pennsylvania Press, 1999.

Corredor Martínez, Consuelo. *Los límites de la modernización*. Bogotá: Cinep, Facultad de Ciencias Económicas Universidad Nacional de Colombia, 1992.

Darío, Rubén. *Obras completas*. Barcelona: Círculo de Lectores, 2007.

De la Campa, Román. "Hispanism and its Lines of Flight" in Moraña, Mabel, ed. *Ideologies of Hispanism*. Nashville: Vanderbilt University Press, 2005. 300-310.

Díaz Rodríguez, Manuel. *Sangre Patricia*. Caracas: Tip. J. M. Herrera Irigoyeb & Ca., 1902.

Foucault, Michel. "Preface to Transgression". Bouchard, Donald, ed. *Language, Counter Memory, Practice: Selected Essays and Interviews*. Ithaca: Cornell University Press, 1980. 29-52.

Franco, Jean. *Decline and Fall of the Lettered City: Latin America* in the Cold War. Cambridge: Harvard University Press, 2002.

Fuguet, Alberto y Gómez. McOndo. Barcelona : Grijalbo Mondadori, 1996.

González, Aníbal. *A Companion to Spanish American Modernismo*. Woodbridge y Rochester: Tamesis, 2007.

—. *Love and Politics in the Contemporary Spanish American Novel*. Austin: University of Texas Press, 2010.

González-Stephan, Beatriz. *Fundaciones: canon, historia y cultura nacional. La historiografía literaria del liberalismo hispanoamericano del siglo XIX*. Madrid: Iberoamericana, Vervuert, 2000.

González Echevarría, Roberto. *La ruta de Severo Sarduy*. Hanover, N.H: Ediciones del Norte, 1987.

—. *The Voice of the Masters: Writing and Authority in Modern Latin American Literature*. Austin: University of Texas Press, 1985.

Gutiérrez Girardot, Rafael. *Modernismo: supuestos históricos y culturales*. Bogotá: Universidad Externado de Colombia y Fondo de Cultura Económica, 1987.

Hannoosh, Michèle. *Parody and Decadence: Laforgue's* Moralités Légendaires. Columbus: Ohio State University Press, 1989.

Hanson, Ellis. *Decadence and Catholicism* . Cambridge y Londres: Harvard University Press, 1997.

Jofre, Álvaro Salvador. *El impuro amor de las ciudades: Notas acerca de la literatura modernista y el espacio urbano*. Madrid: Visor, 2006.

Ludmer, Josefina. *Aquí América Latina: Una especulación*. Buenos Aires: Eterna cadencia, 2010.

Mejías-López, Alejandro. *The Inverted Conquest: The Myth Of Modernity and the Transatlantic Onset of Modernism*. Nashville: Vanderbilt University Press, 2009.

Molloy, Sylvia. "La política de la pose". *Las culturas de fin de siglo en América Latina : coloquio en Yale, 8 y 9 de abril de 1994*. Josefina Ludmer, comp. Rosario: Beatriz Viterbo, 1994. 198-208.

Nicholson, Brantley. "Entrevista a Fernando Vallejo." *Chasqui* 40.2 (2011).

Ortega, Julio. "Título". *Crisis apocalípsis y utopías: Fines de siglo en la literatura latinoamericana*. Cÿanovas, Rodrigo y Roberto Hozven, eds. Santiago: Instituto Internacional de la Literatura, 1998.

Ospina, William. *¿Dónde está la franja amarilla?* Bogotá: Norma, 2009.

Paz, Octavio. *Los hijos del limo*. Barcelona, Seix Barral, 1974.

Pierrot, Jean. *Decadent Imagination, 1880-1900*. Chicago: University of Chicago Press, 1981.

Pratt, Mary Louise. "Los imaginarios planetarios". *El salto de Minerva: Intelectuales, género y estado en América Latina*. Moraña, Mabel y María Rosa Olivera-Williams, eds. Madrid: Iberoamericana; Frankfurt am Maim Vervuert, 2005. 269-282.

Rodó, José Enrique. *Obras completas*. Madrid: Aguilar, 1957.

Silva, José Asunción. *Poesía completa y De sobremesa*. Bogotá: Norma, 1997.

Reed, John. *Decadent Style*. Athens,OH: Ohio University Press, 1985.

Vallejo, Fernando. *Almas en pena, chapolas negras*. Bogotá: Punto de Lectura, 2006.

—. *Años de indulgencia. El río del tiempo*. Bogotá: Alfaguara, 2002.

—. *El desbarrancadero*. Bogotá: Alfaguara, 2005.

—. *El don de la vida*. Madrid: Alfaguara, 2010.

—. *El fuego secreto. El río del tiempo*. Bogotá: Alfaguara, 2002.

—. "El lejano país de Rufino José Cuervo". *El Malpensante* 76 (2007). 1-6

—. *El Mensajero. Una biografía de Porfirio Barba Jacob*. Bogotá: Alfaguara, 2003.

—. *Entre fantasmas. El río del tiempo*. Bogotá: Alfaguara, 2002.

—. *La rambla paralela*. Bogotá: Alfaguara, 2002.

—. *La tautología darwinista*. Bogotá: Taurus, 2005.

—. *La Virgen de los sicarios*. Bogotá: Alfaguara, 1998.

—. *Logoi. Una gramática del lenguaje literario*. México: Fondo de Cultura Económica, 1997.

—. *Los días azules. El río del tiempo*. Bogotá: Alfaguara, 2002.

—. *Los caminos a Roma. El río del tiempo*. Bogotá: Alfaguara, 2002.

—. *Manualito de imposturología física*. Bogotá: Taurus, 2005.

—. *Mi hermano el alcalde*. Madrid: Alfaguara, 2004.

Vargas Vila, José María. *Rubén Darío*. Madrid: V.H de Sanz Calleja Editores, 1920.

Villena Garrido, Francisco. "La sinceridad puede ser demoledora: Conversaciones con Fernando Vallejo". *Ciberletras* 13 (2005). Publicación electrónica.

Volpi, Jorge. *El insomnio de Bolívar: cuatro consideraciones intempestivas sobre América Latina en el siglo XXI*. Barcelona: Debate, 2009.

Weir, David. *Decadence and the Making of Modernism*. Amherst: University of Massachusetts Press, 1995.

THE KING'S TOILET: CRUISING LITERARY HISTORY
IN REINALDO ARENAS' *BEFORE NIGHT FALLS*

Lázaro Lima
University of Richmond

[W]hen I entered a public rest room I became painfully aware that my presence failed to arouse the old expectant feeling of complicity. Nobody paid any attention to me, and the erotic games going on proceeded undisturbed. I no longer existed. I was not young anymore. Right then and there I thought that the best thing for me was to die.
—Reinaldo Arenas, *Before Night Falls*

I. Before Night Falls Twenty Years After

Reinaldo Arenas (1943-1990) opens his last major work in search of sex in a cruisy toilet.[1] In his posthumously published autobiography *Antes que anochezca* (1992; *Before Night Falls*, 1993),[2]

---

1. I thank Rita Geada and the late Roberto Valero for introducing me to Arenas and his work. The Department of Rare Books and Special Collections at Princeton University, Firestone Library, provided timely access to Arenas' papers, photographic archive, and correspondence for this article which forms part of a longer project on Arenas' "afterlives."
2. In what follows, all quotations from Reinaldo Arena's *Antes que anochezca* (1992) refer to Dolores Koch's translation of his autobiography *Before Night Falls* (1993). It is worth noting that while Arenas was finishing his autobiography, he was also rewriting *El color del verano* (translated as *The Color of Summer: or the New Garden of Earthly Delights* in 2000), which was published posthumously by Ediciones Universal in Miami in 1991. The novel is one of his most autobiographi-

Arenas—known as "Rey" or "El Rey" to his friends ("the King" in Spanish)—writes that months before taking his life he had entered a public restroom in search of sex only to find that no one was interested in cruising him much less engaging in any sort of sex.[3] Arenas simply finds himself unwanted by the cruisy queens in the loo who carry on as if he did not even exist. El Rey, in the toilet and distraught, tells us that "[r]ight then and there I thought that the best thing for me was to die" (ix). He buys a ticket to Miami to do just that, but finds that even death is elusive when one wants it most. Lucky for Arenas and for us. The experience of rejection at the loo, that symbolizes his impending death, also functions as the catalyst that allows him to face his literary legacy: "My main regret...was to die without having been able to complete my pentagonía" (x).[4] In *Before Night Falls* Arenas' desire and commitment to completing his "pentagonía" (quintet), a cycle of five novels of which he had already published three: *Singing from the Well* (*Celestino antes del alba*, 1967), *The Palace of the White Skunks* (*El palacio de las blanquísimas mofetas, 1980*), and *Farewell to the Sea* (*Otra vez el mar*, 1982), also announces how he wished his body of work to be understood. So it is that in *Before Night Falls*, more than in any other work, "the King's" literal body becomes indexical to and inseparable from how he wished his body of work to be understood. I take Arenas' tearoom anecdote to be highly instructive of a broader concern regarding the nature of writing for El Rey, his literary legacy, and the queer Cuban literary history his broader work wishes to memorialize. Let me explain why.

In the tearoom, Arenas draws a stark parallel between his

cal were his persona is triangulated in the characters "Skunk in a Funk," his queer nom de guerre, Gabriel "the dutiful straight son," and Reinaldo "the famous 'persecuted' author." It is evident that toward the end of his life the autobiographical impulse took center stage in his last works. Still, the genre demands and constraints of autobiography make *Before Night Falls* a indispensible text and map for studies on Arenas' work and legacies.

3. For a useful discussion of the politics of "tearoom," or toilet sex, at the height of the AIDS crisis see José Esteban Muñoz, "Ghosts of Public Sex: Utopian Longings, Queer Memories," in Ephen Glenn Colter, et al., *Policing Public Sex: Queer Politics And the Future of AIDS Activism* (1996).

4. For an analysis of the *pentagonía* see Francisco Soto's *Reinaldo Arenas: The Pentagonia* (1994). Soto's monograph emerged at a moment were the politics of testimonial literature in Latin America received considerable critical attention. Not surprisingly, Soto perhaps too singularly emphasizes Arenas own declaration that the quintet was "both a writer's autobiography and a metaphor of Cuban history."

physical decline, and concomitant lack of desirability in the face of uninterested tricks who refuse to acknowledge his existence, with his incomplete *pantagonía* and his legacy as a writer confronting imminent death in the face of literary history; put another way, Arenas body becomes a book and the loo's queens his unwilling literary critics. So it is that Arenas takes it upon himself to have *Before Night Falls* serve both as a map of how his work should be understood in relation to his very own queer Cuban literary legacy and, no less significantly, as an occasion to revisit his relation to Cuban literary history after the Revolution of 1959. Rey forestalls death in *Before Night Falls* so that his own literary afterlife may be given a corrective reprieve and opportunity for completion lest it be met with the indifference he found in the tearoom. In the process, *Before Night Falls* becomes Arenas' *ars poetica*.

In this article I will read *Before Night Falls* as Arenas' queer version of Cuban literary history and his relation to it. Against the commonplace assertions that demand that *Before Nights Falls* be primarily understood, if not exclusively, as an invective against Fidel Castro or, in the other extreme, as an *ars moriendi* and AIDS testimonial from a sexual dissident, I wish to revisit this text on the twentieth anniversary of its publication to underscore a missed reading that can help situate how Arenas, one of the most transgresive writers theorized in this collection as the Generation of '72, might also be its most conservative in his attachments to the very modernist aesthetic agencies eschewed my so many of his generational contemporaries.[5] This is not to ignore, of course, the most obvious and sometimes illuminating readings of *Before Night Falls*

---

5. For Arenas as little more than an opportunist critic of communist Cuba see Lourdes Argüelles and B. Ruby Rich's influential article in *Signs: Journal of Women in Culture and Society*, "Homosexuality, Homophobia, and Revolution: Notes Toward an Understanding of the Cuban Lesbian and Gay Male Experience, Part 2." Here Argüelles and Rich's go so far as to suggest that Arenas work represents "the beginning of an unprecedented manipulation of the gay issue by those engaged in the U.S.-financed war against the Cuban revolution" (132). For a more measured analysis of this tendency see Vek Lewis's thoughtful essay, "Grotesque Spectacles: The Janus Face of the State and Gender Variant Bodies in the Work of Reinaldo Arenas" (2009). For a reading of Arenas as AIDS memorist see Nerea Riley's "Reinaldo Arenas' Autobiography Antes que anochezca as Confrontational 'Ars Moriendi'" (1999). Riley considers Arena's autobiography as ushering in an aesthetics of dying where "narrating one's death has become a genre in itself." Rafael Ocasio's *A Gay Cuban Activist in Exile: Reinaldo Arenas* (2007) provides a reading of Arenas' complex relationship to queer writing and queer studies.

that have fallen on either end of the political continuum, or somewhere in between, but rather as an opportunity to revisit Arenas' important autobiography on the anniversary of its publication this year. And so it is to *Before Night Falls'* afterlives that I now turn in order to reconsider and map *el caso* Arenas' literary histories.

II. Before Night Falls' *Afterlives*

El Rey's *Before Night Falls*, beyond the genre constraints of autobiography and its attendant truth claims, is unlike any of Arenas' other works. At the end of his life and near death, much of the autobiography was dictated into a tape recorder, transcribed by his intimate friend Lázaro Gómez Carrilles (who became one the beneficiaries of his estate along with the Cuban exile painter Jorge Camacho [1934-2011]), and finally revised for publication.[6] The spoken quality of the transcribed text figures prominently in the autobiography as the first person narrative voice follows the rhythmic patterns of Arenas' measured but speedy delivery of speech. This is evident to anyone who ever heard Arenas speak in person. His voice in *Before Night Falls* glides from sentence to sentence, anecdote to anecdote, with an urgency that is stoically resigned and mediated by a steady tonality that appears unbroken by pauses. Curiously, this very confusion between the actual writer's voice, with his narrative autobiographical voice, also manifested itself most stridently in *Before Night Falls'* most significant afterlife as a film. The substitution from word to flesh, that is, Arenas' book functioning as a metonym for Arenas himself, was facilitated when Arenas was discovered by a generation of admirers after the release of Julian Schnabel's award winning version of *Before Night Falls* in 2000.[7] Indeed, many of

---

6. The original draft of Arenas's *Antes que anochezca* remained closed to researchers until 2010. There is as yet no study that compares the first edition of *Antes que anochezca* published in Spain by Editorial Tusquets in 1992 with the original draft. See the "Dolores Koch Collection of Reinaldo Arenas, 1974-2005" (bulk 19821993). The collection is stored onsite at Firestone Library. Box 1, Folders 1-4 are stored in special vault facilities. For online resources see the Princeton University Library Manuscripts Division site (http://findingaids.princeton.edu/getEad?eadid=C0984&kw=).

7. The Generation of '72's literary outpouring has resulted in many film adaptations including Fernando Vallejo's *La virgen de los sicarios* (1994), Ricardo Piglia's *Plata quemada* (1997), Ariel Dorman's *Death and the Maiden*, and Antonio Skármeta's *Il Postino* (1996), just to name a few of the most popular.

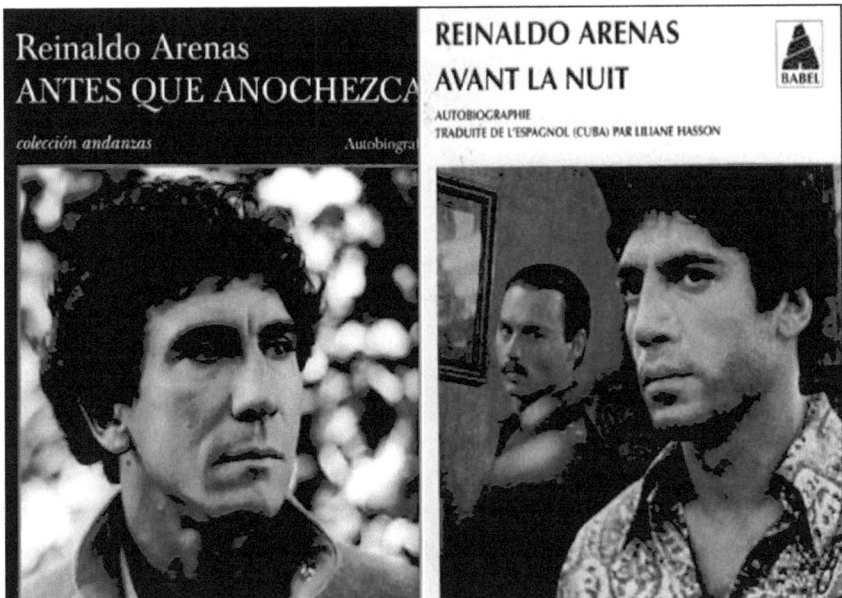

Figure 1: In the French translation of Reinaldo Arenas' *Antes que anochezca* by Liliane Hasson, *Avant la nuit*, Arenas' photograph on the cover is replaced by Javier Bardem playing Arenas in Schnabel's film along with Johnny Depp as Lieutenant Víctor.

these admirers had little or no knowledge of El Rey's broader intellectual project or its relationship to his autobiography and, much less, the extent of his prolific outpouring of work (let alone of his exile through the Mariel Boat Exodus, much less Cuba). And it wasn't just that some popular as well as professional readers confused the generic constraints of the original autobiography, the retrospective accounting of a life, with the genre constraints of the memoir delimited by a finite or thematic moment or preoccupation in a writers' life. The film not only seemed to erase these generic demarcations but it also, wittingly or not, substituted Arenas' own life story with the filmic simulacrum of a queer Cuban life. In the process, Arenas' afterlife became mediated through its filmic simulacrum as represented vis-à-vis the film to the embarrassment of journalists, bloggers and editors who even mistook Javier Bardem's photograph with El Rey's image. This was made blatantly patent, for example, in the French translation of Spanish publisher Editorial Tusquet's *Antes que anochezca* (*Before Night Falls*) when French publisher

Babel's *Avant la nuit* (2000) used Spanish actor Javier Bardem's image on the cover of Arenas' autobiography (see Figure 1). The double, the celluloid simulacrum of Arenas' life, stood inviolate for the original. Schnabel's version of Arenas' life story and those that followed proved problematic, wittingly or not, for various reasons that are worth exploring.

Beyond issues of poetic license, the film ultimately reduced Arenas' life story to a "gay" identity category where the protagonist fundamentally becomes a victim of communist Cuba's repression of artists, if not its most valiant and an admirable one at that, but Castro's victim nonetheless.[8] The film was well received by a U.S. gay and lesbian community who was, as late as 2000, both discovering and starved for queer "Latino" topics that would represent the range of LGBTQ experiences in "America."[9] In *The Advocate*, for example, the oldest continuing LGBT publication in the United States, a review of Schnabel's *Before Night Falls* assured readers that "anyone inclined to romanticize Cuba in these winter years of Fidel Castro's regime needs to take a look at Schnabel's *Before Night Falls*, which presents a harrowing portrait of what it meant for a writer to be gay and out [sic] in the heyday of the revolution. [...] Arenas must run a veritable *Midnight Express* obstacle course of imprisonment and psychological torture before landing on unsteady feet in America [sic]" (57).[10] (Curiously, it is with little irony that *The Advocate*, as the "serious" voice of LGBT issues in the United States, now endorses Cuba's Mariela Castro Espín, President Raúl Castro's Daughter, and her queer rights work in her capacity as the director of Cuba's National Center for Sex Education (CENESEX); an irony that would not have been lost on El Rey.)[11]

---

8. For a reading of Arenas' *Before Night Falls* and Schnabel's film in transnational context see my "Locas al Rescate: The Transnational Hauntings of Queer Latinidad," *Journal of Transnational American Studies* 3.2, Winter 2011 (Reprise). Digital (http://escholarship.org/uc/item/9ch96543).

9. Director Manuel Zayas' documentary *Seres Extravagantes* (2004), released in the United States as *Odd people Out* (2004), attempted to be a corrective of sorts to Shnabele's version of Arenas' life. The documentary, which was clandestinely shot in Cuba, provides interviews with Arenas' colleagues, friends, and relatives. Limited distribution and internet access has limited this important documentary's interlocutors.

10. Jan Stuart, "Havana Heartache," *The Advocate*, December 19, 2000, 57.

11. Michael Rowe, "The New Cuban Revolution," *The Advocate*, September 14, 2009. The online version of the article can be found at the Advocate.com

Not surprisingly, the autobiography, which was rediscovered after the film, and the film's reception itself, also created unusual bedfellows and alliances between formerly irreconcilable camps. Many right-wing media outlets and critics praised both the film and the autobiography by exalting its politics at the expense of its strident emphasis on sexuality, while left-identified queers and their allies praised Arenas' dissident sexuality while mostly ignoring his disillusionment over the most obvious of their sacred cows, the Cuban Revolution of 1959, and what the Revolution has meant to scores of intellectuals and writers outside of Cuba. In the filmic version of Arenas' life story, it appears that the Cuban writer is imprisoned for being a strident *maricón* without taking into account that it was ultimately Arenas' writing, and the subsequent publishing of his work abroad, that led to his incarcerations. The omission is significant. Imprisoned in El Morro, Arenas relates in his autobiography how he finds out through one of his interrogators, Lieutenant Víctor, that his novel *The Palace of the White Skunks* "had been published in France and Germany; he showed me one copy but did not allow me to touch it… The publication of this book was proof of my existence, and that infuriated them" (215). For Arenas, *scripta manent, ergo sum*, that is, if his writing endures, therefore he is.

The most striking feature of these substitutions—between the book and its simulacrum, the celluloid image of the writer with the actual writer—was that it posthumously confirmed Arenas' reputation as a writer and secured his place in the Latin American and, not coincidently, the emerging Unites States Latino literature canon. As a consequence of this, the film also sealed Arenas' reputation as a "gay" anti-Castro zealot on a crusade against "communism," at least as its understood in the United States, and of *Before Night Falls*, the autobiograph—whether it was actually read or not—as the text that proved his singularity of purpose. Such reductionism is, of course, problematic but especially so to a writer like Arenas who understood *Before Night Falls* as a corrective literary supplement to his writerly neglect while he was alive.

The most significant iteration of the Manichean duality that emerged from the success of Schnabel's version of Arena's life story occurred ten years after Schnabel's film with the highly anticipated production of *Before Night Falls* by Cuban American composer

site:<http://www.advocate.com/news/world-news/2009/09/14/new-cuban-revolucion?page=0,0>. Last accessed May 21, 2012>.

Jorge Martín. The opera itself emerged at a propitious moment in the United States where "emerging" cultural centers with large Latino populations such as Dallas and Houston were willing to take risks in "contemporary" productions and establish reputations for not only introducing local audiences to great performances but also to performances that were deemed more relevant than the traditional operatic fare of major venues such as New York, Paris, Munich or Milan.

Before Night Falls, the opera, had been in the works for many years. An initial concert reading from the first act of the opera was performed at the Clark Studio Theatre at Lincoln Center in Manhattan on May 2 in 2005 to considerable acclaim. Following the Lincoln Center performance of the opera's first act, a panel discussion was moderated by Steven Osgood, the conductor and American Opera Projects Artistic Director, and included composer Jorge Martín, and co-librettist Dolores M. Koch. The truncated New York performance, and the panel discussion that attempted to frame it, was but a rehearsal for the world premiere of the complete opera at the Fort Worth Opera in Texas on May 29, 2010.[12] The opera's opening run, however, along with the accompanying 2010 release of a CD performed by the Fort Worth Opera, was met with mixed reviews that are illustrative of the broader tensions that characterized previous iterations of *Before Night Falls'* afterlives from autobiography to film.

Writing for *The Wall Street Journal*, opera reviewer Heidi Waleson repeated and perpetuated many of the standard banalities about the opera that mirrored earlier reviews of Schnabel's film, even calling the opera an adaptation of a "memoir" [sic] by Reinaldo Arenas.[13] Beyond the standard banalities about either left or right political proclivities, or Arenas as a writer in search of freedoms, Waleson's lack of interest in Arenas and, it would appear, the broader themes the production attempted to grapple with were stunning. For Waleson, *Before Night Falls*, the opera, is simply insufferable:

> [I]t's never clear what it was that he [Arenas] wrote that was so threatening to the regime. And as lament follows lament, Rey nev-

---

12. The dates for the performance at the Fort Worth Opera ran from May 29, 2010 until June 6 of that year.

13. See Heidi Waleson, "Imprisoned by Clichés, Laments and Exposition," *The Wall Street Journal Online*. Accessed May 21, 2012.

er seems to change...it's a relief when an actual antagonist—Victor, the Castro hardliner—finally starts *torturing* Rey by burning his manuscript and *knocking him around* in prison. (my emphasis).

Waleson's ahistorical and factually inaccurate review of the opera, as well as the life it was based upon, highlighted the difficulty of apprehending *el caso* Arenas in the public sphere beyond the media sound bite and the unfortunate confluence of events that have made the likes of Arenas, whether one sees him as a Cuban writer, a Cuban American writer, an "American" writer, or a "global citizen," ultimately not worthy of serious or at least thoughtful engagement. Waleson's assertions and mistaken genre associations, in the pages of *The Wall Street Journal* no less, evinced a less than accurate assessment of Arenas' "story of underdevelopment," to borrow a commonplace from the post-revolutionary Cuban and Cuban American vernacular.

Edmundo Desnoes, expanding on his contribution to the classic Cuban film *Memorias del subdesarollo* (1968)—an adaptation of his eponymously named novel—wrote that "El subdesarrollo es la incapacidad de acumular experiencias" (underdevelopment refers to the inability to accumulate experiences). The need to accumulate experiences, understood as a state of yearning from the periphery, versus Waleson's lack of desire or willingness to move beyond her unexamined prejudices, characterizes this misreading of *el caso* Arenas. Waleson's missed opportunity puts into relief the importance of cultivating alternative cultural and critical industries, especially when metropolitan cultural centers are incapable or unwilling to apprehend the objects they ostensibly wish to elucidate. Would a writer in the pages of *The Wall Street Journal* be as unselfconsciously dismissive of, say, an African American writer?

A curious exception to Waleson's depoliticized assessment of the opera appeared in the highly partisan *National Review* by Jay Nordlinger. Yet where Waleson's review was naively ahistorical to the point of actually wishing El Rey's "torture" for the sake of the opera's narrative clarity, or perhaps her own satisfaction, Nordlinger's review evinced a politicized reading mediated through a Cold War era optic that attempted to reconcile conservative homophobia with Castrophobia. Nordlinger called the opera, "a worthy work of art... [that] for telling a truth too seldom told, it makes you grateful." In his review, Nordlinger—who can fortunately distinguish the difference between a "memoir" and an "autobiography"—praises the opera as "a worthy work of art" for the very reasons that Arenas' autobiography was initially reduced to a monochromatic tirade about pro- or contra-Castro subject positions whose "value" was contingent upon how well it represented a particular political agenda for interested constituencies. He begins by establishing a context for his readers noting "that a movie of *Before Night Falls* was made in 2000" before dishing:

> Can we talk about the opera world? We're all adults here, right? We can speak frankly. The opera world is very gay and very left-wing. There are a fair number of conservatives in it. Many are closeted, and they sometimes come out to me (swearing me to eternal secrecy, on pain of death). But the opera world is by and large strongly left-wing, as well as gay. And *Before Night Falls* will pose a dilemma: On one hand, you have your 50-year love affair with the Castro dictatorship; on the other hand...what about gays? It's one thing to persecute filthy capitalists who want to sell toothpaste in the shadows, or who read *National Review*-style literature by candlelight. But *gays*?

Norlinger becomes an apologist for the "gay question" in the *National Review* as the queer theme becomes subservient to the broader appeal of the opera's most important contribution as he sees it: to "speak frankly" and tell the "very gay and very left-wing" opera world about the evils of communism and, presumably, open the eyes of left-wing opera lovers and closeted conservatives alike.

From Nordlinger's jocular but predictable reading of Arenas as a metonym for anti-communism—always through Schnabel's film—to Waleson's disinterest in the politics that Arenas represents to either the left or the right, indeed her disdain for any of Arenas' afterlives, make understanding El Rey's literary legacy all the more urgent twenty years after the publication of his autobiography and how he hoped it would be read and remembered. So it will be useful, however briefly, to distinguish Arenas' afterlife and the use-value of his simulacrum to these partisan constituencies, from the broader concerns that emerged when, after being discarded in the toilet and facing imminent death, El Rey resolves to complete his literary project.

III. The Arts of Cruising

Cruising in *Before Night Falls* is as important as Arenas'

disillusionment with the regime but has received relatively scant critical attention despite its conspicuous presence in the autobiography. From public restrooms, to beaches, changing-rooms, mangroves, trucks, trains, buses, private homes (especially his wretched aunt Agata's), and even at military camps such as the infamous UMAPs,[14] Arenas is constantly cruising. Though the toilet certainly seems like a strange place to begin an autobiography Arenas takes it upon himself to begin in a locus of "unproductive labor," in a scatological social space, engaging in a "nonproductive" activity without any seemingly redemptive or useful ends save his desire to do so. Arenas' laborious cruising is counter to socially "useful" or productive ends and could, with some irony, be said to constitute what Marx called "labor without speech"[15] in order to situate his work—both his literary and sexual labor—in terms of a fundamental modernist proposition: that a work of art is fundamentally an autotelic artifact outside the control of the state or the use-value accorded to it by any system that would delimit the work of art's autonomy. The insistence on the fundamental autonomy of the work of art is, of course, a modernist conceit that Arenas' extends and elaborates in *Before Night Falls* so that his aesthetic proposition here—the art of cruising—requires the recognition that sexual freedom and artistic freedom are inseparable and mutually constitutive of the other; any limitation imposed on one is an affront on the other.

In *Before Night Falls*, laboring unproductively, what I am here calling Arenas' art of cruising, *is* laboring against the state *aesthetically* and so Arenas' writerly critique of the state is further reinforced by his queer acts, the arts of the cruising, that destabilize bodies and pleasures and makes "art" out of queer sociality. Arenas' queer art is ultimately disruptive because it incites reproductive laborers, ostensible subjects of the state, to counter-pleasures they

---

14. Begun in 1965 the "Unidades Militares de Ayuda a la Producción," Military Units to Aid Production, were work camps set up for alternative form of military service for queers and, to a lesser extent, religious groups such as Jehovah Witnesses and Seventh Day Adventists.

15. In the principle English translation of Karl Marx's *Grundrisse* Martin Nicolaus translates Marx's "arebit sans phrase" as "labor pure and simple." The translation misses the ambiguity and force of Marx's assertion where he elaborates, "the harmonies of equality [and] freedom," the structuring force of *pecunia*, or money, in Capitalism resides in alienating labor from speech not just the more commonplace understanding of "alienation" where the subject is severed from her material labor, the material object of production (105).

take out of the toilet and into their state-sanctioned lives. These subjects, who through comportment and deportment are state actors, lose the very subject integrity that the state demands; in the process, they are "interpolated," to borrow an Althusserian commonplace, by the queer imperative of counter(revolutionary) pleasure.[16]

Arenas considers cruising and writing to be a complimentary "great feast." After detailing various sexual escapades at Guanabo Beach with fellow queer writer friends, Arenas relates how they "would all bring [their] notebooks and write poems or chapters of [their] books, and would have sex with armies of men. The erotic and the literary went hand in hand... I could never work in pure abstinence; the body needs to feel satisfied to give free reign to the spirit" (101). Writing for Arenas could not happen without cruising or vice versa:

> I would lock myself in my little room in Miramar, and sometimes write until late into the night. But during the day I roamed all the beaches, barefoot, and enjoyed unusual adventures with wonderful guys in the bushes, with ten, eleven, twelve of the sometimes; at other times with only one, who would be so extraordinary he would satisfy me as much as twelve. (102)

Indeed, Arenas' aesthetic move is strategic, insofar as it allows his recursive cruising in toilets, mangroves, and all manner of recondite places for homosexual erotic fulfillment in *Before Night Falls*, to be understood not only as an affront to a repressive a political regime (Castro's Cuba) that attempts to destroy both unreproductive and unproductive labor—or "the art of cruising"—but also as an indictment of the supposedly "enlightened" regimes of "advanced societies" where, as he notes, queers paradoxically segregate themselves and willingly delimit their own erotic imagination rather than undermine the normative strictures that "tolerate" queerness (107). That is, queerness for Arenas functions as an aesthetic drive, creation *sans* reproduction, an art unencumbered by the potential ends of its use value that can thereby avoid being coerced as much by totalitarian regimes as by purportedly free democratic states.

16. I cite Louis Althusser's ideologeme: "...what thus seems to take place outside ideology (to be precise, in the street), in reality takes place in ideology [....] That is why those who are in ideology believe themselves by definition outside ideology: one of the effects of ideology is the practical *denegation* of the ideological character of ideology by ideology: ideology never says, 'I am ideological'" (118).

Through cruising it might be said that Arenas is extending a broader tradition of Cuban modernist anti-authoritarian aesthetic practice developed by his generational precursor Jorge Mañach (1898-1961) in his classic *Indagacíon del choteo* (1928). Mañach's essay—initially delivered as a lecture at the Institución Hispano-Cubana de Cultura in Havana by the invitation of Fernando Ortiz (1881-1969)—considered "*choteo*" to be an anti-authoritarian *techne* and practice in the face of authority that he strategically understood to be part of the Cuban national character. Manach's *choteo*, and his broader intellectual project, forms part of a wider cultural and political movement, grouped around the *Revista de Avance* (1927-1930) that attempted to counter through cultural agencies the political and economic crisis instantiated by Cuban dictator Gerardo Machado (1871-1939). For Mañach, Cuban *choteo* incarnates individual self-assertion and independence against authority. The practitioner of *choteo*, *un choteador*, is "*un opositor sistemático*," a systematic contrarian who, despite himself, "*no toma en serio nada de lo que generalmente se tiene por serio*" (a *choteador* does not take seriously anything that should be taken seriously), not even the "*presencia sagrada de la muerte*," (the sacred presence of death) (15; 22). It is in this sense that Arenas' cruising extends what Jorge Mañach called "libertinaje mental" (42), literally "mental libertinism," or, more felicitously translated, "unrestrained thinking" in and through the literal body vis-à-vis intercourse with the body politic's forbidden fruits. Perhaps anticipating one of Leo Bersani most important contributions against the orthodoxy of queer theory, and its initial imperative in the 1980s to redeem queer subjectivity by resemanticizing "shame," Arenas refuses to impose the discourse of "dignity" to queer subjects of the state whom the state considers shameful in their unproductive drive, their inability to labor for the Regime, their inability to fashion desire in the image of the state's "Hombre Nuevo" (the New Man).[17] Arenas resists the imperative to rehabilitate what we might call "disabled queer subjects." In this sense, "[g]ay men's 'obsession with sex," as Bersani writes, "far from being denied, should be celebrated—not for its communal virtues, not because of its subversive potential for parodies of machismo [...], but rather because it never

---

17. For an analysis of "el Hombre Nuevo" in Cuban literary studies and its relation to politics see Sonia Béhar, *La caída del Hombre Nuevo: Narrativa cubana del período Especial* (2008):1-34.

stops re-presenting the internalized phallic male as an infinitely loved object of sacrifice" (30). That "object of sacrifice," for Bersani, is the encounter of the self with the incommensurability of absolute otherness; itself understood, as we used to say in literary studies, as an encounter with "the ineffable."

As an aesthetic practice or *techne*, the arts of cruising for Arenas functions as a corporeally coded search for beauty's elusive embrace and an aesthetic response to literary and literal death. Cruising is elaborated in *Before Night Falls* as an aesthetic prerogative of sexual experiences with others from which to lime literary agencies; cruising scandalizes and titillates, to be sure, but it also decenters the spaces ostensibly occupied by what became El Che's compulsory *hombre nuevo*, the Cuban "New Man."[18] The idea of the Cuban New Man was, of course, antithetical to homosexuality as the history of the UMAPs makes clear. Fidel Castro himself had famously pronounced that the "homosexual" could never "embody the conditions and requirements of conduct that would enable us to consider him a true Revolutionary."[19] So it is against the carceral apparatus of forced labor camps and the state's insistence on "productive" labor for the Revolution that Arenas himself labors against as much as for an aesthetic practice of freedom. It is therefore not surprising that it is precisely in a forced labor sugar plantation that Arenas tells us he began to write what became his autobiography, what at the time he called "The Western Diary," his daily record of events, conversations, meetings, and seemingly boundless cruising (130).

Cruising in *Before Night Falls* is both a constant act and an aesthetically principled practice of freedom initiated under state-sanctioned confinement, that is, as much in the forced labor camp as in its metonymic incarnation, the Cuban state. I would go so far as to suggest that cruising for Arena's in *Before Night Falls* is an aesthetic practice that insists on new forms of sociality that are neither dependant on morality or state sanctioned forms of intimacy such as marriage or adherence to the regime's ideals. Arenas' voracious cruising, beyond any moralistic reductionism and collapse into mere promiscuity, constitutes a practical ethics that depends on cultivating a principled openness to otherness. Cruising, like

---

18. Samuel Feijoó, "Revolución y vicios." El Mundo, 15 April 1965 (5).

19. Cited in Carrie Hamilton and Elizabeth Dore, *Sexual Revolutions in Cuba: Passion, Politics, and Memory* (39).

modernism's art for art's sake, is a *techne*, an aesthetic prerogative of confrontation with incommensurable otherness. Cruising for Arenas is a literary practice as much as a corporeal search for the ineffable; aesthetic content inseparable from artistic form.[20]

IV. Before Night Falls' *Queer Literary History*

> [M]y generation, would read the poems, banned under the Castro regime, of Jorge Luis Borges, and we recited from memory the poems of Octavio Paz. Our generation, the generation born in the forties, has been a lost generation, destroyed by the communist regime.
> —Reinaldo Arenas, *Before Night Falls*

The recourse to the concept of a "literary generation" does not emerge *ex nihilo,* or much less disinterested or outside the structuring imperatives it serves, but rather it is created in order to reinforce two of the principal foundational pillars of literary studies as understood within the Western literary tradition: periodization and canonicity. Periodization, the belief in predictable literary thematics or concerns borne of historical circumstances, and canonicity, the means through which literary artifacts are accorded their "value" based on the cultural and historical tastes of the former, are central to the understanding the generational concept in literary studies. The conceptual recourse to literary "generations" has, of course, more notable and linguistically specific genealogies within the languages and canons of the West's list of so-called "great books." But within the Peninsular and Latin American literary tradition, the so-called "Generación del '98" (the Spanish "Generation of 1898), has provided the template from which to understand Julius Petersen's (1878–1941) concept of "literary generations" which he elaborated in 1913.[21]

---

20. Pedro Juan Gutierrez's (1950-) highly sexualized *Trilogía sucia de La Habana* (1998) is the literary inheritor and successor to Mañach's "libertinaje mental" and Arenas' "arts of the toilet." In the face of a broken city, Havana, "un laberinto construido con tablas podridas y pedazos de ladrillos" (293), and a political system confronting its historical legacies, his *Trilogía* expands anti-authroritarian aesthetics in Cuba's "Período especial," or special period of economic hardship after the collapse of the Soviet Union.

21. See Julius Petersen, "Las generaciones literarias," in Emil Ermantinger, *Filosofía de la ciencia literaria* (1946): 75-93. German philologist and literary his-

Petersen's influence was not uniform within the "Hispanic" tradition in the Spanish speaking Americas but it ultimately established the foundation from which critics like Cedomil Goic could term the "Generation of 1972" (1992) to refer to the point of contact and generational affinities between those Latin American writers born between 1935 and 1949.[22] For Goic, Reinaldo Arenas, along with writers as diverse as Mario Vargas Llosa (1936-), José Emilio Pacheco (1939-) and Severo Sarduy (1936-1993), represent a generational cohort of post-Boom writers who break with well-worn and established narrative innovations and who represent a range of *"sectores sociales,"* ("social sectors"), that is, the diversity of experiences made manifest in literature from the vantage point of various social, ethnic, racial and sexually diverse groups that often, though certainly not always, fell outside the standard narratives of postboom aesthetics. The thematic treatment of homosexuality, for example, in texts as diverse as Vargas Llosa' s *La ciudad y los perros* (1963),[23] and the whole of Reinaldo Arenas' writings, make manifest the extent to which Goic attempted to "diversify" Latin American literatures and writers with divergent political and aesthetic concerns despite his structuralist insistence on generational affinities and thematic integrity (even when these affinities were not always driven by generational imperatives or defining zeitgeist).

As the Generation of 1972's queerest of aesthetes, Arenas attempts to explain why his generation of Cuban writers and artists, "has been a lost generation, destroyed by the communist regime" (88). Against Goic's much looser conception of a literary generation, for Arenas the term "generation" refers specifically to those Cuban writers who came of age after the Revolution or who were delimited by the Revolution's insistence on writing that espoused the ideals of the state. It is in this sense that *Before Night Falls*

---

torian Petersen remains central to Cedomil Goic's conception of "literary generations" though by way of José Ortega and Gassett and the Spanish peninsular legacy that Latin American critics of the mid XX inherited as they elaborated an emergent Latin American literature canon.

22. See, Cedomil Goic, *Mitos Degradados: Ensayos de Compresión de la Literatura Hispanoamericana* (1992).

23. In Vargas Llosa's novel the character Paulino, for example, fellates a group of fellow military school cadets with the ruse of awarding a "prize" to the cadet who can last the longest before climaxing. Paulino's labor, is based on favors, whereas Arenas' are based on the premise and expectation, at least as he tells it, of unadulterated pleasure for all parties involved.

becomes both a literary history of Arenas' own trajectory as a writer, his testament to the importance of "un(re)productive labor," as well as a corrective literary history of his generation of Cuban writers that he considers either "lost," "destroyed," or both, by a state that regulates the use-value of artistic creation in general and literature in particular. Arenas' relation to Cuban literary history, as described in *Before Night Falls,* requires an impassioned dialectic between writing and literary futurity; the future aesthetic dividends of his work vis-à-vis an imagined community of readers and critics after his demise.

Before Night Falls is principally divided into three sections or "movements" that correspond with Arenas' early childhood in Cuba in his hometown of Holguín; his late adolescence and adulthood in the early 1960s and 1970s in Havana; and the final decade of his life from approximately 1980 to 1990 that he spent between New York and Miami. These three principal movements are bracketed by an initial introduction that begins in the toilet and Arenas' suicide note, which concludes the autobiography. The first third of the autobiography chronicles Arenas' childhood in terms of "absolute poverty and isolation" that is so anchored to a literalized love of the land that we learn that Arenas, the child, eats dirt in a shed next to "the house where the animals slept" (1). The second movement narrates adolescence and his family life in Holguín before ceding way to his initial exuberance occasioned by the Cuban Revolution's triumph that eventually allowed him to study at university despite coming from abject poverty. This second movement charted in the autobiography is significant because it instantiates the most marked transition form personal biography proper into a story that documents the writerly and artistic censorship he sets out to document in order to liberate himself and his art from increasing state repression. It marks the transition from Arenas' initial uncritical exuberance after the Cuban Revolution to complete disillusionment after learning of the Regime's support of the Soviet invasion of Czechoslovakia in 1968 where "[a]ny hope of a possible democratization of the [Cuban political] system," or "a possible break with the Soviet Union..."died then and there" for Arenas (125).

It is after this transition in *Before Night Falls,* through his second to third movement in the autobiography and the not inconsequential date of 1968, that Arenas' text begins to resemble a literary history. From this point onward, Arenas explains both his *oeuvre*, and his unrelenting attempts at protecting or salvaging his writing, while subjecting the best-known Cuban writers to canonical reevaluation. The list of writers he subjects to reevaluation—sometimes in detail though often in passing—is extensive and includes figures from both the established canon of Cuban literary studies, both on the island and in exile, as well as lesser known Cuban and Cuban American writers. The list is extensive and includes the likes of René Ariza (1940-1994), Antón Arrufat (1935-) , Miguel Barnet (1940-), Lydia Cabrera (1899-1991), Guillermo Cabrera Infante (1929-2005), Alejo Carpentier (1904-1980), Eliseo Diego (1920-1994), Roberto Fernández Retamar (1930-), Fina García Marruz (1923-), Nicolás Guillén (1902-1989), Enrique Labrador Ruiz (1902-1991), José Lezama Lima (1910-1976), Heberto Padilla (1932-2000), Virgilio Piñera (1912-1979), José Rodríguez Feo (1920-1993), Severo Sarduy (1937-1993), Roberto Valero (1955-1994), Cintio Vitier (1921-2009), and many others as well as revered Cuban cultural icons of note such as Alicia Alonso (1921-).

However, Arenas' intentions and his accounting of Cuban literary history, as well as his relation to that literary history, is established early in the autobiography. Arenas' principal break with the Latin American Boom's most famous aesthetic practice begins in the first movement of *Before Night Fall*. At the onset he makes it clear that his reference to "eating dirt," which he does with his cousin Dulce María with whom he also engages in sexual trysts as a child, should not be occasion for readers to take this as an example of an "aesthetic style." He states unequivocally, "I should make it clear right away that to eat dirt is not a metaphor, or sensational act" and, as if requiring further clarification, he continues noting that "[i]t has nothing to do with *magic realism*, or anything of the sort" (11, my emphasis). Banishing the "Macondo aesthetic," so-called "Magic or Magical Realism" from the onset allows Arenas to separate his work from what became the brash commercialization of Gabriel García Márquez's (1928-) fictional Macondo in *One Hundred Years of Solitude* (1967) and the version of Latin America that it represented to a generation of readers, writers, and critics. With this caveat Arenas draws a line in the sand regarding Latin American literature, its commodification, and his absence from the circuits of power that exiled him yet again from the Cuban and Latin American literary canon.

This is significant when one considers that Arenas had won

and shared France's literary prize in 1969, the "Prix du meilleur livre étranger" (the best foreign book prize), for *El mundo alucinante* along with García Márquez and his *One Hundred Years of Solitude*. It is hard to imagine that this irony was lost on El Rey when he notes at the end of *Before Night Falls* how García Márquez stood by Castro after the storming of the Peruvian Embassy that lead to the Mariel Boat Exodus of 1980, which was the catalyst for his leaving Cuba, and applauded when Castro called the defectors "antisocial and sexually depraved" (278). Indeed, Arenas' disdain for what emerged and passed for "authentic" Latin American literary production after the success of *One Hundred Years of Solitude*, and much of what followed, made him acutely aware of the nature of what many years later after his death, the "McOndo generation" derided as an essentializing aesthetics by the likes of Alberto Fuguet (1964-), Giannina Braschi (1953-), Edmundo Paz-Soldán (1967-) and many other writers associated with the McOndo generation.[24]

> It is from his disidentification with Magical Realism that he can, in the second movement in the Autobiography, then establish the conditions that lead to literary death. While elaborating his critique of the Cuban literary canon he writes, "Dictators and authoritarian regimes can destroy writers in two ways: by persecuting them or by showering them with official favors... People of unquestionable talent, once they embraced the new dictatorship. Never wrote anything worthwhile again" (90).

Arenas, having distanced his work from the popularized versions of "lo real maravilloso" that García Márquez and critics turned into a commodity and niche marketing strategy for publishing Latin American literature under the aegis of "Magical Realism, finds its analog, not surprisingly, in Alejo Carpentier whose importance and popularity after the revolution Arenas sees as devoid of merit. "What ever happened to Alejo Carpentier after *El siglo de las luces*?," Arenas rhetorically asks as he continues his surgical dissection of the national literary jugular when he "assesses" his cohorts' legacy beginning with Carpentier:

> His writing [Carpentier's] became slipshod, dreadful, impossible to read to the end. What ever happened to the poetry of Nicolás

---

24. For a reading of the McOndo generation's simultaneous derision and debt to *El Boom* generation see Diana Palaversich's *De Macondo a McOndo: Senderos de la posmodernidad latinoamericana* (2010), especially useful is "Del post*boom* al neoliberalismo": 19-60.

> Guillén? After the sixties his work became irrelevant or, worse, deplorable. What happened to the brilliant essays, though always somewhat reactionary, of the Cintio Vitier of the fifties? What happened to the great poetry written by Eliseo Diego in the Fifties? None of them are what they use to be; they are dead although, unfortunately for UNEAC and even for themselves, they are still living. (90-91)

Arenas does not establish any criterion for his assessment save his privileged position as a writer "fuera del juego," outside the regime's political game.[25] Facing death himself, he pronounces Carpentier, Guillén, Vitier and Diego as already dead as far as their literary afterlives are concerned; a fact, he notes, that is "unfortunate" for the National Union of Writers and Artists of Cuba the Union of Cuban Writers (UNEAC) and, by extension, the national literary canon. Arenas' literary necrology calls attention to and is counterpoised by the vital life affirming "arts of cruising" and, one might be tempted to say, represents an extension of the Cuban national anthem's refrain well-known refrain, "En cadenas vivir es vivir /en afrenta y oprobio sumido," that is, "To live in chains is to die/in dishonour and ignominy," to literalist abandon. Arenas, however, is not the only "survivor" to emerge form what he called "lost generation, destroyed by the communist regime" (88). For every account that he wanted to settle in *Before Night Falls* for real or perceived injustices El Rey is also interested in repaying literary debts.

In his literary accounting Arenas considers José Lezama Lima and Virgilio Piñera to be the foundational pillars of contemporary Cuban literary history. Unlike Alejo Carpentier, who "manipulated information, dates, styles, and numbers like a refined but dehumanized computer," meeting Lezama Lima for Arenas was "an entirely different experience" insofar as Lezama's erudition shared and radiated "creative vitality" (83). Arenas considers Lezama's *Paradiso* (1966) one of the most "heroic" and important works of the Latin American literature canon. In Cuban letters, "I do not think Cuba had ever witnessed the publication of a novel so explicitly homosexual, so extraordinarily complex and rich and

---

25. Heberto Padilla's collection of poems *Fuera del juego* (1968) represented one of the few significant literary attacks by Arenas' generational cohort in Cuba; though Padilla was ultimately made to recant his "antirevolutionary" work in a public *mea culpa*, to Arenas it represented Padilla's death, "he walked like a ghost among the tress" (217).

imagery, so idiosyncratically Cuban, so Latin American, and at the same time, so unique" (84). Arenas' assessment of *Paradiso* hinges on the exaltation of thematic and formal characteristics that make it at once "idiosyncratically Cuban" as well as Latin American. In this sense, *Paradiso* for Arenas is both a national Cuban novel and a transnational Spanish American novel. Crossing genres into the performative, Arenas also exalts the merits of Virgilio Piñera's *Dos viejos pánicos* (1968) for its ability through "the absurd" to reference what it is like to exist under totalitarian rule. Unlike Arenas, however, both Lezama and Piñera remained in Cuba which, according to Arenas, caused their work to suffer under censorship and "internal exile" as they wrote "until death claimed them, knowing that their writings would end up in the hands of State Security, and perhaps the only person to read them would be the policeman assigned to filing or destroying them" (84). What is most curious about Arenas' evaluative assessment of Lezama and Piñera's work is the anxious substitution that takes place when Arenas apparently displaces his fears of being forgotten by the literary establishment with the image of Lezama and Piñera's writings in the hands of an unappreciative representative of the state acting like a literary critic who discards or destroys their work. This anxiety is intensified in *Before Night Falls* when Arenas finds that fulfillment, leaving Cuba, creates another set of challenges he summarized thusly, "the difference between the communist and capitalist system is that, although they give you a kick in the ass, in the communist system you have to applaud, while in the capitalist system you can scream. And I came here to scream" (288).

It is in exile, and feeling ignored by both the left and the right literary establishment, that Arenas' turns his attention to the question of canonicity most directly as he himself becomes a critic of the academic institutions that establish what counts as good writing and in doing so consecrate literary canons. He writes with critical aplomb that in the United States leftist academics and critics have made it nearly impossible for his works, or the works of those Cuban and Cuban American writers he wishes to canonize, to find critical the interlocutors they require:

> When I left Cuba my novels were being used as assigned texts at New York University, and when I adopted a radical position against the Castro dictatorship, Haydée Vitale, professor of literature, started to drop my books from the curriculum until not one

of the remained. She did the same with all other Cuban writers in exile. In the end, the program included only a few of Alejo Carpentier's novels. This happened to me at many universities in the United States and in many other parts of the world. Ironically, while I was in jail and could not leave Cuba, my chances of being published were better because I was not allowed to speak out, and foreign publishing companies with leftist leanings would support a writer living in Havana. (301)

In typically strident fashion Arenas names and seeks an accounting of the literary legacy he feels he has been denied. In Arenas' less than generous analysis of why his work, and that of fellow Cuban exile writers have fallen into disfavor, he signals institutional practices and academic canon formation as the primary reason for being ignored as a writer. For Arenas, it would seem that armchair leftist critics are the worst, unlike many other Generation of '72 writers whose experiences and ideology fed seamlessly into the academic and the New Left zeitgeist that romanticized revolutionary aesthetics and battles on distant shores.

Yet for aficionados of Arenas who are certain that he is an acerbic critic of his contemporaries, even of his once close circle of friends, it should be noted that perhaps El Rey's most powerful invective against those who would belittle his prolific *oeuvre* or, worse, ignore it altogether for political reasons, was reserved for the very oblivion he believed was heaped upon him. Arenas effaces as much as he wishes to redress in *Before Night Falls* as the prospect of his literary erasure clashed head on with canon formation and literary practice in the Unites States academy. The most infamous of the erasures concerning Arenas' literary history is also perhaps the least known and deserves some commentary.

The Cuban exile poet and academic Roberto Valero, in a question and answer forum at the Library of Congress for "Hispanic Heritage month"—and perhaps sensing his own relation to literary history a year before he passed away—related how Arenas was incensed to learn in 1986 that Stanford University professor and, not coincidentally, the Chilean critic of Latin American literary studies, Fernando Alegría had excluded any mention of him whatsoever in the critic's influential *Nueva historia de la novela Hispanoamericana* (1986 [1973]).[26] By the publication of Fernando Alegría's high-

---

26. Roberto Valero's lecture and selected reading from his posthumously published *Este Viento De Cuaresma* (2004) was read at the Library of Congress' "His-

ly influential and augmented *Nueva historia* in 1986, it appeared to El Rey that his work was not going to be valued in the standard canonical literary accounts of the period. Without mentioning Alegría directly in *Before Night Falls*, Arenas is clearly interested in diminishing the critical labor of those who have been dismissive of his literary labor.[27]

Alegría, Valero noted, was said to have dismissed Arenas' work because of his invectives against Uruguayan literary critic Ángel Rama (1926-1983) whom Arenas considered, despite a prior history of conviviality, an opportunist "communist sympathizer." Rama, who had been appointed to a professorship of Latin American Literatures at the University of Maryland, College Park, in the Department of Spanish and Portuguese, was denied a continuation of a work permit under the McCarthy era McCarren-Walter Act which sought to root out "subversive communists" by restricting immigration to the United States.[28] It has been suggested that Arenas was instrumental in the State Department's denial of a work permit extension for Rama and his partner, the well-known critic of Latin American art Marta Traba (1930-1983). Having left the United States and exiled in Paris, after Rama's petition was denied on behalf of the University of Maryland, they died in a plane crash outside of Madrid while en *route* to a conference on Latin American writers at the "Primer Encuentro de la Cultura Hispanoamericana" in Bogotá, Columbia, in 1983.[29] The tragic loss of Rama and Traba

---

panic Heritage Month" celebration at Pickford Theater, Madison Building, United States Library of Congress, Washington, D.C., September 13, 1993.

27. Valero's assertions are substantiated in Arenas' correspondence. See Firestone Library, Department of Rare Books and Special Collections at Princeton University, boxes labeled "Nonfiction" (numbers 23-26) for Arenas' exchanges with Rama, Rodríguez-Monegal, and others.

28. See Rosario Peyrou for a documented discussion of the Arenas-Rama controversy, "Reinaldo Arenas y Ángel Rama: El perseguido como perseguidor" (2012). As a graduate of the University of Maryland, College Park, it was common knowledge for those of us who entered the Department, and well into the mid-1990s, that the effects of both Rama and Arenas' personal histories were tied to the Department's own history. In my experience, the departmental administrative structure remained respectfully neutral about the issue despite the grave loss that the controversy itself represented to the University at the height of Ronald Reagan's establishment of neoliberal policies; policies whose collateral effects throughout the country and the nation's cultural industries we have yet to recover.

29. Peyrou, quoting from another source, ventures the conjecture that "'...desprestigiar a Rama y calificarlo como 'agente castrista', Arenas—con el perman-

has created long-standing animosities that almost thirty years have not been able to quell for interested constituencies.

It would seem from the extant record that neither Arenas nor Alegría were successful in creating the conditions under which canonicity and politics would become wholly integrated and function in unison to either create or destroy literary traditions based primarily on personal vendettas and an impolitic understanding of the politics of canon formation.

V. Conclusion: "The King is Dead. Long Live the King!"

El Rey's literary legacy—twenty years after the posthumous publication of *Before Night Falls*—is still most legible through various instantiations or what I have here called Arena's "afterlives." From book, to celluloid, to stage, and representational points in between, the King's body has been reconstituted as a performative stand-in for a variety of political positions that reduce both his work and his relation to literary practice; most especially, the question of canonicity and periodicity and its relation to Arenas' work. As I have suggested, such reductive performances of the King's body risk ignoring how cruising, as an aesthetic *techne*, provides a significant contribution to a broader history of anti-authoritarian literature within the Cuban literary canon; that is, what Jorge Mañach called *"libertinaje mental,"* literally "mental libertinism," more felicitously, "unrestrained thinking."

Moving beyond such an impasse twenty years later, as *Before Night Falls* implores us to do at its best, might require retiring the figurations of the King that we have inherited so that the generation of '72's queerest of aesthetes may continue to cruise after death, arousing readers and critics alike, to other forms of sociality and political *libertinaje*. The arts of cruising ultimately require us to be less beholden to our own subjection, whatever our political

ente apoyo de Rodríguez Monegal—logró el padrinazgo de otro exiliado cubano que actuaba como asesor de seguridad en la Casa Blanca del gobierno Reagan: Roger Fountain, nacido en Cuba como Rogelio Fuentes'. Sea o no cierta esa conjetura, el episodio en el que este perseguido se convierte en perseguidor es digno de ser conocido. Por cierto no rebajará un ápice el valor literario de su obra, pero al menos a mí, me hace dudar de la calidad de su persona. Y sin duda, asuntos como éste integrarán la peor historia del exilio latinoamericano de esos años" (emphasis in the original).

attachments may be, so that the fiction of an inviolable and unified subject (defender of either left or right agendas) is undressed and we, ideal readers, are reminded that stakes are never as clear cut when we attach ourselves to ideas that impose content over form.

Works Cited

Alegría, Fernando. *Nueva historia de la novela Hispanoamericana*. Hanover, NH: Ediciones del norte, 1986. Print.

Althusser, Louis. *Lenin and Philosophy and Other Essays*. Trans. Ben Brewster. New York: Monthly Review Press, 2001. Print.

Arenas, Reinaldo. *Antes que anochezca (Autobiografía)*. Barcelona: Editorial Tusquets, 1992. Print.

—. *Avant la nuit* [French translation of *Antes que anochezca (Autobiografía)*]. Trans. Liliane Hasson. Paris: Babel, 2000. Print.

—. *Before Night Falls*. Trans. Dolores M. Koch. New York: Viking, 1993. Print.

—. *The Color of Summer: or the New garden of Earthly Delights*. Trans. Andrew Hurley. New York: Viking, 2000. Print.

Argüelles, Lourdes and B. Ruby Rich. "Homosexuality, Homophobia, and Revolution: Notes Toward an Understanding of the Cuban Lesbian and Gay Male Experience, Part 2," *Signs: Journal of Women in Culture and Society* 11 (1), 1985: 120-136. Print.

Béhar, Sonia. *La caída del Hombre Nuevo: Narrativa cubana del periodo Especial*. New York: Peter Lang, 2008.

Bersani, Leo. *Is the Rectum a Grave? and Other Essays*. Chicago: University of Chicago Press, 2010.

Cabrera Infante, Guillermo. "Reinaldo Arenas o la destrucción por el sexo." *Mea Cuba*. Barcelona: Plaza & Janés, 1992. 400-405. Print.

Dorman, Ariel. *Death and the Maiden*. New York: Penguin, 1994. Print.

Ermantinger, Emil. *Filosofía de la ciencia literaria*. Mexico: Fondo de Cultura Económica, 1946 and SS. Print.

Feijoó, Samuel. "Revolución y vicios." *El Mundo*, 15 April 1965 (5).

García Márquez, Gabriel. *One Hundred Years of Solitude*. New York: Harper Collins, 2004 [1967].

Goic, Cedomil. *Los Mitos Degradados: Ensayos de Comprensión de la Literatura Hispanoamericana*. Amsterdam: Editions Rodopi, 1992. Print.

Gutiérrez, Pedro Juan. *Trilogía sucia de La Habana*. Barcelona: Anagrama, 1998.

Hamilton, Carrie and Elizabeth Dore, eds. *Sexual Revolutions in Cuba: Passion, Politics, and Memory*. Chapel Hill: University of North Carolina Press, 2012.

Lezama Lima, José. *Paradiso*. Madrid: Cátedra, 2006 [1966]. Print.

Lewis, Vek. 'Grotesque Spectacles: The Janus Face of the State and Gender Variant Bodies in the Work of Reinaldo Arenas' in *Chasqui: revista de literatura latinoamericana* 8(1): May 2009. 104-24. Print.

Lima, Lázaro. "Locas al Rescate: The Transnational Hauntings of Queer Latinidad," *Journal of Transnational American Studies*, 3.2, Winter 2011 (Reprise). Digital (http://escholarship.org/uc/item/9ch96543).

Mañach y Robato, Jorge. *Indagación del choteo*. Linkgua Digital Books, USA, 2007. Digital Book.

Marx, Karl. *Grundrisse*. Trans. by Martin Nicolaus. London: Penguin, 1993. Print.

Muñoz, José Esteban. "Ghosts of Public Sex: Utopian Longings, Queer Memories," in *Policing Public Sex: Queer Politics And the Future of AIDS Activism*. Edited by Ephen Glenn Colter, David Serlin, et al. Boston: South End Press, 1996. Print.

Ocasio, Rafael. *Political and Sexual Outlaw: Reinaldo Arenas*. Gainesville: UP of Florida, 2003. Print.

—. *A Gay Cuban Activist in Exile: Reinaldo Arenas*. Gainesville: University Press of Florida, 2007. Print.

Olivares, Jorge. A Twice-Told Tail: Reinaldo Arenas's "El Cometa

Halley." *PMLA*, Vol. 117, No. 5 (Oct., 2002), pp. 1188-1206. Print.

Padilla, Heberto. *Fuera del Juego*. Miami: Ediciones Universal, 1998 [1968]. Print.

Palaversich, Diana. *De Macondo a McOndo*. México, DF: Plaza y Valdés, 2005. Print.

Peyrou, Rosario. "Reinaldo Arenas y Ángel Rama: El perseguido como perseguidor," *Vedenuevo: Política, economía, sociedad y cultura*, year 4, Number 43, Wednesday, April 4, 2012. Electronic Resource: <http://www.vadenuevo.com.uy/index.php/the-news/2639-43vadenuevo05>.

Piglia, Ricardo. *Plata quemada*. Madrid: Planeta, 1997. Print.

Rechy, John. *The Sexual Outlaw: A Documentary*. New York: Groove Press, 1977. Print.

Rieley, Nerea. "Reinaldo Arenas' Autobiography *Antes Que Anochezca* as Confrontational 'Ars Moriendi.'" *Bulletin of Latin American Research*, Volume 18, Issue 4, October 1999. 491-496. Print.

Rowe, Michael. "The New Cuban Revolution." *The Advocate.com*, September 14, 2009: <http://www.advocate.com/news/world-news/2009/09/14/new-cuban-revolucion?page=0,0>. Last accessed May 21, 2012.

Sanchez-Eppler, Benigno. "Reinaldo Arenas, Re-writer Revenant, and the Re-patriation of Cuban Homoerotic Desire." *Queer Diasporas*. Ed. Cindy Patton and Sanchez-Eppler. Durham: Duke UP, 2000. 154-82. Print.

Schnabel, Julian. Dir. *Before Night Falls*. Fine Line Features, 2000. Film.

Skármeta, Antonio. *The Postman: A Novel*. New York, W. W. Norton, [1996] 2008. Print.

Soto, Francisco. *Reinaldo Arenas: The Pentagonía*. Gainesville: UP of Florida, 1994.

Stuart, Jan. "Havana Heartache," *The Advocate*, December 19, 2000. Print.

Valero, Roberto. *Este Viento De Cuaresma*. Miami: Ediciones Universal, 2004. Print.

Vallejo, Fernando. *La virgen de los sicarios*. México, DF: Alfaguara, [1994] 2000. Print.

Vargas Llosa, Mario. *La ciudad y los perros*. Barcelona, Spain: Seix Barral, 1963. Print.

Waleson, Heidi. "Imprisoned by Clichés, Laments and Exposition," *The Wall Street Journal Online*. Accessed May 21, 20012

Zayas, Manuel. *Seres Extravagantes*. Barcelona, Spain: Canal Documental TV, 2004. Film.

Postdata

APUNTES SOBRE EL ESPACIO EN LAS NOVELAS DE DIAMELA ELTIT[1]

J. Agustín Pastén B.
North Carolina State University

Sin lugar a dudas, la representación del espacio resulta tan variada como la vida misma. Desde las descripciones del espacio en apariencia reales en textos tales como *Naufragios*, de Álvar Núñez Cabeza de Vaca e *Historia verdadera de la conquista de México*, de Bernal Díaz del Castillo,[2] hasta las representaciones más imaginarias del espacio en obras tales como *Cartas marruecas*, de José Cadalso, *Voyage au bout de la nuit*, de Céline, y *Los pasos perdidos*, de Alejo Carpentier, o incluso los retratos de naturaleza literaria y etnosociológica tales como *El lazarillo de ciegos caminantes*, de Alonso Carrió de la Vandera, y los de carácter casi puramente etnográfico tales como *Tristes Tropiques*, de Claude Lévi-Strauss, así como, finalmente, las travesías netamente literarias de críticos como Guy Davenport y su brillante *The Geography of the Imagination*, pareciera que, necesariamente, el espacio estuviese condenado a ser la víctima de la representación y la teorización (piénsese, por ejemplo, en Gaston Bachelard, Henri Lefebvre, Fredric Jameson, David Harvey, Edward Soja). Pareciera, además, que los grabados en general, seguidos por la primera foto[3] y especialmente por la introducción pública de la fotografía en 1839, enriquecieron enormemente las posibilidades de la representación espacial, haciendo posible directa o indirectamente, en el caso de América Latina, la creación de las deliciosamente íntimas geografías de la novela modernista (*De sobremesa, Amistad funesta*) así como los grandes espacios de textos empecinados en inscribir la nación (*La vorágine, Doña Bárbara*), al decir del crítico Carlos Alonso en relación a las llamadas "novelas de la tierra." Ahora bien, si acaso en la representación narrativa en general el espacio oscila perennemente entre lo que pudiera llamarse un afuera y un adentro, podría argüirse con toda seguridad que la novelista Diamela Eltit privilegia espacios interiores o limitados.[4] Asimismo, podría decirse que, en gran medida—y dejando de lado los temas más conocidos de sus obras[5]—, ella trabaja una estética del espacio. Lo que me gustaría analizar en este breve ensayo es la manera en que, en esta estética del espacio, incluso en las áreas más cerradas, y por muy paradójico que pudiera parecer al principio, se produce una constante tensión entre el interior y el exterior, entre lo local y lo global, y entre lo nacional y lo transnacional. La tensión presente en sus primeras novelas, empero, empieza a desvanecerse en *Mano de obra* (2002),[6] siendo inmisericordemente apabullada en *Impuesto a la carne* (2010)[7]—su penúltima novela—por un biopoder neoliberal demasiado poderoso para ser eliminado. Si en las crónicas urbanas de Pedro Lemebel existe una distinción relativamente clara entre lo local y lo global,[8] y si en la narrativa de Alberto Fuguet hay una confirmación innegable de las transformaciones culturales producidas por la globalización—particularmente en los sectores más adinerados de Santiago[9]—, en las novelas de Eltit resalta el camino de lo que pudiera denominarse un "Chile nacional" a una "nación posnacional." Mi análisis centra la atención sobre todo en *Jamás el fuego nunca* (2007)[10] e *Impuesto* aunque también alude, brevemente, a *Mano*.[11] En primer lugar, no obstante, ofrezco un resumen de algunos juicios críticos respecto de la representación del espacio en la producción narrativa de Eltit anterior a estas tres obras.

    Hay quienes han señalado la presencia de "anti-espacios" (Olea, "El cuerpo" 89) en las novelas de Eltit; otros se han referido al "problema de los límites" (Kirkpatrick 42) que caracteriza su estética del espacio. En el corazón mismo de la esfera privada del hogar, Bernardita Llanos (110) advierte los efectos infames que el poder y la violencia tienen en las relaciones interpersonales en general y entre la madre y el hijo o la madre y la hija en particular. En cuanto a "la plaza" en *Lumpérica* (1983), la primera novela de Eltit, algunos la han visto como un lugar sagrado y de rito construido para la creación de un nuevo tipo de comunidad, la comunidad de los que están social y políticamente marginados (Tafra 49; Avelar 170), mientras que otros, por el contrario, la han visto como "una metáfora de la comunidad ausente" (Ortega 53) e incluso como una cárcel (Brito, *Campos* 122) donde el espacio público ha sido colonizado por "el luminoso" (Donoso 255). En lo tocante a *Por la patria* (1986), su segunda novela, las múltiples geografías que pueblan el texto, o sea, "el bar," "el erial", "el barrio" y "el galpón", han sido entendidas, metafóricamente, como espacios propicios para la construcción de una identidad femenina latinoamericana (Arrate 150). Una novela que "effectively writes a marginal space" (Tierney-Tello), *Por la patria* presenta espacios reales, tales como "el bar," por ejemplo, ya como sitios para el desarrollo del poder subalterno (Tierney-Tello 126), ya como una "'trinchera'" (Tafra 53) de la libertad y la resistencia. Para Raquel Olea, quien se adhiere a las nociones de "lugar" y "no-lugar" del antropólogo francés Marc Augé, "el bar," pero también "el barrio," se contraponen a "el súper" en *Mano* ("El deseo" 101). Simbólicamente, el título de la tercera novela de Eltit, *El cuarto mundo* (1988), podría perfectamente representar el territorio por excelencia de todos los habitantes de su cosmos literario, ora como realidad (degradada) ora como utopía. Un crítico, por ejemplo, entiende este espacio principalmente como un lugar psíquico, recalcando un movimiento que se extiende desde el locus intrauterino de los mellizos a todo el continente americano (Tafra 79, 82). Gisela Norat concibe el útero como "a space subject to patriarchal assault" (124), puesto que es el mellizo hombre y no la melliza mujer quien narra la concepción. Rodrigo Cánovas, por su parte, entiende el espacio uterino como "un taller literario" en el sentido de que "La maternidad, condición biológica, se desplaza hacia la escritura" (27-28).

En lo relativo a *El padre mío* (1989), un fascinante texto testimonial en el que un individuo esquizofrénico provee, paradójicamente, algunos de los primeros relatos verídicos sobre las consecuencias de la política neoliberal en la sociedad chilena, un crítico, con mucha razón, afirma que es precisamente desde "el borde" (Malverde 161) que el discurso subalterno alcanza su pleno potencial. De modo similar a *El cuarto mundo,* el espacio privado de la madre y el hijo en *Los vigilantes* (1994), la quinta novela de Eltit, ha sido analizado como un proceso a través del cual la subjetividad femenina internaliza, tanto psíquica como físicamente, las múltiples fuerzas represivas mediante las cuales el patriarcado oprime a los protagonistas (Medina-Sancho 149). Respecto de *Los trabajadores de la muerte* (1998), su sexta novela, si bien es cierto que la dinámica espacial del texto fluctúa entre un movimiento desde el interior al exterior y viceversa (Olea, "El deseo" 95), es igualmente evidente, como nota Francine Masiello, que en esta obra la autora chilena "revisits sites of congregation" (207) y "takes us to a more archaic sense of the public space when the market was the center of polis" (214). Finalmente, en relación a *Mano*, la crítica ha vertido interesantes juicios. Una estudiosa de su obra, por ejemplo, hace hincapié no sólo en la falta de "public sphere" en el texto sino que se refiere al supermercado, muy apropiadamente, a mi juicio, como "a Wal-Mart-like superstore" (Lynd 16, 23). De acuerdo a Olea, "el súper," que ella califica como "templo panóptico del poder del consumo" ("El deseo" 99), simboliza "un espacio de pseudoneutralidad donde se debilitan las fronteras de lo público y lo privado y de las identificaciones sociales" (97), mientras que Michael Lazzara lo llama "un espacio hiperracionalizado, serializado y panóptico" (158). Otra estudiosa de la obra de Eltit hace referencia al desvanecimiento de las fronteras presente en *Mano*, resaltando cómo la lógica del mercado ha colonizado inclusive la casa donde viven los empleados (Carreño 147-48), lugar que Eugenia Brito denomina, sin más, "casa antropofágica" ("Utopía" 30).

Estas son algunas de las aserciones críticas concernientes a la representación espacial en la novelas de Eltit. Rastreemos a continuación la penetración gradual del neoliberalismo en el espacio nacional en sus primeros textos y luego sigamos con el análisis de *Mano, Jamás*, e *Impuesto*. Escritas durante la dictadura, y como retratos de un país en estado de sitio, tanto en *Lumpérica* como en *Por la patria* la oposición propio/ajeno o nacional/transnacional o neoliberal, se presenta en términos marcadamente raciales, particularmente en la última. En ambas, sin embargo, lo nacional resiste encarnizadamente, y, finalmente, triunfa. "El luminoso" en *Lumpérica*, una metáfora no solamente de la ubicua presencia del control del Estado sino también del mercado, se cierne sobre "L. Iluminada," "los pálidos" y "los desharrapados" en una "plaza" localizada en "Santiago de Chile" (131)—mencionada una cuantas veces en la historia[12]—pero sin poder dominarlos. La dicotomía nacional/extranjero es especialmente palpable en las siguientes líneas: "Porque el luminoso no se detendría. Estaba programado para la noche y su programación no tenía la racionalidad de Chile que paraba su ritmo nocturno" (212). El binario racial es incluso más pronunciado en *Por la patria*, como acabo de afirmar. "Zarco" y "eslavo," presentes a lo largo del texto, aluden no sólo a la piel blanca sino también a los militares en el poder, como en la expresión "uniformados eslavos" (213). Lo interesante de esta novela, sin embargo, y lo que en cierto sentido complica las cosas, es que si algunas de las mujeres en la historia buscan derrotar a "los eslavos," otras se sienten atraídas a ellos (271) e incluso rehúsan ser chilenas: "... no quiero ser más chilena" (106), dice una de las voces narrativas. La oración "loca que quería gringo fuerte y eficaz" (158) contrasta con "ERAN OSCUROS, MORENOS, CHILENOS, ESCURRIDIZOS Y TRAIDORES"[13] (92) y "mi cara imperfecta, mis rasgos oscuros, mis crenchas" (273). En *El cuarto mundo*, lo nacional lo representa el término "sudaca," expresión peyorativa con fuertes tintes raciales que aparece de distintas formas en el texto: "jóvenes sudacas" (52), "familia sudaca" (110), "estigma sudaca" (123, 145, 150), "nuestra raza sudaca" (126), "especie sudaca" (152), etc. En un principio, se tiene la impresión que es la ciudad, descrita como peligrosa (60, 94) y hostil (155), la que amenaza la integridad de la "familia sudaca." Hacia el final de la diégesis, empero, aprendemos que lo que viene a transformar de manera drástica "la especie sudaca" es "la nación más famosa y poderosa del mundo" (130), la cual, aunque no se menciona por nombre en la novela, apunta claramente a la llegada del neoliberalismo: "Afuera la ciudad devastada emite gruñidos ... Se ensayan todas las retóricas esperando el dinero caído del cielo ... En venta los campos de la ciudad sudaca. En venta el sudor (158) ... Sólo el nombre de la ciudad permanece, porque todo lo demás ya se ha vendido en el amplio mercado ... y en el dinero caído del cielo está impresa, nítidamente, una sonrisa de menosprecio a la raza sudaca" (159).

Un retrato sombrío de la ciudad es también evidente en *Vaca sagrada* (1991)—la cuarta novela de Eltit—donde "un viento helado" (155) invade el ambiente. Aun cuando, en contraste con *El cuarto mundo*, no se hace una alusión directa al neoliberalismo, sí se encuentran referencias a algunas de sus consecuencias, por ejemplo referencias al desempleo (128) y a la vigilancia en las calles (130). En *Los vigilantes*, que se publica durante el llamado período de transición en Chile (1990-2010), la escritora chilena vuelve a enmarcar lo propio/ajeno, nacional/neoliberal en términos de un binario. Pero no dentro de parámetros raciales sino culturales y económicos, oponiendo "vida occidental" (88), "perfección occidental," "belleza occidental" (49)—así como "el Occidente" (88) en general—a "edificios públicos," "sitios eriazos," "vagabundaje urbano" (92), "las orillas de Occidente" (107) y "este Occidente secundario" (109). Es justamente esta "vida occidental" la que parece haber ocupado la esfera pública en *Los trabajadores de la muerte*, como puede apreciarse particularmente en la primera y última secciones de la novela. Si bien la observación de Masiello de que Eltit lleva al lector "to a more archaic sense of the public space" es acertada, otro modo de entender las calles saturadas de "vitrinas" (190), "ratones electrónicos", "arañas eléctricas" (191) y una infinidad de objetos de consumo, sería concluir que, en contraposición a la alabanza que hace el peruano Hernando de Soto de la economía informal en su ya clásico *El otro sendero* (1987), la imposición de una economía de libre mercado a cualquier precio sólo puede producir una frágil y extremadamente inestable existencia económica paralela para un gran porcentaje de la población. En el texto no solamente se vigila con cámaras a los vendedores callejeros (192) sino que, además, la policía irrumpe en su espacio laboral y procede a destruir sus productos (194).

La tensión que había caracterizado la narrativa de Eltit entre un espacio nacional que resistía y un espacio transnacional o neoliberal que persistía, comienza a desvanecerse en *Mano*. En ésta, efectivamente, no existe ni un adentro ni un afuera. Para el 2002, resultaba claro que los gobiernos de la Transición, el del socialista Ricardo Lagos (2000-2006) incluido, no estaban dispuestos a transformar significativamente los mecanismos del libre mercado impuestos a la fuerza por Pinochet. Chile se había convertido, según la apropiada frase de Luis Cárcamo-Huechante, en una "*nación-mercado*" ("Hacia" 99).[14] A fin de dramatizar esta situación, la novelista chilena escribe un texto en el que el supermercado se convierte en una incontrovertible metáfora de Chile. Ninguna oración ilustra con mayor precisión esta idea que cuando el narrador homodiegético de la primera parte del texto declara, "El súper es como mi segunda casa" (71). En esta novela, el espacio no se erige como obstáculo contra el neoliberalismo, es, más bien, la encarnación misma del sistema neoliberal. Si en obras anteriores el espacio nacional combatía contra fuerzas amenazantes procedentes del exterior, en *Mano* es el sujeto subalterno mismo quien contribuye al buen funcionamiento del neoliberalismo, como cuando, verbigracia, Gloria acusa a Alberto de querer formar un sindicato en la segunda parte de la novela (89-90), o cuando Enrique, "Más alto que cualquiera de nosotros. Su piel era mucho más blanca" (102), se convierte en uno de los encargados del supermercado.

La presencia de un espacio dialéctico, no obstante, vuelve a relucir en *Jamás*, pero no en el sentido liberador de *Lumpérica* ni en el sentido de redención de *Por la patria*. Lo propio o nacional en el texto, cuyo máximo símbolo es una "célula muerta" (79), se presenta como absolutamente derrotado e inclusive fuera de la historia. La novela se enfoca específicamente en una pareja de ex militantes de izquierda que viven a duras penas en la clandestinidad. En esencia, tres lugares descuellan en el texto: la casa vieja y sin ventanas donde habita la pareja, las casas de los ancianos que la narradora homodiegética visita, y la ciudad, descrita como "una ciudad verdaderamente moderna y colapsada" (154). Ninguno de éstos, empero, es un espacio productivo como sí lo son "el bar" en *Por la patria* y hasta la casa en *Los vigilantes*. Es cierto que existe en *Jamás* un espacio interior y otro exterior, pero ninguno de los dos deviene locus de resistencia. En este texto, Eltit retrata—sin sucumbir a la derecha pero lanzando una feroz crítica contra la izquierda radical—una situación de estancamiento político sin salida. El miembro masculino de la "cúpula," por ejemplo, pasa la mayor parte del tiempo en su cama, "enroscado" (35), convertido en un "ovillo" (61), compartiendo con la voz narrativa femenina que lo interpela incansablemente, "el estrecho colchón arruinado" (34) y sobreviviendo con una ración diaria de arroz y té.[15] La narradora, por su parte, sale de la casa algunos días de la semana no sólo para encontrarse con una calle que parece un "jeroglífico" (62) y que "se torna irreconocible cada día" (115) sino también para lavar los cuerpos de frágiles y moribundos ancianos que no siempre la tratan bien. Ciertos indicios textuales llevan a pensar que, en realidad, esta novela de Eltit le da la bienvenida a los adelantos de la modernidad, como cuando, por ejemplo, la voz narrativa parece arrepentirse de no haberse comprado un televisor y una calculadora (85), o cuando se sintió fuertemente seducida por un vestido rojo detrás de una vitrina (112). Sin embargo, las veces que sí sale a la calle, calles usualmente "custodiadas por ojos técnicos" (102), se encuentra con crimen, violencia y robo: "Desvalijan, desvalijan, desvalijan" (145), afirma la voz narrativa. Lisa y llanamente, esta novela carece de un espacio desde el cual enfrentar el neoliberalismo.

Finalmente, en *Impuesto*, el espacio se ha transformado en un lugar enfermo o para enfermos, un hospital—una alegoría de Chile, ciertamente—donde una madre y una hija, aquélla dentro de ésta, esperan la llegada del Bicentenario mientras se preparan para vender algunos de sus miembros. Si, como afirma Dianna Niebyski, *Impuesto* constituye "a record of the marginal or excluded body in pain" (107), o bien una obra en la que Eltit manifiesta su preocupación en lo relativo a "the future of human bodies in our age of DNA experimentation" y "quick organ transplants" (116), el hecho es que, al igual que en novelas anteriores, el contraste nacional/extranjero aparece en términos claramente raciales. Si madre e hija son descritas por los doctores en el texto como "Bajas/feas/seriadas" (25) y "demasiado morenas" (33), y si la voz narrativa se refiere a uno de los doctores como "bajo, común, opaco, nacional" (27), también hay una alusión a "Un médico blanco, frío, metálico" (13) y, más tarde, una referencia a "una mujer muy correcta, más alta que nosotras" (176). Repetidamente en *Impuesto*, "país," "nación," "territorio," y "hospital" se presentan como vocablos intercambiables, sugiriendo que, aunque madre e hija hablen de librarse de doscientos años de opresión, resulta casi imposible la resistencia contra la explotación económica. Es más, dentro de los parámetros de un espacio totalmente colonizado por el mercado, "un territorio que me saca sangre, me saca sangre, me saca sangre" (80), la única salida posible es vender los órganos del cuerpo.

Como hemos visto, en suma, pareciera que el proyecto narrativo de Eltit ha cubierto todo el "suelo chileno" (*Impuesto* 116), desde la "plaza" a la casa, desde el "bar" al "barrio," desde el "súper" al "hospital" y, en *Fuerzas especiales* (2013), novela que acaba de publicarse, desde los bloques de viviendas sociales al "cíber." Pese a que estoy consciente que no he contestado la pregunta de por qué su cartografía literaria se traza casi siempre sobre la base de una dinámica racial, lo que no puede negarse es que el espacio nacional en sus textos se representa siempre como bajo la amenaza de una fuerza transnacional. Me pregunto al respecto: ¿no ha sido siempre ése el caso en Chile o América Latina? A su vez, ¿sería posible transcender esta dicotomía espacial y reflejar un mundo donde los límites entre la geografía nacional y la geografía neoliberal no aparecieran tan marcados como algún día lo estuvieron?

Notas

1. Este breve ensayo es una versión en español de "Dialectical Geographies in Contemporary Chilean Literature: the Case of Diamela Eltit's Na-

rrative Production," que será publicado el próximo año (2014) en el volumen 54, número 1, de la revista *Romance Notes*. El autor quisiera expresar su gratitud tanto a Vinodoh Venkatesh—editor del número especial donde aparecerá el artículo—como a los editores de la revista por haberle permitido traducir el artículo al español. La versión inglesa fue presentada en la Kentucky Foreign Language Conference (en Lexington, KY, en abril del 2013) y también en LASA (en Washington, D.C., en mayo del 2013).

2. Muy recientemente, el historiador francés Christian Duverger ha puesto en tela de juicio la autoría de Bernal Díaz.

3. La foto "Vue de la fenêtre du domaine du Gras" (1826), del inventor francés Joseph Nicéphore Niépce.

4. Especialmente en las novelas *El cuarto mundo*, *Vaca sagrada*, *Los vigilantes* y *Jamás el fuego nunca*, pero también en *Mano de obra* e *Impuesto a la carne*.

5. La precariedad del sujeto subalterno, la marginalización de la mujer, el cuerpo como *el* lugar de lucha por excelencia entre lo personal y lo político, entro otros temas.

6. *Mano* desde aquí en adelante.

7. *Impuesto* desde aquí en adelante.

8. Si bien, claramente, el espacio en general se hace algo más difuso en su última colección de crónicas, *Háblame de amores*.

9. Ver mi artículo sobre Fuguet y Lemebel.

10. *Jamás* de aquí en adelante.

11. No incluyo en mi análisis *Fuerzas especiales*, la última novela de Eltit que recién acaba de salir y que aún no he tenido la oportunidad de leer. Sólo he consultado la reseña de María Teresa Cárdenas del texto; ésta reseña, a su vez, incluye una extensa entrevista a Eltit donde la autora habla de su nueva novela.

12. Por ejemplo en las páginas 9, 84 y 120.

13. Mayúsculas en el original.

14. En su *Tramas del Mercado*, Cárcamo-Huechante ofrece un excelente análisis de cómo ocurrió este proceso en Chile.

15. Para María Rosa Olivera-Williams—quien designa esta novela de Eltit como "representante de una estética de la desaparición" (58) donde también está presente el tema de "la crisis de la masculinidad" (50)—, esta cama vieja que comparten los ex militantes viene a ser, alegóricamente, no sólo "espacio último" (48) sino también "lugar de excavación, ... ruina, ... donde surj[e]n los retazos, los despojos del pasado" (48).

Obras citadas

Alonso, Carlos. *The Spanish American Regional Novel. Modernity and Autochthony*. Cambridge; New York: Cambridge U P,

1990.

Arrate P., Marina. "Los significados de la escritura y su relación con la identidad femenina latinoamericana en *Por la patria*, de Diamela Eltit." En *Una poética de literatura menor: la narrativa de Diamela Eltit*. Ed. Juan Carlos Lértora. Santiago: Editorial Cuarto Propio, 1993. 141-54.

Avelar, Idelber. *The Untimely Present. Postdictatorial Latin American Fiction and the Task of Mourning*. Durham: Duke U P, 1999.

Brito, Eugenia. *Campos minados (literatura post-golpe en Chile)*. Santiago: Editorial Cuarto Propio, 1990.

—. "Utopía y quiebres en la narrativa de Diamela Eltit." En *Letras y proclamas: la estética literaria de Diamela Eltit*. Ed. Bernardita Llanos M. Santiago: Editorial Cuarto Propio/Denison University, 2006. 19-32.

Cánovas, Rodrigo. "Diamela Eltit. Algunos años antes, algunos años después." En *Diamela Eltit: redes locales, redes globales*. Ed. Rubí Carreño Bolívar. Madrid/Santiago: Iberoamericana/Vervuert/Pontificia Universidad Católica de Chile, 2009. 25-32.

Cárcamo-Huechante, Luis E. "Hacia una trama *localizada* del mercado: Crónica urbana y economía barrial en Pedro Lemebel." En *Más allá de la ciudad letrada. Crónicas y espacios urbanos*. Ed. Boris Muñoz and Silvia Spitta. Pittsburgh: Instituto Internacional de Literatura Iberoamericana, 2003: 99-115.

—. *Tramas del mercado. Imaginación económica, cultura pública y literatura en el Chile de fines del siglo veinte*. Santiago: Editorial Cuarto Propio, 2007.

Cárdenas, María Teresa. "Diamela Eltit, malabarista del lenguaje." Reseña de *Fuerzas especiales*. "Revista libros" de *El Mercurio* (Domingo 16 de junio de 2013). http://letras.s5.com/delt200613.html

Carreño, Rubí. "Eltit y su red local/global de citas: rescates del fundo y del supermercado." En *Letras y proclamas: la estética literaria de Diamela Eltit*. Ed. Bernardita Llanos M. Santiago: Editorial Cuarto Propio/Denison University, 2006.

143-71.

Donoso, Jaime. "Práctica de la Avanzada: *Lumpérica* y la figuración de la escritura como fin de la representación burguesa de la literatura y el arte." En *Diamela Eltit: redes locales, redes globales*. Ed. Rubí Carreño Bolívar. Madrid/Santiago: Iberoamericana/Vervuert/Pontificia Universidad Católica de Chile, 2009. 239-60.

Duverger, Christian. *Crónica de la eternidad. ¿Quién escribió la Historia verdadera de la conquista de la Nueva España?* México: Taurus, 2013.

Eltit, Diamela. *El cuarto mundo*. Santiago: Seix Barral, 1988, 1996.

—. *Fuerzas especiales*. Santiago: Planeta, 2013.

—. *Impuesto a la carne*. Santiago: Seix Barral, 2010.

—. *Jamás el fuego nunca*. Santiago: Seix Barral, 2007.

—. *Los trabajadores de la muerte*. Santiago: Seix Barral, 1998.

—. *Los vigilantes*. Santiago: Editorial Sudamericana, 1994.

—. *Lumpérica*. Santiago: Seix Barral, 1983, 1998.

—. *Mano de obra*. Santiago: Planeta, 2002.

—. *Por la patria*. Santiago: Editorial Cuarto Propio, 1986, 1995.

—. *Vaca sagrada*. Buenos Aires: Planeta, 1991.

Kirkpatrick, Gwen. "El 'hambre de ciudad' de Diamela Eltit: forjando un lenguaje del Sur." En *Letras y proclamas: la estética literaria de Diamela Eltit*. Ed. Bernardita Llanos M. Santiago: Editorial Cuarto Propio/Denison University, 2006. 33-68.

Lazzara, Michael J. "Estrategias de dominación y resistencia corporales: las biopolíticas del mercado en *Mano de obra*, de Diamela Eltit." En *Diamela Eltit: redes locales, redes globales*. Ed. Rubí Carreño Bolívar. Madrid/Santiago: Iberoamericana/Vervuert/Pontificia Universidad Católica de Chile, 2009. 155-64.

Lemebel, Pedro. *Háblame de amores*. Santiago: Seix Barral, 2013.

Llanos M., Bernardita. "Pasiones maternales y carnales en la narrativa de Eltit." En *Letras y proclamas: la estética literaria de Diamela Eltit*. Ed. Bernardita Llanos M. Santiago: Editorial

Cuarto Propio/Denison University, 2006: 103-41.

Lynd, Juliet. "Writing from the Margins of the Chilean Miracle: Diamela Eltit and the Aesthetics and Politics of the Transition." En *Post-Authoritarian Cultures. Spain and Latin America's Southern Cone*. Ed. Luis Martín-Estudillo and Roberto Ampuero. Nashville: Vanderbilt U P, 2008. 12-33.

Malverde Disselkoen, Ivette. "Esquizofrenia y literatura: la obsesión discursiva en *El padre mío*, de Diamela Eltit." En *Una poética de literatura menor: la narrativa de Diamela Eltit*. Ed. Juan Carlos Lértora. Santiago: Editorial Cuarto Propio, 1993. 155-66.

Masiello, Francine. *The Art of Transition. Latin American Culture and Neoliberal Crisis*. Durham: Duke U P, 2001.

Medina-Sancho, Gloria. *A partir del trauma: narración y memoria en Traba, Peri Rossi y Eltit*. Santiago: Editorial Cuarto Propio, 2012.

Niebylski, Dianna. "Blood Tax: Violence and the Vampirized Body in *Impuesto a la carne*." *Arizona Journal of Hispanic Cultural Studies* 15 (2011): 107-21.

Norat, Gisela. *Marginalities. Diamela Eltit and the Subversion of Mainstream Literature in Chile*. Newark: U of Delaware P, 2002.

Olea, Raquel. "El cuerpo-mujer. Un recorte de lectura en la narrativa de Diamela Eltit." En *Una poética de literatura menor: la narrativa de Diamela Eltit*. Ed. Juan Carlos Lértora. Santiago: Editorial Cuarto Propio, 1993. 83-95.

—. "El deseo de los condenados: constitución y disolución del sujeto popular en dos novelas de Diamela Eltit, *Por la patria* y *Mano de obra*." En *Diamela Eltit: redes locales, redes globales*. Ed. Rubí Carreño Bolívar. Madrid/Santiago: Iberoamericana/Vervuert/Pontificia Universidad Católica de Chile, 2009. 91-102.

Olivera-Williams, María Rosa. "La década del 70 en el Cono Sur. Discursos nostálgicos que recuerdan la revolución y escriben la historia." *Romance Quarterly* 57.1 (2010): 43-62.

Ortega, Julio. "Diamela Eltit y el imaginario de la virtualidad." En *Una poética de literatura menor: la narrativa de Diame-*

la Eltit. Ed. Juan Carlos Lértora. Santiago: Editorial Cuarto Propio, 1993. 53-81.

Pastén B., J. Agustín. "Neither Grobalized nor Glocalized: Fuguet's or Lemebel's Metropolis?" *Contemporary Literary Criticism* 308 (Summer 2011): 117-33.

Tafra, Sylvia. *Diamela Eltit: el rito de pasaje como estrategia textual*. Santiago: RiL Editores, 1998.

Tierney-Tello, Mary Beth. *Allegories of Transgression and Transformation. Experimental Fiction by Women Writing Under Dictatorship*. Albany: State U of New York P, 1996.

CRISTINA PERI ROSSI BAJO LA LENTE DE LA GENERACIÓN DEL 72

María Rosa Olivera-Williams
University of Notre Dame

La obra de Cristina Peri Rossi, desde su temprano comienzo en Montevideo, fue acogida y premiada por la crítica. El poder de sus imágenes y la rica textura de su lenguaje marcaban la originalidad de la precoz escritora. Peri Rossi ofrecía un puente alegórico para un mundo que se transformaba por la violencia económica y política que impulsó las revoluciones de la izquierda de la década del 60 y promovió la brutal represión de las dictaduras militares de los 70 en el Cono Sur, manifestaciones regionales de la llegada de la globalización y el neoliberalismo a América Latina. Su obra que abarca todos los géneros literarios la hacen merecedora de la categoría de "clásico contemporáneo", ya que la misma se puede leer en presente, en este presente signado por la inmediatez, la presencia, el directo o como propuso Barthes, el "efecto de (vida) real".

En el contexto de este panel que está dedicado a releer la obra de importantes escritores latinoamericanos contemporáneos como integrantes de la Generación del 72 según la propuesta de Brantley Nicholson y Sophia McClennen en *The Generation of '72: Latin America's Forced Global Citizens*, mi presente trabajo sobre Cristina Peri Rossi intenta mostrar las características de su forzada ciudadanía global más allá de lo analizado en el capítulo sobre *La nave de los locos* que integra el libro de Brantley y Sophia. Para ello voy a referirme a uno de los polos que enmarcan a la Generación del 72, los narradores latinoamericanos del *"boom"* y en particular al texto de José Donoso, *Historia personal del boom* (1972; 1985), así como al suplemento de la edición de 1985 del mismo, escrito por su esposa, María Pilar Donoso, y titulado "El *boom* doméstico". Los textos del matrimonio Donoso subrayan la performance tradicional de la división de los géneros sexuales: masculino/femenino, que articulaba el discurso narrativo del *boom* y la vida diaria de sus integrantes.[1] Pienso que es importante recordar esta representación de las identidades sexuales en las obras del *boom* clásico y la ideología patriarcal de los miembros del grupo para evaluar los cambios en la obra de la Generación del 72. Muchos de los integrantes de esta última, o sea muchos de los escritores del "post-*boom*", son mujeres, las que faltaron en la generación anterior. Ellas ofrecen en su literatura otras performances para lo femenino/masculino, otras maneras de fabricar la realidad, y hacen visibles las diferencias entre el deseo de cosmopolitismo de sus antecesores literarios y el doloroso mareo que produce la forzada ciudadanía global, ya sea en la experiencia de exilio o insilio, el exitoso neologismo de los cientistas sociales Juan Rial y Carina Perelli para referirse al "exilio interno", la marginación de los individuos dentro de las propias fronteras nacionales, producto del terror y la auto-censura originados por regímenes dictatoriales.

Como se sabe el *boom* literario latinoamericano no tuvo mujeres, si bien fue el fruto de la astuta estrategia editorial de una mujer, Carmen Balcells, quien colocó la narración de ficción publicada entre 1962 y 1975 por un grupo de talentosos novelistas latinoamericanos en el centro de la cultura occidental. Según Donoso, Julio Cortázar, Gabriel García Márquez, Carlos Fuentes, Guillermo Cabrera Infante, Mario Vargas Llosa y el propio Donoso constituían "una pandilla masculina" (Donoso 1998: 84). Durante el periodo gestacional del grupo, sus miembros necesitaban una red de amistad para familiarizarse con las últimas corrientes estéticas y las ventas de libros del Primer Mundo. Necesitaban adquirir una identidad autorial más grande que la del autor individual, mientras que cada uno de los miembros de la cofradía literaria anhelaba ser reconocido como el líder de "la pandilla", el más grande novelista latinoamericano del siglo veinte. La dinámica del grupo estaba basada en la división patriarcal de los géneros: los hombres hacían literatura, mientras las mujeres, sus mujeres, mantenían el hogar de los escritores, como indica María Pilar Donoso en "El *boom* doméstico". Paradójicamente, mientras las performances de los géneros lentamente cambiaban en la cultura occidental, incluyendo a América Latina, los creadores de la imagen mundialmente aceptada de Latinoamérica, la cual por medio del realismo mágico se convertía en una nueva representación tropical del continente, resolvieron ignorar esos cambios. Asimismo escogieron no reconocer a las autoras latinoamericanas que desde la década del 40 y especialmente después de importantes logros legales, tales como el derecho político al voto y la igualdad de derechos civiles, abrazaron el género de la narrativa de ficción larga: la novela. Si las contribuciones literarias de predecesores tales como Jorge Luis Borges, Miguel Ángel Asturias, Juan Carlos Onetti, y Juan Rulfo fueron importantes para los integrantes del *boom*, igualmente importantes fueron las silenciadas obras de autoras, como *La última niebla* y *La amortajada* de María Luisa Bombal, *Balún Canán* de Rosario Castellanos, *La mujer desnuda* de Armonía Somers, y *Los recuerdos del porvenir* de Elena Garro, contemporánea del *boom*. Las integrantes mujeres de la generación del 72 constituyen lo que podría llamarse el *boom* femenino de las letras latinoamericanas. Sin embargo este *boom*, al que puede calificarse de tal por la explosión en el número de mujeres novelistas que alcanzan reconocimiento crítico y un lugar importante en el mercado editorial, carece de la dirección de una agente como la Balcells y nunca formó una hermandad como la de "la pandilla masculina" que le dio identidad a los novelistas latinoamericanos en sus primeros años. Junto a las negociaciones y estrategias de la Balcells, la identidad colectiva del *boom* se solidificó por los deseos de sus miembros de ser ciudadanos cosmopolitas de la ciudad letrada. Estos deseos los unió y despertó envidias que podrían leerse como manifestaciones de diferentes crisis de la masculinidad. Asimismo, como Donoso indica, el deseo de cosmopolitismo marcó que el origen del grupo y su final se llevaran a cabo en fiestas y eventos cosmopolitas. Donoso describe las reuniones del grupo de la siguiente manera: "Todo fue muy internacional y moderno—con intérpretes simultáneos y todo—una especie de gran carnaval de intelectuales, con *picnics*, baños de mar, exposiciones, *flirts*, y comidas" (1998: 46). Las mujeres latinoamericanas del *boom* femenino, así como todos los integrantes de la Generación del 72 no ansiaron el estatus cosmopolita. No podían hacerlo porque a partir de los 70, sin ellos quererlo, entraron en la vorágine de la globalización pautada por los movimientos de la economía mercantilista del neoliberalismo.

    Si se comparan dos relatos breves de Cristina Peri Rossi de uno de sus libros de cuentos más logrados del periodo de exilio y que cuenta con un prólogo de Cortázar, *La tarde del dinosaurio*

(1976) se aprecia el cambio en las expectativas que la generación de Peri Rossi tenía con respecto al poder de la literatura. En "En la playa", el segundo cuento de la colección, Peri Rossi presenta a una niña que encuentra y enfrenta a un matrimonio joven en una playa casi desierta por la hora, el momento en que se pone el sol, y la fresca brisa que se levanta al atardecer en las playas del este de la costa uruguaya, si bien el relato no menciona el nombre del balneario.[2] El encuentro de la niña y la pareja en su doble significado: encuentro como el verse y entablar una conversación, así como el choque de dos maneras diferentes de ver y estar en el mundo, intensifica su fuerza de encuentro y choque al tratarse de una pareja joven. La descripción del matrimonio es casi idílica:

> De lejos parecían hermanos. Rubios, de ojos claros, piel delicada, ropa discreta, hablar bajo, caminaban por la playa tomados de la mano y eran de la clase de gente a quienes jamás la brisa del atardecer los sorprende sin un abrigo en el bolso, por cualquier cosa (24).

Se podría decir que esta descripción apunta a un "indicio pánico", como tituló Peri Rossi a su libro de 1970, para dejar testigo del horror que marca a las sociedades gobernadas por regímenes policíacos y que ciertamente en 1970 marcaba a la sociedad uruguaya bajo del pachecato.[3] El indicio que causa pánico en los lectores del cuento radica en que esta pareja de imagen armoniosa es joven. Sin embargo, la fuerza de su juventud está paralizada por su atadura "a las buenas costumbres", por su incapacidad de "desafiar" las convenciones por temor a "los peligros que asechaban a los disidentes, a los marginales, a los evadidos, a los opositores" (24). Peri Rossi abre *Indicios pánicos* con el siguiente epígrafe de Benito Mussolini: "Señores: Es tiempo de decir que el hombre, antes de recibir los beneficios de la cultura, debe recibir los beneficios del orden. En cierto sentido, se puede decir que el policía ha precedido, en la historia, al profesor" (Peri Rossi 1976: 5). En un tiempo en el cual el policía sustituye al profesor y el orden es violencia y silenciamiento de todo lo que pueda ser disidente, el futuro que es siempre cambio no existe. Por eso en el cuento que nos incumbe, cuando el hombre toma una fotografía del sol poniente, el exquisito dominio y juego del lenguaje que caracterizan la prosa de Peri Rossi permiten narrar el acto de tomar la fotografía como un crimen. La voz narradora en tercera persona dice: "Enfocó a distancia y disparó sobre el sol. Lo mató instantáneamente. Satisfecho rebobinó" (25).

La juventud atada a las viejas convenciones por miedo a los peligros que conllevan los cambios mata el futuro, asesina el sol.

El personaje que se enfrenta al peligro de un futuro inmediato sin salida, atado a viejas convenciones: el origen de una vida, la del joven matrimonio que mata el futuro, tiene que provenir de un mundo ajeno a las normas sociales. Ese personaje tiene que representar la niñez. Es una niña pequeña que sin padres visibles en la playa no actúa como la mayoría de los niños y se enfrenta a la pareja con un lenguaje nuevo que desestabiliza todos los valores de la pareja. Sirva de ejemplos los nombres de los tres personajes. Mientras los nombres propios de la pareja, Alicia y Aníbal, comienzan con la vocal "a" y tienen el mismo número de sílabas (3) y letras (6), subrayando la representación de los sexos como el anverso y reverso de una misma moneda: los hermanos complementarios de lo femenino/masculino, el nombre de la niña, Euuuuyllarre, que recuerda la musicalidad rica en vocales del canto VII de Altazor o el viaje en paracaídas de Huidobro, quiebra las expectativas con que se interpretan los significados de los nombres y los géneros. En verdad, la niña y la niñez se presentan como el no-lugar y la invitación a interpretar "la luminosidad" de las cosas y del arte por medio de los sentidos, como proponía Susan Sontang en Against Interpretation and Other Essays (1966), texto al que se refiere el relato. La niñez es el no-lugar de la extranjería, donde se experimenta la falta de normas y códigos conocidos. Ocho años más tarde en La nave de los locos (1984), el discurso sobre la calidad de extranjero logrará su expresión culminante, a la que volverá a revisitar desde distintos géneros, como es el caso de su gran poemario Babel bárbara (1991).

Desde la niñez, "la gatería" en el cuento, la propuesta revolucionaria de sentir/vivir el mundo desde nuevas perspectivas más integradoras y libres—la propuesta política que nunca se llevó a cabo de los Tupamaros, de ahí la mención a los numerosos gatos que hace la niña: C.A.T., Comité de Apoyo a los Tupamaros[4]—la joven pareja conservadora es vencida. El relato termina con el pedido de ellos de que la niña no los abandone: "–Pero no, Euuuuyllarre, quédate, quédate con nosotros... –Bueno, si es así, los acompañaré toda la noche. Siempre hay gente solitaria por la playa. Se aburren y no saben qué hacer" (37).

Muy distinta es la posición y la actitud de la niña que se enfrenta a su padre exiliado en España en "La influencia de Edgar A. Poe en la poesía de Raimundo Arenas", el tercer relato de La tarde del dinosaurio. Si bien esta niña al igual que Euuuuyllarre parece haber adquirido mayor madurez que los adultos, sabe que su padre no la comprende a ella ni a su generación. Ella dice: "Estoy segura de que lo que piensas acerca de nuestra generación es completamente falso" (52). Nicholson y McClennen abren con esta cita la introducción al presente volumen. ¿Qué es lo que no comprende la generación anterior? ¿Cómo se hace arte en el Primer Mundo inundado de inmigrantes, exiliados, migrantes? ¿Qué dice el disfraz de india charrúa que la niña usa para ganar algún dinero en las calles? ¿Importa la imagen aceptada que el Primer Mundo tiene de América Latina? Todas estas preguntas que aparecen en el relato responden a la experiencia de la violencia global que tienen que sobrellevar los miembros de la Generación del 72.

Si la "pandilla masculina" del *boom* pudo tener una *Historia personal del boom* y una "Historia doméstica del *boom*" porque fue un grupo que logró una identidad colectiva sólida, pese a las envidias y rencillas que separaron a alguno de sus miembros definitivamente, la Generación del 72 no contó ni cuenta con tal testimonio. En verdad, la narración de su experiencia como creadores literarios en el contexto de la violencia globalizada hay que encontrarla en otros medios. En el caso de Cristina Peri Rossi, una ávida y talentosa escritora de cartas, parte de esta historia se halla en veinte cartas que le escribió, principalmente durante la década del 90, a una antigua compañera de estudios y colega docente de literatura en la enseñanza secundaria en Montevideo, Iris Pereira. Debo decir desde ya que se trata de una historia solitaria, pues si bien esta generación pudo tener padres literarios, al igual que la hija del exiliado del relato "La influencia de Edgar A. Poe en la poesía de Raimundo Arenas", esos padres no pueden entender la experiencia de aquéllos que les tocó vivir una ciudadanía global forzada. Así, una de las primeras cartas fechada el 13 de febrero de 1989 dice:[5]

> Disculpá si no sé decirlo de otro modo, por el momento, pero me cuesta mucho escribir (¡!) *desde acá a allá*; durante muchos años he sentido que a la gente que más quiero la he dejado entre las paredes grises de Montevideo y a veces escribir cartas es doloroso, por el contraste con la realidad inmediata. (El énfasis me pertenece)

El dolor que le impide escribir a alguien para quien la escritura es la vía más natural de comunicación y que de acuerdo a esta misma carta la lleva a enfrentarse con "el fantasma del suicidio" se origina en la experiencia de dos mundos diferentes y de dos identidades diferentes que se resumen en la distancia entre el "acá" y el "allá". El "acá" es la inmediatez globalizada que obliga a un ritmo extenuante de trabajo para sobrevivir—sobrevivir emocional y materialmente—; el "allá" es la melancolía gris de los sentimientos y el origen de la escritura.

En una carta del 20 de enero de 1990 en la que siente que se ha convertido en "la escritora más famosa de habla española y probablemente en una de las más conocidas del mundo entero"—es el periodo de euforia al haber terminado el manuscrito de *Babel bárbara*[6] y saber que su poemario saldrá en una de las colecciones más importantes de España—habla del ritmo enloquecido que exige la globalización. Con mezcla de orgullo enumera sucintamente lo que hace: un artículo al mes para la Agencia Efe que publica simultáneamente para 125 diarios en todo el mundo, dos mensuales para *Diario 16* (Madrid y el resto de España), tres más para otro de los diarios importantes de España, dicta dos a tres conferencias al mes por todo el país, además de aparecer asimismo dos veces al mes en la televisión, lo que la hace viajar a Madrid. Le dice a Iris: "Llevo una vida tan agitada que no puedo reseñártela meticulosamente: te abrumaría. Hay que ser muy fuerte y muy resistente para poder llevar este tren (mejor dicho: este avión) y seguir en pie." Fuerza y resistencia que con el tiempo tendrán que enfrentarse a las claudicaciones de su propio cuerpo.

Las correspondencia de Peri Rossi a Iris Pereira gira sobre tres puntales: la literatura, su literatura, la enfermedad y los deseos lésbicos. Peri Rossi surge de esta correspondencia a una amiga, con quien por momentos puede confesarse con sinceridad segura de que solo ella leerá lo escrito, como un individuo estoico, aunque no por eso menos orgulloso del único capital que tiene: su obra literaria. Su fortaleza la lleva a detenerse extrañamente en su deterioro físico: los huesos se vuelven polvo con artrosis y artritis, la presión arterial sube, el corazón falla, las hormonas dejan de actuar correctamente haciendo visible su malfuncionamiento en tejidos y órganos: problemas con la glándula tiroides la obligan a tomar yodo sintético, la úlcera fastidia y persiste, el asma le impide respirar y una larga lista de medicamentos y hormonas sintéticas la ayudan y dañan simultáneamente. Parecería que la narración detallada de su claudicación física en el epistolario son los síntomas del mal de su tiempo, más que de los achaques de los años, aunque ella siempre se refiere al paso de los años y deja constancia exacta de los que va cumpliendo. Por ejemplo, el 28 de marzo de 1996 dice: "Quizás esta enfermedad me ha hecho comprender que tengo 54 años y que no puedo seguir viviendo como una mujer de 25... A la vejez hay que casarse ¿no? Los amantes son solo para la juventud".

La literatura le da felicidad, pero es una actividad que tiene que defender de la política editorial y al mismo tiempo vender sus libros, obtener premios y aparecer constantemente en los medios porque es la actividad que en España le da de comer. Si me permiten quiero terminar con una cita larga de una de las cartas más sentidas y sinceras a Iris (30 de junio de 1991). Tras el disgusto de que Planeta ("la editorial más grande y estafadora de este país de asaltantes y usureros") compró la editorial que estaba publicando *Fantasías eróticas* (1990), libro de ensayos de gran éxito de mercado, perdiendo las ganancias que hubiera recibido por derechos de autor, le escribe a Iris:

> Si no fuera porque soy feliz, escribiendo, realmente estaría amargada por esta profesión. No olvides nunca que si he llegado hasta donde he llegado, es porque soy mucho más fuerte que los demás. De lo contrario, habría desaparecido ya, por la crueldad y el expolio del mundo en que me ha tocado escribir y vivir... Tú te quejas de Uruguay y tienes toda la razón del mundo, pero la alternativa no es este modelo de sociedad española. Aquí, reina el puro instinto: la lucha por la supervivencia y el éxito es implacable... No hay amigos: solo intereses. Los intereses, de todo tipo, rigen la conducta de todo el mundo, sin la menor sombra de afecto. También el ser humano se convierte en un artículo de consumo. Nadie se te acerca espontáneamente: solo lo hacen para obtener algo... Es una sociedad absolutamente impía, dura, egoísta y deshumanizada. Te adaptas o mueres. Por supuesto, si yo no fuera como soy, estaría en la cúspide más absoluta. Pero hago favores, no me vendo, ayudo a la gente, y lo que consigo es solo bienestar de conciencia, porque el que no sigue el patrón general, es considerado bobo e idealista, sinónimo de lelo.

No seguir las reglas del juego, la actitud que le permite a Peri Rossi mantener su ética como escritora y forzada ciudadana global, podría ser el denominador común de la Generación del 72. "No seguir las reglas del juego" tiene un precio alto para cada uno de sus integrantes. En el caso de Peri Rossi, significa también una exacerbación en la búsqueda del afecto. Ella trata de tocar a la sociedad dura y deshumanizada por medio de las sensaciones, de la ironía, del humor, de una erótica que inunda todos los aspectos de la vida. Ese choque afectivo que es la meta de su literatura la lleva a la narrativa de ficción breve y a la poesía más que a la novela, aunque en toda la obra de Peri Rossi las divisiones de los géneros literarios fueron porosas. El choque instantáneo del afecto que puede lograr un cuento o un poema coincide con la experiencia del "tiempo cero" sobre la que "especula" Josefina Ludmer. Ludmer explica la nueva experiencia histórica global del Internet como "la travesía del espacio en no tiempo". El tiempo cero, para Ludmer: "incluye experiencias instantáneas como el estallido, el accidente y el atentado, todos puntos sin tiempo o que cortan el tiempo" (18-19). La literatura de Peri Rossi busca el estallido de los sentidos por medio de un corte en la vorágine veloz de nuestra experiencia del tiempo para quebrar por un instante con la soledad virtual y ofrecer una nueva experiencia de la soledad: la soledad del placer de la lectura y los sentidos.

Notas

1. Mi lectura de los textos del matrimonio Donoso se benefició del artículo de Diana Sorensen, "La hermandad ansiosa".
2. Los detalles que se indican en el párrafo inicial del cuento permiten pensar que se trata de un balneario uruguayo de los departamentos de Canelones o Maldonado. Había un hotel de tres estrellas con precio módico donde se comía bien. El hotel estaba frente a la playa, lo que le permite a la pareja cruzar a la playa temprano todas las mañanas. Sin embargo, les es difícil encontrar un lugar donde instalarse porque la playa desde temprano está llena de gente. Asimismo, se describe la arena como "un polvo marrón, más bien grueso, pegajoso..." ("En la playa" 24)
3. El gobierno represivo de Jorge Pacheco Areco (1967-1972) fue llamado popularmente "pachecato".
4. Después del copamiento de la ciudad de Pando por el Movimiento de Liberación Nacional-Tupamaros en 1969, según lo explica Julio Marenales, uno de los fundadores del Movimiento, se dio una aparente paradoja. Frente a la derrota militar (mataron a tres militantes y tomaron presos a veinte) surgió un crecimiento del accionar político. Es en este momento que surgen los Comités de Apoyo a los Tupamaros.
5. Hubo una serie de cartas anteriores, pertenecientes a los primeros años del exilio de Peri Rossi. Sin embargo, el temor que sintió Iris Pereira por tener cartas de una exiliada que dejaba saber por medio de su literatura y artículos lo que pasaba en el país y la región, la llevaron a destruir esa

correspondencia. Esta información fue otorgada por Peri Rossi a la autora de este trabajo en una conversación telefónica del 27 de mayo de 2013.
6. Este poemario fue publicado por Lumen y en 1992 recibió el premio Ciutat de Barcelona.

Obras citadas

Barthes, Roland. "The Reality Effect." *The Rustle of Language*. Trad. Richard Howard. Oxford: Blackwell, 1986. 1441-148.

Donoso, José. *Historia personal del boom*. Santiago de Chile: Alfaguara, 1998.

Ludmer, Josefina. *Aquí América Latina: una especulación*. Buenos Aires: Eterna Cadencia, 2010.

Marenales, Julio. "Breve historia del M.L.N". http://www.chasque.net/mlnweb/historia/brevehistoria.htm (accedido el 2 de julio de 2013).

Peri Rossi, Cristina. *La tarde del dinosaurio*. Prólogo de Julio Cortázar. Barcelona: Plaza y Janés, 1985.

—. *Indicios pánicos*. Barcelona: Bruguera, 1981

—. *La nave de los locos*. Barcelona: Seix Barral, 1984.

—. *Babel bárbara*. Barcelona: Lumen, 1991.

—. "En la playa". (1976). *Cristina Peri Rossi. Cuentos reunidos*. Barcelona: Lumen, 2007. 24-37.

—. "La influencia de Edgar A. Poe en la poesía de Raimundo Arias" (1976). *Cristina Peri Rossi. Cuentos reunidos*. Op.cit. 38-52.

—. Correspondencia de Cristina Peri Rossi a Iris Pereira, 13 de febrero de 1989, 20 de enero de 1990, 30 de junio de 1991 y 28 de marzo de 1996. Colección sin procesar. Los papeles de Cristina Peri Rossi. Hesburgh Library Special Collections. University of Notre Dame, Notre Dame, Indiana.

Sontag, Susan. *Against Interpretation and Other Essays*. New York: Octagon Books, 1978.

Sorensen, Diana. "La hermandad ansiosa". *El salto de Minerva*. Eds. Mabel Moraña y María Rosa Olivera-Williams. Madrid: Iberoamericana-Vervuert, 2005. 227-249.

Contributors

BRANTLEY NICHOLSON is a visiting scholar and President's College Associate in the Department of Latin American and Iberian Studies at the University of Richmond. His research and teaching focus on globalization and cosmopolitanism in Latin America with a focus on modern and contemporary cultural production. He has published articles in journals in Europe and throughout the Americas and is currently preparing volumes on Fernando Vallejo and modernismo and a monograph on literary cosmopolitanism and aesthetic idealism.

SOPHIA A. MCCLENNEN is Professor of International Affairs and Comparative Literature at the Pennsylvania State University, University Park, where she directs the Center for Global Studies. Her most recent books are *Colbert's America: Satire and Democracy* (Palgrave 2012) and *Neoliberalism, Terrorism, Education* co-authored with Jeffrey Di Leo, Henry Giroux, and Ken Saltman (Paradigm 2012). She is also the author of *Dialectics of Exile: Nation, Time, Language, and Space in Hispanic Literatures* (Purdue UP 2004), *Ariel Dorfman: An Aesthetics of Hope* (Duke UP, 2010), and with Henry James Morello, *Representing Humanity in an Age of Terror* (Purdue UP 2010). She is currently working on a study of Latin American Cinema and globalization.

JUANITA ARISTIZÁBAL (PhD Yale University, 2011) is Assistant Professor of Spanish at The Catholic University of America, where she teaches nineteenth, twentieth and twenty-first-century Latin American literature and culture. Her research focuses on comparative approaches to the turn of the twentieth and twenty-first centuries from the perspective of the discourses of modernization, modernity, decadence, marginality, religion, and national identity.

Her current book project explores Fernando Vallejo's dialogue with the modernista tradition in Spanish America. She has published articles on Vallejo, Machado de Assis and female autobiography in nineteenth-century Colombia.

PATRICK DOVE is Associate Professor and Director of Graduate Studies in the Department of Spanish and Portuguese at Indiana University. His research explores intersections between literature, philosophy and politics in Latin America; he has written on Peronism, political violence, and dictatorship and memory, among other topics. His first book, *The Catastrophe of Modernity: Tragedy and the Nation in Latin American Literature* (Bucknell UP, 2004), examines the use of the tragic as a topos for literary considerations of modernity in Argentina (Borges and Piglia), Peru (César Vallejo) and Mexico (Rulfo). Currently he is completing a second book project, "Literature and Interregnum," which looks at literary responses to neoliberalism, the demise of the national popular and the crisis of sovereignty in Argentina and Chile.

GEOFFREY KANTARIS is Senior Lecturer (Associate Professor) in the Department of Spanish and Portuguese of the University of Cambridge and a Fellow of St Catharine's College. He was Director of the Centre of Latin American Studies in Cambridge from 2005-2010 and is currently the Cultural Studies editor of the Bulletin of Latin American Research. His current research is on contemporary urban cinema from Argentina, Colombia and Mexico, and he has published several articles and book chapters in this area, with a forthcoming book entitled *Latin American Film: The Urban Paradigm*. He is co-editor of *Latin American Popular Culture: Politics, Media, Affect* (Boydell & Brewer, forthcoming c. 2012). He has also worked and published extensively on women's writing and dictatorship in Argentina and Uruguay, and is author of *The Subversive Psyche* (Oxford University Press, 1996).

LEILA LEHNEN is Associate professor of Spanish and Portuguese at the University of New Mexico. She specializes in contemporary Brazilian and Southern Cone literature. Her book *Citizenship and Crisis in Contemporary Brazilian Literature* (forthcoming Palgrave Macmillan) examines the representation and critique of disjunctive citizenship (Holston 2008) in contemporary Brazilian literature. Leila Lehnen has published articles on globalization in Brazilian and Spanish American literature, among other topics. She is currently working on the interface between globalization and the formulation of citizenship in present-day Argentine, Chilean and Brazilian literature.

LÁZARO LIMA is the E. Claiborne Robins Distinguished Chair in the Liberal Arts and professor in the Department of Latin American and Iberian Studies and the program in American Studies at the University of Richmond. His publications include *The Latino Body: Crisis Identities in American Literary and Cultural Memory*; *Ambientes: New Queer Latino Writing* (co-edited with Felice Picano); *Trevor Young: The Aesthetics of Displacement*; and the forthcoming *Losing Sonia Sotomayor: An American Life After Multiculturalism*. Lima's interdisciplinary work on inter-American literatures and cultural history has also appeared in *American Literary History*, *Revista Iberoamericana*, *The Wallace Stevens Journal*, *Hispanic Review* and many other journals.

MARÍA ROSA OLIVERA-WILLIAMS (Ph.D., Ohio State University) is Associate Professor of Latin American Literature at the University of Notre Dame and a fellow of the Helen Kellogg Institute for International Studies. She received a Fullbright Award for Scholars (2011-2012) for the book she is currently preparing on tango and modernization in the Río de la Plata region. Her research interests lie in the representation of national subjectivities and identities in Latin America; artistic projects in the Southern Cone; dictatorial literature; democratic transition and traumatic memory. Her books include *El salto de Minerva: intelectuales, género, Estado en América Latina*, co-edición with Mabel Moraña (Madrid: Iberoamericana-Vervuert, 2005), *La poesía gauchesca de Hidalgo a Hernández: respuesta estética y condicionamiento social* (Xalapa, Veracruz, México: Centro de Investigaciones Lingüistico-Literarias. Universidad Veracruzana, 1986), and a wide range of articles. Her latest book is entitled *El arte de crear lo femenino: ficción, género e historia del Cono Sur* (2012) and is available with the Santiago, Chile based Editorial Cuarto Propio.

J. AGUSTÍN PASTÉN B. (Santiago, Chile) has a B.A. in English pedagogy (Universidad de Chile, 1979), a B.A. in History and Germany (Berea College, 1982), a Masters of Divinity (Duke University, 1985), an M.A. in Spanish (University of Kentucky, 1988), and a Ph.D. in Spanish (University of Pennyslvania, 1993). He taught at the University of Nebraska from 1993 to 2008, before becoming an Associate Professor of Latin American Literature at North Carolina State University. His the author of *Octavio Paz: crítico practicante en busca de una poética* (1999) and has published articles in *Revista Hispánica Moderna, Revista Iberoamericana, Revista Canadiense de Estudios Hispánicos*, among others.

RANDOLPH POPE is the Commonwealth Professor of Spanish and Comparative Literature at the University of Virginia, where he has served as Chair of Spanish, Italian and Portuguese (2004–2007) and Director of Comparative Literature (2008–2011). Born in Chile, he studied Spanish Literature and Classics at the Universidad Católica de Valparaíso. He received an M.A. and Ph.D. in Spanish from Columbia University in New York. His field of specialization is the Peninsular novel and autobiography, but he has also written extensively on other topics, such as Latin American literature, cultural studies, literature and architecture, literature and the arts, and literature and philosophy. He has taught at Barnard College, the University of Bonn in Germany, Dartmouth College, Vassar College, where he was Chair of Hispanic Studies, and Washington University in St. Louis, where he served as Chair of Comparative Literature for seven years. He has been Visiting Professor at the University of Colorado at Boulder and at the University of Tübingen in Germany. For four years he directed the Middlebury College Spanish Summer School in Vermont. He was one of the two founders and main editors of Ediciones del Norte and serves on several editorial boards. From 1991 to the Spring issue of 2002 he was editor of the *Revista de Estudios Hispánicos*. He has published three books and over one hundred scholarly essays. He has directed twice an NEH Summer Seminar for College Teachers on Spanish autobiography in the European context.

JOHN RIOFRIO, or "Rio" as he is called by just about everyone besides his parents, earned his PhD in English from the University of Wisconsin-Madison. The son of Ecuadorian migrants, Rio teaches courses in Latin@ studies at the College of William and Mary where he is an Assistant Professor in the Department of Modern Languages and Literatures. Rio has published on the confluence of Latin American and Latino studies in MELUS and LALR, is at work on a book-length manuscript entitled "Continental Shifts: Hemispheric Migrations and the Struggles over Latino/a Identity in the Americas", and occasionally finds the time and emotional energy to publish opinion pieces in *Huffington Post* on topics ranging from Arizona's ban in Ethnic Studies, to a media review of CNN's Latino in America, to cable television's obsession with big, white families.

www.ingramcontent.com/pod-product-compliance
Ingram Content Group UK Ltd.
Pitfield, Milton Keynes, MK11 3LW, UK
UKHW041431180426
11947UKWH00007B/389